APPLIED APL PROGRAMMING

Wilbur R. LePage

Department of Electrical and Computer Engineering
Syracuse University

PRENTICE-HALL, INC., Englewood Cliffs, N.J. 07632

Library of Congress Cataloging in Publication Data

Le Page, Wilbur R.
  Applied APL programming.

  Includes index.
  1. APL (Computer program language) I. Title.
QA76.73.A27L46   001.6´424   78-6619
ISBN 0-13-040063-7

© 1978 by Prentice-Hall, Inc., Englewood Cliffs, N.J. 07632

All rights reserved. No part of this book
may be reproduced in any form or
by any means without permission in writing
from the publisher.

Printed in the United States of America

10 9 8 7 6 5 4 3 2

Prentice-Hall International, Inc., *London*
Prentice-Hall of Australia Pty. Limited, *Sydney*
Prentice-Hall of Canada, Ltd., *Toronto*
Prentice-Hall of India Private Limited, *New Delhi*
Prentice-Hall of Japan, Inc., *Tokyo*
Prentice-Hall of Southeast Asia Pte. Ltd., *Singapore*
Whitehall Books Limited, *Wellington, New Zealand*

To those who would blend an appreciation for precision of thought with a respect for subjective values in the management of human affairs, this book is dedicated.

CONTENTS

CHAPTER 1   PEOPLE AND COMPUTERS   1

    1-1   Communications   1
    1-2   Elementary Operations on Symbols   2
    1-3   Memory   3
    1-4   Language   3
    1-5   The Assignment Operation   5
    1-6   Structuring a Problem for a Numerical Solution (Algorithms)   6
    1-7   Decision-Making   7
    1-8   Illustration of an Iterative Process   9
    1-9   Describing an Algorithm for an Iterative Process   12
    1-10 An Algorithm for Solving a Cubic Equation   15

CHAPTER 2   RUDIMENTS OF APL   21

    2-1   The Nature of an APL Time-Sharing System   22
    2-2   Workspace and Memory Utilization   22
    2-3   Properties of a Workspace   24
    2-4   Diagnostic Messages (error and trouble reports)   24
    2-5   Correcting Typing Errors   25
    2-6   Names and Values of Variables   26
    2-7   Example of an APL Statement   28
    2-8   A List of Numbers or Characters as One Value   29
    2-9   Some Arithmetic Primitive Functions   31
    2-10 Negative Numbers and Negation   33
    2-11 Scaled (Floating Point) Notation   34
    2-12 Statements Having More than One Primitive Function,   36
          Parentheses
    2-13 Introduction to Defined Functions   38
    2-14 Local and Global Variables   41
    2-15 Display of a Function   42
    2-16 Suspended Functions   43
    2-17 A Few Primitive Functions on Vectors   45
    2-18 Use of a Defined Function Within a Defined Function   47
    2-19 Comment About Program Structure   50
    2-20 Monadic Defined Functions   51
    2-21 Printing Values Produced Within a Function   52
    2-22 Other Types of Defined Functions   53
    2-23 Evaluated and Character Input, Execute   54
    2-24 Bare Output, Monadic Format   56
    2-25 Comment Lines   57

CHAPTER 3   ARRAYS   65

    3-1   Terminology for Arrays   66
    3-2   Character Arrays   69
    3-3   Specification of Arrays, the Reshape Function   69
    3-4   Catenate and Laminate   72
    3-5   Ravel   75

vi / Contents

3-6	The Shape Function	75
3-7	The Object Value in Reshape	77
3-8	Illustrations of Manipulations of Arrays	77
3-9	Empty Arrays	79
3-10	Rank of a Value	80
3-11	Arithmetic Functions with Arrays	80
3-12	Reduction Operator	83
3-13	Index Function	87
3-14	Specifying an Indexed Value	90
3-15	Take and Drop	92
3-16	Grade-up and Grade-down	95
3-17	Reverse and Rotate	96
3-18	Transpose of a Matrix	98
3-19	Illustrative Examples Using Arrays	98
3-20	Outer Product for Vectors	103
3-21	Inner Product for Vectors and Matrices	104
3-22	Evaluation of a Polynomial	106

CHAPTER 4 SCALAR FUNCTIONS 115

4-1	Compatibility for the Dyadic Scalar Functions	116
4-2	Domain Restrictions	117
4-3	Floor and Minimum	117
4-4	Ceiling and Maximum	119
4-5	Roundoff Error in Floor and Ceiling, Comparison Tolerance	120
4-6	Absolute Value, Signum	121
4-7	Factorial	123
4-8	Roll	124
4-9	Residue	125
4-10	Generalized Combination	127
4-11	Comparison of Floor, Ceiling and Residue	127
4-12	Summary of the Arithmetic Functions	128
4-13	The Relational Functions	129
4-14	Membership	131
4-15	Comparison Tolerance in the Relational Functions	131
4-16	Summary of the Relational Functions	132
4-17	Logic Functions	133
4-18	Summary of the Logic Functions	136
4-19	Compression and Expansion on Vectors	137
4-20	Transcendental Functions	140
4-21	Summary of Transcendental Functions	147
4-22	Scalar Functions in the Inner and Outer Products	147

CHAPTER 5 BRANCHING AND ITERATION 154

5-1	Unconditional Branching	155
5-2	Conditional Branching	156
5-3	A Control Structure Equivalent of Conditional Branching	159
5-4	Program Loop	160
5-5	Using a Loop to Evaluate a Polynomial	161
5-6	Nested Loops	162
5-7	Successive Approximations	163
5-8	Comment about Convergence	166
5-9	A Control Structure Equivalent to a Loop	166
5-10	Bisection Method of Finding a Zero	168
5-11	Secant Method of Finding a Zero	172
5-12	Use of Execute in Representing a Mathematical Relationship	174
5-13	Recursive Functions	175
5-14	Input-Controlled Loop	177

Contents / vii

```
CHAPTER 6    EXTENDED SCALAR AND MIXED FUNCTIONS                   186

             6-1  Reduction                                        187
             6-2  Scan                                             189
             6-3  Outer Product                                    192
             6-4  Inner Product                                    194
             6-5  Catenate                                         196
             6-6  Laminate                                         198
             6-7  Take and Drop                                    199
             6-8  Compression                                      200
             6-9  Expansion                                        202
             6-10 Index Function                                   204
             6-11 Reverse                                          206
             6-12 Rotate                                           207
             6-13 Monadic and Dyadic Transpose                     209
             6-14 Reduced Dyadic Transpose                         213
             6-15 Decode                                           214
             6-16 Encode                                           217
             6-17 Index Of                                         222
             6-18 Deal                                             225
             6-19 Matrix Divide                                    225
             6-20 Matrix Inverse                                   228
             6-21 Dyadic Format                                    229

CHAPTER 7    REFINEMENTS                                           239

             7-1  Types of Defined Functions                       239
             7-2  Ease of Reading                                  241
             7-3  Convenience to the User                          241
             7-4  Memory Space Utilization                         242
             7-5  Running Time                                     245
             7-6  Roundoff Errors                                  247
             7-7  Branching on Inequalities                        249
             7-8  Roundoff Errors in Computed Index Numbers        250
             7-9  Ambiguous Arguments of Dyadic Functions          250
             7-10 Uses of Execute                                  251
             7-11 APL Functions as Experimental Tools              252
             7-12 System Variables                                 253
             7-13 System Functions                                 255
             7-14 A Function for Creating a One-line Function      257
             7-15 Shared Variables                                 258
             7-16 Establishing a Shared Variable                   258
             7-17 Access Control                                   261
             7-18 Retraction of Sharing                            262
             7-19 Illustration of Shared Variable Operations       263

CHAPTER 8    CONCERNING STRUCTURE                                  266

             8-1  Description of a Data Base                       266
             8-2  Specifications for an Algorithm                  268
             8-3  Subprograms for Testing and Modifying Inputs     269
             8-4  A General Input Function                         273
             8-5  A Structured Realization                         273
             8-6  Files                                            275

APPENDIX 1   WORKSPACE MANAGEMENT                                  278

             A1-1 The Active Workspace                             278
             A1-2 System Commands                                  279
             A1-3 Workspace Identification                         279
             A1-4 Creating a Library Workspace                     280
             A1-5 Conditions for Saving a Workspace                281
             A1-6 Loading a Workspace                              282
```

             A1-7 Copying Objects   282
             A1-8 User Numbers and Passwords   283
             A1-9 Dropping a Workspace   284
             A1-10 Monitoring the Contents of the Active Workspace 284
             A1-11 Removing Objects from a Workspace   285
             A1-12 Signing Off   285

APPENDIX 2 ERROR REPORTS   287

APPENDIX 3 TROUBLE REPORTS   289

APPENDIX 4 NUMBER STORAGE   291

            A4-1 Alphanumeric Characters   291
            A4-2 Boolean Numbers   291
            A4-3 Integers   292
            A4-4 Floating-point Numbers   292
            A4-5 Overhead   292
            A4-6 The Byte Unit   292

APPENDIX 5 SYMBOL TABLE   293

APPENDIX 6 STATE INDICATOR   294

APPENDIX 7 DISPLAYING AND EDITING   296

            A7-1 Displaying a Function   296
            A7-2 Editing a Function   297
            A7-3 Locked Functions   298

APPENDIX 8 STOP AND TRACE CONTROL   299

APPENDIX 9 CONTROL STRUCTURE FOR A LOOP   300

APPENDIX 10 ACCESS CONTROL   301

APPENDIX 11 APL CHARACTER SET   303

INDEX   305

PREFACE

About the Subject

In general terms, this book deals with the use of computers to solve practical problems, using the APL language as a vehicle. Except in the most trivial examples, practical computing involves two activities: analyzing a problem so as to prepare a plan for a solution (an algorithm), and writing a program which a computer can employ to carry out that plan. An algorithm is necessarily slanted toward human modes of comprehension and a program is necessarily slanted toward a computer's "mode of comprehension," as represented by one of the so-called programming languages. Various programming languages succeed in different ways and to different degrees in bridging the gap between the way a person conceives a solution and the instructions a computer can "comprehend." APL is a programming language for which the gap is small.

In relation to the comments above, it is significant to note that APL is both a mathematical notation and a computer language. This means that, as a notation, APL can frequently be used to evolve the plan for a solution. Then, not much additional effort is required to translate the plan into a workable program, and the distinction between the activities of planning and programming tends to vanish. Therefore, APL is an appropriate vehicle for learning both how to prepare problems for computer solutions and how to obtain actual solutions. This is the rationale for presenting APL in a problem-solving context.

In the choice of illustrative examples, an attempt has been made to make them simple enough so as to not detract from the programming concepts being illustrated, but sophisticated enough to illustrate nontrivial features of the language. Examples are chosen from a wide range of applications so that the reader will perceive the pertinence of computing to many fields of activity.

The mathematical level required for most of the book is algebra (the transcendental functions are exceptions). Although the mathematical prerequisite is not high, the subject is treated in depth, and is graduated in difficulty in the expectation that the reader's level of sophistication will rise during progress through the book.

The APL notation has certain features of "style" that tend to provide simpler conceptualizations than would otherwise be evident. To learn APL well is to incorporate these features of style into one's mode of thinking. Therefore, style considerations are stressed, including APL versions of the concepts of structured programming.

Many APL systems operate with files, and they are important in many practical applications. However, file operations are not part of the APL language, they are not particularly pertinent to the concepts of APL, and they are not standardized. Accordingly, the subject of file management is not included. With the knowledge of the language that can be obtained from the book, it is expected that the reader will experience little difficulty in acquiring necessary information about files from locally available information.

About the Book

Chapter 1 gives an overview of computing, emphasizing the importance of developing an algorithmic approach, and is included for the reader who is interested in a philosophical appraisal of what computing is about. The extent to which the chapter will be appreciated will depend on the reader's prior knowledge, and so it is recommended that it be read with whatever thoroughness the reader's background permits. The chapter is not essential to the subsequent chapters and may therefore be considered optional. If Chap. 1 is skipped, the ideas presented therein will be acquired gradually through the experience of studying the remainder of the book.

Chapters 2 through 5 contain the basic information about APL and its application to practical problems. Because these chapters must be learned thoroughly, a series of questions is included, providing the reader with a mechanism for continual self appraisal. In Chaps. 2 through 4 these questions are on the margins of the pages of text; in Chap. 5 they are grouped at the end of the chapter, arranged according to related section numbers. Diligent attention to these questions is highly recommended. Success in learning APL depends to a great extent on acquiring a precise knowledge of the meanings of the notations, and this requires much practice.

The sequence of presentation of topics has been chosen to provide an early emphasis on the essential characteristics of APL: the ease of doing computations with arrays, the breaking of an algorithm into parts which can be represented by separate APL programs, and the blending of user created programs with the primitive functions of the language in a common syntax. Accomplishing this purpose necessitates a certain amount of repetition, to the extent that some of the primitive functions of the language are introduced in simplified forms in early chapters, with complete treatments occurring later. The learning of APL can no more be put on a rigid predetermined schedule than can the learning of a natural language. Therefore, the reader is encouraged to "browse ahead" in the interest of finding alternative methods but, of course, only to the extent of not being confused. However, the premature use of ideas presented in Chap. 5 can interrupt the learning of how to use arrays imaginatively.

Chapter 6 deserves special mention because of its unique nature. It presents general treatments of many of the features of APL which are presented in simplified form in the earlier chapters. Therefore, because the properties dealt with are quite complicated and sometimes subtle, this chapter makes higher intellectual demands of the reader than the earlier chapters. To some extent it should be regarded as a reference chapter, and many rereadings of all or parts of it are to be anticipated. The subtle points dealt with in this chapter are essential in the sophisticated use of APL.

Chapters 7 and 8 deal with further refinements, particularly the use of shared variables, and how the concepts of structured programming can be used in APL. These two chapters contain material that a mature user of APL would be expected to know, but to some extent they may be considered optional in an introductory course of study.

The book is primarily intended for beginning students. However, it is expected that people with considerable knowledge of APL will find useful information in the relatively sophisticated treatments in the later chapters, particularly in the descriptions of general properties of the functions in Chap. 6.

Descriptions of the various APL functions given in the text are generally valid on all system implementations, but some slight variations may be found. In particular, some implementations will handle special cases which are not defined in the language. Such special cases can be investigated by experimentation on an individual computer, but their use is not recommended because resulting programs may be system dependent.

In general, the illustrative examples are designed to serve two purposes: to demonstrate the process of analyzing a problem and converting it to a computer solution, and to illustrate details of the language. Because of the latter, the style of a given program tends to be dependent on the features of APL being treated at that point. Thus, several of the illustrative programs are less sophisticated than they would have been without that constraint.

The various system commands used in executing APL on a computer form a conceptual entity apart from the language itself and are, therefore, covered in a set of appendices. The main text deals almost exclusively with the language, but at appropriate points there are brief references to system operations and to the appendices. Assuming learning will be done with the aid of a computer, selected study of the appendices will be required from time to time.

Acknowledgements

The APL computer language is based on the mathematical notation created by Kenneth E. Iverson and presented in his book "A Programming Language." There is therefore a fundamental indebtedness to Dr. Iverson for the very existence of APL, which is respectfully acknowledged. Concerning the development of "Applied APL Programming," I wish to acknowledge the roles played by my colleagues Garth H. Foster and Edward P. Stabler, whose early enthusiasm for APL had a definitive influence. Also, over the several years while the book was being developed and used in classes in preliminary forms, significant suggestions were obtained from my students and many others, among whom Paul Penfield, Jr., John C. McPherson, and Alan Graham, should receive particular mention. The help of all these people is acknowledged with much gratitude. Concerning the actual production, my sincere appreciation is extended to Anne L. Woods and Karen Raab for their excellent work in typing camera-ready copy from a very difficult manuscript, to Pamela Walker for help in proofreading, and to John McPherson for checking all the APL functions and results.

Wilbur R. LePage

Chapter 1

PEOPLE AND COMPUTERS

INTRODUCTION

Mankind, compared with other living species, is strikingly unique in the ability to employ symbols as vehicles for communicating and for thought. Alphabets, language, numbers, and pictorial objects are obvious examples of such symbols. People use symbols by attaching *meaning* to them, *arranging* them to create new meanings, and recognizing *relationships* among symbols and their arrangements. For example, in writing a sentence a person arranges symbols (words) in a meaningful order. Another person then reads and understands that sentence by recognizing relationships of the symbols of the sentence to his or her understanding of the meanings. Perhaps a more succinct example is provided by arithmetic. The symbols 2, 3, + have universal meanings, and in the arrangement 2 + 3 they have a relationship (equality) with the meaning of the symbol 5.

Computers extend the capability of people in the use of symbols. They have an ability to arrange and recognize symbols, and do arithmetic, in amounts and speeds vastly exceeding human capabilities. However, what they do is abstract; meanings must be provided by people. Thus, computers extend, but do not replace human effort.

The objective of this first chapter is to develop an overview. It is hoped that reading about similarities between what a computer does and what people do with language and symbols will excite your interest and put you in a mood for studying the remainder of the book in depth. In seeking this objective, we introduce some examples and treat them in a semirigorous way. A degree of superficiality is necessary because, at the beginning, only a few concepts of the art of computing can be used. Whether you will understand each example thoroughly will depend to some extent on your background. If you have trouble with some of the details, do not be concerned: general impressions are more important than details, in this chapter.

1-1 Communications

The most prevalent method of communicating symbolic objects among people is by written and spoken language (including numbers), but other means such as pictures, sign language, Braille, and other codes are also used. Computers can receive letters of the alphabet, numeral characters, and certain other symbols (such as +) in the form of codes on punched cards or punched paper tape, from magnetic tape, in some cases from a keyboard terminal connected to a computer, or by optical reading of "stylized" printed characters. In all cases one must use a specific technique to put data in proper form (for example, use a card punch or a typewriter). Special computers have been made which allow inputs consisting of line drawings or photographs, and there has been some success in designing computers that can "recognize" spoken words. While there are some differences in the communication of symbolic data from a person to a computer, compared with communications among people, the differences are minor; and there is reason to speculate that future developments in computer technology will close the gap.

The preceding remarks pertain to the transfer of symbolic data from a person to a computer. About the same can be said about communication from a computer to a person, with the exception that it is somewhat easier to obtain variety. For example, for printed outputs various styles of characters can be obtained by the simple expedient of making a mechanical or electrical change in the printing device.

There is a significant difference in speed: A computer can accept data much faster than a person can convert the data into suitable form, and a machine can print out data much faster than a person can read it.

One computer can communicate with another through direct electrical connection. Also, communications among computers are frequently by means of magnetic tape, punched paper tape, or decks of punched cards. A tape or deck of punched cards is produced by one computer and then transported to the other, which reads the tape or deck of cards directly.

Our principal objective in this discussion of communication of data is to show that computers can receive and deliver symbolic data in forms which are familiar. If you wish to communicate with a computer you can do so without the necessity of new learning, other than possibly the operation of some equipment. Here we refer to the *mechanics* of communication. Learning how to *structure* the communication (programming) is a substantial undertaking.

1-2 Elementary Operations on Symbols

Both people and computers are capable of the following basic operations with symbols:

(a) Determination of whether two or more symbols are identical.
(b) Determination of whether two or more symbols are in a prescribed order (for example, are the letters *DHF* in alphabetical order, or is 124 greater than 273).
(c) Collection of symbols into groups and making decisions (a) and (b) for the groups.
(d) Doing the basic operations of arithmetic on numbers.

With respect to the ability to perform these elementary operations, there is not much difference between people and computers, except that computers are millions of times faster and much less prone to error.

1-3 Memory

The human brain is capable of receiving symbolic data (imagery and ideas) from the outside, through the senses, and also creating new data in the process of thinking. In varying degrees, items of data created in these ways can be recovered at a later time. We use the word "memory" to describe storage of data in the brain. Computers are designed to have a somewhat similar capability. They store data taken in from the outside, and create and store new data as they carry out computations. Because of these similarities, a computer is also said to have a "memory."

The similarity is not complete. A computer memory does not exhibit the dynamic and spontaneous qualities of the human brain. Thus, a computer memory is not subject to the process of forgetting. Also, it does not exhibit the whimsical property of sometimes "remembering" and sometimes not. An item of data stored in a computer memory remains there until it is removed through an explicit action of some sort. These differences make it evident that it is not appropriate to regard a computer as a "giant brain."

1-4 Language

Languages used by people to communicate with computers are called *programming languages*. APL (an acronym for A Programming Language) is one example of a programming language. There are many others. Different programming languages have different characteristics, but they all have in common certain features which we shall consider here. A person's communications with a computer fall into two categories: the transmission of data and the transmission of instructions as to what computations are to be done on that data. Since a programming language provides the means for communications between a person and a computer, it must be compatible with both. The differences between a natural language and a programming language reflect to a great extent the differences between people and computers. Natural languages are often vague and imprecise but are very rich in the nuances they can communicate. On the other hand, a programming language must be completely free of ambiguities and shadings of meanings.

A computer program is made up of *statements* written in the style of a particular programming language. Each such statement is similar to an imperative sentence of a natural language. For example, consider the sentence:

"The average of the ages of John and Mary is one-half the sum of John's age and Mary's age."

To write this as a statement in a programming language, a letter of the alphabet, or combination of letters, is used to represent each concept in the sentence (such as John's age). Also, the actions implied by the sentence are represented by symbols pertinent to the particular programming language being used. In the style of APL the above sentence could be written

$$AVERAGE \leftarrow (AGEJOHN + AGEMARY) \div 2$$

The arrow stands for the word "is"; and the three concepts "average of the ages," "John's age," and "Mary's age" are represented, respectively, by the words *AVERAGE*, *AGEJOHN*, and *AGEMARY*.

In computer terminology, each concept in a sentence is called a *variable*, and the word used to represent it is called the *name* of the variable. In this example the variable "average of the ages" is given the name AVERAGE. A distinction is made between a variable and its name because many names can be used to represent a given variable. Thus, for the computer it would be just as appropriate to use the names Z, Y, and X instead of AVERAGE, AGEJOHN, and AGEMARY, giving

$$Z \leftarrow (Y + X) \div 2$$

as an equivalent statement. Many similar statements could be written, using other names for the variables.

The computations implied by either of the preceding statements cannot be done until each of the variables named on the right of the arrow has been *specified* to have a *value*. In the APL language, such specifications might be as follows:

$$AGEMARY \leftarrow 19$$
$$AGEJOHN \leftarrow 21$$

Each of these is called an *assignment statement*. Thus, an assignment statement causes a variable to be specified. After these two steps have been taken, the statement

$$AVERAGE \leftarrow (AGEJOHN + AGEMARY) \div 2$$

will specify AVERAGE to have the value produced by the computation to the right of the arrow, using the numbers 21 and 19 for AGEJOHN and AGEMARY, respectively.

The purpose of this example is to illustrate a simple computer statement, to relate it to the sentence in a natural language from which it is derived, and to emphasize the differences among variables, names of variables, and values of variables.

A sentence of a natural language must conform to certain rules of structure, or *syntax*. For example, every sentence must include a verb. There are also rules of syntax for a programming language. One such rule is that the parentheses in a statement must occur in pairs. Therefore, if the example above had been written with only one parenthesis, or perhaps as

$$AVERAGE \leftarrow)AGEJOHN + AGEMARY) \div 2$$

there would be an error in syntax. The computer would be unable to do the computation.

With respect to syntax, the main difference between a natural language and a programming language is that the rules of syntax of a programming language must be adhered to very strictly. In a natural language it is possible to take liberties with syntax if the context implies what is correct. For example, in answer to the question "Where were you?" it would be permissible to answer with the syntactically incorrect (incomplete sentence) "In class." The existence of the preceding question implies "I was in class." As this example illustrates, a person can sometimes deduce the meaning of a syntactically incorrect statement by knowing what the situation calls for. A computer has no such ability: it must be provided with statements in which *every detail* of syntax is correct.

When first considering the subject of computing it is normal to think about calculations with numbers. However, computers can also do certain operations with values which are *alpha-numeric* characters. These are letters of the alphabet, numerals, and certain other characters. Ordinary arithmetic cannot be done with character values, but the operation of comparing two characters is possible. This leads to the ability to do such things as alphabetize lists of words or to determine whether a given word is in a list. A character value is created by placing the characters within quote symbols. For example,

    FRIENDS ← *'JOHN AND MARY'*

specifies the variable named *FRIENDS* to have the character value indicated. We postpone consideration of computations with character values until later in the book. It is sufficient here merely to point out that character values are possible.

1-5 The Assignment Operation

It is essential that you understand the process of specifying the value of a variable in an assignment statement. In conventional notation the way we do this is to write, for example,

    Let A = 5

We then interpret the symbol A as standing for the number 5. The arrow symbol ← was introduced in Sec. 1-4 for this purpose because it is the APL style for an assignment statement. There are two reasons for not using the equals sign:

First, we observe that in conventional notation the equals sign has several meanings. For example you might be told that

    $(X - 4)^2 = X^2 - 8X + 16$

Here, the equals sign means "identity," namely that both sides are equal for all values of X. On the other hand, you might be asked to "solve" the equation

    $(X - 4)^2 = X - 2$

There are only two particular values of X (3 and 6) for which the two sides of this expression are equal. These meanings are quite different. Given such an expression, you must determine from its nature (the context) what meaning is intended. This observation is made in the light of the fact, mentioned in Sec. 1-4, that a programming language cannot depend on context. Therefore, there cannot be multiple meanings for the equals sign.

The second reason for not using the equals sign in an assignment operation is that in programming it is convenient to be able to *respecify* a variable, as in the two statements

    A ← 6
    A ← $(A + 4) \div 2$

These are to have the following interpretation: A is specified with the value 6, then A is respecified with the value obtained by adding 4 to the first value of A

(namely, 6) and dividing the result by 2. Thus, the respecified value of A is 5. It would be very confusing to write the second of the lines above as

$$A = (A + 4) \div 2$$

The conventional interpretation would be that A is the same on both sides, and that the expression calls for "solving for" A to obtain the value 4. A practical example using respecification is given in Sec. 1-9.

The assignment operation implies a sequence in time of two events:

(a) First, determine the value on the right-hand side of the arrow.
(b) Second, specify the variable named on the left-hand side of the arrow with the value determined in (a).

As the previous example illustrates, step (a) can involve the evaluation of an expression, and that expression can include in it the same named variable (say A) as on the left of the arrow. In such a case the concept of a sequence of two events is important: on the right A has a value; then at a later time A is given another value.

1-6 Structuring a Problem for a Numerical Solution (Algorithms)

The example given in Sec. 1-4 is very simple. The solution is written directly, based on an assumption that the computations required to find the average of two numbers are obvious. For most problems it is not obvious what computational steps are required, and some cases require a considerable amount of thought. A problem must be analyzed and an organized method of attack developed.

To illustrate, we use a problem which requires only a small amount of effort. Suppose you have liquid A of density D_a and liquid B of density D_b and wish to determine in what proportions they should be combined to give a resulting liquid of density D. Using algebra, you would proceed as follows: Let X be the fraction of liquid A and Y the fraction of liquid B. Then you would write the two equations

$$D_a X + D_b Y = D$$
$$X + Y = 1$$

Solving these for X gives the expression

$$X = \frac{D - D_b}{D_a - D_b}$$

and of course when X is known, $Y = 1 - X$.

Based on this analysis, here is one possible set of directions for obtaining a numerical solution.

Step 1: Subtract the density of liquid B from the desired density.
Step 2: Subtract the density of liquid B from the density of liquid A.
Step 3: Divide the result of step 1 by the result of step 2.
Step 4: Subtract the result of step 3 from the number 1.

The result of step 3 is the fraction of liquid A required; the result of step 4 is the fraction of liquid B required.

This set of directions is an example of an *algorithm*, written essentially in English. Observe that each step calls for a calculation with numbers (arithmetic) but that algebra was used in the derivation. The algorithm is not a computer program because it is not written in the symbolism of a programming language.

This algorithm can be written in a more concise form, similar to APL, by using assignment statements as follows:

Algorithm 1-1

$$DA \leftarrow 0.9$$
$$DB \leftarrow 0.5$$
$$D \leftarrow 0.675$$
$$X \leftarrow (D - DB) \div (DA - DB)$$

Because the coding for computer characters does not recognize subscripts, the variables are named DA and DB, rather than D_a and D_b as in the algebraic analysis.

Any set of explicit directions for attaining a computable solution to a problem is an algorithm. It can be written almost entirely in a natural language, or in symbolic form as in algorithm 1-1. If an algorithm is written in a programming language, in a form that a computer can execute, the result is a *program*. Thus, a workable computer program is also an algorithm.

Observe that although names for variables used in an algorithm (or program) are similar to names used in the algebraic manipulation leading to the algorithm, they are conceptually different. In algebra a variable is a quantity that does not necessarily have a specified numerical value; in an algorithm each variable must be given a value before it can be used. Despite some resemblance between a statement in an algorithm and a line of algebra, they are different.

For complicated problems an algorithm is usually written first and then translated into a program. The reason is that programs frequently must include detailed instructions required by the computer which are not essential to the algorithm.

In this simple example there appears to be little advantage in having a computer make the calculations. It is easy to do a problem as simple as this by hand. However, suppose you want for liquids A and B a table of fractions which will produce 1000 different densities of the mixture. There would be a considerable saving in labor in using the computer to make the 1000 calculations as compared with doing them 1000 times by hand. It is a simple matter to arrange the program so it will run 1000 times automatically, each time for a different value of required density D.

1-7 Decision-Making

Suppose someone gives the following instruction to another person: "If it rains, close the windows; otherwise leave them open." This instruction includes two alternative courses of action, and a precise statement as to how to determine which action to take (determine whether it is raining). The person receiving this instruction is given no freedom to make a value judgement; there would be freedom if the instruction were "close the windows if you think it is necessary." A computer can make a "decision" in accordance with an instruction similar to the first example, but not the second. It has no capability of determining whether it "thinks it is necessary."

When writing a computer program you must anticipate each situation requiring a decision, and include explicit instructions for carrying it out.

A computer makes a decision by comparing two values, in effect obtaining answers to questions such as "Is A equal to B?" or "Is A greater than B?" and other similar questions. If the answer is "yes," the computer produces the number 1; if the answer is "no" the computer produces 0. We are not ready to show how to write a program statement which will produce a decision, but we can consider ways to indicate a decision in an algorithm.

A simple example can be derived from a "business" type of application in which a data base consisting of a list of names and numbers (such as a telephone directory) is to be created in a computer memory. Specifically, we shall consider only the addition of names to the list. This is a case where variables will be characters of the alphabet rather than numbers.

Assume a list exists in the computer memory, and that we want an algorithm such that its related program will permit someone sitting at a terminal to add one or more names at the end of the list, by typing the names one at a time. When all additions have been made, the person at the terminal will signal that fact to the computer by typing the word *END*.

The algorithm can be described in words as a series of steps, as follows:

Algorithm 1-2

    Step 1: Enter a name and specify it as the value of a variable named N.
    Step 2: Ask the question "Is the value of N the word '*END*'?"
    Step 3: If the answer is "yes," stop; if the answer is "no," continue to step 4.
    Step 4: Append the value of N to the list existing in memory.
    Step 5: Return to step 1.

It should be evident that this algorithm provides for "recycling" until the word '*END*' is encountered, thereby making it possible to enter a sequence of names. The algorithm does not explain how a computer executes each step, and is not written in a programming language (it is not a program). Our interest at the moment is in a precise statement of operations to be carried out, including how to specify a decision-making process.

There are many ways to write an algorithm. The same information can be put in a more formalized and concise form as follows:

Algorithm 1-3

    ASSIGN an input word (or words) to N
    IF the value of N is '*END*' *THEN* Stop *OR ELSE* Continue
    APPEND the value of N to the existing list in memory
    RETURN to the beginning

In this form we have chosen to capitalize those words which embody the essential features of the algorithm. Note that all the information about the decision is carried in the second line.

Another way to describe an algorithm is by means of a *flow chart*, as shown in Fig. 1-1. The connecting lines and arrowheads provide a sense of motion. They give a pictorial impression of the sequence of events in the operation of an algorithm. As in the figure, it is customary to place statements which describe operations in rectangular "boxes," and the statements which ask questions in "diamond" shaped enclosures. In N = '*END*', N stands for its character value.

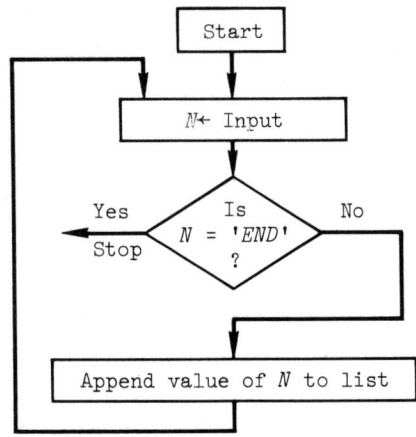

Figure 1-1 Example of a flow chart.

1-8 Illustration of an Iterative Process

We now return to the mixture of two liquids treated in Sec. 1-6. The algorithm described there was arrived at by first developing an analytic solution based on algebra, yielding a formula which could be described in words as the algorithm. That is certainly a reasonable way to solve this problem, but in the interest of expanding on the concept of an algorithm, another approach is considered here.

The general idea is to start with a "guess," and then use a procedure for obtaining a sequence of increasingly accurate approximations for the answer. For example, consider the particular numeric case dealt with previously. The density of liquid A is 0.9, the density of liquid B is 0.5, and the density of the mixture is to be 0.675. The fractional parts, X for liquid A and Y for liquid B, must satisfy the two conditions

$$0.9X + 0.5Y = 0.675$$
$$X + Y = 1$$

Note that the second equation can be "solved" for Y by writing

$$Y = 1 - X \tag{1}$$

and that the first equation can be "solved" for X, as

$$X = \frac{0.675 - 0.5Y}{0.9} \tag{2}$$

Now suppose we "guess" that X is zero, and use this as a first value of X, which we shall call X_1. Equation (1) can then be used to obtain a first value of Y, namely $Y_1 = 1$. This pair of values ($X_1 = 0$ and $Y_1 = 1$) is a solution of Eq. (1) but not of Eq. (2).

The next step is to compute a second value of X (call it X_2) such that the pair of values X_2 and Y_1 will be a solution of Eq. (2). The calculation is

$$X_2 = \frac{0.675 - 0.5}{0.9} = 0.19444$$

Note that because 0.194444 is an approximation for the infinitely repeating decimal 0.19444444..., the values given for X_2 and Y_1 will not be exact solutions of Eq. (2). It is necessary to use a sufficient number of significant digits so that an error such as this (called a *roundoff* error) will be negligible.

We can regard X_2 as a new starting point for a repetition of the above set of two calculations, leading to new values of Y and X to be called Y_2 and X_3, thus:

$$Y_2 = 1 - 0.194444 = 0.805556$$

$$X_3 = \frac{0.675 - 0.5(0.805556)}{0.9} = 0.302469$$

This process can be repeated as many times as we like, until a sufficiently accurate answer is obtained. However, it cannot be continued beyond the point where the roundoff error becomes dominant. This is referred to as an *iterative* process because of its repetitive nature: The words "iterate" and "repeat" are synonyms. The following table (showing the six most significant digits from calculations to ten digits) shows that X and Y approach limiting values as the number of steps increases. The column on the right gives values of the error in density computed from the values of X and Y in the corresponding row. While this column is not part of the iterative process, it provides information as to when to stop. To be specific, you will observe that the error decreases with each successive step. It can be shown, by a proof which we shall omit, that the error would continue to decrease if the table were continued. Therefore, we can be sure that after the 18th step the error in the density is less than 0.000008.

The last value of X in the table is 0.437480 but some of these digits are not accurate. From observing the whole column of values of X, it is seen that some of the digits on the left remain constant beyond a certain point. For example, the first two digits to the right of the decimal point remain unchanged beginning with step 8. This pattern of constancy of digits would continue, for an increasing number of digits, if the table were extended further. Accordingly, since 0.4374 repeats in the last three steps, and values of X are *increasing*, it can be said with certainty

Step Number	Values of X		Values of Y	Values of error in density
1	0.0		1.0	0.175000
2	0.194444		0.805556	0.097222
3	0.302469	⎰Satisfy⎱	0.697531	0.054012
4	0.362483	⎱Eq. (1)⎰	0.637517	0.030007
5	0.395824	⎰Satisfy⎱	0.604176	0.016670
6	0.414347	⎱Eq. (2)⎰	0.585653	0.009261
7	0.424637		0.575363	0.005145
8	0.430354		0.569646	0.002858
9	0.433530		0.566470	0.001588
10	0.435294		0.564706	0.000882
11	0.436275		0.563725	0.000490
12	0.436819		0.563181	0.000272
13	0.437122		0.562878	0.000151
14	0.437290		0.562710	0.000084
15	0.437383		0.562617	0.000047
16	0.437435		0.562565	0.000026
17	0.437464		0.562536	0.000014
18	0.437480		0.562520	0.000008

that the answer is greater than 0.4374 but not greater than 0.4375. Similarly, observation of the last three values of Y shows that since 0.5625 repeats, and the values are *decreasing*, the answer is less than 0.5626 but not less than 0.5625. Thus, after 18 steps of the iterative process, there is an uncertainty in the fifth digit. (The direct method of solution gives the exact values $X = 0.4375$, $Y = 0.5625$.) Do not be misled into believing that an iterative process will always lead to an uncertainty in the fifth digit after 18 steps; how rapidly successive digits become accurate depends on the mathematical relationship involved in the computation of the iterative steps.

The preceding analysis of accuracy is important because it shows that the number of significant digits in the answer depends on the number of steps completed, not the number of digits used in the calculations. This assertion is true only if the number of digits in the calculations is greater than the number of significant digits expected in the answer.

The process described above is said to *converge*, meaning that X and Y approach limiting values (namely, 0.4375 and 0.5625) and the error approaches zero. An intuitive understanding of why it converges can be obtained from Fig. 1-2, which shows graphs of Y vs. X for the two equations. The fact that the lines cross ensures the existence of a solution, and the construction of arrows shows how the steps progress

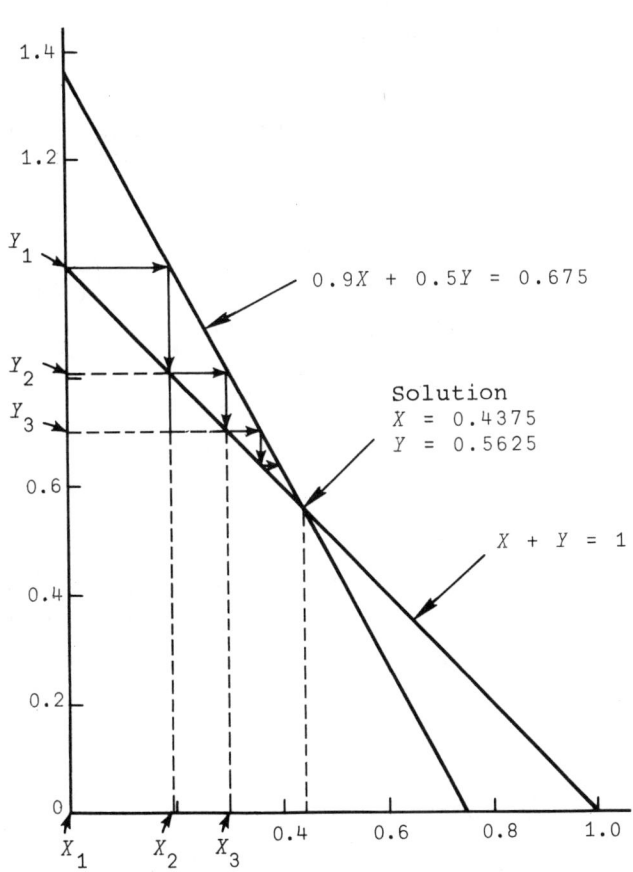

Figure 1-2 Graphical illustration of an iterative process.

12 / People and Computers

with jumps of ever-decreasing size. If the starting value of X is less than the solution value, all values of X obtained in the process will be less than the solution. Conversely, if the starting value is greater than the solution, all values will be greater than the solution. If you will draw some steps on the figure, beginning with an X to the right of the solution, you will see why.

It may seem that this method of solving the problem involves a great deal of unnecessary effort, since a simpler algebraic solution is available. However, the objective here is to illustrate a method which is applicable in many cases where a simpler solution is not possible. An example is given in Sec. 1-10. Furthermore, as you will see when you write programs, an iterative solution is easily done by a computer.

To conclude this section, a word of caution is offered: An iterative process does not always converge to an answer. In fact, the simple case $X - Y = 0$, $X + Y = 1$ does not converge (if you sketch the two graphs for this case, you will see why). Also, the iterative solution shown here converges only if the density of liquid A is greater than the density of liquid B. Interchange the densities and try a few calculations; you will find that the jumps become increasingly large. The case where the density of liquid A is smaller than the density of liquid B is considered in Sec. 1-9.

1-9 Describing an Algorithm for an Iterative Process

The preceding section gave an illustration of an iterative process but not a description of the algorithm. In terms of the same example, we shall use DA, DB and D respectively for the names of the densities of liquids A and B, and the desired density of the mixture. As a first step, we make a simplification based on the fact that the computations of Y are not needed. In Sec. 1-8 we used

$$Y_n = 1 - X_n$$
$$X_{n+1} = \frac{D - DB \times Y_n}{DA}$$

where, in Sec. 1-8, $\begin{cases} D = 0.675 \\ DA = 0.9 \\ DB = 0.5 \end{cases}$

However, these can be combined, giving

$$X_{n+1} = \frac{D - DB \times (1 - X_n)}{DA} \tag{3}$$

Using this formula, values of Y are not computed. At the end of the iteration process the last value of X is a close approximation for the exact solution, and 1 minus that X is a close approximation for the exact Y. The algorithm can be written as follows:

Algorithm 1-4

    ASSIGN values to D, DA, DB
    ASSIGN the desired error tolerance to T
    ASSIGN the initial value 0 to X
    DO the following line *UNTIL* $D - ((DA \times X) + DB \times (1 - X))$ is less than T
        $X \leftarrow (D - DB \times (1 - X)) \div DA$
    $Y \leftarrow 1 - X$

The difference between Eq. (3) and the line following *DO* in the algorithm is to be emphasized. Equation (3) is conventional algebraic notation in which the calculation of a *sequence* of values is implied by the subscripts. There is a different name for the variable (X_1, X_2, X_3, etc.) associated with each of these values. The algorithmic notation employing the assignment symbol ← means that each time the expression on the right is evaluated the variable named X is *respecified* with that value. Thus, X has different values on the right and on the left. Instead of having a sequence of names (X_1, X_2, X_3, etc.), the algorithmic notation has *one* name X which takes on the same sequence of values, one at a time.

The word *UNTIL* implies a decision, and the statement on its right gives the instruction as to when to stop iterating and skip to the last line. The instruction is important; every algorithm must include an instruction for stopping.

This is not a computer program, although it can easily be converted to one. It is a combination of English and mathematical symbolism which gives a concise description of the algorithm. This algorithm is every bit as complete and valid as algorithm 1-1 given in Sec. 1-6.

Next, we shall elaborate on this algorithm to permit its operation for the case where liquid B has a greater density than liquid A. (In Sec. 1-8 it is pointed out that this case does not converge.) For the moment the case of equal densities for the two liquids will be ruled out. One way to modify the algorithm is to arrange so that in the iterations X will always be the fractional part for the liquid of largest density, whether it be A or B. Thus, if the density of liquid B is the larger, the iterative process will produce Y. An algorithm which includes this feature can be written:

Algorithm 1-5

    ASSIGN values to *D*, *DA*, *DB*
    ASSIGN the desired error tolerance to *T*
    ASSIGN the initial value 0 to *X*
    IF DA > DB THEN D1 ← *DA; D2* ← *DB ELSE D1* ← *DB; D2* ← *DA*
    DO the following line *UNTIL D* - ((*D1* × *X*) + *D2* × (1 - *X*)) is less than *T*
    X ← (*D* - *D2* × (1 - *X*)) ÷ *D1*
    IF DA > DB THEN X ← *X ELSE X* ← 1 - *X*
    Y ← 1 - *X*

In this modification there are two instances of the *IF-THEN-OR ELSE* form introduced in Sec. 1-7, except that here the word *OR* has been omitted in compliance with general practice. (*OR* was included in Sec. 1-7 for the sake of completeness.) The first occurrence of an *IF* line means: If it is true that *DA* is greater than *DB*, then assign *DA* to *D1* and *DB* to *D2*; if it is not true, assign *DB* to *D1* and *DA* to *D2*. The result of this action is that *D1* will always be the larger density and *D2* the smaller, no matter what the relative magnitudes of *DA* and *DB*. Note that *D1* and *D2* are used in the iterative part, and that convergence is ensured because *D1* is larger than *D2*. The value produced for *X* in the iterative process is now the fraction for the liquid of larger density (actually *Y*, in the case where *DB* is greater than *DA*). The second *IF* line takes care of this possibility.

14 / People and Computers

The case where *DA* equals *DB* is degenerate and not handled by the algorithm above. This case has no solution unless *D* equals *DA* and *DB*, and then *X* can have any value. Therefore, this case should not be submitted for computation. To prevent its accidental occurrence the algorithm can be changed by replacing the first *IF* line by:

IF DA = DB THEN Stop *ELSE* Continue to next line
IF DA > DB THEN D1 ← DA; D2 ← DB ELSE D1 ← DB; D2 ← DA

It may appear that nothing much has been accomplished, inasmuch as you have not been shown how to write a computer program for this example. However, what we are stressing here is conciseness and orderliness of thought; the fact that before attempting to write a program you should create a *precise* and *complete* set of directions (an algorithm), and that there are systematic and concise ways of doing so.

A flow chart description of algorithm 1-5, including a check to exclude the case of equal densities, is shown in Fig. 1-3. Each of these forms of the algorithm can

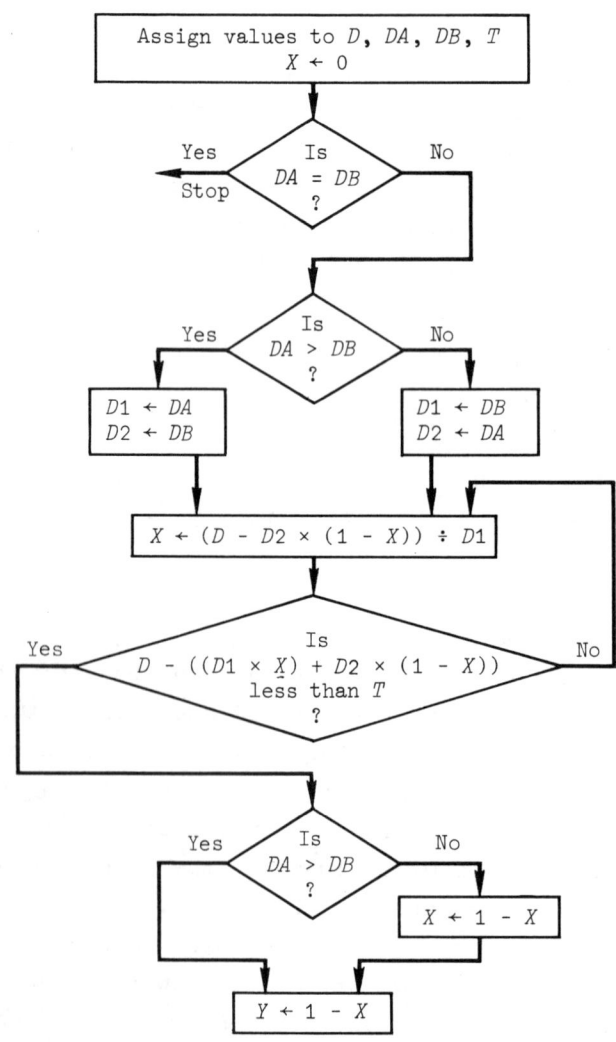

Figure 1-3 Flow chart of the algorithm for a mixture of two liquids.

be converted to a program with very little change, if the programming language is appropriate for that form (the same language is not necessarily the most appropriate for both). There is value in each of these basic styles and so it is worthwhile for you to be aware of both approaches.

1-10 An Algorithm for Solving a Cubic Equation

The next step in our consideration of algorithms deals with the problem illustrated by Fig. 1-4. This figure represents a spherical tank for storing water. The radius of the tank is R and the problem is to find the height of water H which will correspond to a specified volume V.

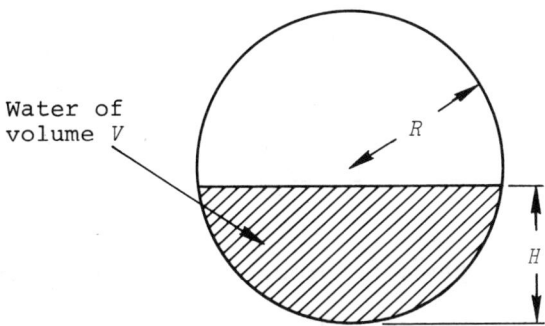

Figure 1-4 A spherical tank partially filled with water.

We shall assume that the formula for the volume of water is known. It is

$$V = \pi H^2 (R - \frac{H}{3})$$

For any specific case, R and V are known, and H is the unknown. One would naturally think of manipulating this expression so as to separate terms with various powers of H, giving the cubic equation

$$H^3 - 3RH^2 + \frac{3V}{\pi} = 0$$

There is a known formula for the roots of a cubic equation but it is too complicated to use conveniently. Therefore, we shall use an iterative solution.

Returning to the first form of the equation, by introducing the variable $W = H^2$, we can obtain the equivalent pair of simultaneous equations

$$W = \frac{V}{\pi(R - \frac{H}{3})}$$

$$W = H^2$$

Graphs of these two relationships between W and H are shown in Fig. 1-5, for the case $R = 5$ and $V = 370$. The main difference between this figure and Fig. 1-2 is that now the lines are curved. The dashed arrows indicate that an iterative process will converge starting from either $H = 0$ or $H = 10$.

16 / People and Computers

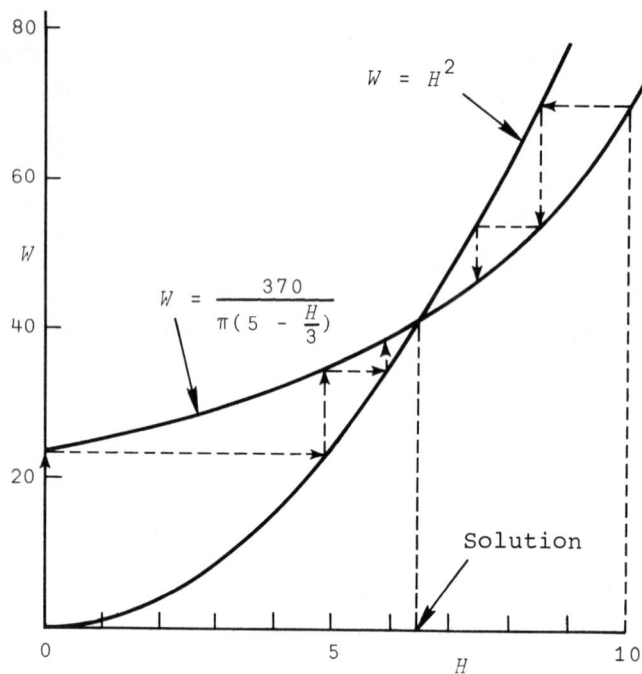

Figure 1-5 An iterative process for a nonlinear case.

Let H_n represent the nth value computed for H, and W_n the nth value computed for W. Assuming H_n is known (assume $H_1 = 0$ or 10) the corresponding W is

$$W_n = \frac{V}{\pi(R - \frac{H_n}{3})}$$

and the next H is

$$H_{n+1} = \sqrt{W_n}$$

Variable W is pertinent to the analysis, but its numerical values are not needed. Therefore, these two formulas can be combined to give

$$H_{n+1} = \sqrt{\frac{V}{\pi(R - \frac{H_n}{3})}}$$

Results for the case $R = 5$ and $V = 370$ (starting from $H = 0$), carried to the point where the error is less than 0.002, are given in the following table. Values in the column on the right are computed from

$$\text{Error} = 370 - \pi H_n^2(5 - \frac{H_n}{3})$$

in order to provide information as to when to stop. Recall that an algorithm for an iterative process must include an instruction for termination.

Step number	Values of H	Values of error in volume
1	0.0	370.000
2	4.85334	119.716
3	5.90099	38.203
4	6.23146	13.438
5	6.34779	4.909
6	6.39033	1.819
7	6.40609	0.678
8	6.41197	0.253
9	6.41416	0.094
10	6.41498	0.035
11	6.41528	0.013
12	6.41540	0.005
13	6.41544	0.002
14	6.41546	0.001

One way to write an algorithm for this example is

Algorithm 1-6

ASSIGN values to R, V
ASSIGN the desired error tolerance to T
ASSIGN the initial value 0 to H

DO the following line *UNTIL* $V - \pi H^2(R - (H \div 3))$ is less than T
$H \leftarrow \sqrt{V \div \pi(R - (H \div 3))}$

Last value computed for H is the approximate answer.

As in algorithm 1-4, when the assignment arrow is used, subscripts on H are not needed. The expression in the assignment to H is not APL notation; in APL other symbols are used for π and the square root.

CONCLUSION

The ability of people to use abstract symbols, such as alphabets and numbers, is the source of their ability to make plans for future actions. Simple plans, such as calculating how much paint is required to cover a house, do not require the aid of a computer. However, in more complex planning, such as the design of an electric power station, or the legislative decisions of a government body, computers enhance tremendously human ability to use symbols, but do not replace it.

A computer is a nonintelligent "slave" capable of following *explicit* directions and doing vast amounts of computing accurately and rapidly. The requirement for explicitness of directions means that one must plan meticulously; namely, write an algorithm and a program. Such planning is sometimes useful in its own right because it can lead to increased understanding. Because of the speed and accuracy of a computer, it is sometimes possible to use types of solutions (such as iterative solutions) which are not otherwise feasible.

A few very simple algorithms were developed in this chapter, and only a hint was given as to the nature of a program. Programs in APL could not be illustrated because only the assignment operation of APL was introduced. The illustrative algorithms are rudimentary. For example, an algorithm for the mixture problem would be better if it included a decision step to prevent cases which are impossible (cases where either X or Y is negative); and the algorithm for the tank problem should include a decision step to prevent computation for the impossible case where the required volume is larger than the volume of the tank.

18 / People and Computers

It is recognized that the extent to which you can appreciate this first chapter will depend on your previous experiences, particularly the degree to which you are comfortable with logical thought. Probably few readers will perceive all of the subtleties of this chapter on a first reading, and therefore it is recommended that you reread all or parts of it from time to time, as you progress through the book. The general principles presented here may be helpful as adjuncts to the later chapters; they may help you obtain a unified viewpoint. What may seem to be a vast amount of detail can blend into a meaningful whole perceived as a collection of relatively few general principles. The chapter is consistent with the general policy of the book, of not merely expounding on the APL computer language, but also developing for you an understanding of the general principles which underlie the use of a computer in managing human affairs.

Problems--Chapter 1

1-1 (a) Suppose, as in the text, the following assignments are made:

$$AGEJOHN \leftarrow 21$$
$$AGEMARY \leftarrow 19$$

Then, doing the following

$$AGEJOHN \leftarrow 22$$
$$AGEMARY \leftarrow 20$$

changes the (variables/values) _____.
(b) If you write

$$P \leftarrow 485$$

and say nothing more about this, the (variable/name) _____ is not known.
(c) You (can/cannot) _____ determine from the name of a variable what the variable is.

1-2 (a) If four named variables are specified with character values, as follows:

$$RED \leftarrow \text{'YELLOW'}$$
$$BLUE \leftarrow \text{'GREEN'}$$
$$GREEN \leftarrow \text{'RED'}$$
$$YELLOW \leftarrow \text{'BLUE'}$$

list the names of the variables in such an order that their values will be arranged alphabetically: (1)_____ (2)_____ (3)_____ (4)_____ .
(b) To say "assign the value 25 to P" (is/is not) _____ equivalent to saying "specify P to have the value 25."
(c) A variable (must/need not be) _____ specified before it can be used in a statement.

1-3 Opposite each of the following write "identity" if both sides are equal for all X, or "to be solved for X" if the sides are not identical for all X.

(a) $(3 + X)^3 = X^3 + 26X^2 + 10$ _____
(b) $(3 + X)^3 = 27 + 9X + 27X^2 + X^3$ _____
(c) $(X + 1)(1 - X) = X^2 - 1$ _____
(d) $\dfrac{1 + X}{1 - \sqrt{1 - X}} = 1 + \sqrt{1 - X} + \dfrac{1}{1 - \sqrt{1 - X}}$ _____

1-4 (a) Suppose the following sequence of steps is part of an algorithm:

$X1X \leftarrow 438$
$PAPER \leftarrow 86$
$PAPER \leftarrow PAPER + X1X$

After these steps have been executed, the value of PAPER is _____; the value of $X1X$ is _____.

(b) Suppose the following sequence of steps is part of an algorithm

$A \leftarrow 5$
$B \leftarrow 2 \times A \leftarrow A \times 3$

After these steps have been executed, the value of A is _____; the value of B is _____.

1-5 Mark each of the following sentences true or false.

(a) An algorithm is a description of a problem to be solved. _____
(b) An algorithm is a specific set of steps for solving a problem. _____
(c) A workable computer program is also an algorithm. _____
(d) Any statement of an algorithm is a computer program. _____

1-6 A set of steps equivalent to algorithm 1-1 is shown below. On each blank line give the value for the variable name indicated (upon completion of the step).

$DA \leftarrow 0.9$
$DB \leftarrow 0.5$
$D \leftarrow 0.675$
$D \leftarrow D - DB$ D is _____
$DA \leftarrow DA - DB$ DA is _____
$X \leftarrow D \div DA$ X is _____
$Y \leftarrow X$ Y is _____

1-7 Compute values for at least five rows of a table similar to the one in Sec. 1-8, but using 1 for the starting value of X.

1-8 For the density of liquids problem described in Sec. 1-6, suppose liquids A and B have densities 0.9 and 0.5, respectively, and the mixture is to have density 0.75.
(a) Compute the fractions X and Y for liquids A and B from algorithm 1-1.
(b) Construct at least five rows of a table similar to the one in Sec. 1-8.

1-9 In sec. 1-9 algorithm 1-4 is given, but it will converge only if DA, the density of liquid A, is greater than DB, the density of liquid B. Suppose the line following DO is changed to

$$X \leftarrow \frac{(DB - D) + DA \times X}{DB}$$

Decide whether the algorithm will then converge for DB greater than DA, but not for DA greater than DB.

1-10 Suppose the second line of algorithm 1-3 begins

IF the value of N is not 'END' THEN

Complete the line so it will be equivalent to algorithm 1-3.

1-11 Refer to algorithm 1-5 and explain why it could not be changed to (excluding the first three lines)

IF $DA > DB$ THEN $DA \leftarrow DA$; $DB \leftarrow DB$ ELSE $DA \leftarrow DB$; $DB \leftarrow DA$

DO the following line UNTIL $D - ((DA \times X) + DB \times (1 - X))$ is less than T
$X \leftarrow (D - DB \times (1 - X)) \div DA$

IF $DA > DB$ THEN $X \leftarrow X$ ELSE $X \leftarrow 1 - X$

$Y - 1 - X$

20 / People and Computers

1-12 For the results tabulated in Sec. 1-10, it can be said that the iterative process has been carried far enough so that we can be sure the height of water is (less/greater)_____ than_____ but not (less/greater)_____ than_____.

1-13 Construct five rows of a table similar to the one in Sec. 1-10 (for the same values of R and V) but beginning with 10 as the initial value of H.

1-14 Complete the following algorithm

    $X \leftarrow K \leftarrow 1$
    DO the next two lines *UNTIL* _____
    $K \leftarrow$
    $X \leftarrow X + (1 \div)$

so that it will compute the sum $1 + \frac{1}{2} + \frac{1}{3} + \ldots + \frac{1}{10}$.

1-15 Construct a flow chart which is equivalent to algorithm 1-6. Assume H starts at zero.

Chapter 2

RUDIMENTS OF APL

Introduction

    Whereas Chap. 1 deals with generalities about computing, the present chapter introduces the detailed study of how APL can be employed to obtain practical results. The APL language can be learned as an abstract notation, without the aid of a computer. However, it is expected that you will use a computer as an aid to learning; to confirm examples given in the text and to try examples on your own. It will be helpful if you keep in mind the idea that your interactions with the computer will be similar to the verbal interactions you would have with a person working under your direction. Specifically:

(a) You will communicate data to the computer. These data are the "raw material" on which the computer does its work.
(b) You will write sets of directions (programs) describing in detail the steps the computer will take in performing a task.
(c) The computer will inform you of any erroneous instructions which it cannot "understand" or carry out.
(d) The computer will transmit results to you in a useful form: numbers and words printed on paper or displayed on a cathode ray tube, and possibly graphs and line drawings.

You can use a computer without dealing with category (b) provided that someone else has written the required programs. However, we are interested in the complete process.

    Beginning with Sec. 2-6 there is a set of questions on the inside border of each page, pertaining to the text on that page. Answering these questions can help you appraise your learning, and provide hints as to what further study might be appropriate. It is suggested that you study an entire page before trying the questions, but use whatever study technique seems best for you.

    This chapter presents enough of the APL language to enable you to perceive its nature, and to write programs for solving simple problems. When you have completed the chapter you will be in a position, in relation to APL, similar to that of a person in the early stages of learning a natural language, when ideas will be expressed in groups of short simple sentences. This chapter is very important; you should study it carefully because it provides the foundation for everything that follows.

22 / Rudiments of APL

2-1 The Nature of an APL Time-Sharing System

In this book it is assumed that you will use the APL language through a keyboard terminal in an *interactive mode*. This may be described as a "conversing" with the computer by means of the keyboard. You will send data and instructions to the computer by typing at the terminal, and the responses from the computer will be automatically typed on the same terminal, or appear on a cathode-ray screen.

In using APL you will be involved with the language itself and also with the control of the system *through the system commands*. The body of this text is about the language, but information about system operations is contained in the appendices.

In the case of some small computers, APL is used by one person at a time. Large computers usually run APL in a *time-sharing* mode, in which many users operate simultaneously. The use of the language to do computations is the same for both types of computers, but there are some differences in the system operations. In the case of time sharing, the main computer (called the *central processor*) will do your work and the jobs of other users, one at a time, giving only a fraction of a second to each one. Except when the computer is overloaded, shifting from job to job occurs so rapidly that each person has the impression of being the only user.

Each authorized person has a *user number* which is recognized by the computer at the time of "signing on." This number may be augmented by a *password* chosen by the user. These two features (number and password) provide security against unauthorized use. The procedure for signing on varies among computers, so it is impossible to give a universally valid description of that procedure. You should obtain information about it from the people who operate your computer.

The "return" key plays an essential role; after you have typed something for the computer to execute, execution is initiated by depressing the return key. For example, you might type

```
      X←35←————————You do a "return" here; the computer assigns 35 to X
      X+6←—————————You do a "return" here; the computer computes X+6
41←———————————————and prints the result at the margin, on this line
```

While computations are in progress the keyboard is inactive, so you cannot use it. Upon completion of computations, the keyboard is released for use, and the printing head (or cursor in the case of a cathode-ray terminal) moves in six spaces. Accordingly, illustrations in the text show items typed by the user indented six spaces (there are a few exceptions, noted where they occur). APL requires a keyboard of special characters, some of which are created by overstriking two symbols (such as o and \ to create ⌽). Overstruck symbols can be typed in either order.

2-2 Workspace and Memory Utilization

While you are using the computer you have access to a certain amount of computer memory called a *workspace* in which you will do your computing and store *objects* such as programs and data. It is never evident to you where in the computer the workspace is stored; it changes from time to time. Sometimes it will be on magnetic disk or tape, and sometimes in the main high speed memory of the computer.

There are certain procedures you will have to learn concerning the "management" of your workspace. In particular, the first time you sign on it will be necessary to give your workspace a name. When you sign on again you will have to put the workspace you named previously into "active" status so you can use it. Also, when you have created data or programs which you want to keep for future use, you will have to "save" them. Objects that are saved in a workspace are stored in the computer memory indefinitely. Objects no longer wanted can be erased. The procedures for managing a workspace are given in Appendix 1.

The amount of memory space available in your workspace will depend on the particular computer system you are using. Some systems employing "virtual" storage have essentially unlimited workspaces. If you have a finite workspace, as you create objects this space will be gradually "used up." Also, the utilization of space usually increases temporarily while computations are in progress. Therefore, it is not possible to fill a finite workspace with objects and still do computing. If you do something that exceeds your workspace size, you will receive the message *WS FULL*, and computation will stop.

There is an object in your workspace called a *symbol table* which records information within the computer about the objects you create. In most systems the symbol table cannot exceed a certain size, so occasionally you may receive the message *SYMBOL TABLE FULL*. When that happens you must reduce the symbol table by employing a special procedure described in Appendix 5. Until this message is received you will be unaware of the existence of the symbol table.

Most APL systems include a facility for copying workspaces (or objects of workspaces) from user numbers other than yours, and from a *public library*. A public library is a collection of workspaces which contain programs of general usefulness. You can obtain information about public libraries from the people in charge of your computer. The copying aspect of workspace management is described in Appendix 1.

The data objects in a workspace are numeric or character values, and the names of variables. A computer recognizes three types of numbers, as follows:

(a) Boolean numbers, used in computations involving logic. They are the numbers 0 and 1.

(b) Integers: plus or minus the ordinary "counting numbers," such as 9 or 354872.

(c) Mixed numbers: numbers that have fractional parts (a number is mixed even if the fractional part is zero). Examples are 27.624 and 5.0.

Technical details about the storage in memory of different types of numbers is given in Appendix 4. Various computer systems differ somewhat in this respect, but in general it can be said that a mixed number requires twice as much memory space as an integer, and a Boolean number requires very much less (of the order of one-thirtieth of the space required by an integer). A character requires about one-quarter as much space as an integer. There is a system-dependent limit on how large integers and mixed numbers can be.

24 / Rudiments of APL

2-3 Properties of a Workspace*

A workspace has five parameters which affect computations done within it. Three of them are mentioned here because they are of immediate interest. They are:

(a) Printing precision (number of significant digits in printed results).
(b) Printing width (maximum number of characters in one line of printed output).
(c) Index origin (starting number, either 0 or 1, for all counting operations done automatically by the computer).

In any given APL system these parameters will automatically have certain nominal values when a workspace is created. These values will remain fixed unless you change them. They are values of three *system variables*: ⎕PP (printing precision), ⎕PW (printing width), and ⎕IO (index origin). You can determine their values by typing the names of these variables. For a typical system (not necessarily yours)

```
      ⎕PP
10
      ⎕PW
120
      ⎕IO
1
```

These can be changed by assigning the values you want, for example

```
      ⎕PP←8
```

to obtain 8 significant digits in numerical answers, and

```
      ⎕PW←80
```

to obtain line lengths of 80 characters maximum, and

```
      ⎕IO←0
```

to cause counting operations automatically done by the computer to start with zero. There is a range of acceptable values for each of these. For example, ⎕IO can be used only if its value is 0 or 1, and ⎕PP cannot be used if its value requests more significant digits than the computer can produce. If you assign an inadmissible value to one of these variables, an error report will occur when its use is invoked.

2-4 Diagnostic Messages (error and trouble reports)

From time to time you will make errors. Some will be typing errors and others will be errors in design of the program steps or in the use of the system. When an error is made which would require the computer to do something impossible it will respond by typing a *diagnostic* message. There are two types of diagnostic messages: those due to errors in use of the language, called *error reports*, and those having to do with operation of the system, called *trouble reports*.

---

*If system variables are not available in your system, refer to Appendix 1 for the system commands which are similar but not completely equivalent. System commands are not variables.

An error report occurs when you make a mistake in the APL language. It consists of a description of the type of error, a reproduction of the statement line in which the error occurred, and a mark below the line to indicate the location where computation became impossible. For example, suppose you type the (incorrect) statement

```
Y←2+4)÷3
```

The computer will respond with

SYNTAX ERROR
```
      Y←2+4)÷3
      ∧
```

The words *SYNTAX ERROR* describe the error; the syntax is incorrect because there is an unpaired parenthesis. Other types of errors elicit other appropriate descriptive words. A list of the various error reports is given in Appendix 2. The mark ∧ will not necessarily point to the error, because the computer does not know what you intended.

A trouble report is similar to an error report, except that it refers to an error in a system command. It does not include the reproduction of an APL statement. To illustrate, suppose you try to copy a workspace, but misspell its name. You will receive the trouble report

WS NOT FOUND

A list of the trouble reports is given in Appendix 3.

Diagnostic messages are very useful as teaching aids. Do not be afraid to experiment on the computer and learn from your mistakes; you cannot damage the computer.

2-5 Correcting Typing Errors

When you make a typing error, and discover it *before* you press the return key, you can correct the error without returning to the beginning. The procedure for correcting errors is not the same in all APL systems, but the following is typical. Suppose you type

```
Y←6325984
```

but intended 6325.984. To make the correction, backspace to the first *incorrect* character (9 in this case) and then press the *ATTN* key. This will print the mark ∨ under the 9, and then you type what is correct. It will look like this:

```
Y←6325984
     ∨          This symbol produced by the computer
     .984
```

Everything above and to the right of the symbol ∨ is wiped out and replaced by what you type then.

If your APL system requires a different procedure, find out about it from someone involved in operating your computer.

2-6 Names and Values of Variables

In this section we shall repeat some of the ideas introduced briefly in Sec. 1-4. Suppose you wish to compute the hypotenuse of a right triangle having sides 3 meters and 4 meters. There are three variables involved in the computation: two sides and the hypotenuse. The variable representing one side has the value 3, the other the value 4. The hypotenuse has the value 5, computed from the expression (in ordinary notation)

$$\sqrt{3^2 + 4^2}$$

An expression in numerical values (such as 3 and 4 in this example) is not normally used on a computer, although it is possible on the APL system. Rather, this is an example of what is usually done on a hand or desk calculator. In computing, expressions (formulas) are written using "words" as names of the variables. By "words" we mean a combination of one or more letters of the alphabet, and numerals, written together without spaces (∆ is accepted as a letter in some systems). A numeral is not permitted as the first character. These are not necessarily words that can be found in a dictionary. Underlines are permitted with letters. For example, X and X̲ can be used as two different names.

To emphasize the difference between a variable and its name, the following possibilities are listed for the example of a triangle (of course, many other names are possible).

	Possible Names			
Variable	Example 1	Example 2	Example 3	Example 4
Side 1	S1	X	A	SIDE1
Side 2	S2	Y	B	SIDE2
Hypotenuse	HYP	Z	H	HYPOTENUSE

Example 4 shows that the name of a variable can be the same, or very nearly the same, as the natural words which describe it, except that it cannot include spaces. The first example shows names which are mnemonically related to (suggestive of) the natural words. The second and third examples show the use of single letters, as is usual in algebra. The choice of a name for a variable is arbitrary so long as it does not conflict with some other use of the same name. If a choice is not made mnemonically it can be on the basis of any convenient rationale, or by whim. However, in the interest of brevity, names of variables should be reasonably short.

For each of the following, on the blank lines list any names that are not acceptable, and explain why.

1) | Variable | Name |
   |---|---|
   | Side 1 | SIDE1 |
   | Side 2 | S2 |
   | Hypotenuse | S3 |

   _____
   _____
   _____

2) | Variable | Name |
   |---|---|
   | Side 1 | SIDE A |
   | Side 2 | SIDE B |
   | Hypotenuse | H |

   _____
   _____
   _____

3) | Variable | Name |
   |---|---|
   | Side 1 | SIDE2 |
   | Side 2 | SIDE1 |

   _____
   _____

4) | Variable | Name |
   |---|---|
   | Side 1 | SIDE |
   | Side 2 | SIDE |

   _____
   _____

5) | Variable | Name |
   |---|---|
   | Hypotenuse | 3RDSIDE |

   _____

Rudiments of APL / 27

In the following, use the specifications in the text.

1) Give the results for

$SIDE2 \times SIDE2$

_____

$SIDE2 \times SIDE1$

_____

2) After doing $SIDE1 \leftarrow 4$ what result is produced by

$SIDE1 \times SIDE2$

_____

3) Give the results for

$5 + SIDE2$

_____

$SIDE2 + 3$

_____

In computing, as in algebra, the use of names for variables makes it possible to write general expressions which are not committed to any particular numerical values. Thus, using the names given in Example 2, the expression for the hypotenuse (again in ordinary algebraic notation) is

$$\sqrt{X^2 + Y^2}$$

or, using the variables of Example 4,

$$\sqrt{SIDE1^2 + SIDE2^2}$$

Of course, these expressions can produce computed results only if the names appearing in them represent numerical values.

Transferring to APL notation, the variables of the last example are specified by writing the two assignment statements

$SIDE1 \leftarrow 3$
$SIDE2 \leftarrow 4$

Until such time as $SIDE1$ might be respecified with another numerical value, it will be equivalent to the numerical value 3 in any statement in which it is used. Thus,

$SIDE1 \times SIDE1$
9

is equivalent to

3×3
9

An attempt to use a name which has not been specified will result in the error report *VALUE ERROR*.

A comparison of $SIDE1 \times SIDE1$ with 3×3 emphasizes a very important fact, that an APL expression can contain either names of specified variables or Arabic numerals. Also, there can be a mixture, as in $3 \times SIDE1$. Numerals used in names for variables, as in $SIDE2$, do not represent numbers; the numeral 2 has no significance to the computer as a numeric value. In this text we make a clear distinction between a numeral (something you write) and a number (an abstract mathematical object). To clarify this, note that the Arabic 5 and the Roman V are two ways to write numerals for the same number "five."

We have emphasized, here and in Chap. 1, that there is a difference between a variable (such as "side 1") and a name for a variable, (such as $S1$, X, A, or $SIDE1$). Therefore, to be precise, we should refer to $SIDE1$ as the "variable named $SIDE1$." However, it is common practice to shorten this to the variable "$SIDE1$," leaving it as understood that $SIDE1$ is the *name* of a variable.

The question now arises as to how to direct a query to the computer so that it will give you the value of a variable. This is done merely by "sending" the name of the variable to the computer, by typing it. Thus, if $SIDE1$ has been specified as indicated earlier, you can *test* its value as follows:

    $SIDE1$
3

This is an illustration of the fact that the computer returns to you the value produced by any expression you type. Also, since a numeral (say 7) is the "name" for a number ("seven"), a query for the value of 7 gives

      7
7

2-7 Example of an APL Statement

Continuing to discuss a right triangle, if the steps

    $SIDE1 \leftarrow 3$
    $SIDE2 \leftarrow 4$

have been done,

    $((SIDE1 \times SIDE1)+(SIDE2 \times SIDE2))*0.5$
5

will produce the value of the hypotenuse. This APL statement is the equivalent of $\sqrt{SIDE1^2 + SIDE2^2}$. $SIDE2 \times SIDE2$ is computed first, then $SIDE1 \times SIDE1$ is computed. The + sign causes these two squares to be added giving the value (25) between the outer parentheses. Finally, the symbols *0.5 on the right mean "raise to the 0.5 power," equivalent to the square root.

Now observe that

    $X \leftarrow 3$
    $Y \leftarrow 4$
    $((X \times X)+(Y \times Y))*0.5$
5

is completely equivalent, emphasizing the principle that the names chosen for variables are unimportant so long as they are used *consistently*.

The result produced by such a computation is a *returned value*, meaning that the value is "returned" to the workspace and can be assigned to a name. Accordingly, continuing to use X and Y as specified above,

    $HYP \leftarrow ((X \times X)+(Y \times Y))*0.5$

assigns 5 to HYP and no printed result appears. To obtain a print in this case, it is necessary to test for the value of HYP, thus

---

1) Using variables specified in the text, what is the result of

    $SIDE2$

_____

2) Using variables specified in the text, fill in between the parentheses in the following, so the result will be the same as for the statement in the text.

    $((\underline{\hspace{1cm}})+$
    $(SIDE1 \times SIDE1))*0.5$

_____

3) What result is produced by

    $S1 \leftarrow 5$
    $S2 \leftarrow 12$
    $((S1 \times S1)+(S2 \times S2))*0.5$

_____

4) What result is produced by

    $9*0.5$

_____

5) What is the result of the following sequence of steps?

    $X \leftarrow 5$
    $Y \leftarrow 12$
    $H \leftarrow ((X \times X)+(Y \times Y))*0.5$
    H

_____

1) What are the results of the following sequence of steps?

    A←2 4 5
    BX←6 11 7
    A+BX

_____

    A×BX

_____

    BX÷2

_____

    3×BX

_____

2) If

    S1←5 4 3 2
    S2←4

show the result produced by

    ((S1×S1)+(S2×S2))*0.5

_____

3) Is there any change in the result of (2) if the specification of S1 and S2 are interchanged?

_____

4) Give the expected computer response to

    2 3 + 5 6 7

_____

```
      HYP
5
```

HYP could be used as a variable in a subsequent statement.

2-8 A List of Numbers or Characters as One Value

A variable can have a value consisting of a row of numbers, specified by typing the numerals with *one or more* spaces between them, as in

```
      W←3 5 8 2
      Y←2 4 3 5
      W
3 5 8 2
      Y
2 4 3 5
```

Such variables can be used in a statement, as in

```
      3+W
6 8 11 5
```

showing that 3 is added to each number of *W*. Another example,

```
      W×Y
6 20 24 10
```

shows that corresponding numbers of *W* and *Y* are multiplied.

In general, a value which is a set of numbers is called an *array*, and an array having numbers in a row is called a *vector*. Each number of a vector is an *element*. To combine two vectors arithmetically, they must have the same number of elements; but a single number can be combined with a vector.

A vector can be specified as in the above only with numerals. Thus, although you might have done A←3 and B←4,

```
      Z←3 4
      Z←A B
```

are not equivalent. The second will yield an error report.

To illustrate the use of a vector, suppose we execute

```
      SIDE1←4
      SIDE2←2 3 4 5
```

and then

```
      ((SIDE1×SIDE1)+(SIDE2×SIDE2))*0.5
4.47214 5 5.65685 6.40312
```

The result is a list of numbers (reading from left-to-right) giving the hypotenuse of each of four right triangles, all having 4 as one side and 2, 3, 4, and 5 as the other sides. As another example, suppose there are two right triangles, one having sides 26.8 and 19.4, and the other having sides 2.5 and 3.6. Both triangles can be solved simultaneously by doing

30 / Rudiments of APL

```
      S1←26.8  2.5
      S2←19.4  3.6
      ((S1×S1)+(S2×S2))*0.5
33.0847  4.38292
```

A vector consisting of a "counting" sequence of positive integers, such as could be created by the assignment

```
      P←1  2  3  4
```

is often useful. There is a special way such a vector can be created, using a function called the *index generator* (monadic use of the symbol ι). It takes the number of elements in the desired vector as its argument. An example is (in origin 1)

```
      ι4
1  2  3  4
```

In ιN, N must be a nonnegative integer. In origin 0, the result of ι4 is 0 1 2 3. The special case ι0 yields a degenerate "vector" having zero elements, called an *empty* vector. The empty vector is treated at greater length in Sec. 3-3.

Keyboard characters are allowed as values. A *character value* is created by typing it within quote symbols (in APL the apostrophe is called the quote symbol) thus

```
      'L'         Name for the value "ell"
L                 Character value "ell"
```

The name of a variable has nothing to do with the character value assigned to it. For example,

```
      M←'L'       Value "ell" assigned to variable M
      M
L
```

A value can also be a vector of keyboard characters, thus

```
      RED←'BLUE'
      RED
BLUE
```

Certain overstruck characters are admissible as character values, as also are nonprinting "characters" such as the backspace (see ⎕AV and ⎕TC in Chap. 7). The character ' is a special case. It is necessary to type it twice, as in

```
      P←'IT WON''T WORK'
      P
IT WON'T WORK
```

because otherwise it would not be distinguishable from ' at the beginning or end. Observe that the character ' appears only once in the displayed value of P.

Numerals can be included in character vectors, as in

```
      'A 5B'
```

---

1) What value is produced by the following sequence of steps?

```
X←2  3  4
Y←3  4  5
H←((Y×Y)+(X×X))*0.5
H
```

──────────

2) Give the value produced (in origin 1) by

```
A←ι5
B←2  4  3  2  1
A+B
```

──────────

```
A+3
```

──────────

3) Give the result for each of the following.

```
LARGE←'SMALL'
SMALL←'VERY LARGE'
LARGE
```

──────────

```
SMALL
```

──────────

4) Specify P so that

```
      P
' IS A ''QUOTE'' SYMBOL
      P←
```

Rudiments of APL / 31

1) Using the specifications for A and B in the text, write the results produced by each of the following.

  B×¯8

  _____

  B÷A

  _____

2) If

  X1←2.5
  X2←16

write the result produced by each of the following.

  X2-X1

  _____

  X2+X1

  _____

  X2÷2.5

  _____

but the 5 does not represent a number. Numbers (as distinct from numerals) and characters cannot be mixed in an array.

2-9 Some Arithmetic Primitive Functions

The APL language has a collection of *primitive functions* which perform basic operations. They are functions in the sense that they produce results which depend on the values on which they operate. They are called "primitive" because they are "built-in" as inherent parts of the language and are always available.

You have seen examples of the + and × primitives. To these we now add - and ÷, and summarize the four basic arithmetic functions. In terms of the variables,

  A←3
  B←5

results are

```
        A+B
8
        A×B
15
        A-B
¯2
        A÷B
0.6
```

A-B produces a result having a *raised* minus sign. This notation is used in recognition of the fact that the regular minus sign (-) represents a function. On the other hand, the raised minus sign (¯) is a *label* on a numeral to signify a negative number. The symbol ¯ *does not* represent a function. The distinction can be clarified by thinking of the "number line" shown below.

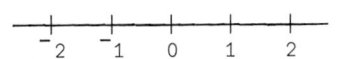

```
    +---+---+---+---+
    ¯2  ¯1  0   1   2
```

The number ¯2 is the point two units to the left of the origin. It is a result of any one of an infinite number of operations, such as 0-2, 4-6, 100085-100087. This distinction is not usually made in ordinary arithmetic, but it enhances the precision of APL.

Each of these function symbols (+, ×, -, ÷) takes a value on its left and another value on its right (represented by *A* and *B* in the examples). These values are called the *arguments* of the function. Any combination of symbols for functions and symbols for values (numerals or names of variables) is called an APL *statement*. Spaces between a function symbol and its argument are optional: *A + B* is equivalent to *A+B*.

32 / Rudiments of APL

The essential points developed so far are:

(a) Variables having numerical values, when used in a statement, behave as if they were the numbers equal to their values.

(b) Typing a statement such as $A+B$ is your instruction to the computer to do the operation described by that statement.

(c) The resulting value is returned to the workspace and can be assigned to a name or displayed (under computer control) at the left margin.

You are reminded that numerals can be used as arguments, as in

```
      9+A
12
      7÷2
3.5
```

The above examples illustrate +, ×, - and ÷ when used as *dyadic* functions. The word *dyad* means "two"; a dyadic function takes *two* arguments. The symbols +, ×, - and ÷ can also represent *monadic* functions (taking one argument). Only the second of these (-) has common monadic usage in ordinary algebra, meaning "change the sign of", or negation. It has the same meaning in APL. The monadic +, - and ÷ functions are defined in terms of their dyadic meanings, as follows (using B as previously specified):

```
     +B      Equivalent to 0+B; called the conjugate* of B
  5
     -B      Equivalent to 0-B; called the negative of B
  ¯5
     ÷B      Equivalent to 1÷B; called the reciprocal of B
  0.2
```

Observe that +B produces no change.

The monadic × can be defined as follows: ×C (where C has a numerical value, positive, negative or zero) produces 1 or ¯1 in accordance with whether C is positive or negative, or zero if C is zero. This function (called the *signum* function) preserves the sign information of a number without regard to its size. The three cases are illustrated by

```
      × ¯4 0 5
¯1 0 1
```

---

*Conjugate is a term derived from the arithmetic of complex numbers. For real numbers, the conjugate of a number equals itself.

1) If
   X1←2.5
   X2←16
what results are produced by the following?
   12×X1
   ───────
   ¯2.5×12
   ───────
   X2-25
   ───────

2) In the 2nd example of (1):
The symbol for the function is
───────
The values for the arguments are
───────
and
───────

3) Show the result produced by each of the following.
   Z←25
   -Z
   ───────
   ÷Z
   ───────
   ÷¯0.4
   ───────

Rudiments of APL / 33

The monadic function *absolute value* (using the symbol `|`) is in a sense the complement of signum. It preserves the magnitude of a number rather than its sign. This function is illustrated by

```
      | ¯4  0  5
4  0  5
```

Next we consider a dyadic function called *exponentiation*, meaning "raise to a power" (as in 3^2). The exponent is not necessarily an integer. The APL notation for A with an exponent B is $A*B$. Using the same variables A and B having the values 3 and 5, respectively,

```
      A*B
243
```

and

```
      B*A
125
```

The square root is an important example of a fractional exponent; the square root of a number is computed as the number to the `0.5` power, as in

```
      A*0.5
1.732050808...
```

Of course, for the square root, the left-hand argument cannot be negative.

We conclude this section by pointing out that `-`, `÷`, and `*` work for vector arguments in a manner similar to `+` and `×`. Some examples are:

```
      2  5  4 ÷ 2  10  5
1  0.5  0.8
      6  3  7 - 3
3  0  4
      4 * 2  3
16  64
```

2-10 Negative Numbers and Negation

In Sec. 2-9 the difference between the signs `-` and `¯` is emphasized; the former being a symbol for the function of subtraction or negation, and the latter a label on a numeral. The raised sign should always be used when entering a negative number, as in the case of an assignment. This is true in spite of the fact that

```
      ¯5
¯5
```

and

---

1) For any numeric variable V, give the result produced by

   `(×V)×|V`

   _____

2) If

   `Z←9  16  25`
   `Y←264  ¯5863  0`

   write results for

   `Z*2`

   _____

   `Z*0.5`

   _____

   `×Y`

   _____

   `|Y`

   _____

3) If A and B are the sides of a triangle, write a statement using `*` instead of `×`, to give the hypotenuse.

   _____

4) Write a statement using the index generator that will produce

   `¯2  ¯1  0  1  2`

   _____

34 / Rudiments of APL

```
        ⁻5
⁻5
```
appear to be the same. In the first case, the input is a negative number, and the response is that same number. In the second case the input 5 is subjected to negation, the negative number ⁻5 being the result. The following examples give additional demonstrations of the difference between ⁻ and -.

```
       ⁻5+7
2                   Sum of negative 5 and positive 7
       -5+7
⁻12                 Negation of 5 plus 7
       4  ⁻7
4  ⁻7               Print of the vector 4  ⁻7
       4-7
3                   7 subtracted from 4
       4⁻7
SYNTAX ERROR
       4⁻7
        ∧           4 and ⁻7 are not separated, as in forming a
                    vector, and have no function symbol between
                    them
       ⁻7  4
⁻7  4               Print of the vector ⁻7  4
       -⁻7  4
⁻7 ⁻4               Negation of the vector ⁻7  4
```

The error report for 4⁻7 emphasizes the fact that the raised minus sign does not represent a function. You should regard the raised minus sign as part of the numeral with which it is associated. It should never be used with anything other than a numeral. Thus, if A and B are variables, ⁻A and A⁻B will produce error reports.

2-11 Scaled (Floating Point) Notation

Because computers are capable of handling numbers ranging from the extremely small to the extremely large, it is convenient to have a notation which will avoid typing many zeros, as in 354200000000 or 0.0000000065725. In ordinary notation it is common to write these as 3.542×10^{11} and 6.5725×10^{-9} respectively. Essentially the same notation can be used with a computer. The only difference is that, because superscripts cannot be used, the exponents are not raised and the usual 10 is replaced by the letter E. A number displayed in this way is said to be in *scaled* (or *floating point*) notation. Examples are:

```
    3.542E11      For 354200000000
    6.572E⁻9      For 0.000000006572
```

---

1) If
$A \leftarrow ⁻6$
$B \leftarrow ⁻3$
give the result (value or error report) produced by each of the following.

A-B _____

⁻B+A _____

-A _____

A-3 _____

-3+A _____

2) If you want to subtract 100 from 75, some of the following are correct, some give the wrong answer, and some an error report. Mark which is which.

75-100   _____
75⁻100   _____
75+⁻100   _____
⁻100+75   _____
-100+75   _____
75-⁻100   _____
⁻100-75   _____
⁻75-100   _____

3) Write each of the following in scaled notation.

20003   _____
0.000423 _____
0.25   _____

Rudiments of APL / 35

1) In usual floating point notation, for the number 0.0234, the value of the mantissa is
_____
and the value of the exponent is
_____

2) If
    $A \leftarrow 2860000000$
what result is produced by each of the following?
$2E9-A$ _____
$A \times 2E^-9$ _____
$A + ^-2E9$ _____
$2E8+A$ _____

3) On the blank line opposite each of the following, mark "correct" for those which yield $^-1.6E^-12$ as a result, and "wrong" for any which do not.
$^-4E^-6 \times 4E^-5$ _____
$4E^-12 \times 0.4$ _____
$4E^-6 \times 4E^-6$ _____

4) It (is/is not) _____ true that the following two statements are equivalent:
    $(2.3E6) \div 2E10$
    $2.3E6 \div 2E10$

The number to the left of E is the *mantissa*, the number to the right is the *exponent*. Usually, the magnitude of the mantissa is greater than or equal to 1 and less than 10.

There are no spaces in a number written in this form, and negative exponents are typed with the raised minus sign. It is not necessary to use parentheses when such numbers appear in statements. That is,

        $3.542E11+8.673E12$
$9.0272E12$

Results typed by the computer may or may not appear in floating point form. The computer uses a rather complicated algorithm to make a decision as to what notation to use. The computer's decision is not dependent on how you may have entered a number. Some examples are

        0.00000675
$6.75E^-6$
        $0.02*4$
$1.6E^-7$
        $2.43E^-2$
0.0243
        75400000000
$7.54E10$
        $7.54E5$
754000

Two of the factors which can affect the notation in a printout are: the printing precision (value of $\Box PP$ in the workspace) and the print format (a row, or rows and columns, for example). As an example of the effect of the printing precision, if it is 10,

        $2.345E6$
2345000

but if the printing precision is 4,

        $2.345E6$
$2.345E6$

To illustrate the effect of print format, suppose the printing precision is 4, and Z is

        $Z \leftarrow 2300 \quad 0.000005 \quad 53690000 \quad 0.000234 \quad 24 \quad 2345$

Printed as a vector, the result is

        Z
$2300 \quad 5E^-6 \quad 5.369E7 \quad 0.000234 \quad 24 \quad 2345$

As is shown in Chap. 3, this can be printed in a row-column format (by using the function $2 \quad 3 \rho Z$ to give 2 rows and 3 columns). Thus, again using 4 for the printing precision,

36 / Rudiments of APL

```
       2  3 ρZ
2.300E3    5.000E¯6    5.369E7
2.340E¯4   2.400E1     2.345E3
```

The vector is printed partially in floating point notation. On the other hand, if floating point notation is necessary for any element in the row-column format, it will appear for all elements. If it were otherwise, columns might not line up uniformly.

2-12 Statements Having More than One Primitive Function, Parentheses

We shall now consider the rules for computing results for statements having a multiplicity of primitive functions. For that purpose, suppose the following variables have been specified:

```
A←6
B←9
C←5
D←2
```

An example of a statement involving these variables and three primitive functions is:

```
A×B-C÷D
```

39

The manner in which the computer arrives at the result is illustrated by the following diagram (written in terms of the values of the variables):

```
6×9-5÷2
     └── Step 1:  2.5,  from 5÷2
   └──── Step 2:  6.5,  from 9-2.5
 └────── Step 3:  39,   from 6×6.5
```

The function written farthest to the right (÷) is executed first, giving the value 2.5 as a result. The next function on the left (- in this case) is then executed, using 9 as its left-hand argument and 2.5 (the result of the previous calculation) as its right-hand argument. This process continues until all functions have been executed. A general description of this process is as follows: The computer scans the statement from *right to left*, executing each function in sequence. For each function its left-hand argument is the value immediately to its left, and its right-hand argument is the result produced by the execution *up to that point*. This order of execution is consistent with certain cases of ordinary notation, as in cos sin x, meaning take sin x first.

The order of execution can be modified by the use of parentheses, as in

---

1) Give the results produced by

¯10+8××¯3
_____

1-1-1
_____

1-1-1-1
_____

2) In each of the following use the values for A, B, C, and D specified in the text. Give the result produced by the statements

A+D×B÷C
_____

B+B×C×D
_____

-B÷A÷D÷C
_____

A-B-C-D
_____

Rudiments of APL / 37

1) Determine the result produced by each of the following:

8÷3-24÷6×4*0.5

_____

(8÷3)-24÷6×4*0.5

_____

(8÷3-24÷6×4)*0.5

_____

2) Determine the result produced by each of the following:

1-2-3-4-5

_____

(1-2)-3-4-5

_____

((1-2)-3)-4-5

_____

(((1-2)-3)-4)-5

_____

3) If the following specifications are made

A←4
B←6
C←¯80

what result is produced by each of the following?

A+(×C)×B-÷A

_____

A+(×C)×B÷-A

_____

A+C××B÷-A

_____

   (A×B)-C÷D
51.5

or, in terms of the equivalent numeric values,

   (6×9)-5÷2
51.5

In this example, ÷ is executed first, giving 2.5 as the right-hand argument of the subtraction. However, the left-hand argument of - is the value produced by the statement within the parentheses, so the execution of - must become interrupted temporarily while 6×9 is computed. Then, the result of the subtraction is obtained as 54-2.5.

When a statement within parentheses includes more than one function, as in (6×9-5), the right-to-left scanning rule applies *within the parentheses*. Furthermore, a statement within parentheses can include portions within "inner" pairs of parentheses. A statement within an inner pair is treated in exactly the same way; its value must be computed before the function on the right of the inner pair can be executed. For example,

   ((6×9)-5)÷2
24.5

Here, 6×9 is computed first, then 54-5 is computed, and then that value is divided by 2.

Parentheses have no effect if they enclose the function on the right and its arguments as in

   6×9-(5÷2)

because the function on the right is executed first anyway.

We now return to the computation of the hypotenuse of a right triangle having sides S1 and S2. The statement given in Sec. 2-7 as ((S1×S1)+(S2×S2))*0.5 can now be written

   ((S1×S1)+S2×S2)*0.5

and its execution, using the values

   S1←3
   S2←4

is as follows:

   ((3×3)+4×4)*0.5
         Step 1: 16, from 4×4
         Step 2: 9, from 3×3
         Step 3: 25, from 9+16
         Step 4: 5, from 25*0.5

The symbol ⎕, called the *quad symbol*, can be used to trace out the execution of a statement by including ⎕← at one or more points. The computer prints the value appearing on the right of the arrow. For example,

38 / Rudiments of APL

```
            (⎕←(⎕←3×3)+⎕←4×4)*0.5
16
 9
25
 5
```

The partial results are printed in the order in which the computer executes them. Think of ⎕ as being the "name" of the terminal so that assigning a value to that name causes the terminal to print that value.

As a final point in this example, note that

```
            ((S1*2)+S2*2)*0.5
 5
```

is another possible statement for the hypotenuse.

An intermediate value produced within a line can be assigned to a variable at the appropriate point. Such an assignment is said to be *imbedded*. For example, if $SQ1$ and $SQ2$ are the squares of the sides, they can be specified in

```
            ((SQ1←S1*2)+SQ2←S2*2)*0.5
 5
            SQ1
 9
            SQ2
16
```

2-13 Introduction to Defined Functions

We have seen that the length of the hypotenuse of a right triangle of sides $S1$ and $S2$ is computed when you type

```
            ((S1×S1)+S2×S2)*0.5
```

and do a return. This "calculator" mode of using the computer is feasible in this example because the program is one short line. In general, where programs may consist of several (possibly long) lines, typing the program each time an answer is wanted is not feasible.

In view of the above comment, it is important to be able to assign a *name* to a program. The program can then be executed by using that name as an input to the computer. A program that has been given a name is called a *defined function*.

Presently we shall consider how to create a defined function, but first let us assume that the name $HYPOTENUSE$ represents a program for computing the hypotenuse. We desire to be able to use it in a statement such as

```
            3 HYPOTENUSE 4
 5
```

to compute the hypotenuse for a triangle of sides 3 and 4, or

---

1) If

$A←3$
$B←5$
$D←7$

for each of the following, show all responses that will be produced by the computer.

(⎕←2*(⎕←D+1)÷D-5)-÷B

_____
_____
_____

(⎕←(⎕←A÷B)+D-4)×2

_____
_____
_____
_____

2) Give results for each of the following.
$E←(F←4×G←÷9+4*2)*0.5$
E

_____

F

_____

G

_____

$J←(K←¯5×(H←×¯3+⍳5)+4)*2$
H

_____

J

_____

K

_____

3) Give results for each of the following.
4 HYPOTENUSE 3

_____

5 HYPOTENUSE 12

_____

4 5 HYPOTENUSE 3 12

_____

DEFINING A FUNCTION

1) Show results for each of the following.

    `12 HYPOTENUSE 1+4`

_____

    `2+4 HYPOTENUSE 3`

_____

    `H←4 HYPOTENUSE 4`
    `(4+3) HYPOTENUSE H`

_____

    `(3+2) HYPOTENUSE 5+2`

_____

2) What symbol do you type first, to put the computer in the definition mode, if it was in the computation mode?

_____

3) In the first example of a header line shown on this page,

`HYPOTENUSE` is called

_____

`A` is called

_____

`B` is called

_____

```
      6.5 HYPOTENUSE 4.3
7.79359
```

to compute the results for a different triangle. Also, we want to be able to assign the result to a variable, as in

```
    HYP←3 HYPOTENUSE 4
    HYP
5
```

The point being illustrated is that the syntax of `3 HYPOTENUSE 4` is the same as for a primitive dyadic function (say `3×4`). Accordingly, `HYPOTENUSE` is also called a dyadic function. The only difference between the use of a defined function and a primitive is that a defined function must be separated from its arguments by at least one space, unless an argument is in parentheses. Next, observe that `HYPOTENUSE` can be part of a more extensive statement, such as

```
    (2+4.5) HYPOTENUSE 1+3.3
7.79359
```

Another example,

```
    6 HYPOTENUSE 3 HYPOTENUSE 4
7.81024
```

illustrates that the execution order is the same as for primitive functions. For this example, `3 HYPOTENUSE 4` produces the value 5, and then the second execution of `HYPOTENUSE` (the one on the left) is equivalent to `6 HYPOTENUSE 5`.

    Having considered some examples of how the defined function `HYPOTENUSE` would be *used*, we now consider the procedure for *constructing* it. The first step is to send a signal to the computer, informing it that a function is about to be *defined* (meaning constructed). The signal is provided by the so-called *header line*, which begins with the symbol ∇. One possible example of a header line for this case is

    `∇ C←A HYPOTENUSE B`   or   `∇C←A HYPOTENUSE B`

We say "one possible example" because, as you will see later,

    `∇ Z←X HYPOTENUSE Y`

and many others, would do just as well. After you do this, the computer is in the *definition mode* (with respect to you) as distinct from its normal state, the *computation mode*. The space following ∇ is optional.

    The header line includes the name of the function (`HYPOTENUSE`) and the names of three variables (`C`, `A`, `B` in the first of the illustrations). The variable names immediately to the left and right of the function name (`A` and `B`) are called *input variables*. The roles they play are indicated by the following comparison of the header line (written in the definition mode) and a statement (written in the computation mode) in which the function is used. The role of `C←` in the header line is discussed later.

    ∇ C←A HYPOTENUSE B   Header line, in definition mode
      3 HYPOTENUSE 4   Use line, in computation mode
       (↓A)   (↓B)   Roles of input variables

In the "use" line the occurrence of the arguments 3 and 4 causes the corresponding variables (A and B) to be assigned these values, as suggested by the encircled arrows. These assignments to A and B are *implied* by their appearance in the header line. There are no actual statements A←3 and B←4. The circles are a fiction, shown here to stimulate your imagination.

Since A and B have the values from which the result is to be computed, these variables appear in the statement line of the program. Thus, to create the function, you will type

    ∇ C←A HYPOTENUSE B
[1]   C←((A×A)+B×B)*0.5 ∇

When you execute the return, after typing the header line, the line number [1] is typed automatically by the computer. (Remember, the computer is now in the definition mode, and the return does not initiate a computation.) You will then type the statement opposite [1]. The ∇ at the end of the line "closes the definition," returning the computer to the computation mode. The ∇ can also be typed on a separate line, thus

    ∇ C←A HYPOTENUSE B
[1]   C←((A×A)+B×B)*0.5
[2]   ∇

Here, a return was executed after line [1] was typed, causing the computer to be ready for a second line (the [2] was typed by the computer). Then, typing ∇ will close the definition.

The role played by `C←` in the header line will now be explained. It identifies C as an *output variable*, and allows the function to produce a *returned value*. This means that the computed result produced by the function is a value which *can be used in further calculations*, as in

    2×3 HYPOTENUSE 4
10

Also, a returned value can be assigned to a variable, as in

    HYP←3 HYPOTENUSE 4
    HYP

---

1) Suppose you define the function

    ∇ Z←X HYP Y
[1] Z←((X*2)+Y*2)*0.5
[2] ∇

In the process of doing this, what part of it will the computer type?

_____

2) In terms of the function defined in (1) above, if you do

    X←2.5
    Y←5

and then

    (2+X) HYP Y*2

during execution of HYP, values of X and Y will be

    X
_____
    Y
_____

3) A function defined as

    ∇ C←A HYP B
[1] Z←((A×A)+B×B)*0.5 ∇

will not give a returned value. Modify it so it will do so.

1) Suppose you have the two functions

∇ Z←A HYP1 B
[1] Z←((A×A)+B×B)*E ∇

∇ X←A SUMSQUARES B
[1] X←E←(A×A)+B×B ∇

and you do the following sequence. Fill in the blanks showing the responses.

E←0.5
1 HYP1 1

_____

1 SUMSQUARES 1

_____

1 HYP1 1

_____

2) Now let the header line of the second function be changed to

∇ E←A SUMSQUARES B

Again fill in the blanks for the sequence of operations:

E←0.5
1 HYP1 1

_____

1 SUMSQUARES 1

_____

1 HYP1 1

_____

3) Answer the following "true" or "false."

Names for input variables must be A and B.

_____

Using $C←$ in a header line does not ensure that the function will produce a returned value.

_____

It is important to recognize that the output variable must be *identified* (by including it in the header line) and *also* that it must be *assigned a value* (as in line [1] of *HYPOTENUSE*). If either of these incidences of the output variable is missing, the function will not return a value. In the absence of a returned value each of the examples above requiring a computation on the *result* of 3 *HYPOTENUSE* 4 would produce a *VALUE ERROR* report.

At the beginning of this section it was stated that Z, X and Y could just as well have been used in the header line. It is now seen that these variables would be a different set fulfilling the same roles as C, A and B, on the condition that they would also be used on line [1] as in

∇ Z←X HYPOTENUSE Y
[1] Z←((X×X)+Y×Y)*0.5 ∇

This function is completely equivalent to the one written in terms of C, A and B.

There is much more to be said about defined functions than is contained in this section. The subject is continued in later chapters.

2-14 Local and Global Variables

The input and output variables of a defined function are *local* to the function, meaning that they have values only while the function is being executed. Thus, after 3 *HYPOTENUSE* 4 has been executed, the input and output variables will not appear in the workspace. This is an important feature. It ensures that there will be no conflicts if the same name is used in two or more functions.

A general variable in your workspace, such as would be created by a specification

E←0.5

is called a *global* variable. A global variable can be used within a function, but it must be different from each local variable. Using the above specification of E, a function for the hypotenuse of a right triangle could be

∇ C←A HYPOTENUSE B
[1] C←((A×A)+B×B)*E ∇

This will give correct results only if E is assigned the value 0.5 in an operation *external* to the function. Suppose the value of E were to become modified at a later time, perhaps inadvertently in some unrelated computation. Then *HYPOTENUSE* would no longer yield correct results. Because of such a possibility, using a global variable in this way is to be discouraged except when the nature of a program requires it.

Sometimes a variable (other than an input or output variable) is needed temporarily during execution of a defined function, but for no other purpose. Such a variable should be made local by including it in the header line, separated from the remainder of the header line by a semicolon. This is illustrated in the following version of *HYPOTENUSE*:

```
        ∇ C←A HYPOTENUSE B;T
[1]     T←(A×A)+B×B
[2]     C←T*0.5  ∇
```

When this function is executed, using 3 *HYPOTENUSE* 4, *T* is assigned the value 25 on line [1], but when execution is complete *T* will have no value. If *T* were not in the header line, *T* would have the value 25 in the workspace, after the execution of 3 *HYPOTENUSE* 4. Additional variables can be designated local by appending them on the right of the header line, separated by semicolons.

2-15 Display of a Function

The computing system provides a means whereby you can inspect the contents of an existing defined function. This is accomplished by typing ∇ followed by the function name (but no local variables) to open the definition, and then the symbols [□] and an optional second ∇ as explained below. Two examples, using the first version of *HYPOTENUSE*, are:

```
        ∇HYPOTENUSE[□]∇          ←——— You type
        ∇ C←A HYPOTENUSE B
[1]     C←((A×A)+B×B)*0.5        ←——— Computer types
        ∇
```

or

```
        ∇HYPOTENUSE[□]           ←——— You type
        ∇ C←A HYPOTENUSE B
[1]     C←((A×A)+B×B)*0.5        ←——— Computer types
        ∇
[2]
```

In the first case, the inclusion of the second ∇ causes the definition to close after the display is completed. In the second, where the second ∇ is omitted, the definition remains open after the lines are displayed. Then you would have the option of adding a second line, or closing the definition by typing ∇ to the right of [2].

The symbols [□] are your instruction asking the computer for a display of the function. You may type [□] opposite a

---

1) Referring to the text, suppose *T* is not in the header line of *HYPOTENUSE*. The following sequence of steps is then executed. On the blank lines show the results.

    1 *HYPOTENUSE* 2
    _____

    T HYPOTENUSE 12
    _____

    T
    _____

2) The following function has been defined.

    ∇ Z←X HYP Y
    [1] R←(X×X)+Y×Y
    [2] Z←R*0.5

Show what change should be made so *R* will be a local variable.

3) To open the definition of the function described in (2), after it has been defined, which should you type?

    ∇ Z←X HYP Y

or

    ∇ HYP
    _____

4) A beginner is sometimes not sure whether the computer is in the definition mode. It is in the definition mode if (choose 1) the last thing typed by the computer is

    ∇

or

    a line number
    _____

Rudiments of APL / 43

1) Opening a definition does not cause a display. To obtain a display, after opening a definition, what should you type?

_____

Does this have to be typed on the same line as the definition-opening statement?

_____

2) Suppose a function has the following incorrect definition:

```
    ∇ C←A HYP B;G
[1] G←(A×A)+B×B
[2] C←G 0.5 ∇
```

What will be the response to

   3 HYP 4

_____

After this, what will be obtained from

   A

_____

   B

_____

   C

_____

   G

_____

line number any time the definition is open. For example, you can open the definition with

[2]   ∇ HYPOTENUSE   or   ∇HYPOTENUSE

If you decide not to add a line but want to see a display, you can type [□] opposite [2] thus

[2]   [□]

to get a display and leave the definition open after the display has been presented, or you can include ∇, as

[2]   [□]∇

to obtain a display and to close the definition after the display is completed.

There are other possibilities for displaying single lines or selected parts of a function. Further details are given in Appendix 7.

2-16 Suspended Functions

Suppose *HYPOTENUSE* is incorrectly defined as

```
     ∇ C←A HYPOTENUSE B
[1]  C←((A×A)+B×B*0.5 ∇
```

Then, an attempt to execute it will yield an error report

```
      3 HYPOTENUSE 4
SYNTAX ERROR
HYPOTENUSE[1] C←((A×A)+B×B*0.5
                        ∧
```

After this happens the function is in a *suspended* state, meaning that the local variables exist in the workspace and that if a correction is made in the function, execution can be resumed in a manner described below. See Appendix 6 for further information about suspended functions.

An error in a function can be corrected by opening the definition and retyping the incorrect line, or by editing the line (inserting corrections without retyping parts that are correct). Editing is described in Appendix 7. For the example above, you can replace the line as follows: type ∇HYPOTENUSE[1], to open the definition and designate line [1]; retype the line; close the definition. In the following example, you would type everything except [1] at the margin:

```
     ∇HYPOTENUSE[1]
[1]    C←((A×A)+B×B)*0.5∇
```

The header line can also be changed, by treating it as line [0]. Any line, including the header, can be corrected while

44 / Rudiments of APL

the definition is open. Merely type the line number in brackets opposite whatever line number was last printed by the computer, as in either of the following:

```
       ∇HYPOTENUSE                        ∇HYPOTENUSE
[2]       [1]              or      [2]       [1] C←((A×A)+B×B)*0.5∇
[1]    C←((A×A)+B×B)*0.5∇
```

Having corrected the function and closed the definition, it is possible to *resume* computation by executing

```
       →1
```

where the number 1 is the line number where computation is to be resumed. If the error has been successfully corrected, computation will go to conclusion; if not, another error report will appear and the correction process can be tried again. If execution goes to completion, the suspension becomes *cleared* (local variables disappear and workspace returns to the normal state).

If for any reason a resumption of computation is not wanted, the suspension should be cleared by executing

```
       →
```

or

```
       →0
```

Further insight can be obtained from the two-line version of *HYPOTENUSE* given in Sec. 2-14. Suppose this is incorrectly defined as

```
       ∇ C←A HYPOTENUSE B;T
[1]      T←(A×A)-B×B
[2]      C←T*0.5 ∇
```

When this is executed with arguments 3 and 4, line [1] is executed first (assigning ¯7 to T) and then the response will be

DOMAIN ERROR
HYPOTENUSE[2] C←T*0.5
                ∧

Inspection shows nothing wrong with line [2], so there must be something wrong with T. As a first step in debugging you can test its value. Although T is a local variable, it exists while the function is suspended. This test gives

```
       T
¯7
```

and shows the reason for the error report. Negative numbers are not in the *domain* of numbers which have square roots. This result provides the hint that the error is on line [1], and we see that - was used instead of +.

1) Under what condition (after a suspension) should you use

   →

rather than

   →(a line number)

2) Refer to the suspension of *HYPOTENUSE* on this page of the text. While the function is suspended, give the results for

   A
   _____

   B
   _____

   T
   _____

   C
   _____

3) Suppose you have just finished correcting a suspended function. It (is/is not)_____ necessary to close the definition before using the right-pointing arrow to continue the execution or clear the suspension.

Rudiments of APL / 45

1) For the suspension of *HYPOTENUSE* described on the previous page, complete the following statement of assignment to T such that

    →2

will give the correct result.

    $T←$

2) Suppose you have the incorrectly defined function

    ∇ A←B HYP C
    [1] A←((B×B)+C×C*0.5 ∇

and do

    3 HYP 4

After the error report, give the responses you will get from the following tests for values.

    B
    _____
    C
    _____
    A
    _____

Then, you do

    6 HYP 5

Now, the responses are

    B
    _____
    C
    _____
    A
    _____

3) The system command

)SI

is used to (choose one):

(a) Clear the state indicator.

(b) Produce a record of past suspensions.

(c) Remove the last suspension.

Assume this error is corrected. Then, if you remember that computation stopped on line [2], you may be inclined to resume execution by doing

    →2

However, this will again produce an error report because the incorrect value of T remains. In this case, execution should be resumed by returning to the line where the correction was made. Therefore,

    →1

will resume execution properly.

It is *very important* that suspensions be cleared, either by correcting the function and resuming computation to a successful conclusion, or by executing

    →   or   →0

This is important because a workspace contains all variables pertinent to a suspension until such time as the suspension is cleared. Many suspensions can exist simultaneously. For example, suppose a function has two errors, and you obtain a suspension from trying to run it. If you then correct the error causing that suspension, and *initiate* another execution instead of *resuming* the suspended execution, the function will become suspended a second time. Meanwhile, the original suspension remains. In this way an unwary beginner can build up a long list of suspensions which can eventually result in a *WS FULL* report.

In case you are not sure whether you have any suspended functions, the system command

)SI

is available. It produces a print of the contents of the *state indicator*, an object in your workspace in which the computer keeps a record of the suspensions. See Appendix 6 for further information about the state indicator.

2-17 A Few Primitive Functions on Vectors

There are many functions considered in later chapters which perform a wide variety of operations on vectors. We include a brief introduction of five of them here, using the vector

    V←21 15 23 31

for illustration.

46 / Rudiments of APL

VECTOR FUNCTIONS

(a) Reduction

All of the individual elements of a vector can be added or multiplied by using the symbols +/ or ×/ with the vector as an argument on the right. Thus,

```
      +/V         Equivalent to 21+15+23+31
90
      ×/V         Equivalent to 21×15×23×31
224595
```

These are called, respectively, *add reduction* and *multiply reduction*. Reductions using the subtract and divide symbols are also possible, as follows:

```
      -/V         Equivalent to 21-15-23-31
¯2
      ÷/V         Equivalent to 21÷15÷23÷31
1.03871...
```

Reduction is really an *operator* rather than a function; the difference is clarified in Chap. 3 but is not important here.

(b) Take

Given a vector such as V, it is possible to use the dyadic function *take* (employing the symbol ↑) to select a prescribed number of elements from either end. The given vector is the right-hand argument. The left-hand argument is an integer which specifies how many elements are to be taken; positive for taking from the left and negative for taking from the right. Examples are:

```
      3↑V
21  15  23
      ¯2↑V
23  31
```

Take can also be used on a character vector, as in

```
      3↑'ANDOR'
AND
```

(c) Drop

The dyadic function *drop* (employing the symbol ↓) causes a prescribed number of elements to be dropped from either end of a vector which is the right-hand argument. The left-hand argument is a positive or negative integer, depending on whether elements are to be dropped from the left or right. The absolute value of that argument determines how many elements are dropped. Examples are:

---

1) Show statements that will compute the sum of: The squares of the integers from 1 to 10, inclusive

The odd integers from 1 to 15, inclusive

The even integers from 2 to 16, inclusive

2) Write an expression using reduction that will compute the factorial of 8.

3) Give the result for

$÷/⍳4$

4) If W has the value
   $W←2\ 6\ 9\ 5\ 4$
give the result for each of the following.
   ¯1↑4↑W

   1↑¯2↑W

5) For W as given in (4) give two statements using take which will produce

6 9 5

6) What would you expect as the result of take, with a zero argument on the left?

Rudiments of APL / 47

1) Using the vector
$$W \leftarrow 2\ 6\ 9\ 5\ 4$$
give the results of
$$2 \downarrow {}^-1 \downarrow W$$
_____

$$2 \downarrow 4 \uparrow W$$
_____

2) For W given in (1), give the results for
$$\rho\ {}^-2 \downarrow W$$
_____

$$\rho 1 \uparrow W$$
_____

3) Using W as given in (1) give the results for
$$\rho W,\ 5\ {}^-9$$
_____

$$\rho W, W$$
_____

4) In terms of A and B given in the text, show a statement which will produce the result

TWO AND ONE

5) What would you expect as a result of dropping all the elements of a vector?
_____

6) What is the shape of an empty vector?
_____

```
      1↓V
15  23  31
      ¯3↓V
21
```

Drop also works on character vectors.

(d) Shape

The number of elements in a numeric or character vector can be determined by using the monadic function *shape* (employing the symbol ρ) with the vector as its argument. Thus,

```
      ρV
4
      ρι9
9
      ρ'ANDOR'
5
```

This result is called the *shape* of the vector.

(e) Catenate — *dyadic*

Given two vectors, say V and W, the dyadic function *catenate* (employing the symbol ,) with V and W as the arguments creates a new vector by placing V and W end to end. V and W must be of the same type; both numbers or both characters. For example, if

```
      W←54  43
      V,W
21  15  23  31  54  43
```

Either vector can be empty (V,ι0 produces V). Also,

```
      A←'ONE AND '
      B←'TWO'
      A,B
ONE AND TWO
```

These primitives are subject to the same rule concerning the order of execution as the arithmetic primitives.

2-18 Use of a Defined Function Within a Defined Function

It has been pointed out that a dyadic defined function can be used in a statement line, its use being governed by the same syntax as a primitive function. This being the case, a defined function can be used within another defined function.

Example 2-1

As an illustration, consider the diagram of Fig. 2-1 which shows a point at an elevation E outside the surface of a sphere

48 / Rudiments of APL

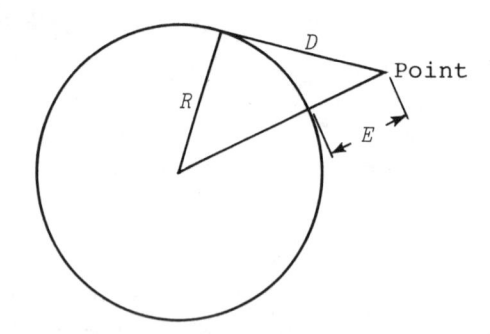

Figure 2-1 Distance to horizon of a point outside a sphere.

of radius R (say the earth) and at a distance D from the horizon. E is to be found, when R and D are given. It is evident from Fig. 2-1 that the algorithm is: Subtract R from the hypotenuse of a right triangle having sides R and D.

A defined function which will take R as the left-hand argument and D as the right-hand argument, and return the value of the elevation, is

```
      ∇ EL←RAD ELEVATION HORIZ
[1]     EL←(RAD HYPOTENUSE HORIZ)-RAD ∇
```

In this, *HYPOTENUSE* is any one of the programs given in Sec. 2-13.

Example 2-2

As another example, let *STRING* be a defined function which will compute the length of a string stretched between the ends of a stick and over a support, as in Fig. 2-2. The height of the support is one-quarter of the length of the stick and it may be located anywhere along the stick at a distance D from the center. L is the length of the stick.

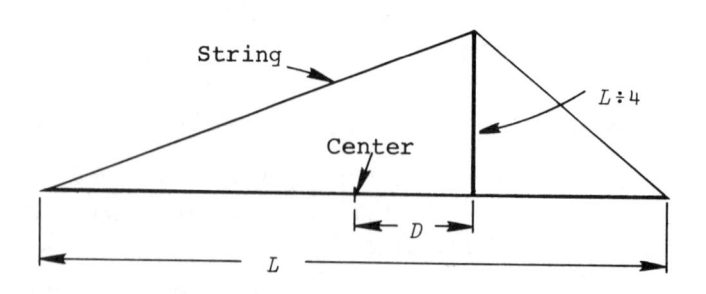

Figure 2-2 String stretched between the ends of a stick.

---

1) In the defined function *ELEVATION* given on this page, suppose *HYPOTENUSE* is

```
     ∇A←B HYPOTENUSE C
[1]    A←((B×B)+C×C)*0.5 ∇
```

During the execution of

    120 ELEVATION 90

give the values of the variables:

A
_____

B
_____

C
_____

2) Is the following a possible realization of *ELEVATION*?

```
     ∇ E←R ELEVATION H
[1]    E←(((R×R)+H×H)*0.5)-R ∇
```
_____

3) Is the following a possible realization of *ELEVATION*?

```
     ∇ E←R ELEVATION H
[1]    E←R HYPOTENUSE H
[2]    E←E-R ∇
```
_____

1) Another version of STRING (partially completed) is

```
     ∇ P←X STRING Y;H;L;M
[1]  H←X÷4
[2]  L←(X÷2)-Y
[3]  M←(X÷2)+Y
[4]  P←H HYPOTENUSE L
[5]  P←P+
[6]  ∇
```

Complete line [5].

For the following three questions, suppose you have the definitions:

```
     ∇S←L STRING C;T;U
[1]  T←2×U←L÷4
[2]  S←U HYP T+C
[3]  S←S+U HYP T-C ∇

     ∇ Z←C HYP L;T
[1]  T←(C×C)+L×L
[2]  Z←T*0.5 ∇
```

Then you execute

```
     24 STRING 5
```

2) Give values for the following variables at the time line [1] of STRING is just completed.

L _____
C _____
T _____

3) Give values for the following variables during the execution of line [2] of HYP, for HYP on line [2] of STRING.

L _____
C _____
T _____

4) Give values for the following variables during the execution of line [2] of HYP, for HYP on line [3] of STRING.

L _____
C _____
T _____

An algorithm for this problem is: Compute the hypotenuse for each triangle, and add the results. This computation is carried out by the statement

```
     ((L÷4) HYPOTENUSE D+L÷2)+(L÷4) HYPOTENUSE (L÷2)-D
```

In defining a function for this problem, let the length of the stick be the left-hand argument and let the distance of the support from the center of the stick be the right-hand argument. One possible version is

```
     ∇ P←A STRING B
[1]  P←((A÷4) HYPOTENUSE B+A÷2)+(A÷4) HYPOTENUSE (A÷2)-B ∇
```

This is not in particularly good style, for two reasons:

(a) The values A÷4 and A÷2 are each computed twice.

(b) There is a proliferation of parentheses.

In these respects, a better form is

```
     ∇ P←A STRING B;HL;SUP
[1]  HL←2×SUP←A÷4
[2]  P←(SUP HYPOTENUSE HL+B)+SUP HYPOTENUSE HL-B ∇
```

In this function, let us assume HYPOTENUSE is

```
     ∇ C←A HYPOTENUSE B
[1]  C←((A×A)+B×B)*0.5 ∇
```

and suppose you execute

```
     24 STRING 5
```

In STRING, A is 24, B is 5, SUP is 6 and HL is 12. Then, on the first execution of HYPOTENUSE, the A local to HYPOTENUSE is 6, because its value is the same as SUP. Also, the B local to HYPOTENUSE is 7, because its value is the same as HL-B (where this B is local to STRING). For the second execution of HYPOTENUSE, A and B local to that function are 6 and 17, respectively (you can verify this). This example illustrates the use of the same names (A and B in this case) to represent different variables which are local to different functions. There are three variables named A (one in STRING and one in *each* of the two uses of HYPOTENUSE). Similarly, there are three variables named B.

Example 2-3

Recall that the algorithm for the string problem calls for computing the hypotenuse of each of two triangles, and adding them. In example 2-2 there is a separate appearance of HYPOTENUSE for each triangle. However, HYPOTENUSE can handle more than one triangle at the same time. Therefore, it is possible to use HYPOTENUSE only once, with the vector of the two horizontal sides, given by

50 / Rudiments of APL

```
    (L÷2)+ 1 ¯1 ×D
```

as one argument, and $L \div 4$ as the other. To check that the above expression gives the vector of the two horizontal sides, suppose L is 10 and D is 2. The above yields `5+ 1 ¯1 ×2` or `5+ 2 ¯2` or `7 3`. The sum of the elements of the vector produced by HYPOTENUSE with these arguments can be obtained from add reduction. Thus, another program is

```
    ∇ P←A STRING1 B
[1] P←+/((A÷2)+ 1 ¯1 ×B) HYPOTENUSE A÷4 ∇
```

1) In STRING1, suppose the + sign immediately to the right of (A÷2) is replaced by a - sign. Show what other changes are necessary so the function will be correct.

Example 2-4

Now suppose the vertical strut supporting the string in Fig. 2-2 has a height H (rather than $L \div 4$). We shall define a function STRING2 which will be dyadic, taking L as its left-hand argument and a two-element vector (having D as its first element and H as its second element) as the right-hand argument. An example of the use of this function is

```
    6 STRING2 1 3
8.60555
```

2) Write a function similar to STRING1, but not using a multiplication by 1 ¯1.

The take function can be used to extract D as the first element of the right-hand input variable, and H as the second element. One possible realization is

```
    ∇ P←A STRING2 B
[1] P←+/((A÷2)+ 1 ¯1 × 1↑B) HYPOTENUSE ¯1↑B ∇
```

3) Write a version of STRING2 using drop instead of take.

2-19 Comment About Program Structure

The possibility of using one program within another is very important, particularly for problems that are more complicated than the simple examples of Sec. 2-18. In the case of example 2-1 it enables us to think of the algorithm in two parts:

(a) Identification of a hypotenuse.
(b) Identification of a computation to be made, using that hypotenuse as one of the arguments.

Problems more complicated than this can have a greater number of parts for which separate functions can be written. The principle of breaking a problem into independent parts, and writing separate programs for the parts, is the main idea in what is called *structured programming*. The more complicated a problem the greater are the advantages of proceeding in this way whenever possible.

Example 2-1 is so simple that the advantage of regarding the computation of the hypotenuse as a separate entity may be too subtle to be recognizable. Example 2-4 provides a somewhat more tangible illustration. A nonstructured approach to

1) Write a version of *SATELLITE* similar to the one in the text, but taking an argument which is the height expressed as a fraction of the earth's radius.

2) The velocity *V* (in meters/sec) of a freely falling body, starting from rest, (in conventional notation) is related to distance fallen *D* (in meters) by

$V^2 = 19.6D$

Write a monadic function *FALL* which will take distance fallen as its argument, and give velocity as the returned value. For example,

   FALL 2.8
7.408

3) Write a monadic function *SATVEL* which will take the height of a satellite above the earth (in km) as its argument, and return a value which is the velocity of the satellite (in km/hr). Use *SATELLITE* as given in the text as a subfunction.

this problem would lead to a program such as the following:

```
     ∇ P←A STRING2A B;HL;D;HS
[1]    HL←A÷2
[2]    D←1↑B
[3]    HS←(¯1↑B)*2
[4]    P←((((HL+D)*2)+HS)*0.5)+(((HL-D)*2)+HS)*0.5 ∇
```

Compared to the structured version in Sec. 2-18, it is evident that the present one is encumbered with many more details. The same numerical calculations are carried out by either version, but the structured version gives a better picture of the nature of the computing process. The structured approach yields a simpler viewpoint of the algorithm, and leads to a program which is simpler to write and understand.

The principles illustrated by these simple examples become more significant as problems become more complicated. They will be dealt with again as we get into more advanced programming, particularly in Chap. 5.

2-20 Monadic Defined Functions

As with primitive functions, some of which are monadic, it is possible to create defined functions which are likewise monadic.

Example 2-5

We shall develop a function named *SATELLITE* which will compute the time required for one revolution (the period) about the earth of a satellite in a circular orbit. From principles of mechanics it can be shown that the period *T* in hours (in conventional notation) is

$$T = \frac{\pi}{1134000}(R + H)^{(3/2)}$$

where *R* is the radius of the earth (6371 km) and *H* is the height of the orbit above the earth's surface, in km. The required monadic function will take *H* as its argument. One possible version is

```
     ∇ Z←SATELLITE H
[1]    Z←(3.1416÷1.134E6)×(6371+H)*1.5 ∇
```

As you will see in Chap. 4, it is not necessary to enter the numeric value of π; the symbol ○ stands for a monadic primitive function which causes its argument to be multiplied by π. Thus, another possible version is

```
     ∇ Z←SATELLITE H
[1]    Z←○((6371+H)*1.5)÷1.134E6 ∇
```

52 / Rudiments of APL

For a height of 500 km, this gives

```
      SATELLITE 500
1.57785
```

Example 2-6

A function for computing a hypotenuse can be defined in monadic form. To do so, we make the argument a vector of two elements representing the sides of the triangle. Such a function is

```
      ∇ H←HYPOTENUSE1 S
[1]     H←(+/S×S)*0.5 ∇
```

To obtain the hypotenuse of a triangle of sides 3 and 4 this function would be used in the following way:

```
      HYPOTENUSE1 3 4
5
```

Example 2-7

A monadic function MEAN is to be defined which will compute the mean (average) value of the elements of a vector argument. For example,

```
      MEAN 2 8 3 5
4.5
```

The algorithm is: Add the numbers in the vector and divide by the number of elements in the vector. This is easily accomplished by

```
      ∇ M←MEAN N
[1]     M←(+/N)÷ρN ∇
```

2-21 Printing Values Produced within a Function

The use of the *quad output* ☐← within a statement line to produce a print of partial results was illustrated in Sec. 2-12. The same technique can be used within a defined function, to provide printouts of intermediate results while the function is running. Such intermediate results are often helpful in finding errors ("debugging"). To illustrate, suppose HYPOTENUSE is written incorrectly, as

```
      ∇ C←A HYPOTENUSE B
[1]     C←((☐←A×A)+☐←A×B)*0.5 ∇
```

The location of the error can be found from a trial, as follows:

```
      F←3 HYPOTENUSE 4
12
9
      F
4.5826
```

1) Although the function HYPOTENUSE1 defined on this page is for a triangle, it will work for a vector of more than 2 numbers. Give the result produced by

```
   T←2 2 4 4 3
   HYPOTENUSE1 T
```
_____

2) The geometric mean of two numbers is the square root of their product; for three numbers it is the cube root of their product, etc. Define a monadic function GEOMEAN which will return the geometric mean of a vector argument.

3) Suppose the function
```
   ∇R←A TEST B
[1] R←☐←(☐←A×☐←B+1)*2 ∇
```
has been defined. Show the results of

```
   A←2 TEST 1
```
_____
_____
A
_____

Rudiments of APL / 53

1) For the version of HYPOTENUSE on this page, show what printed results will be obtained from

$F←⎕←3\ HYPOTENUSE\ 4$

2) Show how to modify line [2] of the version of HYPOTENUSE on this page so that + is not used to the left of T, but the function will perform in exactly the same way.

3) Referring to the version of HYPOTENUSE on this page, explain why the value of T will not print if the + to its left is omitted and there is no other change.

A simple test case was used (arguments 3 and 4) and obviously the answer (value assigned to F) is wrong. The partial results 12 and 9 resulting from the two quad outputs show that the first number printed is not the square of a side; it is 12 rather than 16, and inspection of the function shows A×B rather than B×B. These quad outputs are not to be confused with the returned value, which is assigned to C within the function, and to F externally.

After all errors have been found, the ⎕← symbols can be removed so that the corrected function will run without producing extraneous printed results. (See Appendix 7 for the procedure for removing symbols from a line of a function.) Other aids for debugging are described in Appendix 8.

Another way to obtain a printed result, if it is the last value produced by a statement line, is to *not* assign it to a variable. That value will automatically print upon execution of the line. An example is

```
      ∇ C←A HYPOTENUSE B;T
[1]     'THE SUM OF THE SQUARES OR THE SIDES IS'
[2]     +T←(A*2)+B*2
[3]     C←T*0.5 ∇
      F←3 HYPOTENUSE 4
THE SUM OF THE SQUARES OF THE SIDES IS
25

      F
5
```

Execution of line [1] produces a character value consisting of the words within quotes. Since this value is not assigned to a variable, it prints. Also, on line [2] the sum of the squares is assigned to T, but the last operation on the line is +T. The monadic + leaves its argument unchanged. Furthermore the value computed from +T is not assigned to a variable, so the value of T prints as execution of the line goes to completion.

2-22 Other Types of Defined Functions

The functions illustrated in this chapter are characterized by two properties; namely, during execution:

(a) Data "enters" the function by virtue of one or two input variables.

(b) The result of the calculations "leaves" the function by virtue of an output variable.

Names of the input and output variables appear in the header line.

54 / Rudiments of APL

This type of function is used most frequently because it permits the blending of defined functions with primitive functions without any modification of syntax. That is,

```
    2+3×4
```

and

```
    2+3 HYPOTENUSE 4
```

are syntactically equivalent.

Functions can be written which do not take arguments or do not return a value. Such functions cannot be used with the same syntax as the primitive functions. For that reason they are used rather rarely. An example of a function which takes no arguments is given in Sec. 2-23.

A function which returns a value is said to give an *explicit* result. If the output variable is omitted, a function will produce a *printed result*. A comprehensive discussion of the various types of defined functions is given in Sec. 7-1.

2-23 Evaluated and Character Input, Execute

A function not having arguments is sometimes desirable in situations where the user is expected to know nothing about the syntax of arguments, or may need instruction as to what data are required. In such a case data can be entered from the keyboard, using ←⎕ (called *evaluated input*) in a statement line. The following is an illustration:

Example 2-8

```
      ∇ C←HYPOTENUSE2;A;B;P
[1]     (P←'ENTER SIDE '),'1'
[2]     A←⎕
[3]     P,'2'
[4]     B←⎕
[5]     C←((A×A)+B×B)*0.5 ∇
```

An example of the execution of this function is

```
      T←HYPOTENUSE2
ENTER SIDE 1
⎕:
      3
ENTER SIDE 2
⎕:
      4
      T
5
```

After each display of a line of instructions, the input statement ←⎕ causes ⎕: to appear at the margin. This is a signal to the user that input is awaited, and that it will be evaluated. The numbers 3 and 4 were typed by the user. Because there are no arguments, this is called a *niladic* function.

---

1) Write a version of *HYPOTENUSE*2 which uses a global variable *P* having the same value as the local variable *P* specified on line [1] of the version in the text.

2) Complete lines [1] and [2] of the following function

```
      ∇C←HYPO;A
[1]
[2]
[3]   C←1↑A
[4]   A←¯1↑A
[5]   C←((C×C)+A×A)*0.5
      ∇
```

so that a possible execution would be

```
      T←HYPO
ENTER THE SIDES
⎕:
      3 4
      T
5
```

3) Explain why parentheses are needed in line [1] of *HYPOTENUSE*2 in the text.

1) Create a defined function *ADDWORD*1 using evaluated input, such that if
   P←'ONE TWO'
   P←*ADDWORD*1 P
□:
   'THREE'
P
ONE TWO THREE

In this example, 'THREE' is your input.

2) If
   A←4
   B←'A+3'
write the results for
   ⍎B
   ─────────────
   ⍎'3×',B
   ─────────────
   A×⍎B,'-1'
   ─────────────

If you program a statement calling for evaluated input, such as

   A←⎕

it will assign to A the value produced by whatever you type following

□:

For example, if a variable B has a value 15, all of the following evaluated inputs:

□:
      15
□:
      3×5
□:
      B

are equivalent, causing A to be assigned 15. Also, the input can be a character value, as in

□:
      'MONEY'

If a character value is wanted, without requiring the quote symbols, the above statement can be changed to a *character input*

   A←⍞

In this case, the □: does not appear when the function runs, and the printing head remains *at the margin*. Anything you type (not using quotes) will be assigned to A as a character value. This is a case where the computer *does not* indent six spaces while awaiting input.

To illustrate character input it is convenient to introduce the monadic primitive function *execute* (using the symbol ⍎ made by overstriking ⊥ and ∘). It takes a character vector as its argument. This vector must describe a computable statement, in terms of numerals and previously specified variables. The result is the value produced by executing that statement, as in

      ⍎'3×5'
15
      2×⍎'345'
690
      B←15
      ⍎'5+B×B'
230

Example 2-9

A niladic function *HYPOTENUSE*3 using character input can be written as follows:

56 / Rudiments of APL

```
      ∇ C←HYPOTENUSE3;A;B;P
[1]     (P←'ENTER SIDE '),'1'
[2]     A←⍎⎕
[3]     P,'2'
[4]     B←⍎⎕
[5]     C←((A×A)+B×B)*0.5 ∇
```

An execution of this might be

```
      T←HYPOTENUSE3
ENTER SIDE 1
3
ENTER SIDE 2
4
```

emphasizing the absence of prints of ⎕: and the fact that the inputs 3 and 4 appear at the margin. The function execute converts the characters 3 and 4 to numeric values.

If the execution of a function has stopped at a call for evaluated input, you can exit from the function by typing a right-pointing arrow,

```
⎕:
      →
```

In some systems, exiting from a call for character input is accomplished by overstriking the letters OUT; in other systems this interrupts execution, resulting in a suspension.

Of course, character input can be used in functions which are monadic or dyadic. This permits data to be entered which are not included in the arguments, perhaps in response to a question.

2-24 Bare Output, Monadic Format

In rare cases a function is wanted such that a printed result will include an explanatory statement. Such a function usually does not give an explicit result. If HYPOTENUSE4 is designed in this way, its use might be as follows:

```
      HYPOTENUSE4
ENTER SIDE 1
3.4
ENTER SIDE 2
4.6
HYPOTENUSE IS 5.72014
```

The last line is printed by the computer. It must be a character vector because characters and numbers cannot be mixed in one vector. Thus, the computed number 5.72014 must be converted to a vector of characters. The function *format* (represented by the symbol ⍕ made by overstriking ⊤ and ∘), in monadic form, converts a numeric argument to its character equivalent. Two examples (using 5 digits printing precision

---

1) Create a defined function ADDWORD2 using character input such that

```
   P←'ONE TWO'
   P←ADDWORD2 P
THREE
   P
ONE TWO THREE
```

In this example, THREE is your input.

2) Describe the difference in the way the computer acts for evaluated input and character input.

3) Answer the following true or false:

(a) The value entered on an evaluated input can be a character vector.
_____

(b) On a character input, the entered characters must be typed between quote symbols.
_____

(c) Exiting at an evaluated input is accomplished by typing OUT overstruck.
_____

(d) Numerals can be entered on character input.
_____

Rudiments of APL / 57

1) Show results for

   '2 CUBED IS',⍕2*3

———————————

   '2 CUBED IS','2*3'

———————————

   ⌽⍕2564

———————————

   ⌽25 64

———————————

   ⌽⍕25 64

———————————

(Note: ⌽ reverses the order of elements of a vector: see p. 96)

2) Write a function similar to HYPOTENUSE2, but taking the two sides as an evaluated input vector. Adjust the printed statements accordingly.

3) Write a niladic function ENTER which will give an explicit result in accordance with the following example.

   A←ENTER
ENTER DATA 21 13 7.5
   A
7.5 13 21

where 21 13 7.5 would be your entry of data. The result is a numeric vector.

4) referring to HYPOTENUSE5, explain the reasons for the spaces in '1 ' and '2 '.

are:

    ⍕263.723
263.72

    ⍕4.63   12.78
4.63   12.78

From these displays it seems that ⍕ has no effect. However, the shapes of these results are 6 and 11, respectively, so it is evident that the results are characters. The number of significant digits in a print of ⍕N is the same as in the print of N.

Using this function, the definition of HYPOTENUSE4 can be

```
    ∇ HYPOTENUSE4;A;B;P
[1]   (P←'ENTER SIDE '),'1'
[2]   A←⍎⎕
[3]   P,'2'
[4]   B←⍎⎕
[5]   'HYPOTENUSE IS ',⍕((A×A)+B×B)*0.5 ∇
```

Another variation of this function is possible in which data are entered on the same lines as the printed instructions, as in

   HYPOTENUSE5
ENTER SIDE 1 3.4
ENTER SIDE 2 4.6
HYPOTENUSE IS 5.72014

The computer will print a character vector such as ENTER SIDE 1, and stop without a return, if the character vector is assigned to overstruck symbol ⍞. An output produced in this way is called *bare output*. Thus, the function can be written

```
    ∇ HYPOTENUSE5;A;B;P
[1]   ⍞←(P←'ENTER SIDE '),'1 '
[2]   A←⍎⍞
[3]   ⍞←P,'2 '
[4]   B←⍎⍞
[5]   'HYPOTENUSE IS ',⍕((A×A)+B×B)*0.5 ∇
```

A character input following a bare output will have leading spaces corresponding to the characters in the bare output. Thus, the input resulting from entering 3.4 at ⍞ on line [2] will be 13 spaces followed by the characters 3.4. The leading spaces are ignored by the execute function.

2-25 Comment Lines

Once a defined function has been constructed and saved, it is important that you keep the following documentation about it:

   (a) What the function does.
   (b) What its arguments should be.
   (c) In the case of complicated programs, hints about how the program carries out the prescribed operations.

58 / Rudiments of APL

An adequate documentation will be a help if you want to use the function a long time after it was written, or if someone else wants to use it. One way to provide documentation is to maintain a separate written description for each function. This is a good method. However, an APL system permits the inclusion of *comment lines* within a function. Such lines appear in a display, but are ignored during computation. A comment line begins with the symbol ⍝ (∘ overstruck with ∩), followed by the comment, *not* enclosed within quote symbols.

The second version of STRING given in Sec. 2-18 (example 2-2) can be used as an example. A reasonable set of comment lines is as follows:

```
      ∇ P←A STRING B;HL;SUP
[1]   ⍝COMPUTES LENGTH OF A STRING STRETCHED BETWEEN ENDS
[2]   ⍝OF A STICK AND PASSING OVER A SUPPORT OF HEIGHT 1÷4 THE
[3]   ⍝LENGTH OF STICK: LEFT ARGUMENT IS LENGTH OF STICK
[4]   ⍝RIGHT ARG.IS DISTANCE OF SUPPORT FROM CENTER OF STICK
[5]    HL←2×SUP←A÷4
[6]   ⍝HL IS HALF-LENGTH OF STICK,SUP IS HEIGHT OF SUPPORT
[7]    P←(SUP HYPOTENUSE HL+B)+SUP HYPOTENUSE HL-B
[8]   ⍝HYPOTENUSE COMPUTES THE HYPOTENUSE FOR ONE TRIANGLE ∇
```

Even if complete documentation is not incorporated within a function (because it is unnecessary or recorded elsewhere), it is good practice at least to include a statement describing what the function does and what are its arguments. It is disconcertingly easy to forget this basic information.

1) Rewrite the function *ELEVATION* of Sec. 2-18 with documentation, describing what the function does and its arguments.

CONCLUSION

The treatment of the APL language in this chapter is relatively complete in the sense that it presents the essential features concerning the style of the language. However, many details are missing or treated superficially. Many primitive functions are not dealt with at all, and those in Sec. 2-17 are described incompletely. Also, the important question of how to incorporate decision-making steps in a program has not been considered.

Chapter 2 deals thoroughly with the concepts of variable, name, and value, and also the nature of APL statements and the rule of execution, and how to create defined functions. You must have a good understanding of these ideas before going on, and they are so important that they are summarized here.

APL statements consist of symbols for primitive functions, or names for defined functions, combined with symbols for arguments of these functions. Values can be designated in any one of the following three forms:

(a) Numerals (the Arabic symbols), as in

6×4

(b) Named variables, whose values have been previously specified, as in

```
A←6
B←4
A×B
```

(c) Computed values which are not assigned to a name, as in

```
C←5
(1+C)×4
```

where the left-hand argument of × is computed from 1+C.

From studying this chapter you should be well versed in writing and interpreting APL statements having more than one primitive or defined function. Specifically, you should understand the rule of execution.

The nature of a defined function (whether it is monadic or dyadic, or gives an explicit result) is determined by the contents of the header line. What a function computes is determined by the contents of the statement lines. Input and output variables must appear in the header line. They are always local to the function. Other variables can be designated as local by including their names in the header line, separated by semicolons. Any variable used within a defined function but not appearing in the header line will be global.

Because this chapter is introductory, the examples of defined functions are relatively simple, but they are sophisticated enough to demonstrate something about style.

Problems--Chapter 2

Comment: In each of these problems you are asked to define a function. Before you start writing in APL, be sure you have planned the algorithm. Also, be particularly aware of opportunities for structuring programs in accordance with the principles outlined in Sec. 2-19. Hints are given in the descriptions of those problems for which this is a possibility. All of the problems can be done using only the primitives introduced in this chapter. In each problem except the last, the function is to produce an explicit result.

2-1 (a) Construct a dyadic function which returns a value, such that its left-hand argument is the hypotenuse of a right triangle and the right-hand argument is one of the sides of that triangle. The returned value is to be the value of the other side. Call the function $SIDE$.
(b) Imagine a circle of radius R and a radial line bisecting a chord of the circle at a distance X from the nearest point on the periphery. Design a dyadic function $CHORD$ which will return the length of the chord. The left-hand argument is to be the radius R, and the right-hand argument the distance X. Use $SIDE$ as specified in part (a) as a subfunction.

2-2 Suppose a certain amount of money M is placed in a bank to draw interest at an annual percentage rate I, compounded quarterly. At the end of one year the amount of money will be

```
M×(1+0.01×I÷4)*4
```

(a) Create a dyadic function $BANK$ which will return a value which is the amount of money in the account after a specified number of years. The left-hand argument is to be the initial principal amount (M), and the right-hand argument is to be a two-element vector: the percentage annual interest, and the number of years.

60 / Rudiments of APL

(b) Create a monadic function *INTEREST* which will take as its argument the same vector as specified as the right-hand argument of *BANK*, and will return a value which is the effective percentage interest for the number of years specified in that argument. Use *BANK* as a subfunction.

2-3 Suppose you go to the store and buy 5 units of an item A, 3 units of an item B, and 7 units of an item C. Items A, B and C are priced, respectively, at 3.45, 5.25 and 6.95. A dyadic function *COST* is to be constructed such that the total cost of the purchase can be obtained as a returned value from

```
      5   3   7 COST 3.45   5.25   6.95
81.65
```

The function is to work for any number of items, not only three as in the example, and for any vector of costs.

2-4 Define a monadic function *SECTOR*. It will take a two-element vector as its argument, in which the first element is a radius and the second element is an angle of a sector of a circle in degrees. The returned value is to be the area of the sector.

2-5 For the right triangle shown

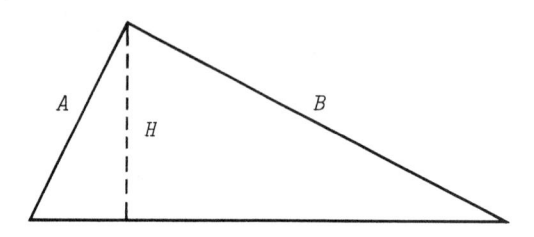

design a dyadic function *ALT* which will take *A* and *B* as its argument and produce *H* as a returned value. Use *HYPOTENUSE* as a subfunction. It is not necessary to use trigonometric functions. Hint: consider the area of the triangle.

2-6 Suppose a vector *S* contains three elements which are the edges of a rectangular parallelepiped. Define a monadic function *DIAG* which will take *S* as its argument and return the length of a diagonal. Use *HYPOTENUSE* as a subfunction an appropriate number of times.

2-7 Imagine a sphere of diameter *D* inside a cube having dimension *D* on a side. Define a monadic function *CSVOL* which will take *D* as its argument and return a value which is the volume within the cube and outside the sphere.

2-8 Assume

```
    ALPH←'ABCDEFGHIJKLMNOPQRSTUVWXYZ'
```

is available as a global variable. Write a monadic function *LETTER* which will take an integer from 1 to 26 (inclusive) as its argument and return, as a character value, the letter of the alphabet corresponding to that argument. For example,

```
    LETTER 5
E
```

2-9 Define a monadic function *COINS* which will return the total value of an assortment of coins. The argument will be a vector which represents the assortment of coins in the following way:

```
    1st element - number of half-dollar pieces
    2nd element - number of 25 cent pieces
    3rd element - number of 10 cent pieces
    4th element - number of 5 cent pieces
    5th element - number of 1 cent pieces
```

An example is

```
      COINS 3 5 2 1 6
3.06
```

2-10 Imagine an automobile trip in N segments, where each segment is traveled at a constant velocity. Let D be a vector of distances in kilometers for the sequence of segments, and V a vector of velocities in kilometers per hour for corresponding segments.

(a) Write a dyadic function *TRIPTIME* that will take D as its left-hand argument and V as its right-hand argument. Its returned value is to be the elapsed time of the trip, in hours.
(b) Use *TRIPTIME* as a subfunction in another dyadic function *TRIPVEL*. The arguments for *TRIPVEL* are the same as for *TRIPTIME*, but the returned value of *TRIPVEL* is to be the average velocity for the trip.

2-11 Design a monadic function *SIGN* which will take a positive or negative number as its argument, and return the following as character values:

Argument	Returned Value
Any positive number	*POSITIVE*
Any negative number	*NEGATIVE*
Zero	*ZERO*

Hint: Note that for a number N, `1-|×N` is 1 if N is 0, and otherwise zero. Another approach will be available after you have studied Chap. 4.

2-12 Suppose time is reckoned on a 24-hour clock, and that during any one day $T1$ and $T2$ are two instants of time, each given as a three-element vector (first element hours, second element minutes, third element seconds). A dyadic function *ELAPSE* is to take $T1$ and $T2$ as arguments (either one on the left or right) and return a value which is the elapsed time from the earliest to the latest instant. The result is to be one decimal number, in hours.

2-13 Suppose you are mixing any number of liquids of known densities. These densities can be the elements of a vector D. Suppose the proportions are stated as: so many parts of the first, so many parts of the second, etc., and that these form another vector P. Define a dyadic function *MIXTURE* that will take P as its left-hand argument and D as its right-hand argument and return a value which is the density of the mixture.

2-14 If a missile is sent vertically from the earth with an initial velocity $V0$ (meters/sec), the velocity at any height H (meters) is approximately

$$V = \sqrt{V0^2 - (19.6 \times H)}$$

The approximation is good up to a few thousand meters; it is based on the assumption that the pull of gravity does not vary with elevation.

(a) Write a monadic function *MAXHGT* which will take $V0$ as its argument, and produce the maximum height that will be attained, as an explicit result, in meters.
(b) Design a monadic function *VELS* which will take $V0$ as its argument and return a vector of velocities at 0, 20, 40, 60, 80 and 100 percent of the maximum height. Use *MAXHGT* as a subfunction. Note: Depending on the characteristics of your computer, you may see evidence of roundoff error at the highest point.

2-15 Do both parts of Prob. 2-14, but using the more exact formula (in conventional notation)

$$V = \sqrt{V0^2 - 19.6\left(\frac{R \times H}{R + H}\right)}$$

62 / Rudiments of APL

where $R = 6371000$ meters is the radius of the earth. This formula takes into account the decrease in the pull of gravity with increasing distance from the earth. Call the functions *MAXHGTM* and *VELSM*.

2-16 Let *C* be a vector of the coefficients of a quadratic equation, arranged in decreasing powers of *X*. For example (in conventional notation)

$$3X^2 - 7X + 2 = 0$$

would have *C* specified by

```
    C←3 ¯7 2
```

(a) Design a monadic function *QUADR* which will take a vector such as *C* as its argument and, for any case where the roots are real, return a two-element vector of the two roots.
(b) Design a monadic function *QUADC* which will take a vector such as *C* as its argument and, for any case where the roots are complex, return a four-element vector in which the first two elements are the real and imaginary parts of one root, and the last two elements are real and imaginary parts of the other root. Note: It is possible to design a function which will handle both cases, but not conveniently with the primitive functions introduced so far.

2-17 For this problem it is assumed you have *QUAD* from Prob. 2-16. If a ball is thrown vertically with an initial velocity *V0*, at any instant *T* (sec.) after it is thrown the height *H* (meters) is given (in conventional notation) by

$$H = (V0 \times T) - (4.9T^2)$$

Define a dyadic function which will take a value of *V0* as its left-hand argument and *H* as its right-hand argument, and return the value of *T* at that height (on the way up). Use *QUAD* as a subfunction.

2-18 A quadratic expression can be factored. For example (in conventional notation),

$$(X - 3)(X - 4) = X^2 - 7X + 12$$

You are to define a dyadic function *LINFAC* which, for this example, would take 3 and 4 as its arguments (either one on the left) and return a three-element vector which has as its elements the coefficients of *X* in the resulting polynomial, in decreasing powers of *X*. For example,

```
      3 LINFAC 4
1 ¯7 12
```

If you have *QUAD* from Prob. 2-16, specify two variables (say *A* and *B*) with trial values, and then execute

```
    QUAD A LINFAC B
```

2-19 Write a monadic function *STDEV* which will return the "standard deviation" of a vector of numbers. The standard deviation is computed by first computing the mean (average) of the numbers, subtracting that mean from each number, squaring each result, obtaining the mean of these squares, and then taking the square root. This is easily demonstrated by example. If $V \leftarrow 9\ 2\ 8\ 5$, the mean is 6, and so the standard deviation is the square root of the mean of $(9-6)^2$, $(2-6)^2$, $(8-6)^2$, $(5-6)^2$, or

$$\sqrt{\frac{9 + 16 + 4 + 1}{4}} = \sqrt{\frac{30}{4}} = 2.73861$$

The vector of numbers will be the argument, and the standard deviation will be the returned value. Use *MEAN* as defined in the text as a subfunction as many times as is appropriate.

2-20 The figure shows a graph of four data points, as representative of any number of points. Let X be a vector of the horizontal coordinates, and Y a vector of the vertical coordinates. (In the example, X is ¯2 3 7 12 and Y is 1 4 2 6.)

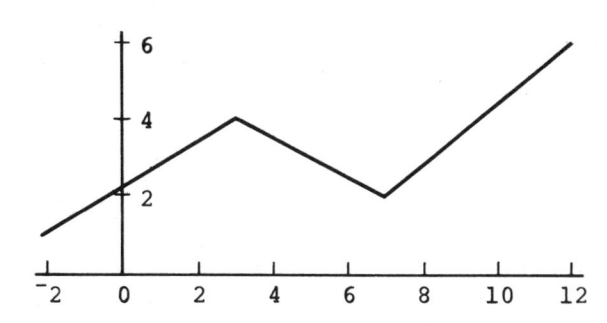

Design a dyadic function called *LENGTH* which will take X as the left-hand argument and Y as the right-hand argument, giving the total length of the straight lines joining the points, as a returned value. Use *HYPOTENUSE* as a subfunction.

2-21 (a) A monadic function *FN1* is to be defined so as to return a vector of values of Y for the mathematical relationship (in conventional notation)

$$Y = 4X - \frac{X^2}{2}$$

for a given vector of values of X. Specifically, a vector of values of X is to be the argument, and Y the returned value.
(b) A dyadic function *FN2* is to give values of Y as computed from the formula given in part (a), but for a set of uniformly spaced values of X. The left-hand argument is to be a positive integer stating how many values are to be computed, and the right-hand argument is to be a two element vector: the smallest value of X, and the increment in X between successive points. Design *FN2* using *FN1* as a subfunction.

2-22 In conventional notation we have the approximate equality, valid for X between ¯1 and 1 (not inclusive)

$$\frac{1}{1 + X} = 1 - X + X^2 - X^3 + X^4 - X^5 + \ldots \pm X^N$$

which becomes increasingly accurate as the number of terms on the right increases. Design a dyadic function *R1PX* which will take the highest power in the series approximation as the left-hand argument, and a value of X as the right-hand argument. It is to return the value of the series, and also print the exact value of ÷1+X. Try this function repeatedly for the same X, with increasing numbers of terms in the series, to observe the increasing accuracy.

2-23 Write a niladic function *COSTN* which will perform the calculation specified for *COST* in Prob. 2-3, but using evaluated input. It should return a value. An example of execution might be

```
      R←COSTN
ENTER THE NUMBER FOR EACH ITEM
☐:
      5 3 7
ENTER THE PRICE FOR EACH ITEM
☐:
      3.45 5.25 6.95
      R
81.65
```

2-24 Write a niladic function *BANKN* which will perform the calculation specified for *BANK* in Prob. 2-2a, but using character input. It should return a value. A typical execution would be

```
      R←BANKN
ENTER THE PRINCIPAL AMOUNT
4800
ENTER THE ANNUAL INTEREST, IN PERCENT
6
ENTER THE NUMBER OF YEARS
4
      R
6091.13
```

2-25 Write a niladic function *BANKM* which will perform the calculations specified for *BANK* in Prob. 2-2a, but with all data being entered in one character input statement following the statement of what to enter. It should return a value. A typical execution would be

```
      R←BANKM
ENTER PRINCIPAL, ANNUAL INTEREST, YEARS 4800 6 4
      R
6091.13
```

2-26 Write a function *BANKL* which will have the same properties described in Prob. 2-25, except that it is to have a printed result (no returned value) as illustrated in the following example:

```
      BANKL
ENTER PRINCIPAL, ANNUAL INTEREST, YEARS 4800 6 4
THE PRINCIPAL AFTER 4 YEARS WILL BE 6091.13
```

Chapter 3

ARRAYS

INTRODUCTION

The previous chapter includes an introduction to vectors; sets of numbers or characters arranged in a line. In the present chapter this idea is extended, allowing sets of numbers or characters to have a variety of geometrical arrangements similar to the arrangements used in ordinary writing. Some examples (including a repetition of the vector case) are as follows:

(a) Line (Vector)

```
2  8  26  3  9  18  258  7  3        or        INTELLIGENCE IS
```

There can be any number of *elements* (numbers or characters) in a line. This numerical example has 9 elements (each number of more than one digit is one element). The character example has 15 elements (including one space character). In a numerical case, spaces between numbers act as separators but are not part of the list.

(b) Page (Matrix)

```
2   8  6  3                    INTELLIGENCE
9  18  5  7        or          IS NECESSARY
3   2  5  4                    IN PROGRAMMING
```

There can be any number of elements in a row and any number of elements in a column. Each row must have the same number of elements, and each column must have the same number of elements. For the character page on the right, each row has 14 characters. There are two spaces at the ends of the first and second rows, because each row must have the same number of elements.

(d) Book

```
2  8  6  3  9  ⎫                 INTELLIGENCE  ⎫
8  5  7  3  2  ⎭ Page 1          IS NECESSARY  ⎭ Page 1

5  4  2  7  1  ⎫                 IN PROGRAMM-  ⎫
8  5  3  9  2  ⎭ Page 2    or    ING AN ELEC-  ⎭ Page 2

6  8  5  1  3  ⎫                 TRONIC DIGIT- ⎫
4  2  9  4  2  ⎭ Page 3          AL COMPUTER   ⎭ Page 3
```

These are examples of arrays. The present chapter presents the basic ideas, with emphasis on:

66 / Arrays

(a) How arrays can be constructed on the computer.
(b) How computations can be done on arrays.
(c) How arrays can be used in practical problems.

This chapter deals mainly with vectors and matrices; arrays of greater complexity are treated more extensively in Chap. 6.

3-1 Terminology for Arrays

The objective of this section is the development of a precise terminology for the description of arrays, using for illustrations the examples given in the introduction. In what follows, the word "display" refers to the form typed by the computer. Illustrations are for origin 1.

(a) Vectors

A *vector* displays as a row of numbers or typewriter characters. A display of a vector consists of nothing but the elements themselves, but associated with the display you should *imagine a coordinate axis* and a set of *index numbers*, as in the following:

```
[1]  [2]  [3]  [4]  [5]  [6]  [7]  [8]  [9]   ←— Index numbers
                                              ←— Axis 1
 2    8   26   3    9   18  258   7    3     ←— Display
```

The index numbers may be thought of as coordinate positions along the axis, at which the elements of the vector are located. Every coordinate position must be occupied by an element. An element can be zero.

When a vector is a line of characters, each character occupies an index position, as in the example

```
[1][2][3]...[13][14][15]
 ↓  ↓  ↓     ↓   ↓   ↓
INTELLIGENCE IS
```

For any vector (numeric or character) the total number of coordinate positions along the axis is called the *dimension* of the vector (also called its length). In the above numerical example the dimension is 9. In the character example the dimension is 15. The number of axes is called the *rank* of an array. Thus, a vector is an array of rank 1.

(b) Matrices

A *matrix* displays as one page of numbers or characters. Such a display has *two* coordinate axes and two sets of index numbers, as in the following example.

---

1) For the numeric vector

   283   475

the element at index position [2] is (choose one: 8, 475)

_____

the element at index position [3] is (choose one: a space, 3, non-existent)

_____

2) For a vector having the following display,

   SAVE TIME

the element at index position [5] is (choose one: a space, T)

_____

3) The dimension of the vector given in question (1) is

_____

The dimension of the vector given in question (2) is

_____

4) The dimension of a vector (is/is not) _____ the same as its length.

(5) If an array has one axis it is called a _____

If an array has two axes it is called a _____

Arrays / 67

1) A vector whose elements are the dimensions of the axes of an array is called the

_____

of the array.

The number of axes in a display of an array is called the

_____

of the array.

2) The dimension of the shape vector of an array equals (mark any of the following that are true):

The rank of the array.

_____

The number of axes of the array.

_____

3) For an array having the following display:

```
2  8  7  6
4  3  2  1
```

the element at index position [2] for axis 1 and index position [3] for axis 2 equals

_____

The dimension of axis 1 equals

_____

The dimension of axis 2 equals

_____

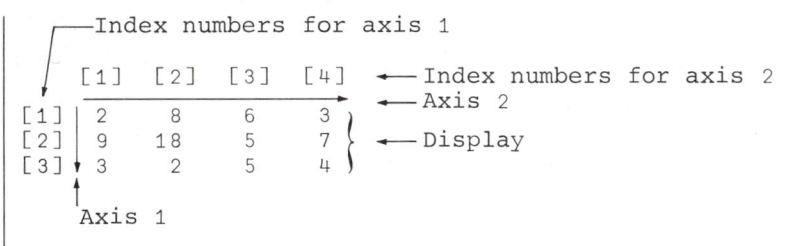

```
                ┌─── Index numbers for axis 1
                │   [1]  [2]  [3]  [4]   ◄── Index numbers for axis 2
            [1] │   2    8    6    3  ┐  ◄── Axis 2
            [2] │   9   18    5    7  ├── Display
            [3] ▼   3    2    5    4  ┘
              Axis 1
```

The axes and index numbers are included to aid your visualization; they do not appear in a computer display. Each axis has a dimension. In the example, axis 1 has dimension 3 and axis 2 has dimension 4. A vector obtained by listing the dimensions of the axes in order, as for this example,

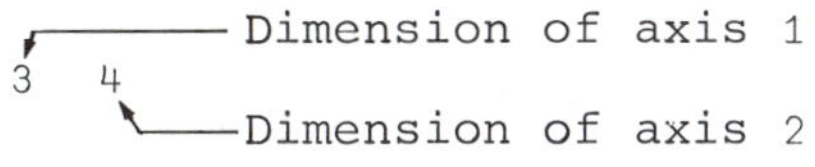

```
          ┌──── Dimension of axis 1
        3   4
            └── Dimension of axis 2
```

is called the *shape* of the matrix. Since a matrix has two axes, it is an array of rank 2.

(c) Arrays of Rank Higher than 2

A computer value can have a rank higher than 2. The following displays show two portrayals of an array of rank 3 (requiring 3 axes). The way the computer displays such an array (augmented with axis and index labels) is shown on the left. A perspective portrayal which makes the axes more evident is shown on the right.

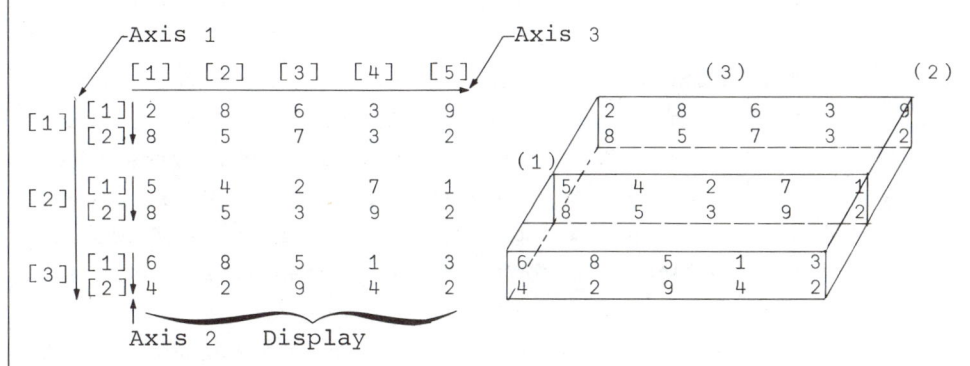

```
              ┌─Axis 1                              ┌─Axis 3
              │  [1]  [2]  [3]  [4]  [5]             (3)          (2)
          [1] │[1]  2   8   6   3   9
              │[2]▼ 8   5   7   3   2              2  8  6  3  9
                                                   8  5  7  3  2
          [2]  [1]  5   4   2   7   1        (1)
               [2]▼ 8   5   3   9   2             5  4  2  7  1
                                                  8  5  3  9  2
          [3]  [1]  6   8   5   1   3
               [2]▼ 4   2   9   4   2             6  8  5  1  3
                                                  4  2  9  4  2
              Axis 2    Display
```

In the example the dimensions of axes 1, 2, and 3 are, respectively, 3, 2, and 5. The list of these dimensions, namely the vector

3 2 5

is the shape of this array.

The computer can handle arrays having more than 3 axes. For example, an array of rank 4 has a display as illustrated by the following example (augmented with axis and index labels).

68 / Arrays

```
              [1]  [2]  [3]  [4]  [5]
                                         Axis 4
         [1] [1] │ 2    8    6    3    9  ⎫
             [2] ↓ 8    5    7    3    2  ⎪
                                           ⎪
         [2] [1] │ 5    4    2    7    1  ⎬ Book 1
     [1]     [2] ↓ 8    5    3    9    2  ⎪
                                           ⎪
             [1] │ 6    8    5    1    3  ⎪
         [3] [2] ↓ 4    2    9    4    2  ⎭

         [1] [1] │ 3    6    7    6    5  ⎫
             [2] ↓ 9    8    1    5    4  ⎪
                                           ⎪
     [2] [2] [1] │ 9    2    2    5    3  ⎬ Book 2
             [2] ↓ 5    8    7    8    6  ⎪
                                           ⎪
         [3] [1] │ 1    6    5    4    4  ⎪
             [2] ↓ 3    2    1    8    9  ⎭

Axis 1  Axis 2  Axis 3
```

This array is of rank 4 and its shape vector is

    2   3   2   5

Axis and index numbering depends on the index origin. The labeling shown in these examples is for origin 1. For origin 0 each axis number and index number would be less by one.

The following comments are made concerning the display of arrays by the computer:

(1) The last (highest numbered) axis is always horizontal.
(2) For ranks higher than 3, the largest vertical spaces represent jumps between index numbers of the first axis, the next largest vertical spaces represent jumps between index numbers of the second axis, etc.
(3) The axis lines and bracketed index numbers shown in the illustration above do not appear in a display; they must be imagined.
(4) The dimensions of the axes in these examples are merely illustrative; the dimension of an axis can be any nonnegative integer. The only restriction is the availability of memory space.
(5) The elements of the shape vector are the dimensions of the axes, in the order of the axis numbering.

(d) Scalars

A value which is a single number can be viewed as a degenerate "array" having no axis (rank 0). Such a value is called a *scalar*. The single numbers used in the examples of

---

1) For the display of an array of rank 3, double vertical spaces correspond to the counting of index numbers for axis number
_____

2) For each of the following, designate the rank:

Scalar _____

Vector _____

Matrix _____

3) If a vector corresponds to a geometrical line, a matrix corresponds to a geometrical rectangle, then a scalar corresponds to a geometrical
_____

4) In origin 0, for a matrix of shape 5 3 answer the following:

The axis numbers are
_____ and
_____

The lowest index number for each axis is
_____

The highest index number for the lowest numbered axis is
_____

The highest index number for the highest numbered axis is
_____

Chap. 2 are scalars. A single character value can also be a scalar. Thus, the variables

$A \leftarrow 5$

and

$B \leftarrow 'H'$

have scalar values.

3-2 Character Arrays

Each of the previous examples of arrays could have been illustrated using character elements. For example

INTELLIGENCE
IS NECESSARY
IN PROGRAMMING

is a matrix having the shape vector 3 14. There are 3 rows and 14 characters in each row (including two space characters at the ends of rows 1 and 2). Also,

INTELLIGENCE
IS NECESSARY

IN PROGRAMM-
ING AN ELEC-

TRONIC DIGIT-
AL COMPUTER

is an array of rank 3, having 3 2 13 as its shape vector.

Numerals can be elements of an array of characters, a fact that can be confusing to the unwary. For example,

816234

can be a display of the character vector 816324 (having the dimension 6) or it can be the scalar number 816324.

3-3 Specification of Arrays, the Reshape Function

In Chap. 2 we assigned a value to a variable by doing an operation such as

$A \leftarrow 5$

The variable named A then has the scalar 5 as its value. We now proceed to review how vectors are specified, and consider the specification of arrays of ranks 2 and higher.

(a) Specification of a Vector

The basic method for creating a vector (introduced in Sec. 2-8) is to enter a row of numeric or character values, as in the examples

---

1) For each of the following arrays give the information requested.

APL IS A PRO-
GRAMMING LANGUAGE

Shape
_____

Rank
_____

Dimension, axis 1
_____

Dimension, axis 2
_____

AS YOU STUDY,
YOU SHOULD

MAKE DELIBER-
ATE AND

STEADY
PROGRESS

Shape
_____

Rank
_____

Dimension, axis 1
_____

Dimension, axis 2
_____

Dimension, axis 3
_____

2) Punctuation marks (are/are not) _____ admissible as elements in vectors of characters.

3) If you do the following assignments, show the computer responses to tests for values of the variables.

$VA \leftarrow 12345$
$VB \leftarrow '12345'$
VA
_____
VB
_____

70 / Arrays

```
    V1←2  8  26  3  9  18  258  7  3
    V2←387.29   0.87625   7.293
    V3←'INTELLIGENCE IS'
```

For numeric vectors there must be at least one space between elements, but additional spaces are permitted. While numerals and other characters can be mixed in a character vector, as in V←'34 AND 35', *numbers* cannot be mixed with character values. For example, V←34 'AND' 35 is not possible because 34 and 35 are numbers (not within quotes).

DYADIC ρ

If a vector having a cyclic repetition is wanted, it is not necessary to list the repetitions in an assignment statement. Instead, the *reshape* function (using the symbol ρ in dyadic form) can be used. For example,

```
      V4←9ρ 1  2  3
      V4
1  2  3  1  2  3  1  2  3
```

Other examples are

```
      V5←15ρ8
      V5
8 8 8 8 8 8 8 8 8 8 8 8 8 8 8
```

and, using characters,

```
      V6←21ρ'-O'
      V6
-O-O-O-O-O-O-O-O-O-O-
```

The left-hand argument of ρ determines the number of elements in the resulting vector (its dimension). The right-hand argument is the *object value*; the value which supplies the elements from which the vector is formed. The computer "reads" the object value from left to right until its elements have been exhausted, and then reads it again a sufficient number of times to provide all the elements needed. If there are more elements in the object value than required, the unused elements are ignored. For example, using the previously specified V4 and V5,

```
      7ρV4
1  2  3  1  2  3  1
      3ρV5
8  8  8
```

The left-hand argument of ρ must be a nonnegative integer. If it is not, an error report will be received.

An interesting case occurs when the left-hand argument is 1, as in

```
      1ρ6
```

6

---

1) If you do the specification

   V←'78 AND 9,10'

the first element of V is
_____

and the 9th and 10th elements are
_____

What are the 3rd and 7th elements of V?
_____

2) Give results produced by

   5ρ4

_____

and

   5ρ'4'

_____

3) Using 3 5 7 as an object value, show how to use reshape to produce

3 5 7 3 5 7 3
_____

4) Write statements that will produce each of the following:

--*-*-*
_____

*-**-**-**-*
_____

----*--*--*
_____

Arrays / 71

1) Mark the correct one of the following statements. The notation ι0 produces an empty vector:

Only in origin 0
_____

Only in origin 1
_____

In either origin
_____

2) Mark the correct one of the following statements. The notations ι1 and 1ρ1 are equivalent:

Only in origin 0
_____

Only in origin 1
_____

In either origin
_____

Under no condition
_____

This produces a result which prints like a scalar, but it is really a vector having one element.

(b) Empty Vector

The result of

    $V8 \leftarrow \iota 0$

is of particular interest. It is a vector of zero elements, called an *empty vector*. This is not to be confused with the number 0. The value of an empty vector is not zero, its value is a vector in which there are no elements.

Because an empty vector has no content, a test for its value produces no print other than an up-space. Thus, having specified $V8$ as above,

    $V8$

where the space immediately below $V8$ is the blank-line response from the computer.

The reshape function

    $0 \rho 5$

where 5 represents any numeric object value, also produces an empty vector, because the number of elements called for by the left-hand argument is 0. There are many ways to create empty vectors. Two others are: a pair of quote symbols with nothing between them, thus

    ' '

and

    $0 \rho 'K'$

(where 'K' stands for any character object value).

These last two are called empty vectors of *character type* because they are limiting cases of character vectors having zero elements. The two previous examples are empty vectors of *numeric type*. In some applications empty vectors of numeric type and character type are equivalent, in some they are not.

(c) Matrices

The reshape function can be used to create a matrix, by using the shape vector of the desired matrix as the left-hand argument of ρ. For example,

```
      M1←3 4 ρ 2 8 6 3 9 8 5 7 3 2 5 4
      M1
   2  8  6  3
   9  8  5  7
   3  2  5  4
```

An example yielding a character matrix is

```
      M2←3  14 ρ'INTELLIGENCE  IS NECESSARY  IN PROGRAMMING'
      M2
INTELLIGENCE
IS NECESSARY
IN PROGRAMMING
```

As indicated for vectors, it is not necessary that the object value have exactly the same number of elements as required by the left-hand argument. Thus,

```
      3  4 ρι6
1  2  3  4
5  6  1  2
3  4  5  6
```

and

```
      3  4 ρι50
1  2  3  4
5  6  7  8
9 10 11 12
```

(d) Arrays of Rank Higher than Two

The reshape function can be used to create an array of any rank, by using the desired shape vector as the left-hand argument of ρ. For example, to create an array of 3 pages, with 4 rows and 5 columns per page, the left-hand argument would be 3 4 5. As a case in point,

```
      A1←3  4  5 ρι60
      A1
 1  2  3  4  5
 6  7  8  9 10
11 12 13 14 15
16 17 18 19 20

21 22 23 24 25
26 27 28 29 30
31 32 33 34 35
36 37 38 39 40

41 42 43 44 45
46 47 48 49 50
51 52 53 54 55
56 57 58 59 60
```

3-4 Catenate and Laminate

We shall now consider two functions which can be used to attach two arrays in various ways. The function *catenate* was treated briefly in Sec. 2-17 for vectors, but it also applies to arrays of ranks higher than 1. It combines two arrays along an existing axis. The function *laminate* combines two arrays in such a way as to create a new axis.

---

1) The following specifications are done:

```
MX←3  2 ρ 6  5
MY←2  3 ρ 6  5
```

Write out the display obtained when each is tested for value.

```
MX
```

```
MY
```

2) A variable *C* is to have this display

```
C
DON'T WALK
ON THE GRASS
```

Write a specification for *C*.

---

3) Show a statement using reshape which will produce a matrix *I* having the display

```
    I
1 0 0 0
0 1 0 0
0 0 1 0
0 0 0 1
```

Arrays / 73

1) Show how to produce
1 2 3 1 2 3
from
    A←⍳3
(a) by reshape
_____
(b) by catenation
_____

2) If you have the two variables
    VA←'TIME'
    VB←'FLIES'
show how to use catenation to produce the value
    TIME FLIES
_____

3) Is there any difference between values assigned to A by
    A←2 2 3 3
and
    A←2 2,3 3
_____

A general treatment of these functions for ranks higher than 2 is given in Chap. 6. In this section we treat catenation for vectors and matrices, and lamination for vectors.

(a) Catenate   DYADIC

We summarize catenation for vectors, pointing out that either argument can be a scalar. Suppose we have the vectors

```
    V1← 2  8  26  3  9  18  258  7  3
    V2← 386.29  0.87625  7.293
    V3←'AP'
```

Then,

```
      V1,V2
2  8  26  3  9  18  258  7  3  386.29  0.87625  7.293
      V1,5
2  8  26  3  9  18  258  7  3  5
      21.9,V2
21.9  386.29  0.87625  7.293
      V3,'L'
APL
```

It is not possible to catenate V3 with V1 or V2 because this would be an attempt to mix numbers and characters in one vector.

To illustrate catenation of matrices, assume the following three matrices have been specified:

```
      M1
2  8  6  3
9  4  3  7
3  2  5  4
      M2
5  5  5  5
5  5  5  5
      M3
6  6
6  6
6  6
```

M2 can be appended above or below M1 (catenated *along* axis 1) in the following two ways:

```
      M1,[1]M2
2  8  6  3
9  4  3  7
3  2  5  4
5  5  5  5
5  5  5  5
```

and

```
      M2,[1]M1
5  5  5  5
5  5  5  5
2  8  6  3
9  4  3  7
3  2  5  4
```

74 / Arrays

The words "along axis 1" are implied by the *axis operator* [1]. Catenation along axis 2 is obtained by using [2] as the axis operator, as in

```
    M1,[2]M3
2 8 6 3 6 6
9 4 3 7 6 6
3 2 5 4 6 6
```

For matrices, there is an important condition on compatibility: Catenation along the first axis requires that arguments must have second axes of equal dimensions; catenation along the second axis requires that arguments must have first axes of equal dimensions. The illustrations above of axis operators are in origin 1, in origin 0 they would be 1 less. This compatibility condition can be violated if one argument is a matrix and the other a scalar, or vector of compatible length. In such a case the scalar or vector is automatically extended to a compatible matrix (1 row or 1 column). For example,

```
    M1,[1]5    is equivalent to   M1,[1] 1 4 ρ5
```

and

```
    M1,[2]ι3   is equivalent to   M1,[2] 3 1 ρι3
```

The axis operator can be omitted if catenation along the highest-numbered axis is intended. Thus, M1,M3 is equivalent to M1,[2]M3.

(b) Laminate   DYADIC

In terms of the two vectors

```
W1←5 4 7 3
W2←9 2 5 6
```

one example of laminate is (in origin 1)

```
    W1,[0.5]W2
5 4 7 3
9 2 5 6
```

There is a similarity with catenation, but the "axis operator" includes a noninteger. The number 0.5 could be any number between 0 and 1 (exclusive). Being less than 1, this means: Create an array having a new axis which *precedes* what was axis 1 of the arguments. In origin 0 the number in the axis operator would be between ¯1 and 0 (exclusive).

An array can be created in which a new axis *follows* axis 1 of the arguments, by executing (**in origin 1**)

In the following questions use

```
A←2 6 5
B←1 3 ρA
C←3 1 ρA
D←2 3 ρ 4 7 8 3
```

Answer the questions for origin 1.

1) Give results for the following:

   A,ι3

   B,[1]ι3

   C,[2]ι3

   A,[1]B

2) Give results for the following, or mark "incompatible"

   B,[1]D

   B,[2]D

   D,[2]ι2

   5,[1]D

   5,[2]D

Arrays / 75

1) Give results for (in origin 1)

    6,⍳4

    6,[0.5]⍳4

    6,[1.5]⍳4

2) If

    B←'BOOK'

show a specification for A so that (in origin 1)

    A,[0.5]B
    PEN
    BOOK

    B,[1.5]A
    BP
    OE
    ON
    K

_____

3) Write a statement using ravel, laminate, and the index generator to produce the vector

    1 1 2 2 ... N N

where N N stands for a repetition of any positive integer.

_____

4) If A is any array, and

    B←,A

the dimension of B is equal to (choose one)

⍴A _____
×/⍴A _____
+/⍴A _____

```
    W1,[1.5]W2
5   9
4   2
7   5
3   6
```

The number 1.5 could be any number between 1 and 2 (or between 0 and 1 in origin 0).

The general condition for compatibility is that the lengths of the vectors must be the same. However, one argument can be a scalar. In that case the scalar is automatically extended to form a compatible vector. For example,

```
    W1,[0.5]9
5   4   7   3
9   9   9   9
```

3-5 Ravel   [MONADIC ,]

Let A2 be an array of rank 3 which displays as follows:

```
    A2
8   7  ¯2
6  12  15

1  ¯8  ¯9
4  ¯5   6

2   9   9
7   6   3
```

The *ravel* function (represented by the monadic use of the symbol ,) with A2 as the argument produces the following vector:

```
    ,A2
8 7 ¯2 6 12 15 1 ¯8 ¯9 4 ¯5 6 2 9 9 7 6 3
```

This result is the vector obtained by reading the display of A2 in the *normal* reading order. The ravel of an argument of any rank is produced in the same way. Ravel always produces a vector. In particular, the ravel of a scalar is a vector of one element. Thus,

[CONVERT SCALAR TO VECTOR]

```
    ,5
5
```

converts the scalar 5 to a vector of one element having 5 as the element. The result is the same as 1⍴5.

3-6 The Shape Function   [⍴ MONADIC & DYADIC FUNCTIONS]

The *shape function* was introduced for vectors in Sec. 2-27. We now extend it to arrays of higher ranks, but first we review the vector case. If V is some vector,

    ⍴V

yields a vector of *one element* (its shape). That element is

76 / Arrays

the number of elements in *V* (its dimension). There is a subtle difference between the shape and dimension of a vector. They are the same number, but the dimension is a scalar and the shape is a vector of one element.

If *M* is a matrix,

    ρ*M*

yields a two-element vector; the number of rows in *M* (the dimension of the first axis) followed by the number of columns (the dimension of the second axis). That is, ρ*M* yields the shape of *M*. To illustrate the shape function, suppose we have

    V11←'COMPUTERS WORK RAPIDLY'
    M3←6 4 ρ(4ρ5),4ρ6
    A3←5 3 6 ρι150

then

    ρV11
22
    ρM3
6 4
    ρA3
5 3 6

The *number* of elements in the result of monadic ρ equals the number of axes of the argument. Since a scalar has zero axes, the monadic ρ of a scalar produces a result which has no elements, and hence is an empty vector. Thus,

    ρ(any scalar)
empty vector

The monadic function ρ always produces a vector.

We now see how it is possible to distinguish between a scalar 5 and the one-element vector ,5 (or 1ρ5). Although they both yield a print of the numeral 5, the shape function gives different results, as follows:

    ρ5
empty vector
    ρ,5
1

Also, now we can distinguish between a character vector and a scalar number which exhibit the same printed result. It is evident that

    ρ618234
empty vector
    ρ'618234'
6

---

1) Give the result for each of the following:

  ρ,89

  ρ1ρ89

  ρι0

---

2) For each of the variables having the displays shown below, indicate the result of the shape function and the ravel function.

  MP
2 4
3 1

6 5
4 3
  ρ*MP*

  ,*MP*

  MQ
2 4

3 1
  ρ*MQ*

  ,*MQ*

  MR
2 4
3 1
  ρ*MR*

  ,*MR*

Arrays / 77

1) If $A\leftarrow\iota 0$ and $V\leftarrow ,6$ the result of

   $A\rho V$

is (choose one)

Vector 6 _____

Scalar 6 _____

Neither _____

2) If M is any matrix,

   2 3 ρM

(is/is not) _____
the same as

   2 3 ρ ,M

3) If A has a value which displays as

```
      A
   2  8  6
   3  2  1

   4  9  5
   8  7  3
```

give the results of

   3 6 ρA

and

   2 1 4 ρA

Let us consider how to convert a vector of one element to an equivalent scalar. The shape of a scalar is an empty vector, and so a scalar can be produced by using an empty vector as the left-hand argument of the reshape function. Thus,

   $(\iota 0)\rho ,5$

and

   $''\rho ,5$

both produce the scalar 5. There are other ways to do this.

3-7 The Object Value in Reshape

In Sec. 3-3 the reshape function is always shown with a vector (or possibly a scalar) as its object value. However, the object value can be an array of any rank. Then, $B\rho A$ produces the same result as $B\rho ,A$. As an example, if A has the display

```
       A
   8  6  3
   4  9  7
```

then

```
      2  2  2 ρA
   8  6
   3  4

   9  7
   8  6
```

3-8 Illustrations of Manipulations of Arrays

The following two examples are offered to illustrate operations on arrays which have been considered up to this point.

Example 3-1

A niladic function $TICTAC$ is to give an explicit result which is a diagram for the game of "tic-tac-toe," as a character matrix. Specifically, the diagram is to be

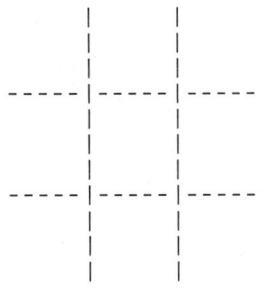

```
         |     |
         |     |
         |     |
   ------|-----|------
         |     |
         |     |
         |     |
   ------|-----|------
         |     |
         |     |
         |     |
```

For the algorithm, observe that the figure is made up of two types of lines:

78 / Arrays

Type 1: (5 spaces),'|',(5 spaces),'|',(5 spaces)
Type 2: (5 '-'chars.),'|',(5 '-'chars.),'|',(5 '-'chars.)

The figure can be created by first arranging these lines as a vector and then reshaping that vector. The following steps describe the algorithm.

   (1) Create a line of type 1.
   (2) Create a vector of three of the vectors created in step 1.
   (3) Append a vector of type 2 on the right of the result of step 2.
   (4) Make a vector of three repetitions of the result of step 3, and reshape it into 11 rows and 17 columns.

One function which will carry out these steps is

```
     ∇ L←TICTAC
[1]    L←17ρ(5ρ' '),'|'
[2]    L←51ρL
[3]    L←L,17ρ(5ρ'-'),'|'
[4]    L←11 17 ρL  ∇
```

Use is made of the fact that the reshape function repeats elements in its object value. In line [1], the part

   (5ρ' '),'|'

creates a vector of six elements, 5 spaces and '|'. Then this is repeated 3 times by reshaping it into a vector of 17 elements, except that the third '|' is dropped (because 17 is 1 less than 3 times the 6 elements). Line [2] makes L a vector of three copies of the L specified in line [1]. On line [3] a vector of characters for a line of type 2 is catenated on the right of L. To explain line [4], observe that L from line [3] has 68 characters, and that 11 rows and 17 columns require 187 characters. This is 17 less than 3×68, and so the last 17 elements of L are used only twice, which is correct because a line of type 2 is not wanted at the bottom.

Example 3-2

Suppose M is a numeric matrix of any shape, and you want a function ADDLINE which can be used to insert an additional line at any index position. For example, suppose M is

```
        M
    1   2   3   4
    5   6   7   8
    9  10  11  12
```

and you want to change it to

```
    1   2   3   4
    5   6   7   8
   13  14  15  16
    9  10  11  12
```

1) Refer to line [1] of TICTAC given in the text. Write an equivalent statement using ρ only once and no other primitive.

2) Write an equivalent for line [2] of TICTAC not using ρ.

3) Write an equivalent of TICTAC in one line.

4) Suppose TICTAC has the following first 2 lines:

```
     ∇ L←TICTAC;M
[1]    L←3 17ρ17ρ(5ρ' '),'|'
[2]    M←17ρ(5ρ'-'),'|'
[3]
```

Use catenate to complete line [3] so that this function will give the same result as the version in the text. Use catenate only.

Arrays / 79

1) Refer to step (3) of the algorithm on this page. Suppose the result for that step is to be obtained from $D\downarrow M$ instead of $T\uparrow M$. Write a statement for making an assignment to D.

───────────

2) Write a version of ADDLINE using D as described in (1) above instead of T.

3) Answer the question as to whether ADDLINE as given in the text can be used with a vector argument, to form a matrix of two rows.

───────────

4) Modify ADDLINE as given in the text so it will work for a character matrix.

The function is to be dyadic, taking the line number of the added line (in origin 1) as its left-hand argument, and M as its right-hand argument. The value of the added line will be entered as character input, and a message should indicate when to enter it. For the above example, using the original M,

```
      M←3 ADDLINE M
ENTER NEW LINE
13   14   15   16
      M
 1    2    3    4
 5    6    7    8
13   14   15   16
 9   10   11   12
```

Possible steps for an algorithm are:

(1) Determine the shape of M, and call it S. From S determine the number of columns in M, and call it C.

(2) Assign to M the ravel of M.

(3) If R is the row number for the row to be added, there will be $C \times R-1$ elements before it in the ravel produced in step 2. Call this T, and then take T elements from the left of vector M and assign it to $M1$.

(4) Drop the T elements from the left of vector M and call the result $M2$.

(5) Form the catenation ($M1$,the new data,$M2$) and reshape it with one row more than the original M.

The following is an example of an actual program:

```
     ∇ A←R ADDLINE M;C;M1;S;T
[1]    C←¯1↑S←ρM
[2]    M1←(T←C×R-1)↑M←,M
[3]    'ENTER NEW LINE'
[4]    A←(S+ 1  0)ρM1,(⍎⎕),T↓M ∇
```

A simpler program is possible, using functions not yet introduced, in which the matrix is not changed to a vector. However, here we wish to illustrate ravel and reshape. Line [1] corresponds to step 1, line [2] carries out steps 2 and 3, and line [4] does steps 4 and 5. Note the following: Execute is applied to the character input, $S+$ 1 0 increases the number of rows by 1, and $T\downarrow M$ is used without giving it the name $M2$.

3-9 Empty Arrays

It has been shown that ι0 and 0ρ5 produce a vector having an axis of zero dimension (empty vector). This idea of "emptiness" extends to arrays. For an array to be empty, one or more of its axes must have zero dimension. Some examples are:

80 / Arrays

```
        A←0  3 ρ5         Zero dimension of first axis
        B←4  0 ρ5         Zero dimension of last axis
        C←0  0 ρ5         Zero dimension of first and last axis
        D←4  0 2 ρ5       Zero dimension of second axis
```

The right-hand argument is unimportant (5 is representative of any value). These examples show that an empty array can be of any rank; variables A, B, and C are of rank 2, D is of rank 3.

Empty arrays can be distinguished from empty vectors by applying the shape function. For the above cases:

```
            ρA
    0  3
            ρB
    4  0
            ρC
    0  0
            ρD
    4  0  2
```

while for an empty vector,

```
            ρι0
    0
```

3-10 Rank of a Value

The rank of a value is the number of axes in its display. This is also the number of elements in the shape vector. Therefore, for any variable A,

```
            ρρA
```

yields the rank of the value of A. Perhaps it is useful temporarily to think of this as ρ(ρA) although the computer does not require the parentheses.

3-11 Arithmetic Functions with Arrays

Suppose M3 and M4 are matrices having the displays

```
        M3
    3  ¯5  8
    2   4  3

        M4
    2   3  ¯2
    9   5   4
```

Any of the computations M3+M4, M3-M4, M3×M4, M3÷M4 and M3*M4 are possible. The operation (+, × etc.) combines elements in corresponding positions to produce the result. Some examples are:

---

1) For an array to be classified as empty, the dimension of (only one axis/at least one axis) _____ shall be zero.

2) If
```
    A←4  0 ρ10
    B←0  4 ρ'AB'
```
give results for
   ρA _____
   ρB _____
   ρ,A _____
   ρρB _____

3) Consider the function ADDLINE of example 3-2. Specify N so that if you execute

```
    T←1 ADDLINE N
ENTER NEW LINE
2 9 4 3 5
```

the value of T will be the 1-row matrix
2 9 4 3 5
   N←

4) If A is a vector
      B is a matrix
      C is an array of rank 3
write the result produced by each of the following.
   ρρA _____
   ρρB _____
   ρρC _____
   ρρι0 _____
   ρρ,1 _____

Arrays / 81

1) In terms of the following matrices, give answers for the computations indicated.

$M3$
```
 3  ¯5   8
 2   4   3
```

$M4$
```
 2   3  ¯2
 9   5   4
```

$M4-M3$

$M4\div M3$

$2\times M4$

$M4*3$

$\div M3$

$\times M3$

2) For the following three statements, mark OK if the statement is permissible, or ERROR if it will give an error report.

$2+\iota 0$ _____

$2\ 3\ +\iota 0$ _____

$(3\ 0\ \rho 5)+\iota 0$ _____

$(\iota 0)+7$ _____

```
       M3+M4
 5  ¯2   6
11   9   7
       M3×M4
 6  ¯15 ¯16
18   20  12
       M3*M4
9.0000E0    ¯1.2500E2   1.5625E¯2
5.1200E2     1.0240E3   8.1000E1
```

Results are similar for arrays of any rank.

Observe in these examples that the shapes of the arguments are the same. Except for the special case treated in the next paragraph, this is a necessary condition for an arithmetic operation between two arrays.

The exception is that if one argument is a scalar (or one-element vector) the other argument can be of any rank, as in

```
      5+M3
 8   0  13
 7   9   8
```

In such a case the computer automatically *extends* the scalar by repetition, to the same shape as the other argument.

The above principle applies if an argument is an empty array. If one argument is an empty array the other can be a scalar and the result will be empty and of the same shape as the empty argument. For example, $7+\iota 0$ produces an empty vector, and $5*0\ \ 2\ \rho 6$ produces an empty array of zero rows and two columns.

The monadic forms of the arithmetic functions can be used with array arguments, as in

```
       -M3
¯3   5  ¯8
¯2  ¯4  ¯3
       ×M4
 1   1  ¯1
 1   1   1
```

The monadic function (- or ×) acts on each element separately.

Applications of arithmetic functions occur repeatedly throughout the book. At this point we consider one illustrative example, done in a manner appropriate for this stage of your learning.

Example 3-3

Suppose you are in charge of five weather stations each of which reports temperature and wind velocity four times a day, at equal intervals of time. For one day, the results could be stored in two matrices, say

82 / Arrays

```
     TEMP                          VEL
 ¯5  ¯2   1  ¯7  ¯4         12  35  29  42  18
¯10 ¯12  ¯4  15 ¯12         14  40  31  39  25
 ¯4   6  ¯3  ¯9  ¯3          6  15  40  23  34
 ¯8   0   2  ¯8  ¯6         21  32  45  42  19
```

where temperatures are in Celsius and velocities are in km per hour. Axes 1 and 2 represent time and location, respectively. For example, column 1 gives data for station 1. For a given temperature T and velocity V, the "apparent" temperature TA (due to the "wind chill factor") is given (in conventional notation) by

$$TA = 33 - (33-T)F(V)$$

where $F(V)$ has a rather complicated relationship to the velocity V, shown in Fig. 3-1. A good approximation for $F(V)$ is given by the polynomial

$$F(V) = 1 + A_2 V^2 + A_3 V^3 + A_4 V^4 + A_5 V^5 + A_6 V^6 + A_7 V^7 + A_8 V^8$$

where

$A_2 = 6.35866E^{-}4$
$A_3 = 9.76462E^{-}5$
$A_4 = {}^{-}8.956E^{-}6$
$A_5 = 2.98218E^{-}7$
$A_6 = {}^{-}4.91985E^{-}9$
$A_7 = 4.03582E^{-}11$
$A_8 = {}^{-}1.31417E^{-}13$

The approximation is good up to a value of 80 for V.

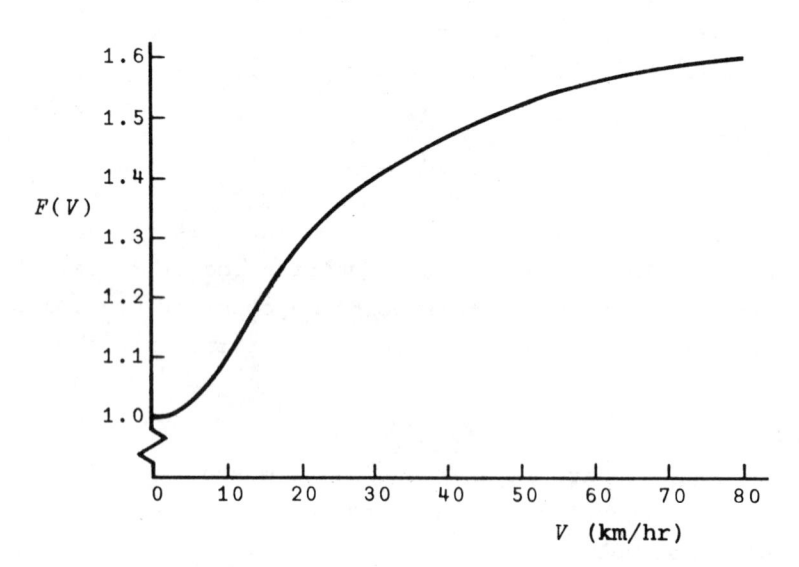

Figure 3-1 Curve for computing "windchill" effect.

---

1) Show an assignment statement for VEL, assuming you have

   $A \leftarrow 12\ 35\ 29\ 42\ 18$
   $B \leftarrow 14\ 40\ 31\ 39\ 25$
   $C \leftarrow 6\ 15\ 40\ 23\ 34$
   $D \leftarrow 21\ 32\ 45\ 42\ 19$

2) Suppose you have an incomplete variable $TEMP$ in which the last line is missing. Show how to use $ADDLINE$ given in example 3-2 to add the last line.

3) In the execution of

   $33 - TEMP$

   it is possible to regard the scalar 33 as being extended to a nonscalar form. Show a display of it.

Arrays / 83

1) Would F operate if VEL were a matrix of 6 rows and 8 columns?

_____

2) Would $WINDCHILL$ operate if $TEMP$ and VEL were both matrices, but having different shapes?

_____

3) Suppose $TEMP$ and VEL are of rank 3 and shape 30 4 5, where each page is a record for one day and the entire array is for a month of 30 days. Will $WINDCHILL$ work with these arguments, assuming there is sufficient workspace?

_____

4) If

   $V \leftarrow 4\ ^-6\ 9\ 5\ ^-2.5$

give results for

   $+/V$

_____

   $-/V$

_____

   $\times/V$

_____

We are to write a dyadic function $WINDCHILL$ which will take a matrix such as $TEMP$ as a left-hand argument and a matrix such as VEL as a right-hand argument. The explicit result is to be a matrix of apparent temperatures. The algorithm is: Compute $F(V)$, and then compute TA. It is convenient to employ a subfunction F for $F(V)$, which can be

```
    ∇ Z←F V
[1] Z←¯4.91985E¯9+V×4.03582E¯11+V×¯1.31417E¯13
[2] Z←9.76462E¯6+V×¯8.956E¯6+V×2.98218E¯7+V×Z
[3] Z←1+V×V×6.35866E¯4+V×Z
```

The function $WINDCHILL$ can be

```
    ∇ Z←T WINDCHILL V
[1] Z←33-(33-T)×F V ∇
```

The statements in F may not appear to evaluate the polynomial in question. However, if you trace out these statements it will be evident that $^-1.31417E^-13$ is multiplied by V eight times, $4.03502E^-11$ is multiplied by V seven times, and so forth. The important point is that the + and × operations in F take matrix arguments, giving a matrix result from F in $WINDCHILL$.

For the given data (with a printing precision of 2)

```
    T←TEMP WINDCHILL VEL
    T
¯10     ¯18    ¯12    ¯27    ¯13
¯18     ¯33    ¯19    ¯38    ¯28
 ¯5.3   ¯14    ¯20    ¯23    ¯19
¯21     ¯14    ¯14    ¯28    ¯17
```

More elegant versions of F can be written in several ways, using functions described in Chap. 6.

3-12 Reduction Operator   *fn / object*

In this section we consider how the reduction operator (introduced for vectors in Sec. 2-17) extends to arrays of rank higher than 1. Given a vector such as

   $W \leftarrow 7\ 2\ 6\ 3\ 8$

it is recalled that

   $+/W$
26

is equivalent to $7+2+6+3+8$, and

   $\times/W$
2016

is equivalent to $7\times2\times6\times3\times8$. Results for $-/W$ and $\div/W$ are determined in a similar way. In each case the result is a scalar.

84 / Arrays

The symbol / is used in conjunction with the symbol for one of the primitive functions (+ or × in the examples). In this usage, / alone does not stand for a function and so it is an *operator*; it effectively places the associated primitive function between elements of the vector.

It is possible to use * with the operator /, but this operation is usually wanted only for vectors of two elements, as in

```
     */ 3  4
81
```

In Chap. 4 you will learn many other primitive functions that can be used in reduction.

Reduction can also be used on a matrix argument. We shall use +/ for the purpose of illustration (you can try ×/, -/, and ÷/) on the matrix

```
      M5
   4  8  6  2
   9  7  8  7
   6  2  8  5
```

Because a matrix has two axes, there are two kinds of add reduction.

One type of add reduction on M5 produces a vector having the following elements:

    1st element: *Add reduction of 1st row of M5*
    2nd element: *Add reduction of 2nd row of M5*
    3rd element: *Add reduction of 3rd row of M5*

The APL notation which produces the result described above is

```
     +/[2]M5   (in origin 1)       +/[1]M5   (in origin 0)
20  31  21
```

This is called reduction along the second axis. The [2] (or [1]) to the right of / is an *axis operator*. It identifies the axis along which the additions are to be made.

The other possible add reduction on M5 produces a vector having the following elements:

    1st element: *Add reduction of 1st column of M5*
    2nd element: *Add reduction of 2nd column of M5*
    3rd element: *Add reduction of 3rd column of M5*
    4th element: *Add reduction of 4th column of M5*

In these four separate add reductions, each column is treated as a vector. This result is produced by

```
     +/[1]M5   (in origin 1)       +/[0]M5   (in origin 0)
19  17  22  14
```

---

1) Show a statement that will take as its argument a positive integer N, and produce the factorial of N. This is not to be the factorial primitive given in Chap. 4.

_____

2) Give results for

   */ 2 2 2

_____

   */ 2 8

_____

   */ 8 2

_____

3) Fill in the following table with axis numbers in the two possible origins, for a matrix.

	Origin 1	Origin 0
First axis	____	____
Last axis	____	____

Arrays / 85

1) For the following matrix M, give the results indicated.

$$M$$
$$\begin{array}{rrrr} 9 & 2 & ^-4 & 6 \\ 5 & 8 & 7 & ^-3 \\ 2 & ^-8 & 9 & 5 \end{array}$$

$+/[1]M$
_____

$+/[2]M$
_____

$\times\neq M$
_____

$-/M$
_____

2) For the following A, give the results indicated.

$A \leftarrow 2\ 3\ 4\ \rho(\iota 12),,M$

$\times/[1]A$

$+/[2]A$

The statement
$\quad \times/[2]A$
is equivalent to (choose one answer for each origin):

	Origin 0, Origin 1
$\times\neq A$	_____ _____
$\times/A$	_____ _____
Neither	_____ _____

In this case reduction is along the first axis, as indicated by the axis operator [1] (or [0]).

For an array $A1$ of rank 3, three add reductions are possible. The notations for them are (in origin 1):

$\quad +/[1]A1$
$\quad +/[2]A1$
$\quad +/[3]A1$

Further consideration of reduction for arrays of rank higher than 2 is given in Sec. 6-1.

There are alternative notations for reductions along the *highest* numbered and *lowest* numbered axes. These notations, which are origin independent, are

$\quad +/\quad$ along the last (highest numbered) axis
$\quad +\neq\quad$ along the first (lowest numbered) axis

These alternative notations are useful in cases where the argument is not necessarily always of the same rank.

Reduction always yields a result of rank 1 less than the rank of the argument; reduction of a vector yields a scalar, and reduction of a matrix yields a vector.

Reduction on a single element is a special case, defined to yield that element no matter what primitive accompanies the reduction operator. Thus, each of

$\quad +/6\quad,\quad \times/6\quad$ etc.

and

$\quad +/,6\quad,\quad \times/,6\quad$ etc.

produces the scalar 6.

Reduction of an empty vector is another special case. The result depends on the primitive function used in the reduction. A complete consideration of all functions applicable to reduction is given in Chap. 6. For the present we note the following:

0 $\quad +/\iota 0$

1 $\quad \times/\iota 0$

0 $\quad -/\iota 0$

1 $\quad \div/\iota 0$

It is important to recognize that the reduction operator can be used only with certain primitive functions, those considered in Chap. 4. Defined functions cannot be used in reduction.

86 / Arrays

Example 3-4

It is often required to find the mean values of the columns or rows of a matrix. If M is the matrix, in origin 1 the means of the columns are produced by

$$(+/[1]M)\div 1\uparrow\rho M$$

In this, $+/[1]M$ produces a vector which is the sums of the columns, and $1\uparrow\rho M$ is the number of elements in each column. Similarly, the means of the rows are produced by

$$(+/[2]M)\div {}^-1\uparrow\rho M$$

A function *MEANMAT* is to be defined which will yield either of these results. The function is to be dyadic. Its left-hand argument will control which result will be produced. A zero on the left is to produce means of the columns; a one on the left is to produce means of the rows. The right-hand argument will be the matrix. The function can be written (in origin 1)

```
    ∇ R←I MEANMAT M
[1]   R←(+/[I+1]M)÷(1-2×I)↑ρM ∇
```

Example 3-5

The function *MEANMAT* of the previous example requires a matrix argument, because of the axis operator. If the function is used with 1 on the left and a vector on the right, an error report will result because a vector has no second axis. This raises an interesting question as to whether the function can be modified to accept a vector and treat it as if it were a matrix of one line (or a scalar and treat it as if it were a matrix of one element). This can be done in accordance with the following algorithm.

If M is the input variable, reshape it in accordance with the table

If M is	$\rho\rho M$ is	Required shape of result
Scalar	0	1 1
Vector	1	1,ρM
Matrix	2	ρM

It is evident from the tabulation that

$$^-2\uparrow\ 1\ \ 1\ ,\rho M$$

will give the correct shape of the result in all cases.

From the above, a function can be written

```
    ∇ Z←SVM M
[1]   Z←(¯2↑ 1  1 ,ρM)ρM ∇
```

and used as a subfunction in *MEANMAT* as follows:

---

1) Write a version of *MEANMAT* which uses drop instead of take.

2) Write a version of *MEANMAT* which will operate in origin 0.

3) Write a function *TIMEMEANWCH* which will produce the means, for various sample times, of apparent temperatures as produced by *WINDCHILL*.

4) The left-hand argument of the reshape function in *SVM* can be of the form

$$(\qquad)\downarrow 1\ \ 1,\rho M$$

if a suitable statement is placed within the parentheses. Write that statement within the parentheses.

Arrays / 87

1) Given the vector

   W←2 8 10

If MEANMAT has the modified form given on this page, give the results of

   0 MEANMAT W

   _____

   1 MEANMAT W

   _____

2) Write a function SVM3 which is similar to SVM but will convert a scalar, vector, matrix or array of rank 3 to an array of rank 3.

3) For M1 given on this page, in origin 1 show results for

   M1[1;3]

   _____

   M1[3;1]

   _____

```
     ∇ R←I MEANMAT M
[1]  M←SVM M
[2]  R←(+/[I+1]M)÷(1-2×I)↑ρM ∇
```

Now, if MEANMAT is inadvertently used with a scalar or vector on the right, it will run.

3-13 Index Function

Suppose we have the three variables:

```
     V11
COMPUTERS WORK RAPIDLY

     M1
 2  8  6  3
 9  4  3  7
 3  2  5  4

     A1
 1   2   3   4   5
 6   7   8   9  10
11  12  13  14  15
16  17  18  19  20

21  22  23  24  25
26  27  28  29  30
31  32  33  34  35
36  37  38  39  40

41  42  43  44  45
46  47  48  49  50
51  52  53  54  55
56  57  58  59  60
```

In each case the complete array is regarded as the value of the variable. We shall now discuss the *index function* which permits the selection of one or more elements of an array. Such selection may be merely for the purpose of display, or to create a value which *can be used in computation*. In this section, all examples are in origin 1. The first example is

```
     V11[14]
K
```

The 14 in brackets is an *index value*; the index number of the element to be selected. This is in origin 1; in origin 0 the number would have been 13. The letter K is the 14th element in vector V11. In the case of a matrix, two index values are required to select one element; a row index number and a column index number. Using M1 for illustration,

```
     M1[2;4]
7
```

This is the element in row number 2 and column number 4. The semicolon does not represent an APL primitive, it is a mark which separates the row index from the column index.

88 / Arrays

For the rank 3 array, an example of indexing is

    $A1[2;3;1]$

31

The numbers within brackets designate page 2, row 3 and column 1.

    The number of semicolons must always be one less than the rank.

    In each of the previous examples the result is a scalar. However, indexing can also produce a result of rank 1 or higher. As the first example, consider

    $V11[\iota 9]$

COMPUTERS

Here, $\iota 9$ is the index value which selects each of the first 9 elements. Another illustration is

    $V11[10+\iota 4]$

WORK

    Index numbers can be repeated or given in any order, as in

    $V11[1\ \ 2\ \ 3\ \ 3\ \ 19\ \ 6\ \ 6\ \ 7\ \ 7]$

COMMITTEE

    A vector can have a matrix (or array of rank higher than 2) as its index value. For example, if I is

```
          I
  1   2   3   4   5   6   7   8   9
 17   8   7  15  15  15  15  15  15
 17   1   1   5   8  17   6   7  15
```

    $V11[I]$

COMPUTERS
ARE
ACCURATE

    In the last three examples, observe that the rank and shape of the result is the same as the rank and shape of the *index value*. Having made this observation, decide what result is produced by $V11[,6]$.

    Of course, indexing a numerical vector works in the same way. If

    $V1$

2   8   26   3   9   18   258   7   3

    $V1[7]$

258

    $V1[3\ \ 8\ \ 1\ \ 4]$

26   7   2   3

    In the case of a matrix or array of higher rank, an index value can be a vector, or of rank higher than 1. An illustration of indexing a matrix with vectors is

---

1) Using $A1$ as given in the text, give the results for the following.

    $A1[3;4;2]$

    _____

    $A1[3;2;4]+A1[1;4;3]$

    _____

2) If M is a matrix, what is wrong with

    $M[2\ \ 2]$

    _____

3) If

$W\leftarrow{}'ABCDEFGHIJKLMNOP'$

give the following results (use origin 1).

    $W[17\ \ 6\ \ 16\ \ 17\ \ 13\ \ 6]$

    _____

    $I\leftarrow 17\ \ 6\ \ 15\ \ 1\ \ 2$
    $I\leftarrow I,15\ \ 5\ \ 1\ \ 10$
    $I\leftarrow I,15\ \ 12$
    $W[I]$

    _____

4) For origin 1, show a display of J such that for W as specified in (3)

    $W[J]$
PEN
AND INK

and a K such that

    $W[K]$
PEN
AND
INK

1) Using *M*1 as given on this page, show displays of

 *M*1[2 2;4 3 3]

 *M*1[3 2 1 3;4 1]

 *M*1[2;]

 *M*1[;3]

2) If *V* is a vector of at least 5 elements, the shape and rank of *V*[1 1 4 3] are

shape____, rank____

The shape and rank of *V*[6 5 ρ 2 3] are

shape____, rank____

3) If *M* is a matrix of shape 4 4, the shape and rank of *M*[2;3] are:

shape____, rank____

the shape and rank of *M*[,2;3] are:

shape____, rank____

the shape and rank of *M*[2 2;] are:

shape____, rank____

```
     M1
  2  8  6  3
  9  4  3  7
  3  2  5  4
     M1[1 3 ; 2 4]
  8  3
  2  4
```

The result consists of those elements of *M*1 located in the 1st and 3rd rows and 2nd and 4th columns.

 An illustration of indexing an array of rank 3, using the previously specified *A*1, is

```
     A1[2 3 ;2; 3 5 4]
  28  30  29
  48  50  49
```

This yields elements from pages 2 and 3, row 2, and columns 3, 5 and 4 of *A*1.

 If *all* the index numbers for *one of the axes* are wanted, those index numbers may be omitted. For example, the entire second row of page 3 of *A*1 is produced by

```
     A1[3;2;]
  46  47  48  49  50
```

and the complete 2nd rows of all pages are given by

```
     A1[;2;]
   6   7   8   9  10
  26  27  28  29  30
  46  47  48  49  50
```

 It is important to realize that the semicolon must be retained even when index numbers are omitted.

 Sometimes an index value is a computed result, as in *M*1[1+ι2; 1 3]. Note that it is not necessary to place 1+ι2 in parentheses.

 The index function is very rich in the variety of results it can produce. A more comprehensive and general treatment is given in Chap. 6.

Example 3-6

 The ordinal numbers are 0th, 1st, 2nd, etc. This example involves creating a monadic function which will return a character array of ordinal numbers from 0 to 9, when the argument is a scalar or vector of arabic numerals from 0 to 9. If the name of the function is *ORDINAL*, examples of its use are

```
     ORDINAL 2
  2ND
     ORDINAL 5 8 3
  5TH
  8TH
  3RD
```

90 / Arrays

The algorithm is: Create a matrix of all the ordinal numbers from 0th to 9th, and index it according to the argument. A possible realization is (in origin 1)

```
      ∇ Z←ORDINAL N;OR
[1]   OR←10  3 ρ'0TH1ST2ND3RD4TH5TH6TH7TH8TH9TH'
[2]   Z←OR[N+1;] ∇
```

This can also be written in the one-line form

```
      ∇ Z←ORDINAL N
[1]   Z←(10  3 ρ'0TH1ST2ND3RD4TH5TH6TH7TH8TH9TH')[N+1;] ∇
```

In origin 0 the index value would be N instead of $N+1$. The second form emphasizes the fact that a value can be indexed even though it has not been assigned to a name.

When a function works properly for only one value of the index origin, as in this example, it is a good idea to include an adjustment of the index origin within the function. This can be done by recognizing that the system variable □IO can be local (see Chap. 7). Thus, referring to the first version above, if we change the header to ∇ Z←ORDINAL N;OR;□IO and include □IO←1 as a first statement, the function will be independent of the workspace index origin. Also, executing ORDINAL will then have no effect on the workspace value of □IO. Setting the index origin locally in this way is good policy for functions which are sensitive to origin.

3-14 Specifying an Indexed Value

Suppose we have the variable

```
      M1
2  8  6  3
9  4  3  7
3  2  5  4
```

We can think of the notation for an indexed value

```
      M1[2;4]
```

as being a temporary name for the indexed element. This being the case, a new assignment can be made, as in

```
      M1[2;4]←¯6
      M1
2  8  6   3
9  4  3  ¯6
3  2  5   4
```

Other examples are:

```
      M1[2;]←ι4
      M1
2  8  6  3
1  2  3  4
3  2  5  4
```

1) For either version of ORDINAL given in the text, if the argument is a scalar, the returned value is a (vector/matrix)

_____

If the argument is a vector, the returned value is a

_____

2) Modify the index value in either version of ORDINAL given in the text so that the returned value will always be a matrix, whether the argument is a scalar or a vector.

_____

3) Complete the following so it will be equivalent to the version in the text, use origin 0.

```
      ∇Z←ORDINAL N;OR
[1]   OR←'0TH1ST2ND3RD'
[2]   OR←OR,'4TH5TH6TH'
[3]   OR←OR,'7TH8TH9TH'
[4]                    ∇
```

Line [4] is to be completed.

Arrays / 91

1) If

    `M←5 8 ⍴⍳40`

show how to use indexing to change each element of column [3] to 5

Show how to use indexing to change row [2] of M to

1 0 1 0 1 0 1 0

---

2) If G has the value specified in example 3-7, show a statement that will change the center square to

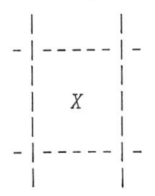

```
    |     |
 -  |-----|-
    |     |
    |  X  |
    |     |
 -  |-----|-
    |     |
```

and

```
      M1[2 3;]←2 4 ⍴ 10 15
      M1
 2   8   6   3
10  15  10  15
10  15  10  15
```

These last two cases show that the value assigned has the same rank and shape as the indexed value. This relationship must be true in all cases unless the value being assigned is a scalar or a one-element vector, as in

```
      M1[2 3;]←4
      M1
2  8  6  3
4  4  4  4
4  4  4  4
```

Example 3-7

Recall the program *TICTAC* described in example 3-1. Let a global variable *G* be specified by

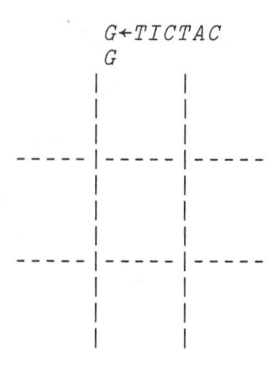

```
      G←TICTAC
      G
      |     |
      |     |
      |     |
 -----|-----|-----
      |     |
      |     |
      |     |
 -----|-----|-----
      |     |
      |     |
      |     |
```

We are to write a dyadic function *PLAY* which can be used alternately by two persons, to play the game of "tic-tac-toe." The computer will not be one of the players; it will merely keep the record.

The left-hand argument of *PLAY* will be a character '0' or 'X', to be placed, by the computer, at the center of one of the squares. The position of each square will be specified by a vector giving the number of squares down and the number to the right (the square in the lower left-hand corner would be designated by the vector 3 1). This vector will be the right-hand argument of *PLAY*. Global variable *G* will change when *PLAY* is executed; there will be no explicit result.

An example of the use of *PLAY* is

92 / Arrays

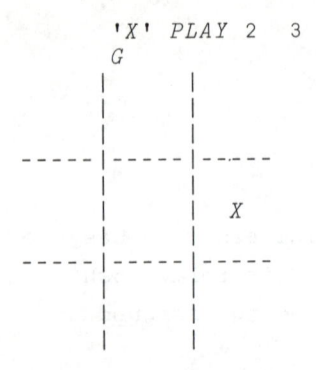

```
      'X' PLAY 2 3
       G
      |     |
      |     |
      |     |
-----|-----|-----
      |     |
      |     | X
      |     |
-----|-----|-----
      |     |
      |     |
      |     |
```

The essential feature of the algorithm is the conversion of the integers 1, 2, or 3 to index values for matrix G. Index values are different for the two axes, as indicated by the following table (given in origin 1):

Location number	Index, axis 1	Index, axis 2
1	2	3
2	6	9
3	10	15

The tabulated index numbers are obtained from observations of the figure. It is evident that if a scalar N is the location number, the index number is given by

 ¯2+4×N   For axis 1
 ¯3+6×N   For axis 2

It is only necessary to index G to these values, and assign the character obtained from the left-hand argument.

One way to write the function (for origin 1) is

```
        ∇ C PLAY N
[1]       G[¯2+4×N[1];¯3+6×N[2]]←C ∇
```

After using TICTAC to initialize G, PLAY can be used alternately by two players, with the computer keeping the record. Each time PLAY is executed, G will be "updated" with another mark.

3-15 Take and Drop

In this section we augment the basic description of take and drop on vectors given in Sec. 2-17, and extend the treatment to matrices. For the vector

```
         V1
2  8  26  3  9  18  258  7  3
```

examples of take are:

```
         3↑V1
2  8  26
         ¯4↑V1
18  258  7  3
```

---

1) Write a version of PLAY which will operate in origin 0.

2) Write a version of PLAY, in origin 1, but where vertical counting of squares is from the bottom.

3) For the vector V1 given in the text, give results for

 ¯2↑5↑V1
_____

 2↑¯5↑V1
_____

4) If V is a vector of more than one element, use take to produce the same result as

 V[¯1 0 +ρV]
_____

Arrays / 93

1) Show displays of

   2 4 ⍴8↑⍳4

and

   2 4 ⍴ ¯8↑⍳4

2) For any vector V, mark the following true or false. 1↑V is completely the same as

V[1] _____

V[,1] _____

3) If V is a vector of more than one element, show a statement using drop that will produce the same result as

   V[¯1 0 +⍴V]

_____

4) If V is any vector and S is its shape, give the shapes of

0↓V

_____

S↓V

_____

The absolute value of the left-hand argument determines how many elements are selected, and the sign of that argument determines which end. A positive sign means take from the left, a negative sign means take from the right. The left-hand argument must always be an integer; a scalar or one-element vector. From this description you should be able to decide what is the result of 0↑V1.

A scalar can be converted to a vector of one element by using 1 or ¯1 as the left-hand argument of take on that scalar. This is because the result of take on a scalar or vector is always a vector.

It is possible to take more elements than there are in a vector. Examples are:

```
      12↑V1
2  8  26  3  9  18  258  7  3  0  0  0
      ¯15↑V1
0  0  0  0  0  0  2  8  26  3  9  18  258  7  3
```

It is evident that zeros appear as the extra elements. Observe from the examples how the sign of the left-hand argument determines on which end the zeros will appear.

When more elements are taken than are in a character vector, the appended elements are spaces. Thus,

```
      'X',¯3↑'X'
X   X
```

For drop, again using

```
      V1←2  8  26  3  9  18  258  7  3
```

two examples are

```
      2↓V1
26  3  9  18  258  7  3
      ¯3↓V1
2  8  26  3  9  18
```

Elements are dropped from one end or the other; the number of elements dropped being determined by the magnitude of the left-hand argument, and the end from which they are dropped being determined by the sign of the left-hand argument, in the same way as for take. The left-hand argument must be an integer (a scalar or one-element vector).

If the number of elements dropped from either end is greater than or equal to the dimension of the vector, the result is empty.

The result of drop on a scalar or vector is always a vector. Therefore, 0↓6 will produce a vector of one element, the same as 1↑6.

94 / Arrays

Example 3-8

Refer to the function *ADDLINE* developed in example 3-2. It is repeated here, slightly modified for adding a line to a character matrix.

```
      ∇ A←R ADDLINE M;C;M1;S;T
[1]   C←¯1↑S←ρM
[2]   M1←(T←C×R-1)↑M←,M
[3]   'ENTER NEW LINE'
[4]   A←(S+ 1  0)ρM1,⌷,T↓M ∇
```

Suppose its argument is a matrix of names, such as

```
      NAMES
JONES, ROBERT
SMITH, JULIA
WILLIAMSON, MARY
```

The point of this example is to emphasize that due to varying lengths of names, there are varying numbers of spaces on the right of each row. Suppose the matrix has 25 columns. For the above function to work it would be necessary for the user to count characters and add spaces, as follows.

```
      4 ADDLINE NAMES
ENTER NEW LINE
BROWN, ARTHUR            ↑
                  space over to here (12 spaces)
```

This inconvenience for the user can be avoided by changing line [4] of the function to

```
[4]   A←(S+ 1  0)ρM1,(25↑⌷),T↓M
```

The value produced by 25↑⌷ will always be a vector of 25 elements. If fewer than 25 are entered, spaces will be added on the right; if more than 25 are entered, the first 25 will be accepted.

For matrices, take or drop must have a two-element vector as the left-hand argument. The first element specifies the take or drop for the first axis of the matrix; the second element specifies the take or drop for the second axis of the matrix. Along each axis, take and drop are the same as for a vector. If

```
      M1
   2  8  6  3
   9  8  5  7
   3  2  5  4
```

an example of take is

```
      2 ¯3 ↑M1
   8  6  3
   8  5  7
```

The argument 2 ¯3 means: take the first 2 rows and the last 3 columns. Another example is:

---

1) Give the result of

$(4↑'X'),'Y'$

Complete the following so that it will produce the same result as the above, using take on `'Y'`.

`'X',`

---

2) The function *YN* partially defined below is to return *NO* if its argument is 0, and *YES* if its argument is 1.

```
      ∇Z←YN P;W
[1]   W←'YESNO'
[2]   Z←_____↑W ∇
```

Complete the function as it is given. Then write line [2], using drop.

---

3) For *M1* given in the text, show how to use take to produce from it the result

```
8 5
2 5
```

Arrays / 95

1) Given a matrix

   M←2 3 ρι6

show statements using take or drop that will produce

```
0 1 2 3 0
0 4 5 6 0
```

```
0 0 0
0 2 3
0 5 6
```

----

2) Show a statement using take that will give

```
0 0 0
0 9 0
0 0 0
```

----

3) In A↑B or A↓B, if B is a matrix, ρA must equal

----

and if B is a vector, ρA must equal

----

or

----

4) Given

   V←5 ¯2 8 9 7 ¯4

give the results produced by

   ⍋V

   ⍋⍋V

```
  ¯4  6 ↑M1
0  0  0  0  0  0
2  8  6  3  0  0
9  8  5  7  0  0
3  2  5  4  0  0
```

Zeros appear because the absolute value of each element of ¯4 6 is greater than the dimension of the corresponding axis of M1.

Some examples of drop are

```
      2 ¯1 ↓M1
3 2 5              This is a matrix of one row

      0 2 ↓M1
6 3
5 7
5 4
```

The result of take or drop on a matrix is always a matrix. A two-element left-hand argument can also be used in take or drop on a scalar, as in the examples

```
       ¯2 3 ↑5
0 0 0
5 0 0

       1 1 ↑5
5                  This is a matrix of one element
```

Take and drop on arrays of ranks higher than 2 are treated in Chap. 6.

3-16 Grade-up and Grade-down   *rearranges indices*

Consider the vector V displayed below along with its index numbers (in origin 1)

```
[1]   [2]   [3]   [4]   [5]   [6]   [7]   [8]    Indices
2.5  ¯1.8   5.6   5.6  ¯3.2   8.4   6.1   2.5    Vector V
```

Now rearrange the elements of V in nondecreasing order (rearranging the original index numbers in the same way) to produce

```
[5]   [2]   [1]   [8]   [3]   [4]   [7]   [6]    Original indices
¯3.2 ¯1.8   2.5   2.5   5.6   5.6   6.1   8.4    Rearranged value
```

The vector formed from these rearranged *index numbers* is produced by the function *grade-up* of V (represented by the monadic symbol ⍋, formed by overstriking ∆ and |). Accordingly,

```
         V
2.5  ¯1.8   5.6   5.6  ¯3.2   8.4   6.1   2.5
         ⍋V
5    2      1     8    3      4     7     6
```

In origin 0, each element of ⍋V would be 1 less.

Since grade-up yields index numbers corresponding to the elements of V arranged in nondecreasing order, the elements can be obtained in that order by using ⍋V as an index value

96 / Arrays

for V, thus

```
        V[⍋V]
¯3.2 ¯1.8  2.5  2.5  5.6  5.6  6.1  8.4
```

This result is the same in either origin.

A similar function, producing indices corresponding to an arrangement of elements in nonincreasing order is called *grade-down* (employing the monadic symbol ⍒, formed by overstriking ∇ and |). Again using V for illustration,

```
         V
 2.5 ¯1.8  5.6  5.6 ¯3.2  8.4  6.1  2.5
        ⍒V
 6   7   3   4   1   8   2   5
        V[⍒V]
 8.4 6.1 5.6  5.6  2.5  2.5 ¯1.8 ¯3.2
```

3-17 Reverse and Rotate

In this section we consider two functions, *reverse* and *rotate*, which cause systematic rearrangements of elements of an array, along an axis. These functions apply to arrays of any rank, but in this section we treat only vectors and matrices. General treatments are given in Chap. 6.

(a) Reverse   monadic ⌽

The function reverse (monadic use of the symbol ⌽, o overstruck with |) reverses the order of a vector argument. Thus, if

```
        V
 6  5  9  3  8
        ⌽V
 8  3  9  5  6
```

For a matrix argument this function requires an axis designation. Thus, for

```
        M1
 2  8  6  3
 9  4  3  7
 3  2  5  4
```

there are the two possibilities:

```
        ⌽[1]M1
 3  2  5  4
 9  4  3  7
 2  8  6  3
        ⌽[2]M1
 3  6  8  2
 7  3  4  9
 4  5  2  3
```

---

1) If V is

$V \leftarrow 4\ \ ¯2\ \ ¯2\ \ 4$

give the result for each of the following.

⍋V

_____

⍒V

_____

V[⍋V]

_____

V[⍒V]

_____

2) For any numeric vector V, in origin 1 it is true that

(⍋⍋V)[⍋V]

is always equivalent to ⍳ρV. Is this relationship also true in origin 0?

_____

3) For any numeric vector V, is it true that ⍋V is equivalent to ⌽⍒V?

_____

Also, is it true that V[⍋V] is equivalent to ⌽V[⍒V]?

_____

1) If M is a matrix, in origin 1 show statements equivalent to $\phi[1]M$

———————

and equivalent to $\phi[2]M$

———————

2) In origin 0, give results for

  $\phi[0]$ 3 4 ⍴⍳12

and

  $\phi[1]$ 3 4 ⍴⍳12

———————

3) For a vector V having D elements, and an integer N, it is true that $N\phi V$ is equivalent to $(N-D)\phi V$ (choose 1):

If N is any integer, positive, negative, or zero

———————

Only if N is positive

———————

Only if N is positive, negative, or zero, and $|N$ is less than or equal to D

———————

Reverse with respect to the *last* axis is implied if the axis operator is omitted. Also, reverse with respect to the *first* axis can be designated by ⊖ (○ overstruck with -) without the axis operator. Thus, $\phi M1$ is equivalent to $\phi[2]M1$, and $⊖M1$ is equivalent to $\phi[1]M1$ (in origin 1).

(b) Rotate   *dyadic* ϕ

The function rotate (dyadic use of the symbol ϕ) shifts elements of a vector argument to the left or right. The amount and direction of shift is determined by the left-hand argument. Using the same $V←6\ 5\ 9\ 3\ 8$, two examples are

    $2\phi V$
9 3 8 6 5
    $^-2\phi V$
3 8 6 5 9

The left-hand argument must be an integer. Its absolute value determines how many index positions each element is shifted, and the sign determines the direction. A positive argument causes a shift toward the end where index numbers are low; a negative argument causes a shift in the other direction. The examples above are portrayed in the following diagrams:

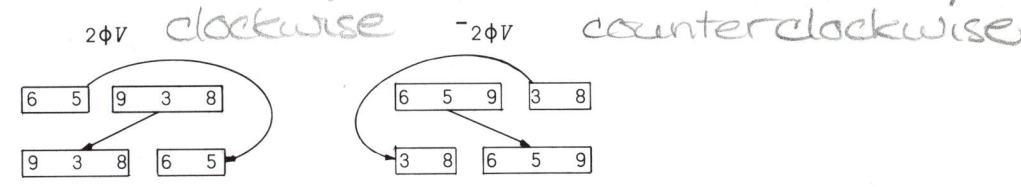

   $2\phi V$ *clockwise* $^-2\phi V$ *counterclockwise*

   | 6 5 | 9 3 8 | | 6 5 9 | 3 8 |
   | 9 3 8 | 6 5 | | 3 8 | 6 5 9 |

Elements that "drop off" one end reappear on the other end.

If the absolute value of the left-hand argument is greater than the dimension of the vector, the result is the same as if the dimension of the vector were added to or subtracted from the argument. Thus, $12\phi V$, $7\phi V$, $2\phi V$ and $^-3\phi V$ are all equivalent. A zero left-hand argument produces no rotation.

For a matrix an axis operator must be designated. Using

   $M1$
2 8 6 3
9 4 3 7
3 2 5 4

as an example, rotation along the first axis is illustrated by

    2 1 0 $^-1\ \phi[1]M1$
3 4 6 4
2 2 3 3
9 8 5 7

Each element of the left-hand argument acts as if it were the argument of rotate of the corresponding column, considered as a vector. An example of rotation of this matrix along the

98 / Arrays

second axis is

```
       2 ¯1  3 ⌽[2]M1
   6   3   2   8
   7   9   4   3
   4   3   2   5
```

In this case each row is rotated in accordance with the corresponding element on the left.

A scalar argument can be used on the left. The computer automatically extends it to a compatible vector. Thus,

   2⌽[1]M1   is equivalent to   2 2 2 2 ⌽[1]M1

and

   2⌽[2]M1   is equivalent to   2 2 2 ⌽[2]M1

The axis operator can be omitted if the *last* axis is intended, or ⊖ can be used to imply the *first* axis.

3-18 Transpose of a Matrix

Consider the matrix

```
       M1
   2   8   6   3
   9   4   3   7
   3   2   5   4
```

Its transpose (produced by the symbol ⍉, formed by overstriking ○ and \) in monadic form is

```
       ⍉M1
   2   9   3
   8   4   2
   6   3   5
   3   7   4
```

Thus, the transpose function operating on a matrix causes an interchange of rows and columns. The transpose function has a dyadic form, of particular importance with arrays of rank higher than 2. This form is considered in Chap. 6.

3-19 Illustrative Examples Using Arrays

Array values are central to programming in APL, and much additional information about their use is given in later chapters. Meanwhile, the following examples are offered as illustrations of concepts developed up to this point.

Example 3-9

Consider a triangle located in the x-y plane having vertices numbered in a counterclockwise sense, as shown in Fig. 3-2. We shall consider the computation of the area of the triangle.

---

1) For M1 given on this page, give results, in origin 1, for

   (⍳4)⌽[1]M1

and

   (⍳3)⌽[2]M1

2) Assume origin 1 and let I be an integer 1 or 2. If A is a vector of integers and B a matrix, in order for A to be compatible in A⌽[I]B, it is necessary that ρA and ρB be related as (choose 1):

ρA equals ρB
_____

ρA equals (-I)↑ρB
_____

ρA equals (¯3+2×I)↑ρB
_____

3) Refer to problem (2) but assume origin 0, and that I is 0 or 1. Give the compatibility condition for A.
_____

4) Give the result of
   1 ¯1 2 ⌽⍉ 4 3 ρ⍳12

1) Each side of the triangle, taken with two of the vertical dashed lines and the x axis, forms a trapezoid. Write expressions for the areas of the three trapezoids, and from them obtain an expression for the area of the triangle.

2) In the expression for the area given in the text, determine the effect on the result if x and y values are interchanged.

3) Write a version of *AREATRI* similar to the one in the text, but with rotate on X rather than on Y.

4) Write a version of *AREATRI* using indexing instead of rotate.

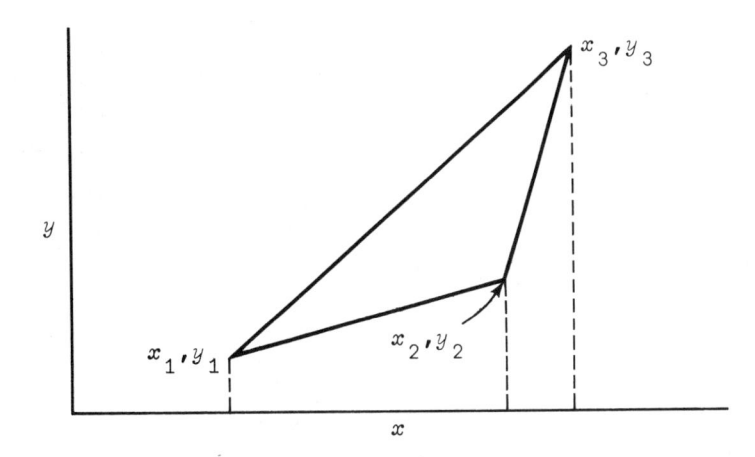

Figure 3-2 Specifying a triangle by coordinates of vertices.

It can be shown that in conventional algebraic notation

$$\text{Area} = \tfrac{1}{2}[x_1(y_2-y_3)+x_2(y_3-y_1)+x_3(y_1-y_2)]$$

The algorithm implied by this expression can be converted to APL by specifying two three-element vectors (say X and Y) as the three x coordinates and the three y coordinates. That is, the elements of X are x_1,x_2,x_3; those of Y are y_1,y_2,y_3.

The formula for the area indicates the following operation (in APL notation but with elements shown explicitly),

$$0.5\times \ +/(x_1,x_2,x_3)\times(y_2,y_3,y_1)-(y_3,y_1,y_2)$$

Since Y represents y_1,y_2,y_3, it is seen that

$1\phi Y$ represents y_2,y_3,y_1

$^{-}1\phi Y$ represents y_3,y_1,y_2

We are to define a dyadic function *AREATRI* which will take X as a left-hand argument and Y as a right-hand argument, each being a vector of three elements. The returned value is to be the area of the triangle whose vertices are the elements of X and Y. It is assumed that the counterclockwise numbering rule given above has been obeyed. In view of the previous analysis, the function can be written

```
      ∇ Z←X AREATRI Y
[1]    Z←0.5×+/X×(1ϕY)-¯1ϕY ∇
```

Example 3-10

A numeric vector can be regarded as representing a mathematical relationship such as might be portrayed by a graph. For instance the vector F specified by

100 / Arrays

$F \leftarrow {}^-2\ 4\ 9\ 10\ 8\ 3$

can represent the vertical coordinates of a graph at the values 0 1 2 3 4 5 for x, the horizontal coordinate. The graph for this F is shown in Fig. 3-3, with straight lines between the data points. We are interested in computing the area between the graph and the horizontal axis. We shall use origin 0 in developing the solution, because then values of x on the graph are index numbers in F.

1) Show a specification of F that will describe the relationship (in conventional notation)

$$y = x^2$$

for x an integer from 0 to 6, inclusive.

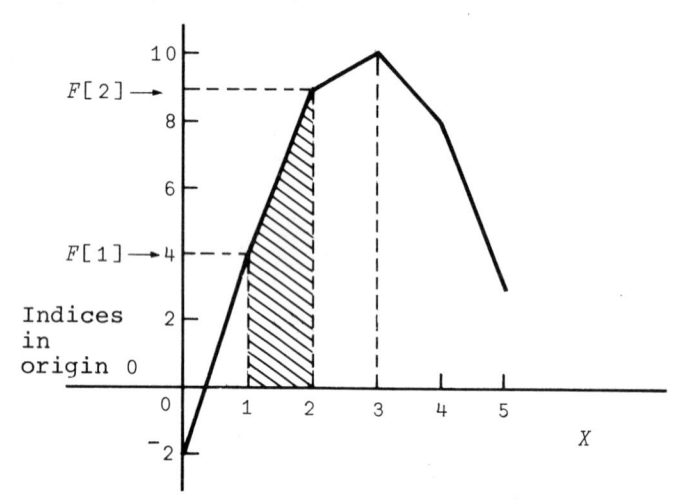

Figure 3-3 Graph of a mathematical relationship.

The total area is the sum of areas of trapezoids similar to the one shown shaded. The area of that trapezoid is

$0.5 \times F[1] + F[2]$

Similarly, the area of the trapezoid on its right is

$0.5 \times F[2] + F[3]$

and the sum of the areas of these two trapezoids is

$F[2] + 0.5 \times F[1] + F[3]$

$F[2]$ is not multiplied by 0.5 because it is counted twice, once with each of the two adjacent trapezoids. This sharing of an ordinate (element of F) occurs for each element of F except the first and last.

This indicates that the algorithm is: Add together all the "internal" elements and one-half the first and last. The internal elements of F are given by

$(1 \downarrow {}^-1 \downarrow F)$

and a vector of the first and last is

$(1 \uparrow F), {}^-1 \uparrow F$

2) For the vector F obtained in problem (1) compute the area in accordance with the algorithm given on this page.

3) Give the result of the algorithm for finding area, if F has the specification

$F \leftarrow {}^-2\ {}^-6\ {}^-4\ 0\ 2$

Arrays / 101

1) For *AREA* as defined in the text, give the results for

AREA ,6

_____

AREA 6

_____

AREA ι0

_____

2) Define a version of *AREA* which has no take or drop functions, but uses indexing.

3) Write two versions of *DIFF* which use rotate and one application of drop.

Using 1ϕP

Using ¯1ϕP

4) State what result is produced by *DIFF* if its argument is:

A vector of one element

_____

A scalar

_____

Therefore, a possible definition of a monadic function *AREA*, which takes a vector such as F as an argument and returns the area, is

```
       ∇ Z←AREA Y
[1]    Z←+/(1↓¯1↓Y),0.5×(1↑Y),¯1↑Y ∇
```

It is suggested that you consider what values this gives for the degenerate cases where the argument is a scalar, a vector of one element, or an empty vector.

Although the concept of indexing was used in developing the algorithm, there is no indexing in the function. Therefore, *AREA* is independent of origin.

Example 3-11

Considering a vector representing a graph, such as

```
           F
 ¯2  4  9  10  8  3
```

it is sometimes useful to derive from it another vector whose elements are successive differences; that is, the successive vertical jumps from data point to adjacent data point. The algorithm is: Form a vector by dropping the last element from F, and subtract from it the vector formed by dropping the first element of F. Thus, for the example, the vector of differences is

```
    6  5  1  ¯2  ¯5
```

It can be derived from

```
    4  9  10  8  3 - ¯2  4  9  10  8
```

The dimension of the vector of differences is one less than the dimension of F.

One version of a monadic function *DIFF* which makes this computation, taking the vector as its argument and giving a returned value, is

```
       ∇ Z←DIFF P
[1]    Z←(1↓P)-¯1↓P ∇
```

Example 3-12

Consider a "sports league" (say baseball) in which there is a given number of teams (4, for example). Each team (labeled A,B,C, and D) plays each of the other teams a certain number of times during the season. On any day, the record of the league can be portrayed as a matrix, as indicated below.

```
        A   B   C   D
    A │ 0   5   5   6        won
    B │ 4   0   3   5
    C │ 5   6   0   6
    D │ 4   5   4   0
      ▼
        lost
```

Each row lists the number of games the team identified by the row labels has won from each of the teams identified by column labels. Let this matrix be given the name *SPORTS*, and assume it exists as a global variable.

We shall consider the following computational tasks to be done on this matrix. We are to compute:

(a) The number of games won (or lost) by each team.
(b) The total number of games played by each team.
(c) The fraction of its total games won by each team.

These tasks offer the opportunity to illustrate one way the concepts of "structured programming" apply in APL. Each task depends on the preceding task, and therefore can be programmed using the solution of the previous task as a subfunction. Origin 1 is used.

For task (a), the games won by each team is the sum of the corresponding row of *SPORTS*. Similarly, the games lost by each team is the sum of the corresponding column of *SPORTS*. Let *WONLOST* be a monadic function taking 0 or 1 as its argument. *SPORTS* will be a global variable. For the argument 0, the explicit result is to be a vector of games lost by each team; for 1, the result is to be a vector of games won. For example, using the sample variable *SPORTS*

```
        WONLOST 0
13 16 12 17         Team A has lost 13, B has lost 16, etc.
        WONLOST 1
16 12 17 13         Team A has won 16, B has won 12, etc.
```

A suitable function for this task is

```
      ∇ R←WONLOST I
[1]     R←+/[I+1]SPORTS ∇
```

For task (b), the total games played by each team is the sum of the number won and the number lost. Hence, it is given by the niladic function *TOTALGAMES* defined as

```
      ∇ R←TOTALGAMES
[1]     R←(WONLOST 0)+WONLOST 1 ∇
```

Task (c) requires that the games won be divided by the total games played. If *FRACTIONWON* is a niladic function giving that explicit result, a possible definition for it is

---

1) Refer to the matrix *SPORTS* and answer the following questions.

How many games has team *B* won?
_____

How many games has team *B* lost?
_____

How many games has team *B* played?
_____

How many games has team *B* won from team *A*?
_____

How many games has team *B* lost to team *A*?
_____

2) Write a version of *WONLOST* which will operate in origin 0.

3) If *SPORTS* has the value given in the text, give the result of

  TOTALGAMES

_____

4) Write a version of *TOTALGAMES* which does not use subfunctions, and is not dependent on origin.

Arrays / 103

1) Write a function FRACTIONLOST which will yield, for each team, the fraction of its total games that it has lost.

```
        ∇ W←FRACTIONWON
[1]     W←(WONLOST 1)÷TOTALGAMES ∇
```

In appraising these examples we comment again on the emphasis on style; the use of existing functions as subfunctions for new programs. Using this approach produces programs which are good algorithms (meaning easy to read), and avoids many repetitions of program steps that would otherwise be required.

3-20 Outer Product for Vectors

We shall now consider a class of dyadic functions produced by an operator called the *outer product*. The operator is represented by the pair of symbols ∘. which are then followed by one of the arithmetic symbols, as in ∘.× or ∘.+ etc. (or one of the additional functions given in Chap. 4). To consider a specific example, suppose the variables

```
    P←3 5 ¯2 4
    Q←6 ¯3 7 9 2
```

2) Write out the results for the following outer products.

```
    2 6 3 ∘.× ¯4 5

    ¯4 5 ∘.× 2 6 3

    2 6 3 ∘.+ ¯4 5
```

have been specified. The effect of the operator ∘. in P∘.+Q or P∘.×Q is explained in terms of the auxiliary matrices

```
  3  3  3  3  3              6 ¯3  7  9  2
  5  5  5  5  5     and      6 ¯3  7  9  2
 ¯2 ¯2 ¯2 ¯2 ¯2              6 ¯3  7  9  2
  4  4  4  4  4              6 ¯3  7  9  2
```

Formed by repeating P as columns, as many times as there are elements in Q.

Formed by repeating Q as rows, as many times as there are elements in P.

3) Write a dyadic defined function named OP which does not use the primitive outer product, but which performs the same operation as A∘.×B when A and B are vectors.

The arithmetic function (say + or ×) operates between these matrices to produce the result. For example,

```
        P∘.×Q
   18  ¯9  21  27   6
   30 ¯15  35  45  10
  ¯12   6 ¯14 ¯18  ¯4
   24 ¯12  28  36   8
        P∘.+Q
    9   0  10  12   5
   11  ¯2  12  14   7
    4  ¯5   5   7   0
   10   1  11  13   6
```

The computer does not actually produce the pair of auxiliary matrices, they are used here as "visual aids." Note that the dimensions of P and Q are not necessarily equal.

Another way to visualize the formation of the result is

4) Give the results produced by

```
    4 3 5 2 ∘.- 3 2

    4 3 5 2 ∘.* 3 2
```

```
        P∘.×Q
   18  ¯9  21  27   6 ←—— P[1]×Q  ⎫
   30 ¯15  35  45  10 ←—— P[2]×Q  ⎬ Equivalent computation
  ¯12   6 ¯14 ¯18  ¯4 ←—— P[3]×Q  ⎭ for each line
   24 ¯12  28  36   8 ←—— P[4]×Q
```

The arguments of the outer product can be arrays of any rank; the explanation for ranks higher than 1 is given in Chap. 6. If either argument is a scalar, the outer product will work, but the operator has no effect.

Defined functions cannot be used with the outer product operator.

Example 3-13

If an amount of money is deposited in a bank at an annual percentage interest I and compounded quarterly, at the end of Y years the amount will have increased by the factor

```
(1+I÷400)*4×Y
```

Suppose we want to compute this result for the five rates of interest in the vector

```
I←5  5.5  6  6.5  7
```

and for years specified by

```
Y←⍳5
```

This can be accomplished by using the outer product

```
      (1+I÷400)∘.*4×Y
1.05095  1.10449  1.16075  1.21989  1.28204
1.05614  1.11544  1.17807  1.24421  1.31407
1.06136  1.12649  1.19562  1.26899  1.34686
1.06660  1.13764  1.21341  1.29422  1.38042
1.07186  1.14888  1.23144  1.31993  1.41478
```

Each row is for a fixed rate of interest, and each column represents a year. A general defined function for this computation could easily be created.

3-21 Inner Product for Vectors and Matrices

The inner product is an operator represented by the symbol . which becomes a dyadic function when an arithmetic function is placed on each side of the dot, as in +.× , ×.+ , ×.× etc. The primitive functions -, ÷, and *, and others given in Chap. 4, can also be used.

The inner product works for arguments of any rank, provided that the shapes of the arguments meet certain conditions of compatibility. Here we shall only consider matrices and vectors; arguments of higher ranks are treated in Chap. 6. We shall illustrate the structure of the inner product in terms of the matrices

---

Note: Both of the problems on this page are based on, and use, the notation of example 3-13.

1) Write a dyadic function DAILYINT which will produce a matrix similar to the result described in example 3-13. A vector such as I will be the left-hand argument, and a vector such as Y will be the right-hand argument. For this case the interest is compounded daily (assume 365 days in a year).

2) Write a dyadic function QUARTINT which will take a vector I as a left-hand argument and a vector Y as a right-hand argument. The explicit result is to be an array of rank 3. Each page is to correspond to a year, each row a rate of interest, and each column a quarter of a year. The number of pages will equal ⍴Y, the number of rows will equal ⍴I, and there will be 4 columns. Assume interest is compounded quarterly.

Arrays / 105

Note: For the following problems *MA* and *MB* are as given in the text.

1) Give the results of:

   MB+.×*MA*

   (⌽*MB*)+.×⌽*MA*

2) Give the results of:

   MB×.+ 8 3

   8 3 5 ×.+*MB*

3) Explain why

   8 3 ×.+*MB*

is not possible.

```
        MA
    9   1   3
    2   4   6
        MB
    6   4
    2   7
    3   5
```

as arguments. For the +.× case, an example is

```
         MA+.×MB
    65   58
    38   66
```

Each element of the result is an *add* reduction of a *multiplication* of a *row* of *MA* by a *column* of *MB*, as follows:

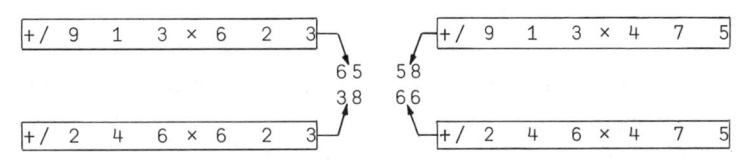

```
+/  9  1  3  ×  6  2  3          +/  9  1  3  ×  4  7  5

                        65  58
                        38  66

+/  2  4  6  ×  6  2  3          +/  2  4  6  ×  4  7  5
```

For matrices it is evident that the condition for compatibility is: 'The dimension of the second axis of the left-hand argument must equal the dimension of the first axis of the right-hand argument.

One argument can be a matrix and the other a vector, provided that the vector has the proper dimension to be compatible. Two examples are

```
      MA+.× 2  5  3                          +/  9  1  3  ×  2  5  3
    32    42            where   32   42
                                             +/  2  4  6  ×  2  5  3
```

and

```
                                             +/  5  2  ×  9  2
       5  2  +.×MA                           +/  5  2  ×  1  4
    49  13   27         where  49  13  27
                                             +/  5  2  ×  3  6
```

For the case of a vector and a matrix the conditions for compatibility are: If the vector is on the right, its dimension must equal the dimension of the *second* axis of the matrix; if the vector is on the left, its dimension must equal the dimension of the *first* axis of the matrix.

With two vectors the result of *V1*+.×*V2* is the same as +/*V1*×*V2*. The dimensions of *V1* and *V2* must be the same.

All of these examples conform to the following condition for compatibility between the arguments: The dimension of the last (highest numbered) axis of the left-hand argument of an inner product must equal the dimension of the first (lowest numbered) axis of the right-hand argument.

This condition does not apply in the special case where an argument is a scalar. If *S* is a scalar and *A* is a vector

106 / Arrays

or matrix, $S+.\times A$ is equivalent to $+/S\times A$ and $A+.\times S$ is equivalent to $+/A\times S$.

Defined functions cannot be used with the inner product operator.

Example 3-14

Suppose the results of an examination consisting of four questions taken by six students are stored in a matrix such as

```
      EXAM
15 18 14 19 10 20
20 15 15 13 17 14
18 16  9 20 20 16
10 12 18 12 15 18
```

Each column corresponds to a student, and each row gives the scores on one question. From this we are to create a matrix of "weighted" total scores as follows: first row, with the first question given double weight; second row, with the second question given double weight, etc.

If we specify

```
      WEIGHT←4 4 ρ2,4ρ1
      WEIGHT
2 1 1 1
1 2 1 1
1 1 2 1
1 1 1 2
```

then,

```
      WEIGHT+.×EXAM
78 79 70 83 72 88
83 76 71 77 79 82
81 77 65 84 82 84
73 73 74 76 77 86
```

gives the desired result.

Let us define a monadic function *WGTEXM* which will take any matrix such as *EXAM* as its argument and produce the above as an explicit result. One way to define this function is

```
      ∇ S←WGTEXM T;P
[1]   P←1↑ρT
[2]   S←((P,P)ρ2,Pρ1)+.×T ∇
```

Note the use of local variable P, specified as the dimension of the first axis of T.

3-22 Evaluation of a Polynomial

There are many ways in APL to evaluate a polynomial, including a primitive function (decode) described in Chap. 6. Here we shall consider a method that uses the inner and outer products.

1) Give a statement different from the one in the text, for creating matrix *WEIGHT*.

2) Would the program *WGTEXM* given in the text work if:

(a) The number of students were other than 6?

(b) The number of questions were other than 4?

3) Suppose, in example 3-14, that matrix *EXAM* had rows corresponding to students and columns corresponding to tests. Rewrite *WGTEXM* so it will give exactly the same results as the example.

Suppose we are given a polynomial such as (in conventional notation)

$$c_0 + c_1 x + c_2 x^2 + \ldots + c_n x^n$$

and wish to evaluate it at a set of values $x_1, x_2, \ldots x_m$. Let us develop an algorithm, and then convert it to a defined function. The algorithm is:

Step 1: Create a matrix PX as follows:

$$\begin{array}{cccccc} 1 & x_1 & x_1^2 & x_1^3 & \ldots & x_1^n \\ 1 & x_2 & x_2^2 & x_2^3 & \ldots & x_2^n \\ \cdot & \cdot & \cdot & \cdot & & \cdot \\ 1 & x_m & x_m^2 & x_m^3 & \ldots & x_m^n \end{array}$$

Step 2: Multiply each row of this matrix (as if it were a vector) by the vector C whose elements are the coefficients.

$$c_0, c_1, c_2, \ldots c_n$$

Step 3: Add the elements of the result of step 2, along rows, to give m separate results, as elements of a vector.

To put this into APL notation, let us assume origin 0. Then, `⍳⍴C` will be the sequence of exponents, and if X is a vector of the values of x,

   `PX←X∘.*⍳⍴C`

This statement accomplishes step 1. Steps 2 and 3 are then combined in one statement

   `PX+.×C`

A defined function *POLY*, which includes a step to ensure operation in origin 0, is

```
      ∇ R←C POLY X;⎕IO
[1]     ⎕IO←0
[2]     R←(X∘.*⍳⍴C)+.×C ∇
```

This function will not work for the trivial case where C is a scalar, representing a degenerate polynomial having only a constant term. This is because `⍴C` will be an empty vector, and `⍳⍴C` will produce an error report. The function can be changed so it will work for this case merely by replacing `⍳⍴C` by `⍳⍴,C`.

---

1) If
`C←2 ¯4 3 1`
`X←1 2 3`
do the hand calculations required to compute (in origin 0)

   `PX←X∘.*⍳⍴C`
   `PX`

Then do the calculations by hand to produce the result of

   `PX+.×C`

2) Referring to line [2] of *POLY* as given in the text, complete the following version so it will be equivalent.

`[2] R←C+.×`

3) Rewrite *POLY* as given in the text, to operate in origin 1.

Arrays / 107

CONCLUSION

This chapter contains important background material concerning the concept of an array as a value. By now you have seen that scalars, vectors and matrices differ in numbers of coordinate axes, that the number of axes is called the rank of a value, and that a list of the dimensions of the coordinate axes is the shape of a value. The imaginative use of arrays in programming depends on an ability to visualize them, and working with vectors and matrices is an important step in attaining that ability. Matrices offer more opportunity than vectors for illustrating the importance of positions of elements, and for demonstrating the usefulness of those primitive functions which serve to modify positional arrangements. Therefore, matrices are a significant part of this chapter.

It is particularly important that you recognize that rank and shape of an array are themselves values which are useful in computations. It is also important to recognize the difference between dimensions of axes and the shape vector. The dimension of each axis is a scalar, and the shape vector is the catenation of these dimensions. This distinction tends to be lost in the case of a vector, because its shape vector has only one element, and therefore looks like its dimension.

A fundamental feature in the use of array structures in APL is the possibility of changing rank and shape during the execution of a program. Also fundamental is the generality provided by empty arrays.

There is much more for you to learn about arrays and their use. In particular, there are many functions not yet considered which manipulate and compute with arrays (these are given in Chap. 6) and, as you mature in programming, frequently it will be necessary for you to think in terms of arrays of ranks higher than 2.

Problems--Chapter 3

Comment: With only a few exceptions, these problems can be done by using only those primitive functions introduced through Chap. 3. The exceptions are noted in Probs. 3-17, 23, 24, 25. For Prob. 3-17 it is suggested that you have in your workspace the defined function (L is described in Chap. 4)

```
     ∇ Z←CENTS N
[1]    Z←0.01×⌊0.5+100×N ∇
```

which will round its argument to the nearest second digit to the right of the decimal point.

3-1 Construct a dyadic function *CKRBOARD* which will produce a print of a checkerboard design, as in the following example.

```
      2 CKRBOARD 4
xx  xx
xx  xx
  xx  xx
  xx  xx
xx  xx
xx  xx
  xx  xx
  xx  xx
```

The left-hand argument specifies the number of rows and columns in the individual squares, and the right-hand argument specifies the number of squares on a side. Either argument can be even or odd.

3-2 Construct a dyadic defined function called *CALENDAR* having the following properties:

(a) Left-hand argument is the day of the week (as a number) on which the 1st of the month falls (Sunday is day 1).
(b) Right-hand argument is the number of days in the month.
(c) The output is to be a print of a calendar for the month, as shown below.

```
      4 CALENDAR 30

SUN MON TUE WED THU FRI SAT
                  1   2   3   4
  5   6   7   8   9  10  11
 12  13  14  15  16  17  18
 19  20  21  22  23  24  25
 26  27  28  29  30
```

3-3 Construct a monadic function *DATE* which will take as its argument a vector of three positive integers representing month, day, and last two digits of the year, as in *DATE* 7 3 78. The explicit result is to be a character vector of the name of the month, the number for the day, and the complete year (assuming the twentieth century). Thus, as an example,

```
      DATE 7  3  78
JULY 3 1978
```

3-4 Assume there is a global matrix of two rows. Each column contains the ages of a married couple: the ages of women in the first row and the ages of men in the second row. Construct a monadic function *AVAGE* which will take 0 or 1 as its argument. If the argument is 0, the value returned by the function should be a vector of the average ages of individual couples. If the argument is 1, the returned value is to be a two-element vector: the average age of all men, the average age of all women.

3-5 Write a monadic function *POWERS* that will take a vector of numbers as its input and print a table of the squares, cubes, and 4th powers of those numbers. The explicit result is to be a matrix: the numbers in the first column, the squares in the second column, the cubes in the third column, and the 4th powers in the fourth column.

3-6 Refer to the program *PLAY* described in example 3-7 in the text, and assume the function *TICTAC* described in example 3-1 is available. Define a modified function *PLAYM* which is similar to *PLAY* except that its left-hand argument is to be 0 or 1, to cause, respectively, the arrangements

```
   \ /                  ┌─── This is the underbar
                        ‾
    o      or     ( _ )
                        _
   / \                  └─── This is the overbar
```

to be centered in the designated square. The right-hand argument will be the same as for *PLAY*: a two element vector in which the first element designates the number of squares down and the right-hand argument designates the number of squares across. Hint: place the arrangements of characters in an array of rank 3. The function will not give an explicit result; it will cause a change in a global variable *G*.

3-7 Assume you have a character matrix containing any number of names, such as

```
         M
ADAMS
BROWN
ROBERTS
```

You are to define a monadic function LINENUMB which will take such a matrix as an argument and return the same matrix with line numbers on the left, within parentheses. Leave room within the parentheses for up to 2 digits, as in

```
(  1)  ADAMS
(  2)  BROWN
(  3)  ROBERTS
```

3-8 Suppose a global variable NAMES is a matrix of names such as described in Prob. 3-7. The number of rows will vary with the size of the list. Assume the number of columns is 25. Design a monadic function ADDNAME which will take as its argument a character vector representing a name of 25 characters or less, to be added at the bottom of the list. The function is to employ NAMES as a global variable, and cause the new name to be added as a new row at the bottom of NAMES.

3-9 In the accompanying figure a vector X represents three numbers on an x axis, as indicated by x_1, x_2, and x_3 (x_1 is not necessarily less than x_2, but neither x_1 nor x_2 can be larger than x_3). Assume a circle is drawn with the axis from 0 to x_3 as a diameter. A triangle is then constructed as indicated in the figure.

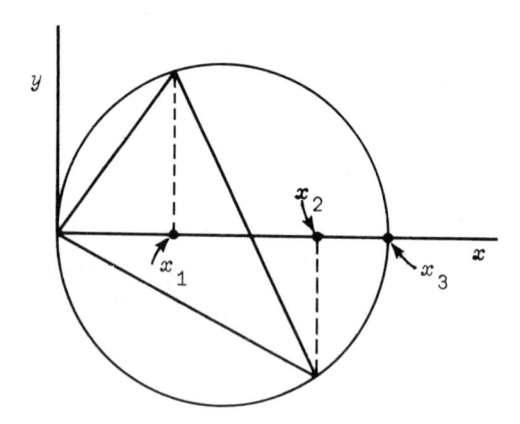

Design a monadic function CIRCTRI which will take X as its argument and return the area inside the circle but outside the triangle. Use AREATRI (given in example 3-9) as a subfunction. Note: in conventional notation the equation of the circle is

$$x^2 - xx_3 + y^2 = 0$$

3-10 Refer to the function AREATRI given in example 3-9 in the text. Prove that if B is any scalar,

(B+X) AREATRI Y   and   X AREATRI Y+B

are both equal to X AREATRI Y. Do this by using APL notation to analyze the statement line of the function for these two cases.

3-11 Refer in the text to the defined functions TOTALGAMES, WONLOST, and FRACTIONWON for making the various computations from a matrix such as SPORTS, described in example 3-12. Assume there is also a character matrix TEAMS, each row of which is the home city of one of the teams. Row 1 of TEAMS is the name for team A, row 2 for team B, etc. Create a niladic function ORDERTEAMS which will employ SPORTS and TEAMS as global variables and print a listing of the cities, in accordance with the fraction of games won. The team with the best percentage is to be at the top of the list. The fraction of games won should appear opposite each name of a city.

3-12 Refer to the matrix SPORTS described in example 3-12 of the text, but assume it can represent the record of as many as 8 teams labeled A through H. Design a dyadic function which will use SPORTS as a global variable and provide a means

Arrays / 111

of changing entries in *SPORTS*. The name of the function will be *BEAT*. To consider how this function will be used, suppose you want to add to the record in *SPORTS* the fact that team F beat team B. This is to be done in the manner

    'F' BEAT 'B'

There is no returned value or print; the result will be a change in *SPORTS*.

3-13 Design a monadic function *LENGTH* which will give, as an explicit result, the length of a curve of straight line segments passing through a series of points in the x-y plane. Values of x at the points are to form the first row of a matrix argument; corresponding values of y are to be in the second row.

3-14 Suppose you are given a vector such as

```
        V
2   8   3   4   9
```

and consider the four arrays

```
        M1                      M2
2   8   3   4   9       2   8   3   4   9
0   2   8   3   4       8   3   4   9   0
0   0   2   8   3       3   4   9   0   0
0   0   0   2   8       4   9   0   0   0
0   0   0   0   2       9   0   0   0   0

        V1                      V2
2  10  13  17  26      26  24  16  13   9
```

Matrices *M1* and *M2* are derived from *V* in obvious ways. In *V1*, the *n*th element from the left is the sum of *n* elements of *V* counting from the left. In *V2*, the *n*th element from the right is the sum of *n* elements of *V* counting from the right.
(a) Construct a dyadic function *SHIFT* which will take 0 or 1 as its left-hand argument and a vector such as *V* as its right-hand argument. Its explicit result is to be a matrix such as *M1* if the left-hand argument is 0, or a matrix such as *M2* if the left-hand argument is 1. The right-hand argument will be a vector of any length.
(b) Using *SHIFT* as a subfunction, design a dyadic function *SCAN* which will take a vector such as *V* as its right-hand argument and return vector *V1* if the left-hand argument is 0, or vector *V2* if the left-hand argument is 1. Note: 0 *SCAN V* gives the same result as the operator scan described in Chap. 6.

3-15 Design a monadic function *CROSS* which will perform as indicated by the examples

```
    CROSS 6                 CROSS 7
x       x               x       x
  x   x                   x   x
    x x                     x x
    x x                      o
  x   x                     x x
x       x                 x   x
                        x       x
```

The integer argument determines the dimensions of the cross figure. Note the difference when the argument is odd or even. The result is to be a print.

3-16 Refer to example 3-3 of the text, and assume the defined functions *F* and *WINDCHILL* are available for obtaining a matrix of apparent temperatures from a matrix *TEMP* of actual temperatures and a matrix *VEL* of wind velocities. Also assume the functions *SVM* and *MEANMAT* given in example 3-5 of the text are available. Design a dyadic function *WEATHER* which will take *TEMP* as its left-hand argument and *VEL* as its right-hand argument. Its explicit result is to be an array of rank 3 having the following properties:

112 / Arrays

Page 1: First row, means over time at the four locations; second row, means over locations at the four values of time.
Page 2: First row, standard deviations over time at the four locations; second row, standard deviations over locations at the four values of time.

Use the functions noted above as subfunctions, but do not use them more frequently than required. Note that the standard deviation of a vector of numbers is the square root of the mean of the squares of the differences between the numbers of the vector and their mean.

3-17 In a common method used by banks to make personal loans, a certain principal amount P is loaned at a monthly interest I. The loan is paid back in N fixed monthly payments of amount M. For each monthly payment a part MP is used to reduce the principal, and the other part MI is interest for the preceding month. It can be shown that (in conventional notation)

$$M = \frac{P \times I \times (1 + I)^N}{(1 + I)^N - 1}$$

$$MP = \frac{P \times I \times (1 + I)^{n-1}}{(1 + I)^N - 1}$$

I is in percent divided by 100,

for the nth payment. You are encouraged to try deriving these formulas. Write a monadic function $LOAN$ which will take as its argument the three-element vector:
(principal amount),(annual interest, in percent),(number of payments).
Assume the number of payments is a multiple of 6. The result is to be printed, as indicated by the following example. Use the function $CENTS$, given under "Comment" at the beginning of these problems, to print answers to the nearest cent.

```
      LOAN 1000  10  12
MONTHLY PAYMENTS 87.92
TOTAL INTEREST 54.99
    79.58      80.25      80.91      81.59      82.27      82.95
     8.33       7.67       7          6.33       5.65       4.96

    83.65      84.34      85.05      85.75      86.47      87.19
     4.27       3.57       2.87       2.16       1.45       0.73
```

The displayed array is a matrix of rank 3. On each page, row 1 is the payment against the principal, and row 2 is the interest. Each column represents one month.

3-18 Refer to the function $AREA$ developed in example 3-10 of the text. It interprets the elements of a numeric vector argument as the ordinates of points on a graph plotted against unit values of an abscissa, in similarity with Fig. 3-3. The returned value is the area between the graph and the horizontal axis, assuming the data points are joined by straight lines. You are to design a dyadic function $GENAREA$ which is general in the sense that it will find the area between any two points of the vector argument. Use $AREA$ as a subfunction. For example,

    2 5 GENAREA ¯2 6 9 12 11 8

is to return the area between the points with ordinates 6 and 11. The significance of the argument 2 5 is that 2 is the position number of ordinate 6, and 5 is the position number of ordinate 11. For this function it is assumed that the two elements of the arguments on the left are positive integers, in increasing order, and that the largest is not larger than the dimension of the argument.

3-19 For this problem it is assumed you have created $GENAREA$ as described in Prob. 3-18. Using $GENAREA$ and $AREA$ as subfunctions, design a function $MGENAREA$ which is similar to $GENAREA$ except that it will accept a left-hand argument which is a vector of two elements in nondecreasing or nonincreasing order. That is, $GENAREA$ will work properly only with an increasing argument, such as 2 4 but $MGENAREA$ is to accept arguments such as 4 2 or 2 4. With 4 2 as the argument

Arrays / 113

the result is to be the negative of the result for 2 4. Also, if both elements in the left-hand argument are the same, the result is to be zero.

3-20 For this problem it is assumed that you have produced the function SCAN described in Prob. 3-14. Assume a numeric vector exists whose elements represent the ordinates of points on a graph plotted against unit values of an abscissa, in similarity with Fig. 3-3. You are to design a dyadic function AREAFN which will take such a vector as an argument and return a vector having the following elements:

    Element 1: Zero
    Element 2: Area from 1st to 2nd point
    Element 3: Area from 1st to 3rd point
    Element 4: Area from 1st to 4th point
    etc.

Use SCAN as a subfunction. It is assumed points on the graph are joined by straight lines.

3-21 Design a dyadic function OPM that will simulate the outer product for vectors, with multiplication as the primitive function. Be sure it works properly if either argument is a scalar.

3-22 This problem involves writing functions to multiply complex numbers. A single complex number has two parts. To consider a particular case, if the real part is 3 and the imaginary part is 4, the usual way to write this is $3 + i4$. Since it is a single complex number it can be called a complex scalar, and written in APL as a two-element vector

    3 4

Now suppose we have the three complex numbers $1 + i2$, $3 + i4$, and $5 + i6$ forming what might be called a complex vector. One way to represent these in APL notation is as the matrix

    1 3 5
    2 4 6

In both cases the first axis has real parts in the first index position and imaginary parts in the second index position.

(a) Design a dyadic function CM1 which will take a complex scalar as each argument and return their product.
(b) Design a dyadic function CM2 which is similar to CM1 except that each argument can be a complex scalar or complex vector (APL vector or matrix). When one argument is a complex scalar and the other a complex vector, the scalar is to multiply each complex number in the vector.

3-23 This problem involves designing a monadic function PTPLOT which will take a vector of integers and plot them as a graph, as a printed result. An illustration is

    PTPLOT 2 5 4 ¯3 0 2
      ×
       ×
    ×   ×
    - - - - -×- -

         ×

The dashed line is the horizontal axis, and data points marked by × symbols are to occur every two horizontal spaces. One unit in the argument corresponds to one vertical space. In order to determine the dimensions for the matrix, and the location of the horizontal axis, use the functions ⌈/V and ⌊/V which give,

114 / Arrays

respectively, the largest and smallest values in a vector V (the functions ⌈ and ⌊ are given in Chap. 4). The horizontal axis should always print, even when the graph does not cross it, as in the examples

```
      PTPLOT 2 4 5 3                          PTPLOT ¯2 ¯4 ¯5 ¯3
                                              - - - - -
  x
              x                                     x
      x                                                   x
x                                                                x
- - - - -                                                  x
```

3-24 You are to design a monadic function *TWOPLOT* which will take a matrix of two rows of integers as its argument and plot two sets of data points. Except that the argument involves two sets of data, requiring two data point symbols ∗ and o, the output is to be similar to that described for Prob. 3-23. You should read that problem in preparation for doing this one. For any data point common to the two sets of data, use the symbol ⊛. An example is

```
         M
    2 5 4 ¯3 0 2
    1 3 4  2 1 0
       TWOPLOT M
  *
     ⊛
  o
  *       o    *
  o       o
- - - - -*-o-


         *
```

3-25 This problem involves designing a monadic function *BARPLOT* which will take a vector of nonnegative integers and plot them as a bar graph, as a printed result. An illustration is

```
       BARPLOT 2 4 6 3 1 0 4
           □
           □
        □  □        □
        □  □        □
        □  □  □     □
     □  □  □  □     □
     □  □  □  □     □
    -□-□-□-□-□-□-□-
```

The height of each stack of □ symbols (not including the bottom one) equals the corresponding element of the argument. In order to determine the size of the matrix it is necessary to compute the largest integer in the argument. For this you can use the function ⌈/V which gives the largest element in V (this function is described in Chap. 4).

3-26 Suppose you have two polynomials in x such as (in conventional notation)

$$2 + 4x^2 + 3x^3 + x^4 \quad \text{and} \quad 1 + 3x + 5x^2 + 2x^3 + 2x^4$$

The polynomials can be described by vectors of their coefficients; for these examples

```
    P1←2 4 3 1
    P2←1 3 5 2 2
```

Design a dyadic function *MULTPOLY* which will take vectors such as $P1$ and $P2$ as arguments and return the vector of coefficients for the products of the polynomials represented by the arguments. The arguments can represent polynomials of any degree.

Chapter 4

SCALAR FUNCTIONS

INTRODUCTION

In Chap. 3 it was shown that functions such as + or - are valid for array arguments. As dyadic functions they perform arithmetic operations between *corresponding* elements as if those elements were scalars, and as monadic functions they operate on each element as if it were a scalar. Using two-element vectors as an example, 3 5 + 6 8 yields the result 9 13 which is equivalent to the *two* scalar operations 3+6 and 5+8, and -3 5 yields ¯3 ¯5, the result of the *two* scalar operations -3 and -5. Because of this property of treating individual elements of an array as if they were scalars, these are called *scalar* functions.

The APL language includes many other scalar functions. They can be classified under the following headings:

   (a) Arithmetic
   (b) Relational
   (c) Logic
   (d) Transcendental

Some of the arithmetic functions have already been considered. Relational functions perform operations such as determining whether two numbers are equal, or if not which is larger. Logic functions give "true" and "false" answers to propositions in two-valued logic. Transcendental functions compute the trigonomic and other standard functions used in applied mathematics.

The objectives of this chapter are to describe those scalar functions not yet considered, to give examples of their use, and to provide tables of the properties of all the scalar functions, for later reference.

Three primitives which are not scalar functions are also included in this chapter. One of them is closely related to one of the scalar functions, and the other two permit the inclusion of interesting applications of the logic functions.

In the interest of conciseness, in the tabulations and a few other places we shall use the symbol ↔ to stand for "is equivalent to". This is *not* an APL symbol, and does not stand for an operation. One use of this symbol is to indicate a result for sample values of arguments; the other is to indicate an equivalent expression, as in

$A \times B + C \leftrightarrow A \times (B + C)$

116 / SCALAR FUNCTIONS

When this symbol is used it implies equivalence of the *complete* expressions on the two sides of the double arrow.

4-1 Compatibility for the Dyadic Scalar Functions

For the purpose of discussion, let the letter s stand for any one of the scalar functions (+, etc. or any of those still to be presented). It has been explained that if A and B are arrays,

    AsB

is executed by having s operate between *corresponding* elements of A and B, as in

    2 3 7 s 4 5 6

which is equivalent to (2s4), (3s5), (7s6). If we attempt

    2 3 s 4 5 6

there is no third element on the left to correspond with the third element on the right, and the report *LENGTH ERROR* will be the result. However,

    3 s 4 5 6

and

    (,3) s 4 5 6

can each be interpreted as (3s4), (3s5), (3s6). The computer uses this interpretation.

These examples illustrate that the arguments must meet a condition of *compatibility*. The condition can be stated: Variables A and B are compatible in the dyadic scalar operation

    AsB

if either

  (1) The shapes of A and B are identical, or
  (2) A or B is a scalar or one-element vector.

When condition 1 is satisfied, the rank and shape of the result are the same as for either argument. If condition 2 is satisfied, the rank and shape of the result are the same as the rank and shape of whichever argument is *not* a scalar or one-element vector; or, if one argument is a one-element vector and the other a scalar, the result has shape 1.

Consideration of condition 2 shows that an empty vector or empty array can be combined with a scalar or one-element vector, producing a result which is empty and of the same rank and shape as the empty argument.

---

1) Mark any of the following which are not of the form AsB.

  2 3 + 4 5 _____

  2⌽ 4 5 3 _____

  2 3 ÷2 _____

2) If

  A←2 3 ⍴⍳6
  B←3 2 ⍴⍳6
  C←6 7 8

Write results for any of the following that are possible.

  A+C

  A+(⍴A)⍴C

  A+⌽B

  3+C

  A+5

  B+A

  A[1;]+C

  A[,1;]+C

3) Give the shape of the result for each of the following that are possible, or write *ERROR* for those that are not possible.

  2 3 × 4 5
  _____

  4× 2 4 ⍴6
  _____

  4 2 +⍳10
  _____

  4+⍳10
  _____

Scalar Functions / 117

1) Mark any of the following that will yield a *DOMAIN ERROR*.

```
    2 0 ÷ 6 3 ¯5 3
_____
    2 4 ÷ ¯6 ¯3 + 6 4
_____
    (¯2 2 × ¯1 0)*0.5
_____
    (2 3 - 2 4)*0.5
_____
```

2) Give the result for each of the following.

```
    ⌊100.6
_____
    ⌊¯100.01
_____
    ⌊ ¯98 ¯0.01 0.01
_____
    ⌊ 2 5 ρ ¯1+0.2×ι10
(in origin 1)
```

4-2 Domain Restrictions

In

$A s B$

there may or may not be special arguments for which the function will not work, depending on s. For the functions considered so far, the following restrictions apply:

$A+B$ ⎫
$A×B$ ⎬ A and B are unrestricted
$A-B$ ⎭

$A÷B$ A is unrestricted, B cannot be 0 unless A is 0

$÷B$ B cannot be 0

$A*0.5$ A cannot be negative

Of course, in all cases, A and B must be numeric.

In these stipulations, the word "unrestricted" means there is no theoretical restriction, but there is a practical restriction imposed by the limited range of numbers that can be represented in an actual computer. No argument and no result can be outside that range. Thus, even though A and B might be small enough to be represented, A×B might be too large.

An attempt to execute one of these functions with an improper argument will produce an error report. If a function will not work on certain numbers, it is said to require a *restricted domain* for its argument(s). When a function is dyadic, it is necessary to designate to which argument a restriction applies.

If arguments are arrays, domain restrictions apply to each element. For example,

    2÷ 4 0 3

will produce an error report.

4-3 Floor and Minimum

The primitive function *floor* (using the symbol ⌊ in monadic form) computes the largest integer which is not greater than the argument. Examples are:

```
      ⌊4.327
4
      ⌊4
4
      ⌊¯5.614
¯6
      ⌊¯5
¯5
```

118 / Scalar Functions FLOOR L   DYADIC L MINIMUM

Note that "largeness" is in an algebraic sense; that is why ¯5.614 is larger than ¯6.

    The function *minimum* (using the symbol L in dyadic form) yields the smaller of the two arguments when they are different, or their common value when the two arguments are the same. Examples are

```
        4.6L5.2
4.6
        ¯0.2L¯0.25
¯0.25
        4L4
4
```

    It is interesting to observe that the minimum function can be used to place an *upper* limit on the elements in an array of numbers. To illustrate, suppose

```
        C←(ι9),⌽ι8
        C
1 2 3 4 5 6 7 8 9 8 7 6 5 4 3 2 1
```

Then,

```
        6LC
1 2 3 4 5 6 6 6 6 6 6 6 5 4 3 2 1
```

    The minimum function can be used in reduction. Thus, if

```
        D←2 4 ¯5 6 ¯3 7 2
        L/D
¯5
```

This is equivalent to 2L4L¯5L6L¯3L7L2. Thus, *minimum reduction* on a vector produces the smallest element in the vector, as a scalar. Minimum reduction on an empty vector yields the *largest* number the computer can produce.

    There is no restriction on the domains of the arguments for the floor and minimum functions, except that they must be numeric.

Example 4-1

    Sometimes an output is wanted in which numbers are rounded to the nearest digit in a specified position. This is almost always true when the numbers represent money, as for the rounding of dollars to the nearest cent. A general purpose dyadic function that will accomplish this, called *DECDIG* is to be designed. Its left-hand argument is to be the number of decimal digits desired, and its right-hand argument the value to be rounded. As a step in developing the algorithm, consider how we would round the number 26.3728 to three decimal digits. On paper, one way is to add 0.0005 to give 26.3733 and then drop the last digit. However, there is no function for "dropping the last digit." But the floor function can be used

---

1) Give results for each of the following.

   ¯2L¯5+ι9

   (¯4+ι9)L0

   ¯4+(ι9)L0

   ¯3 4 ¯5 L ¯2 3 ¯6

2) If

   A←2 ¯3 4 ¯5

give results for

   L/¯6×A

   L/2÷A

3) To compare *DECDIG* as given in the text with the effect of printing precision, suppose

   A←345.678 24.387

For printing precision 5, give results for

   A

   2 *DECDIG* A

Scalar Functions / 119

1) Another algorithm for *DECDIG* is

(a) Add 5 at the position immediately to the right of the last digit to be kept.
(b) Multiply by 10 to the number of decimal digits wanted.
(c) Take the floor.
(d) Divide by the power of 10 used in step (b).

Write a function *DECDIG1* using this algorithm.

in the following sequence:

```
        1000×26.3728
26372.8
        0.5+26372.8
26373.3
        ⌊26373.3
26373
        26373÷1000
26.373
```

Thus, the algorithm is

(1) Multiply by 10 raised to the power: the number of decimal digits wanted.

(2) Add 0.5.

(3) Take the floor.

(4) Divide by the power of 10 used in step 1.

A possible defined function is

```
      ∇ R←D DECDIG N
[1]     D←10*D
[2]     R←(⌊0.5+D×N)÷D ∇
```

2) Write the results for

⌈ ¯8.7 5 9.4

⌈ 24 ¯25 6.5÷4

4-4 Ceiling and Maximum

The primitive function *ceiling* (using the symbol ⌈ in monadic form) computes the smallest integer which is not less than the argument. Examples are

```
      ⌈4.327
5
      ⌈4
4
      ⌈¯5.614
¯5
      ⌈¯5
¯5
```

3) Give results, in origin 1, for

¯2⌈¯5+⍳9

-2⌈¯5+⍳9

¯2⌈3-⍳9

(¯4+⍳9)⌈0

¯4+(⍳9)⌈0

(-4+⍳9)⌈0

The function *maximum* (using the symbol ⌈ in dyadic form) yields the larger of the two arguments if they are different, or their common value when the arguments are the same. Thus,

```
      4.6⌈5.2
5.2
      ¯0.2⌈¯0.25
¯0.2
      4⌈4
4
```

Also, for the previous vector C,

```
      6⌈C
6 6 6 6 6 7 8 9 8 7 6 6 6 6 6
```

showing that the maximum function can be used to put a *lower* limit on a set of numbers.

120 / Scalar Functions

Maximum reduction over a vector is similar to minimum reduction but it yields the largest element. For the previous `D`,

⌈/D

7

is equivalent to `2⌈4⌈¯5⌈6⌈¯3⌈7⌈2`. Maximum reduction on an empty vector yields the negative of the largest number the computer can produce.

There is no domain restriction on the arguments of the ceiling and maximum functions, except that they must be numeric.

4-5 Roundoff Error in Floor and Ceiling, Comparison Tolerance

The representation of a number in a computer is limited to a finite number of digits. Therefore, any fractional part of a mixed number requiring an infinite number of digits cannot be represented exactly. A computer carries enough significant digits so that the resulting errors are usually negligible. However, as we shall show, the floor and ceiling functions are especially sensitive to such errors. To explain, consider that in ordinary arithmetic, if we compute

3÷3

the result is 1. Ideally, the same result should be obtained from

3×÷3

However, in the decimal system, ÷3 can only be represented by an approximation such as

0.333333

Therefore, using this approximation, 3×÷3 yields

0.999999

There is a *roundoff* error in the decimal representation of ÷3. In the decimal system there is no way to obtain exactly 1 from a computation of 3×÷3.

In most cases we learn to live with this problem: we would interpret 0.999999 as 1, recognizing that the error is small. However, in applications of the floor and ceiling functions the problem becomes more acute. For example, using the decimal approximation given above, ⌊3×÷3 is ⌊0.999999 which yields 0 instead of 1. This is a gross error, compared with the error 0.000001 in 3×÷3. Similar problems occur when numbers are represented in binary form.

---

1) If

A←2 ¯3 4 ¯5

give results for

⌈/¯6×A

_____

⌈/2÷A

_____

⌈/A×A

_____

2) Compute by hand ÷7 to six significant digits.

_____

Give the result of multiplying this by 7.

_____

Scalar Functions / 121

1) Without comparison tolerance, give the results, in the decimal system, for

⌊1-3×÷3

_____

⌈1-3×÷3

_____

2) With a comparison tolerance of 1E¯13, and

P←1E¯14× 1 100

give results for each of the following.

⌊1-P

_____

⌈1+P

_____

⌊100-P

_____

⌈100+P

_____

⌊100-100×P

_____

⌈100+100×P

_____

The APL system alleviates this problem, but does not completely eliminate it, by automatically making a check of how close the argument of the floor and ceiling is to an integer. Specifically, it will yield an integer I for both ⌊A and ⌈A if |$A-I$| is less than or equal to a small positive number which we shall call T. This is conveniently portrayed on the number line shown in Fig. 4-1.

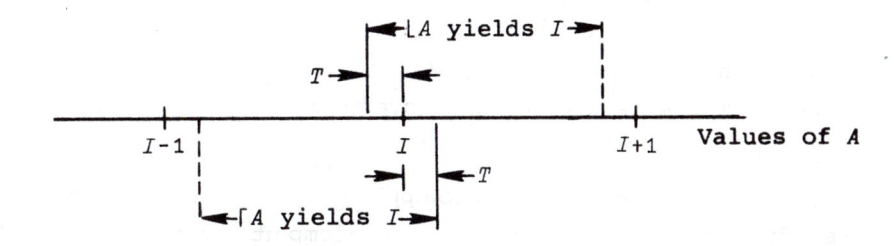

```
                    ├─⌊A yields I─┤
          ┌─T─┤ ├─
──────────┼───┼───┼─────────────┼──── Values of A
      I-1 │   I   ├─┤T          I+1
              ├─⌈A yields I─┤
```

Figure 4-1 Interpretation of tolerance for floor and ceiling.

You do not consciously use a variable T; we use it here as an aid in describing what the computer does "internally". Its value has a rather complicated dependence on |A| and on a system variable ⎕CT called the *comparison tolerance*. As a rough approximation*, T is

⎕CT×|A

⎕CT is a parameter of a workspace, and a normal value (in a clear workspace) is 1E¯13. It can be assigned other values in a normal specification statement.

4-6 Absolute Value, Signum

The absolute value (represented by monadic |) and signum (represented by monadic ×) functions were treated in Chap. 2. They can be summarized by the examples

```
      | ¯2 0 4 ¯6 5
  2 0 4 6 5
      × ¯2 0 4 ¯6 5
  ¯1 0 1 ¯1 1
```

_____

*The way the value of T depends on |A| is system dependent, being quite different in a pure binary machine as compared with a machine which uses a hexadecimal representation.

122 / Scalar Functions

In considering them again, we emphasize a complementary relationship between these two functions. If we think of a signed number as representing a point on the number line:

(a) Its absolute value designates the distance of the point from the origin.
(b) Its sign designates on which side of the origin the point is located.

The absolute value and signum functions are useful because there are situations where a separation of these properties of a number is useful.

These functions accept any numeric arguments.

Example 4-2

To illustrate an application of these functions, suppose a farmer wishes to keep a computer record of haystacks in a field. Let Fig. 4-2 represent the field, the small circles representing haystacks. The farmer might establish a vector giving the east-west locations of the haystacks, with respect to the centrally located road. For the figure, such a vector is

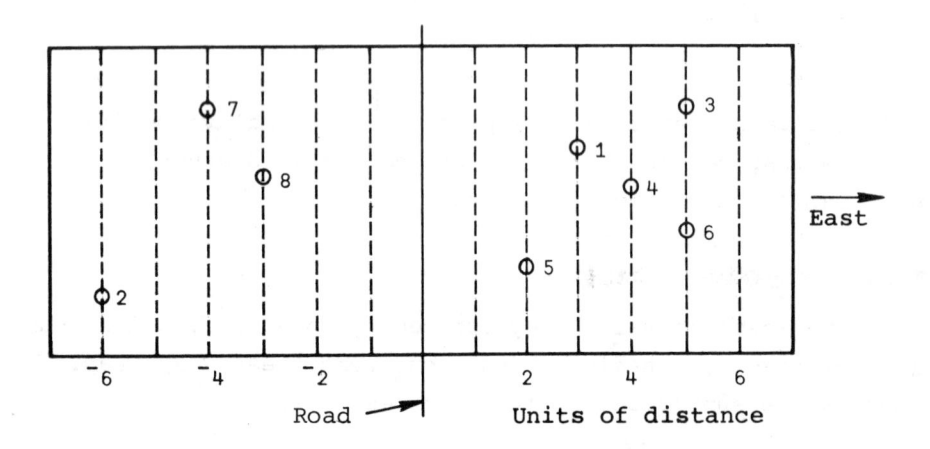

$D \leftarrow 3\ ^-6\ 5\ 4\ 2\ 5\ ^-4\ ^-3$

Figure 4-2 Locations of haystacks in a field.

The numbers next to the circles in the figure are index numbers for this vector. The absolute value of each element of the vector is the distance of the corresponding haystack from the road; positive numbers represent haystacks which are east of the road.

Given this vector, the farmer might want to know the total distance all haystacks must be moved to bring them to the

---

1) Determine results for
   $|(2-^-5)\times\times 4-6$

   $\times(2-^-5)\times|4-6$

   $\times^-4+\iota 7$

2) If A is any number, is it true that
   $(\times A)\times|A$
   is identical to A?

   Is it true that
   $(|A)\times\times A$
   is identical to A?

   How does
   $(A*2)*0.5$
   compare with $|A$?

3) Write a statement that will produce a "signed square" of a number N: the square, but with the same sign as the number.

Scalar Functions / 123

1) Using the vector *D* referred to in the text, write a statement which will give the number of haystacks in the field, excluding any that are on the road.

─────────

2) Give the result produced by

    `! 3 5 4 0 1`

─────────

3) If *N* is a nonnegative integer, write a statement using *N* as an argument, and multiply reduction, which will simulate `!N` for such an argument. Be sure it gives the correct result if *N* is zero.

─────────

road (moving them perpendicularly to the road). The distances of haystacks from the road are given by elements of the vector

```
       |D
3  6  5  4  2  5  4  3
```

and so the total distance they must be moved is the add reduction of this vector, or

```
      +/|D
32
```

Now suppose the farmer wishes to keep approximately the same number of haystacks on each side of the road. Then, whenever he intends to remove some, he would like to determine which side has the most. The signum function is used, giving

```
       ×D
1  ¯1  1  1  1  1  ¯1  ¯1
```

where each 1 represents a haystack east of the road and each ¯1 represents one west of the road. Then,

```
      +/×D
2
```

indicates that the number of haystacks east of the road is 2 greater than the number west of the road. Note that since ×0 is 0, any haystacks at the road will not be counted.

4-7 Factorial

The primitive function *factorial* (monadic use of the symbol `!`) yields the ordinary factorial, for positive integer arguments. Thus,

```
      !6
720
```

The computer function `!N` accepts other values of *N*, but not negative integers. For nonintegers, `!N` has no meaning as a *product of integers*, but the result is the "gamma function" of *N*+1. (The gamma function is one of the standard functions of mathematics, but you are not expected to be familiar with it. It is mentioned only to indicate that `!N` has meaning when *N* is not an integer.) When *N* is zero, `!N` is defined as 1; and `!N` does not exist (goes to infinity) when *N* is a negative integer.

The domain restriction for the factorial function is that its argument shall be numeric but not a negative integer. Because `!N` increases very rapidly with positive *N*, and near negative integers, the size of the result places restrictions on *N*.

4-8 Roll

The primitive function *roll* (monadic use of the symbol ?) takes a positive integer as its argument. If we designate the argument by *N*, the function ?*N* returns an integer selected randomly from the integers in ⍳*N*. Since ⍳*N* is sensitive to origin, ?*N* is also. In origin 1, the result is a random choice from the integers 1 to *N*; in origin 0 the selection is from integers 0 to *N*-1.

Each of the possible results occurs with equal probability. This means that if ?6 is done a very large number of times, in origin 1 approximately one-sixth of the results will be 1's, one-sixth will be 2's, etc. It is possible to do an experiment, say by using

　　?1200⍴6

This does the roll operation 1200 times, each time producing a random integer from 1 to 6. The result will be a vector of 1200 elements in which there are *approximately* 200 of each of the integers from 1 to 6.

In reality, the numbers are not selected in an exactly random way. They should preferably be called "pseudo random" numbers. The difference is that a sequence of real random numbers will never form a repeating pattern, whereas computed "random" numbers will repeat after a very long sequence. This difference is not important in most practical applications.

The roll function is very important in computer simulations of processes involving chance events. For example,

　　+/? 6 6

will simulate the roll of a pair of dice. (Note that 1+?11 yields numbers from 2 to 12, but with uniform probability for all possible results, whereas with an actual throw of two dice 2 and 12 are least probable and 7 is most probable.)

The result obtained from an execution of ?*N* depends on a workspace parameter called the *random link*. It is the value of the system variable ⎕RL. It changes each time the roll function is executed. A set of results from the repeated execution of ?*N* can be duplicated by starting with the same value for ⎕RL. To illustrate, suppose the current value of ⎕RL is saved by

　　I←⎕RL

Then, an execution of ? 6 6 6 6 might yield

　　? 6 6 6 6
2 4 3 1

---

1) Suppose you execute

　　?200⍴4

The result will be a vector of how many elements?

_____

Among these, there will be approximately how many 3's?

_____

2) Write two statements that will simulate *N* tosses of a coin. The result is to be a vector in which 0 means "tail" and 1 means "head".

In origin 1
_____

In origin 0
_____

3) Write a monadic function *DICE* that will take a positive integer *N* as its argument. If *N* is that argument, the value returned shall be the simulation of the sum of *N* throws of a die.

Scalar Functions / 125

1) Suppose you execute
```
    ⎕IO←1
    A←?400⍴10
```
Give highly probable results for

⌊/A

_____

⌈/A

_____

2) Suppose you execute
```
    ⎕IO←0
    A←?500⍴10
```
Give highly probable results for

⌊/A

_____

⌈/A

_____

3) Compute remainders for

283÷21

_____

5843÷47

_____

4) Prove that

(X×A)|X×B

is mathematically equivalent to

X×A|B

The value of ⎕RL will have changed in the process, and another execution of the above might be

```
      ? 6 6 6 6
    5 1 1 2
```

However, if we assign ⎕RL its original value

```
      ⎕RL←I
      ? 6 6 6 6
    2 4 3 1
```

will be a repetition of the first result. ⎕RL has a predetermined value in a clear workspace. It can be set to any positive integer up to the largest integer that can be stored in the machine.

The function roll is the only scalar function that is dependent on the origin, and ?1 yields the origin. Therefore, an indexing operation such as A[I+?1] is origin independent.

4-9 Residue *dyadic* |

Consider the division of the number 161 by 13, carrying the division algorithm far enough to obtain the complete integer part of the quotient. It is found that 161÷13 is equivalent to

12+(5÷13)

The number 5 is called the *remainder*. We are interested in how the remainder can be computed using APL functions. First, note that if the number 12 is known, the remainder R is computed by

R←161-13×12

Furthermore, observe that 12 is the result of

⌊161÷13

Therefore,

R←161-13×⌊161÷13

The primitive function *residue* (dyadic use of the symbol |) yields the equivalent of the above statement. Thus,

```
      13|161
    5
```

In general terms, A|B is equivalent to

B-A×⌊B÷A

if A is not zero. For positive integers, A|B is the remainder when B is divided by A. For other arguments, for which the concept of a remainder does not apply, the result is called the *residue*. When A is zero, the definition above is augmented by

126 / Scalar Functions

the stipulation that $A|B \leftrightarrow B$.*

  Some examples with noninteger arguments are

```
        1.3|161
1.1
        1.3|¯161
0.2
        0.13|161
0.06
        13|16.1
3.1
```

The residue function is useful in situations which are cyclical with respect to some ongoing variable. For example, suppose TIME is a variable whose value is the number of minutes since the previous midnight. The minutes of an hour "recycle" at the beginning of every hour. Thus, the number of minutes into any hour corresponding to a specific value of TIME is given by

        60|TIME

The hours (0 to 23) can also be computed, to form a vector of hours and minutes, by

        (24|⌊TIME÷60),60|TIME

There is a primitive function called encode, described in Chap. 6, which can produce this result in one operation.

  The remainder function can be used in reduction on a vector. As with the other dyadic scalar functions, reduction effectively places the function symbol between each pair of adjacent elements in the vector. Thus,

        |/ 3 5 14

is equivalent to 3|5|14.

  The residue function accepts unrestricted numeric values as its arguments. However, it is sensitive to roundoff errors which can occur for nonintegers.** Therefore, it is best to use integer arguments whenever possible. Thus, although the statements 0.2|0.1×⍳4 and 0.1×2|⍳4 are mathematically equivalent, they can yield different computed results because there are no roundoff errors in 2|⍳4.

---

*In terms of the primitive "equals" given in Sec. 4-13, the complete definition of $A|B$ is given by the statement $B-A×⌊B÷A+A=0$. In some APL systems (particularly APL/360) the definition of residue is $B-(|A)×⌊B÷|A$, with DOMAIN ERROR if $A=0$ and $B<0$.
**The performance of residue when there are roundoff errors is not necessarily the same in all APL systems.

---

1) Compute results for

    17 15 |210

    ———————

    17 15 | 210 78

    ———————

2) Show a statement taking a vector V having elements which are integers and producing a result which is a count of the number of odd integers in V.

3) Compute results for

    22.3|186.2

    ———————

    22.3|¯186.2

    ———————

4) Let M represent an amount of money in dollars (including two decimal places for cents). Write a statement which will give that part of M which cannot be converted to quarters. For example, if M is 6.47, the result is to be 0.22. Arrange the statement so that the arguments of the residue function are integers.

Scalar Functions / 127

1) Write statements that will give a two-element vector which is:

The number of combinations of 20 things taken 12 and 15 at a time.

_____

The number of combinations of 12 and 15 things taken 12 at a time.

_____

2) Compute values of

  4!6

_____

  4!7

_____

3) Write a statement that will give the coefficients for increasing powers of X in the expansion of $(1+X)*6$.

4-10 Generalized Combination   *[handwritten: DYADIC USE OF !]*

If A and B are positive integers, with A less than or equal to B, then

   $(!B) \div (!A) \times !B-A$ *[handwritten: $\frac{B!}{A!(B-A)!}$ combinations]*

gives the number of combinations of B things taken A at a time. This statement has a primitive equivalent, called the *generalized combination* (dyadic use of the symbol !) written

   $A!B$

For an application of the generalized combination, consider the binomial expansion of $(1+x)^8$ (in conventional notation)

   $(1+x)^8 = 1 + 8x + 28x^2 + 56x^3 + 70x^4 + 56x^5 + 28x^6 + 8x^7 + x^8$

The coefficient of x^N where N is any one of the exponents from 0 to 8, is the number of combinations of 8 things taken N at a time. Thus, the APL statement

```
      (0,ι8)!8
1 8 28 56 70 56 28 8 1
```

produces a vector of the coefficients.

At the elementary level assumed for this text, it is expected you will not have an opportunity to use the generalized combination for arguments other than positive integers. However, the domain of the function is less restricted than this. The general domain restrictions for the generalized combination are

(a) If B is any number not a negative integer, A can have any value.

(b) If B is a negative integer, A or $B-A$ must be a negative integer.

For nonintegers, the noninteger interpretation of the factorial is used in the equivalent $(!B) \div (!A) \times !B-A$.

The generalized combination can be used with the reduction operator.

4-11 Comparison of Floor, Ceiling and Residue

It is useful to view $\lfloor X$, $\lceil X$, and $A|X$ as mathematical functions of a variable X, as in Fig. 4-3. The gaps labeled "break" represent the fact that a discontinuous relationship cannot be shown exactly on a graph. For example $\lfloor 1.999$ and $\lfloor 1.999999999$ yield 1, but $\lfloor 2$ yields 2. For the residue function $4|7.999$ yields 3.999 and $4|7.999999999$ yields 3.999999999, but $4|8$ yields 0.

128 / Scalar Functions

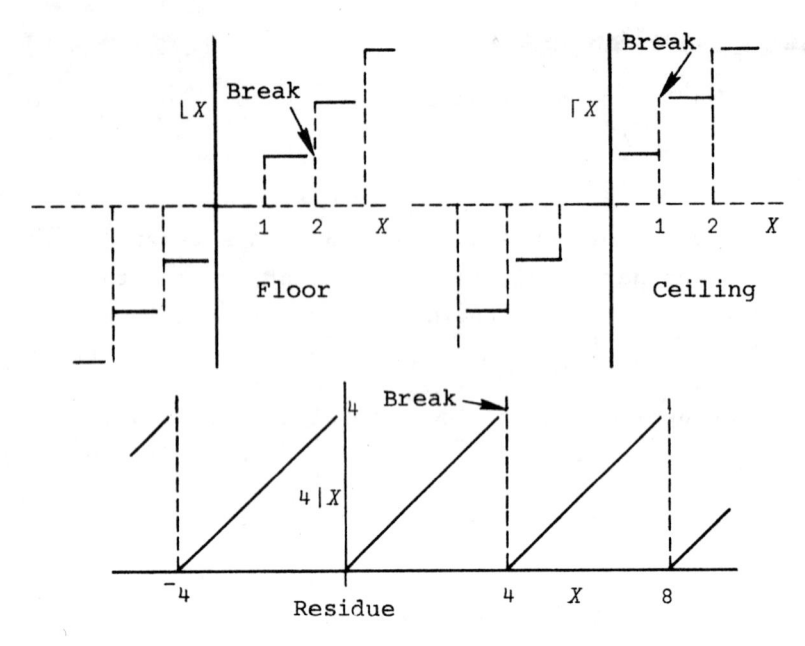

Figure 4-3 Comparison of floor, ceiling and residue.

1) Mark any of the following that are equivalent to ⌈X.

1+⌊X _____
-⌊-X _____
⌊1+X _____

2) Write statements that will produce the following functions of X.

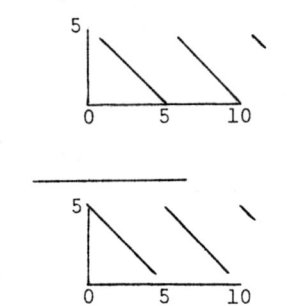

4-12 Summary of the Arithmetic Funcions

The arithmetic scalar functions and their properties are summarized in the following table.

Table 4-1

Sample values	A←3 5 6	B←4 ¯2 5	C←¯2.3 4.6 8.8	N←any positive integer
	Monadic		Dyadic	
Symbol	Name	Example	Name	Example
+	Conjugate	+B ↔ 4 ¯2 5	Addition	A+B ↔ 7 3 11
-	Negation	-B ↔ ¯4 2 ¯5	Subtraction	A-B ↔ ¯1 7 1
×	Signum	×C ↔ ¯1 1 1	Multiplication	A×B ↔ 12 ¯10 30
÷	Reciprocation	÷B ↔ 0.25 ¯0.5 0.2	Division	A÷B ↔ 0.75 ¯2.5 1.2
*	Monadic form defined later		Exponentiation	A*B ↔ 81 0.04 7776
⌊	Floor	⌊C ↔ ¯3 4 8	Minimum	A⌊C ↔ ¯2.3 4.6 6
⌈	Ceiling	⌈C ↔ ¯2 5 9	Maximum	A⌈C ↔ 3 5 8.8
|	Absolute value	|B ↔ 4 2 5	Residue	A|B ↔ B-A×⌊B÷A+A=0
!	Factorial	!A ↔ 6 120 720	Generalized combination	A!B ↔ (!B)÷(!A)×!B-A
?	Roll	?N ↔ Integer selected at random from ⍳N.	Dyadic form not a scalar function (defined later).	

Scalar Functions / 129

1) If
$$A \leftarrow 2\ 8\ 6\ 3\ 5\ 9$$
$$B \leftarrow 3\ 8\ 6\ 4\ 5\ 7$$
write the results for each of the following.

$A=B$

_____

$3=A,B$

_____

2) Given a vector V, write a statement that will give as a result the number of elements of V which are multiples of 3.

_____

Write a statement that will give the number of integers in V.

_____

3) Given a vector V of integers, write statements that will give: The number of odd integers in V.

_____

The number of even integers in V.

_____

The values used in these functions are unrestricted except as follows:

$\div B$	B cannot be zero.
$!N$	N cannot be a negative integer.
$?N$	N must be a positive integer.
$A \div B$	B cannot be zero unless A is zero. $0 \div 0$ is interpreted as 1.
$A*B$	If A is zero, B must be nonnegative; if A is negative, B must be an integer or close to a rational number which is the ratio of an integer to an odd integer. For example, ¯2*0.5 is not possible because it is the square root of a negative number; but ¯2*÷3 is possible.
$A!B$	B cannot be a negative integer unless A or $B-A$ is a negative integer.

Of course, for some functions listed as having unrestricted arguments (such as multiply) the arguments are restricted in the sense that a result exceeding the largest number the computer can handle will produce DOMAIN ERROR.

4-13 The Relational Functions

One of the important concepts in computing involves testing a given proposition, such as "is the value of J equal to the value of K?" and giving an answer in two-valued logic represented by the *Boolean* numbers 0 (for "no") and 1 (for "yes"). Boolean numbers have the appearance of regular integers, but they can be only 0 or 1.

There are six primitives which serve to test relationships between values, such as determining whether they are equal, not equal, or which one is larger. They are called *relational* functions, and are members of the class of scalar functions. They will be illustrated in terms of three sample variables,

$$A \leftarrow 3$$
$$B \leftarrow 6$$
$$C \leftarrow 6$$

(a) Equality, Inequality

A question such as "does A equal B?" is written $A=B$. Thus, in terms of the variables specified above, two examples are

    $A=B$
0
    $B=C$
1

130 / Scalar Functions

There is also the complementary question "is A *not equal* B?" which is asked by using the symbol ≠, as in the examples

```
      A≠B
1
      B≠C
0
```

Equality and inequality admit character values as arguments. Equality of character values means they are the same character. If we have two variables

```
      X←'PLANT'
      Y←'PAINT'
```

then

```
         X=Y
1 0 0 1 1
         X≠Y
0 1 1 0 0
```

Also, numbers can be compared with characters, using = and ≠, as in

```
      6='A'
0
      6≠'A'
1
```

(b) Order

Given two different numbers, if they are placed on a number line

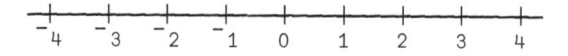

```
  ──┼──┼──┼──┼──┼──┼──┼──┼──
   ¯4 ¯3 ¯2 ¯1  0  1  2  3  4
```

we say that the one to the right on the line is larger than the one to the left. In this sense 0 is larger than ¯1, ¯2 is larger than ¯50, etc. There are four relational functions which establish order between two arguments.

Questions such as "is A less than B?" and "is A less than or equal B?" are represented, respectively, by A<B and A≤B. Examples are

```
         0< ¯2 ¯1 0 1 2
0 0 0 1 1
         0≤ ¯2 ¯1 0 1 2
0 0 1 1 1
```

Questions such as "is A greater than B?" and "is A greater than or equal B?" are represented, respectively, by A>B and A≥B. Examples are

```
         0> ¯2 ¯1 0 1 2
1 1 0 0 0
```

1) Write a statement that will give the total number of occurrences of the letter E in a character matrix M.

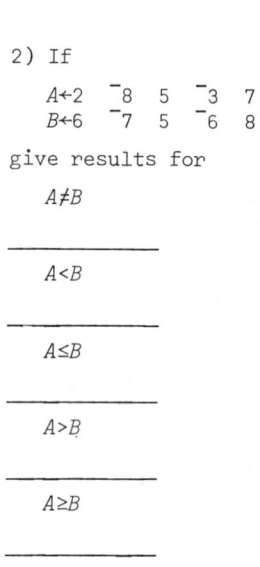

_____

2) If

A←2 ¯8 5 ¯3 7
B←6 ¯7 5 ¯6 8

give results for

A≠B

_____

A<B

_____

A≤B

_____

A>B

_____

A≥B

_____

3) Given a numerical vector V, write a statement which will determine how many of its elements are between ¯5 and 5, inclusive.

_____

Scalar Functions / 131

1) If

```
    A
2 8 3
4 9 1
    B
6 8 3 5 4
```

give results for

$A \epsilon B$

and

$B \epsilon A$

```
      0≥ ¯2 ¯1  0  1  2
   1  1  1  0  0
```

Example 4-3

Due to roundoff errors, results of lengthy calculations often yield a very small number, such as $6.938893904E^{-}16$, instead of zero. We shall define a monadic function ZERO which will convert to zero all numbers smaller in absolute value than some specified number (say $1E^{-}10$). The function is

```
     ∇ Z←ZERO W
[1]  Z←W×1E¯10≤|W  ∇
```

In explanation, $1E^{-}10<|W$ will produce an array of 1's for those elements of W which are to be kept; and zeros otherwise. Multiplying this by W preserves the numbers to be kept and makes the others zero.

2) Write a monadic function PCS which will take a character vector or matrix as its argument and return a value which is a count of the number of periods, commas, and spaces in the argument. This is to be a scalar result, one number which is a count of all the occurrences of the three specified characters.

4-14 Membership   ∈

The function *membership* (employing the symbol ∈ in dyadic form) is not a scalar function but is closely related to the equals function. For each element of the left-hand argument, it answers the question "is that element a member of the right-hand argument?". There is no compatibility condition, each argument can be of any rank. To illustrate this function, assume

```
        A
   MEMBERSHIP
   IS A DYADIC
   FUNCTION
        B
   ABCDEFXYZ
        A∈B
   0 1 0 1 1 0 0 0 0 0 0
   0 0 0 1 0 1 1 1 1 0 1
   1 0 0 1 0 0 0 0 0 0 0
```

The result would be the same for $B←3\ 3\ \rho\text{'}ABCDEFXYZ\text{'}$. Thus, $A\epsilon B$ is the same as $A\epsilon,B$. The result is always a Boolean array of the same rank and shape as A. Of course, the arguments can also be numeric.

3) Write a monadic function LETTERS which will take an argument as specified in (2). It is to return a value which is a count of the number of characters in the argument which are not spaces, commas, or periods. Use PCS as a subfunction.

4-15 Comparison Tolerance in the Relational Functions

In similarity with the floor and ceiling functions, roundoff errors can lead to erroneous results from the relational and **membership** functions. Accordingly, the computer automatically incorporates the comparison tolerance in these functions. If T is some very small positive number, suppose we agree that

$A=B$

shall yield 1 if $(|A-B)$ is less than or equal to T, also that

132 / Scalar Functions

$A<B$

shall yield 1 if $B-A$ is greater than T, and that

$A>B$

shall yield 1 if $A-B$ is greater than T. These relationships are portrayed in Fig. 4-4.

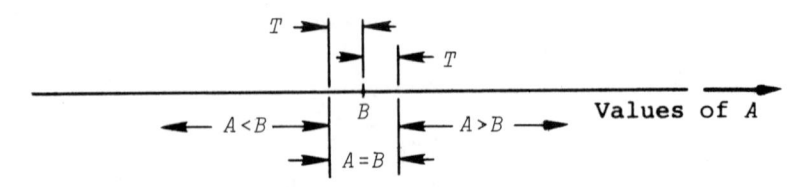

Figure 4-4 Interpretation of tolerance for the relational functions.

The computer gives this interpretation to the relational functions and membership, where T is approximately equal to

$□CT×(⌈|A)⌈|B$

The exact relationship between T and $□CT$, depends on the computer system. Note that $□CT$ is the same system parameter referred to in Sec. 4-5.

We are purposely somewhat vague about the comparison tolerance, because an exact analysis depends on the computer system. With the information given here we cannot say precisely how large $|A-B|$ can be while having $A=B$ yield a result as if they were equal. However, this vagueness is not serious because usually $□CT$ can be set large enough so that roundoff errors are very small compared with the equivalent T. If a function which depends on the comparison tolerance gives an erroneous result, the possibility of roundoff error should be investigated.

4-16 Summary of the Relational Functions

The properties of the relational functions, and membership are summarized in Table 4-2. They are all dyadic.

The relational functions accept all numerical values as arguments, and in the case of =, ≠, and ϵ character values are also valid*. Results from these functions are always Boolean numbers.

---

*Some systems recognize an ordering for character values, in accordance with their positions in the atomic vector $□AV$ (see Chap. 7).

---

1) Suppose, for a certain value of $□CT$, an experiment on the computer yields

　　$10=10+2E^-13$

0

　　$10=10+1E^-13$

1

The value of $□CT$ is between

_____

and

_____

2) For the same setting of $□CT$ as in (1) above, pick the smallest number $N1$ such that you are sure

　　$100=100+N1$

0

_____

and the largest number $N2$ such that you are sure

　　$100=100+N2$

1

_____

Scalar Functions / 133

1) If
   A←1 2 3 4
   B←2 3 4 5
   give results for
   A=B
   _____
   AϵB
   _____
   BϵA
   _____
   A=3
   _____
   Aϵ3
   _____

Table 4-2

Sample values	A←3 8 ¯6 C←'BOX'	B←3 4 ¯5.9 D←'BOG'
Symbol	Name	Example
=	Equal	A=B ↔ 1 0 0 C=D ↔ 1 1 0 A=C ↔ 0 0 0
≠	Not equal	A≠B ↔ 0 1 1 C≠D ↔ 0 0 1 A≠C ↔ 1 1 1
≤	Less than or equal	A≤B ↔ 1 0 1
<	Less than	A<B ↔ 0 0 1
≥	Greater than or equal	A≥B ↔ 1 1 0
>	Greater than	A>B ↔ 0 1 0
ϵ	Membership (not a scalar function)	Aϵ 8 5 4 3 ↔ 1 1 0

2) Apply the algorithm for determining whether a year is a leap year to the following years. Opposite each year, place 1 if it is a leap year, 0 if it is not.

2000 _____
1900 _____
2020 _____
1896 _____
1985 _____

3) Write an APL expression that will yield 1 if Y is divisible by 100, otherwise 0.

_____

The relational functions can be used with the reduction operator, but normally they are used only on two elements, as in

```
      >/ 5 4
1
```

4-17 Logic Functions

Logic functions carry out operations representing statements of logic, using Boolean values as arguments. To illustrate, suppose Y is a variable representing a year in the Gregorian calendar. We are to consider what computation will determine whether Y represents a leap year. In words, Y is a leap year if*

(Y is divisible by 400)
OR
(Y is divisible by 4) AND (Y is NOT divisible by 100)

Each of the capitalized words in the statement above represents a logic function.

The logic functions apply in a realm of *two-valued* logic, where every proposition is either true or false. There are five logic functions. Except for one, each one has four possible results, which are conveniently presented in tabular form.

_____

*For years later than 1582.

(a) Not

The function *not* (represented by the symbol ~) is monadic. It yields the opposite of a Boolean argument. Its meaning parallels usage in natural language: "not true" means "false," and "not false" means "true." The two cases are

A	~A
0	1
1	0

(b) Or

The dyadic primitive function *or* (represented by the symbol ∨) is the equivalent of the English word "or" when used in a logical statement such as: "I will go if the sun shines or if someone can give me a ride." If A represents whether the sun shines and B whether someone can give me a ride, then A∨B represents whether I will go. The result is 1 if either A or B is 1 (or if both are 1), otherwise the result is 0. The possible results are given in the following *truth* table.

A	B	A∨B
0	0	0
0	1	1
1	0	1
1	1	1

(c) And

The dyadic primitive function *and* (represented by the symbol ∧) is the equivalent of the English word "and" when used in a logical statement such as "I will go if I am ready in time and if I have enough money." If A represents whether I am ready in time, and B represents whether I have enough money, the result of A∧B indicates whether I will go. The result is 1 if A and B are both 1, otherwise the result is 0. The possible results of this function are given in the follow- table.

A	B	A∧B
0	0	0
0	1	0
1	0	0
1	1	1

---

1) Give results for each of the following.

1∧~1∨0

_____

(1∨0)∧~1∧0

_____

(3≤16)∧4≥16

_____

~(3>16)∨4<16

_____

The last two parts are in origin 1.

2) Make a truth table for

(~A)∨~B

3) Make a truth table for

(~A)∧~B

4) Write statements that will answer the questions:

Does A equal 5 or 6?

_____

Is A less than 5 and greater than 0?

_____

5) Give two statements which do not use ≠, but are equivalent to

A≠B

_____

_____

Scalar Functions / 135

1) An operation called "exclusive or" combines two Boolean arguments to give 0 if both arguments are the same (both 0, or both 1), and otherwise 1. Let *EXOR* be the name of a defined function having these properties. Write a definition of *EXOR*.

2) Line [1] of *LPYR* is of the form

   $A \vee B \wedge C$

If Y is 2000, fill in the values of A, B, and C.

A _____
B _____
C _____

Repeat the above for the year 1800.

A _____
B _____
C _____

(d) Nor, Nand

The operation *not or* is performed by the dyadic function *nor* (represented by the symbol ⩖, ∨ overstruck by ~). Thus,

   $A \overline{\vee} B$

and

   $\sim A \vee B$

are equivalent. Similarly, *not and* is performed by the dyadic function *nand* (represented by the symbol ⩑, ∧ overstruck by ~). Thus,

   $A \overline{\wedge} B$

and

   $\sim A \wedge B$

are equivalent.

Example 4-4

The introduction to this section includes directions (essentially the algorithm) for finding whether a given year is a leap year. We shall now define a monadic function which will accept the designation of a year as its argument, and return a Boolean result which indicates whether the year is a leap year. Such a function is

```
     ∇ Z←LPYR Y
[1]    Z←(0=400|Y)∨(0=4|Y)∧0≠100|Y ∇
```

To interpret this, recall that $A|B$ is zero if B is a multiple of A. The right-hand argument of ∧ is $0 \neq 100|Y$, which is 1 if Y is not a multiple of 100. The left-hand argument of ∧ is 1 if Y is a multiple of 4. Thus, the right-hand argument of ∨ is 1 if Y is not a multiple of 100 and is a multiple of 4. The algorithm is completed by including $0=400|Y$, which is 1 if Y is a multiple of 400.

The logic functions can be used in reduction. Thus,

   ∨/ 1 1 0 1 1 0 0   Equivalent to   1∨1∨0∨1∨1∨0∨0
1

   ∧/ 1 1 0 1 1 0 0   Equivalent to   1∧1∧0∧1∧1∧0∧0
0

To illustrate the use of reduction, suppose you have a vector V of integers, and you want to ask the question "are all the numbers in V multiples of 3?" The answer is given by

   ∧/0=3|V

Another question, "is there at least one letter Q in a character vector V?" is answered by

136 / Scalar Functions

$$\vee/'Q'=V$$

There are alternative ways to answer these two questions. The first one can be represented by

$$\sim\vee/0\neq 3|V$$

Similarly, the second question can be represented by

$$\sim\wedge/'Q'\neq V$$

Concerning reduction, because $A \barwedge B \leftrightarrow \sim A \wedge B$ (and $A \veebar B \leftrightarrow \sim A \vee B$) it might be thought that $\barwedge/A$ is equivalent to $\sim\wedge/A$ (or that $\veebar/A$ is equivalent to $\sim\vee/A$). However, they are not equivalent, as the following examples show.

```
      ⊽/ 0 1 0 0 1
1
      ~∨/ 0 1 0 0 1
0
      ⊼/ 1 0 0 1 0
0
      ~∧/ 1 0 0 1 0
1
```

Reduction of an empty vector using ∨ or ∧ is possible, as follows:

```
      ∨/ ⍳0
0
      ∧/ ⍳0
1
```

4-18 Summary of the Logic Functions

The properties of the logic functions are summarized in Table 4-3.

Table 4-3

A	B	$\sim A$	$\sim B$	$A \vee B$	$A \wedge B$	$A \veebar B$	$A \barwedge B$	$(\sim A) \wedge \sim B$	$(\sim A) \vee \sim B$
0	0	1	1	0	0	1	1	1	1
0	1	1	0	1	0	0	1	0	1
1	0	0	1	1	0	0	1	0	1
1	1	0	0	1	1	0	0	0	0

The two cases on the right are included to demonstrate that

$$A \vee B \leftrightarrow \sim(\sim A) \wedge \sim B$$

and

$$A \wedge B \leftrightarrow \sim(\sim A) \vee \sim B$$

These two identities are really only one, because if A and B are replaced by $\sim A$ and $\sim B$ in the second identity, the first

1) Give the result for each of the following.

∧/ 1 1 1 1
_____

∧/ 1 0 0 1
_____

∨/ 1 0 0 1
_____

⊼/ 1 1 1 1
_____

⊼/ 1 1 1 1 1
_____

⊽/ 1 1 1 1
_____

⊽/ 1 1 1 1 1
_____

2) In the expression

$$A \wedge B \leftrightarrow \sim(\sim A) \vee \sim B$$

replace A and B, respectively, by $\sim A$ and $\sim B$, to obtain the expression

$$A \vee B \leftrightarrow \sim(\sim A) \wedge \sim B$$

1) According to DeMorgan's theorem, complete

$A \barwedge B \leftrightarrow$ _____

in terms of the $\wedge$ function. Also, complete

$A \barvee B \leftrightarrow$ _____

in terms of the $\vee$ function.

2) Let V be a character vector of any length. Write a statement that will yield a scalar 0 if V has no spaces among its elements; otherwise 1.

_____

3) Let V be a vector of numbers. Write a statement that will give a scalar 1 if all the elements of V are integers; otherwise 0.

_____

will be obtained. The property represented by either of these identities is a fundamental relationship in logic, known as DeMorgan's theorem.

DeMorgan's theorem can be used to obtain an alternative statement which will determine whether a specified year is a leap year. The statement used in example 4-4 was

$(0=400|Y) \vee (0=4|Y) \wedge 0 \neq 100|Y$

First look at the arguments of $\wedge$ in this statement. The *NOT* of $0=4|Y$ is $0 \neq 4|Y$, and the *NOT* of $0 \neq 100|Y$ is $0=100|Y$. Thus, using DeMorgan's theorem,

$\sim(0=4|Y) \wedge 0 \neq 100|Y \leftrightarrow (0 \neq 4|Y) \vee 0=100|Y$

and applying the theorem again, to the *OR* in the original statement, we obtain the alternative

$\sim(0 \neq 400|Y) \wedge (0 \neq 4|Y) \vee 0=100|Y$

4-19 Compression and Expansion on Vectors

A brief digression from the main subject of the chapter is included here for the pragmatic reason of showing some applications of the Boolean results obtained from the relational and logic functions. Two nonscalar functions will be introduced.

(a) Compression on Vectors

The primitive function *compression* is dyadic (employing the symbol /). It takes a Boolean vector as its left-hand argument and an array on the right. At this point we consider only vectors on the right (compression on arrays of higher ranks is treated in Chap. 6). If we have the variables

```
    V← 2 4 6 8 3
    C← 'ABCDE'
    I← 0 1 0 0 1
```

then

```
    I/V
4 3
    I/C
BE
```

These results are easily understood by imagining the Boolean vector I written above the other vector, as in

```
0 1 0 0 1 ←——— imagined
2 4 6 8 3
```

or

```
01001
ABCDE
```

138 / Scalar Functions

The result consists of those elements corresponding to the 1's. Observe the compatibility condition, that both arguments must be of the same length. If all elements on the left are zero except one, the result is a vector of one element.

One use of compression is to select from a vector those elements satisfying a certain criterion, such as all elements greater than 5. For example, if

```
    V←15 8 2 3 7 9 1 1 8 4
```

then

```
       (5<V)/V
15 8 7 9 8
```

because `5<V` is `1 1 0 0 1 1 0 0 1 0`.

If the Boolean vector on the left has all zeros, the result is an empty vector. For example, `(0>V)/V` yields an empty vector, meaning that there are no elements in V less than 0. A simple and useful application is to use compression to obtain the *index numbers* of elements meeting a certain criterion. Thus, using the same V,

```
       (5<V)/⍳⍴V
1 2 5 6 9
```

yields the index numbers in V of those elements that are greater than 5.

(b) Expansion

The primitive function *expansion* is dyadic (using the symbol \). It takes a Boolean vector as the left-hand argument and an array on the right. Here we consider only vectors on the right (expansion on arrays of higher ranks is treated in Chap. 6). Expansion is complementary to compression. It can increase the length of the right-hand argument by inserting zeros (if the argument is numeric) or spaces (if the argument is a vector of characters). Using the vectors

```
V← 2 4 6 8 3
C← 'ABCDE'
I← 1 0 1 1 0 0 1 0 1
```

expansion is illustrated by

```
       I\V
2 0 4 6 0 0 8 0 3
       I\C
A BC  D E
```

Observe that zeros (or spaces) are inserted in positions corresponding to the locations of zeros in I. The relationship to compression is evident from the fact that `I/I\V` is equivalent to V.

---

1) If V is a vector of alphabet characters, spaces, and commas, write a statement that will produce a vector of only the alphabet characters.

————————

2) If V is a vector of integers, write a statement that will produce a vector consisting of all the odd numbers in V.

————————

3) If V is a vector of alphabet characters and spaces, write a statement that will produce the indices in V of the locations of the spaces.

————————

4) Using

```
V←2 8 3 6
```

give the results for the following.

⍴ 1 0 1 1 /V

————————

⍴ 0 0 1 0 /V

————————

⍴ 0 0 0 0 /V

————————

Does ⍴A/V equal +/A for the general case?

————————

5) Does `(5<V)/⍳⍴V` give index numbers which can be used in either origin?

————————

Scalar Functions / 139

1) Specify a vector I such that

$I\backslash\text{'INTHEDARK'}$
IN THE DARK
$I\leftarrow$

2) In the text it is stated that, for any suitable I,

$I/I\backslash V \leftrightarrow V$

Is it also true that

$I\backslash I/V$

is equivalent to V?

___

3) How is

$\rho I\backslash V$

related to some property of I?

___

4) Suppose V is a vector of integers. Write two statement lines that will cause all elements which are the numbers 5 or 6 to be replaced by zeros.

___

5) Suppose V is a vector of alphabet characters. V is to have any length. Write a statement that will put a space between the 3rd and 4th elements, between the 6th and 7th, etc.

___

The condition for compatibility is that the number of 1's in the argument on the left shall equal the dimension of the vector on the right.

Example 4-5

Suppose a variable W has a character vector as its value, consisting of words, spaces, and punctuation marks. This character vector may have been created by a careless typist; there may be missing spaces following punctuation marks or perhaps extra spaces between words. A monadic function $FORM$ is to be defined which will condition the contents of W to a standard form by: (1) placing a space after any punctuation mark not followed by a space, (2) removing extra spaces.

Consider 1 above, for the example

$W\leftarrow\text{'RED,BLUE,GREEN, YELLOW'}$

In view of the fact that extra spaces will be removed under (2), we can place a space after each comma. This means that the last comma will be followed by two spaces, one to be removed later. It is evident that $T\backslash W$ will produce the required spaces if

T
1 1 1 1 0 1 1 1 1 1 0 1 1 1 1 1 1 0 1 1 1 1 1 1 1

In origin 1, observe that the commas in W are at index positions $IP\leftarrow 4\ \ 9\ \ 15$, and that in T the zeros are at index positions 5 11 18 (or $IP+\iota\rho IP$). We can obtain IP from

$IP\leftarrow(W\epsilon\text{'.,:;'})/\iota\rho W$

and

$T\leftarrow\sim(\iota(\rho IP)+\rho W)\epsilon IP+\iota\rho IP$

It is convenient to place these steps in a subfunction

```
      ∇ Z←SAFTP N;IP
[1]   IP←(Nε'.,:;')/ιρN
[2]   Z←(~(ι(ρIP)+ρN)εIP+ιρIP)\N ∇

      SAFTP W
RED, BLUE, GREEN,  YELLOW
```

Now consider step (2), the removal of extra spaces. If W is the character vector with extra spaces, we require a vector R such that R/W will not have extra spaces. A possible criterion for creating R is: An element of R is to be 1 if it corresponds to a nonspace in W, or is a space in W following a nonspace. This vector can be created by

$R\leftarrow W\neq\text{' '}$
$R\leftarrow R\vee\bar{1}\phi R$

However, this does not take care of unwanted spaces at the ends of W. The rotation effectively makes the last element of W the one that precedes the first. If the last element of W is a

140 / Scalar Functions

space, it will cause a leading space to be removed, but not otherwise. A convenient way to take care of this is to add a trailing space, and then remove it in a final step. Such a function is

```
      ∇ Z←REMS N;R
[1]   R←' '≠N←N,' '
[2]   Z←¯1↓(Rv¯1⌽R)/N ∇
```

Note that if there is an unwanted space at the end, the appended space becomes a second space, which will be removed in the compression; and the original extra space will be removed by the drop. These two functions can now be incorporated in FORM as follows:

```
      ∇ Z←FORM N
[1]   Z←REMS SAFTP N ∇
```

One purpose in giving this example is to show that an initial modification can sometimes eliminate a special case.

(c) Special Cases

For compression, the condition that both arguments shall be of the same length can be violated if one argument is a scalar. In that case the scalar argument is automatically extended, by repetition, to the same length as the vector. Two examples of this are

```
      1/ 8 7 6
8 7 6
      1 0 1 /7
7 7 7
```

For expansion, the condition that the number of 1's in the left-hand argument shall equal the dimension of the right-hand argument can be violated if the right-hand argument is a scalar. That argument is automatically extended, by repetition, to the required length, as in

```
      1 1 0 1 \7
7 7 0 7
```

Both arguments can be scalars, as in 1/7 and 1\7, each of which yields 7 as a one-element vector. Also, 0/7 yields an empty vector. Some systems accept empty vectors as arguments.

4-20 Transcendental Functions

The transcendental functions considered here are the exponential (the base of natural logarithms, *e*, raised to some power), the logarithm, the trigonometric, and the hyperbolic functions.

---

1) Analyze the operation of *SAFTP* when its argument is `'AB,C; D'` by writing out values for the following variables or statements during execution.

IP

—————

IP,⍳ρ*IP*

—————

(⍳(ρ*IP*)+ρ*N*)∊*IP*,⍳ρ*IP*

—————

2) Write a version of *REMS* which uses 1⌽*R* instead of ¯1⌽*R*.

3) Describe the result produced by

0/5

—————

Scalar Functions / 141

1) If

    $A \leftarrow *2$

write statements involving A that are equivalent to

    $*^{-}2$

———————

    $*4$

———————

2) Give the results produced by

    ⍟*⍳3

———————

    10⍟ 10 100 1000

———————

3) Write a statement that will give the largest value A can have in each of the following, in terms of L, the largest number the computer can handle.

    $*A$

———————

    $3*A$

———————

(a) **Exponential**

The dyadic * is classified in Sec. 4-3 as an arithmetic function, and called exponentiation. The exponential function of a variable X can be approximated by

    2.7182818*X

where 2.7182818 is an approximation of e, the base of natural logarithms. This result is given more accurately by the *exponential function* (use of the symbol * in monadic form). An example giving some values of the exponential function is

```
   *  -2       -1       -0.5     0   0.5     1        2
   0.135335  0.367879  0.606531  1   1.64872 2.71828  7.38906
```

The domain for the exponential function is unrestricted.

(b) **Logarithm**

The *logarithm* has two forms, dyadic and monadic (using the symbol ⍟, o overstruck with *). The monadic form yields the natural logarithm of the argument (to base e); the dyadic form gives the logarithm of the right-hand argument, to the base designated by the left-hand argument. Some examples are

```
        ⍟ 1       2        3        4        5        6        7
        0 0.693147 1.09861  1.38629  1.60944  1.79176  1.94591

       10⍟ 1      2        3        4        5        6        7
        0 0.30103 0.477121  0.60206  0.69897  0.778151 0.845098

        2⍟ 1      2        3        4        5        6        7        8
        0 1       1.58496   2        2.32193  2.58496  2.80735  3
```

The logarithm of one number to several bases can be obtained by using a vector of the bases on the left, as in

```
       2 10 100 ⍟5.67
   2.50335  0.753583  0.376792
```

Also, since this is a scalar function, both arguments can be vectors; the logarithm of 4.5 to base 2 and 3.85 to base 10 are are obtained from

```
       2 10 ⍟ 4.5 3.85
   2.16993  0.585461
```

Both arguments of the logarithm must be greater than 0, although on some systems 0⍟0 yields 1.

Example 4-6

The decay of radioactive material obeys an *exponential law*. Specifically, if B is the amount of material at zero time (whenever observations begin), the amount at any instant of time T is given by (in conventional notation)

$$A = Be^{-\alpha T} \tag{1}$$

142 / Scalar Functions

where e is the base of natural logarithms, and α is a constant related to the half life H, the time at which half the original material remains. Therefore, $0.5 = e^{-\alpha H}$ or

$$\alpha = \frac{\log_e 2}{H} \qquad (2)$$

We are to write a dyadic function *DECAY* which will take a half life as its left-hand argument, and a scalar or vector of values of time as its right-hand argument. The returned value is to be a matrix having values of time in the first row and corresponding fractions of material remaining in the second row. The algorithm is: Compute α from Eq. (2), and then compute values of $A \div B$ from Eq. (1). A suitable program is

```
      ∇ R←HALF DECAY TIME
[1]     R←(⍟2)÷HALF
[2]     R←TIME,[0.5]*R×-TIME←,TIME ∇
```

(c) Pi

Multiplication of an argument by π is accomplished by the function *pi* (monadic use of the symbol ○). Thus,

```
       ○ 1 2 3
3.14159  6.28319  9.42478
```

Practical computing often requires the conversion of angle values from degrees to radians, or vice versa. Therefore, it is convenient to have general purpose defined functions for this purpose. The function

```
      ∇ Z←RAD X
[1]     Z←○X÷180 ∇
```

converts an argument in degrees to an output in radians. The following function will convert from radians to degrees.

```
      ∇ Z←DEG X
[1]     Z←180×X÷○1 ∇
```

(d) Trigonometric Functions

The three basic trigonometric functions *sine*, *cosine* and *tangent* (produced by the dyadic symbol ○) are as follows:

```
1○A   ↔   sin A
2○A   ↔   cos A
3○A   ↔   tan A
```

In all cases A must be in radians. The left-hand argument can be a vector, providing the opportunity to obtain more than one trigonometric function in one operation. Thus,

```
        1 2 3 ○○÷3
0.866025  0.5  1.73205
```

---

1) Write a statement giving the circumference of a circle in terms of its radius R.

_____

2) Using *DEG* given in the text, give the result produced by

  DEG ○(⍳3)÷6

_____

3) Using *RAD* as given in the text, give the results produced by

  1○*RAD* 0 30 45 60

_____

  2○*RAD* 0 30 45 60

_____

  3○*RAD* 0 30 45 60

_____

4) The number π is produced by (choose one):

  ○ _____

  ○1 _____

5) Write a statement not using the square function and using 1 only once, that will produce the square of π.

_____

Scalar Functions / 143

which are respectively the sine, cosine, and tangent of π÷3.

The domains for the right-hand arguments of the trigonometric functions are unrestricted. As indicated above, the left-hand argument must be 1, 2, or 3.

The corresponding *inverse* trigonometric functions (using the dyadic ○) are

¯1○A ↔ arcsin A
¯2○A ↔ arccos A
¯3○A ↔ arctan A

Given A, the "angle whose sine is A" is not unique. A similar assertion can be made for the other inverse trigonometric functions. The reason is evident from Fig. 4-5 where it is shown that at least* two angles have the same sine (also cosine and tangent). The computer must produce a unique value for each

1) Using *DEG* as given in the text, give the results produced by

DEG ¯1○0.5×1,3*0.5

___

DEG ¯2○0.5×1,3*0.5

___

DEG ¯3○1 ¯1

___

T←1,3*0.5
DEG ¯3○(÷¯1↑T),T

___

2) Give the results produced by

DEG ¯1○1○RAD 150

___

DEG ¯2○2○RAD ¯30

___

DEG ¯3○3○RAD 225

___

3) Give the results produced by

DEG ¯2○1○RAD 30

___

2○¯3○1

___

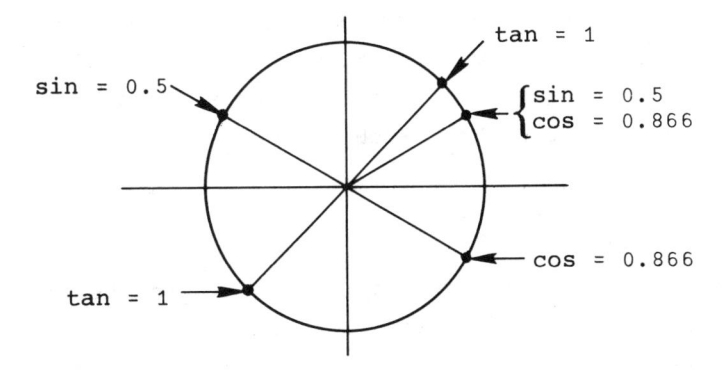

Figure 4-5 Multivaluedness of the inverse trigonometric functions.

inverse trigonometric function, and accordingly the results are in the following ranges.

¯1○A   (-○÷2)≤ result ≤ ○÷2
¯2○A   0≤ result ≤ ○1
¯3○A   (-○÷2)< result < ○÷2

The inverse tangent function accepts values from an unrestricted numeric domain, but for the inverse sine and inverse cosine the absolute value of the argument cannot be greater than 1.

___

*We say "at least" because if any integral multiple of 2π is added to an angle its sine, cosine, and tangent are unchanged.

144 / SCALAR FUNCTIONS

Example 4-7

The function ¯3○A always yields a result in quadrants 1 or 4 of Fig. 4-5. This is in spite of the fact that according to Fig. 4-5 the arctangent of 6÷6 is ○0.25 but the arctangent of ¯6÷¯6 is ○¯0.75. The result depends on individual signs of the numerator and denominator, not on the sign of their ratio. This suggests that, if X and Y are the usual coordinates in Fig. 4-5, the arctangent should be viewed as a function of the *two* variables X and Y. The following algorithm describes how to do this.

    Case 1: If $X>0$, make the result ¯3○Y÷X
    Case 2: If $X=0$, make the result ○0.5×$×Y$
    Case 3: If $X<0$, make the result (¯3○Y÷X)+○1-2×Y<0

In case 3 we have chosen ○1 (rather than ○¯1) for $X<0$ and $Y=0$ in accordance with usual practice.

A defined function *ARCTAN* can be written almost literally from this algorithm. The function is dyadic, taking a scalar or array of values of X on the left and a scalar or array of values of Y on the right. Such a function is

```
       ∇ Z←X ARCTAN Y
[1]    Z←(X≠0)×¯3○Y÷X+X=0
[2]    Z←Z+○((X=0)×0.5××Y)+(X<0)×1-2×Y<0  ∇
```

In line [1] it is necessary to include $X=0$ on the right to avoid an infinite argument when X is zero. The result of ¯3○ is then unimportant because it is multiplied by $X≠0$. If X and Y are both zero, there is no defined angle, but the function yields zero.

(e) Unit Circle (Pythagorean) Functions

Three dyadic functions which compute relationships for the unit circle (using the dyadic ○) are called the *unit circle* or *Pythagorean* functions. Their definitions are as follows:

    4○A ↔ (1+A*2)*0.5 A unrestricted
    0○A ↔ (1-A*2)*0.5 |A less than or equal to 1
    ¯4○A ↔ (¯1+A*2)*0.5 |A greater than or equal to 1

The geometrical properties of these functions are shown in Fig. 4-6.

---

1) For arctan, when $X<0$, ○1-2×Y<0 is used in the text. Complete the following, in the simplest way, so it will be equivalent.

    ○($Y=0$)+ _____

2) Write a monadic version of *ARCTAN* which will take a vector argument X,Y or a matrix in which values of X are in the first row and values of Y are in the second row. The function is to work properly for either type of argument.

3) Using trigonometric and inverse trigonometric functions, write statements which are equivalent to

    4○A
    _____

    0○A
    _____

    ¯4○A
    _____

Scalar Functions / 145

1) If

$B \leftarrow \star A$

in terms of B write statements to complete the equivalencies asked for below.

5○A ↔ _____

6○A ↔ _____

7○A ↔ _____

2) In the following, fill in the blank spaces to make the identities true.

5○A ↔ _____ ¯1+⋆A+A

6○A ↔ _____ 1+⋆A+A

7○A ↔ _____ 1+⋆A+A

3) Prove each of the identities

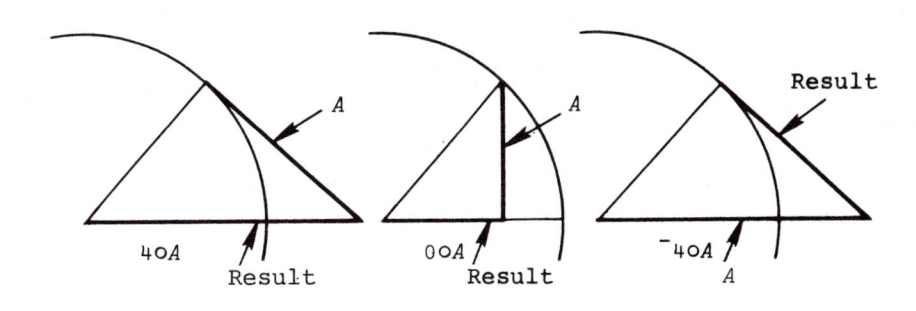

¯5○A ↔ ⍟A+4○A

¯6○A ↔ ⍟A+¯4○A

¯7○A ↔ 0.5×⍟(1+A)÷1-A

Figure 4-6 The Pythagorean functions.

(f) **Hyperbolic Functions**

There are three functions which can be related to the trigonometric functions through theoretical proofs which are beyond the scope of this text. Here we are only interested in defining the functions and giving their APL representations. The names of these functions are the same as the trigonometric functions, with the word "hyperbolic" used as a prefix; and their abbreviations are the same as for the trigonometric function with the letter "h" appended. For practical purposes these three functions can be defined in terms of the exponential function, as follows:

>   hyperbolic sine of A ↔ sinh A ↔ 0.5×(⋆A)-⋆-A
>   hyperbolic cosine of A ↔ cosh A ↔ 0.5×(⋆A)+⋆-A
>   hyperbolic tangent of A ↔ tanh A ↔ ((⋆A)-⋆-A)÷(⋆A)+⋆-A

These three functions (using the dyadic ○) are

>   5○A ↔ sinh A
>   6○A ↔ cosh A
>   7○A ↔ tanh A

For each of these, A is unrestricted.

The inverses of the hyperbolic functions are

>   ¯5○A ↔ inverse sinh of A (arcsinh A)
>   ¯6○A ↔ inverse cosh of A (arccosh A)
>   ¯7○A ↔ inverse tanh of A (arctanh A)

The domain restrictions are as follows:

>   arcsinh A, A is unrestricted
>   arccosh A, A must be greater than or equal to 1
>   arctanh A, |A must be less than 1

Of course, in a computer the domain restrictions are influenced by the largest realizable number. For ¯6○A the computer produces a result with a positive sign. Practical problems using

Table 4-4

Sample values	$A \leftarrow 0\ 0\ 1\ 1$ $C \leftarrow 0.5$	$2 \div 6$ 2	$B \leftarrow 0\ 1\ 2\ 3$ $D \leftarrow 0\ 0.4\ 0.8$	$\left.\begin{array}{c}E\\F\end{array}\right\}$ any value admissible for the function in which it is used

Symbol	Name	Monadic	Dyadic	Domain restrictions
*	Exponential	$*B \leftrightarrow 1\ 2.718\ 7.389\ 20.086$ $*-B \leftrightarrow 1\ 0.368\ 0.135\ 0.0498$	See arithmetic functions	$*F$; F unrestricted
⊛	Logarithm	$\circledast C \leftrightarrow \bar{}0.693\ 0\ 0.693$ (Natural logarithm)	$10 \circledast C \leftrightarrow \bar{}0.30103\ 0\ 0.30103$ $2 \circledast C \leftrightarrow \bar{}1\ 0\ 1$ $2\ 10\ 10\ \circledast C \leftrightarrow \bar{}1\ 0\ 0.30103$ (logarithm is to base specified by left-hand argument)	$\circledast F$; $0<F$ $E \circledast F$; $0<E$, $0<F$
○	Pi	$\circ C \leftrightarrow 1.5708\ 3.1416\ 6.2832$ (Multiply by π)		$\circ F$; F unrestricted
○	Trigonometric: Argument in radians		$1 \circ A \leftrightarrow 0\ 0.5\ 0.8660$ (sine) $2 \circ A \leftrightarrow 1\ 0.8660\ 0.5$ (cosine) $3 \circ A \leftrightarrow 0\ 0.5774\ 1.7321$ (tangent)	$\left.\begin{array}{l}1 \circ F\\2 \circ F\\3 \circ F\end{array}\right\}$ F unrestricted
○	Inverse trigonometric: Result in radians		$\bar{}1 \circ D \leftrightarrow 0\ 0.4115\ 0.9273$ (inverse sine) $\bar{}2 \circ D \leftrightarrow 1.5708\ 1.1593\ 0.6435$ (inverse cosine) $\bar{}3 \circ D \leftrightarrow 0\ 0.3805\ 0.6747$ (inverse tangent)	$\bar{}1 \circ F$; $1 \geq |F|$ $\bar{}2 \circ F$; $1 \geq |F|$ $\bar{}3 \circ F$; F unrestricted
○	Unit circle (Pythagorean)		$4 \circ F \leftrightarrow (1+F*2)*0.5$ $0 \circ F \leftrightarrow (1-F*2)*0.5$ $\bar{}4 \circ F \leftrightarrow (\bar{}1+F*2)*0.5$	$4 \circ F$; F unrestricted $0 \circ F$; $1 \geq |F|$ $\bar{}4 \circ F$; $1 \leq |F|$
○	Hyperbolic		$5 \circ F \leftrightarrow 0.5 \times (*F) - *-F$ (hyperbolic sine) $6 \circ F \leftrightarrow 0.5 \times (*F) + *-F$ (hyperbolic cosine) $7 \circ F \leftrightarrow (5 \circ F) \div 6 \circ F$ (hyperbolic tangent)	$5 \circ F$ $6 \circ F$; F unrestricted $7 \circ F$
○	Inverse hyperbolic		$\bar{}5 \circ F \leftrightarrow$ Inv. hyper. sine of F $\bar{}6 \circ F \leftrightarrow$ Inv. hyper. cos of F $\bar{}7 \circ F \leftrightarrow$ Inv. hyper. tan of F	$\bar{}5 \circ F$; F unrestricted $\bar{}6 \circ F$; $1 \leq F$ $\bar{}7 \circ F$; $1 > |F|$

Scalar Functions / 147

hyperbolic functions are for the most part beyond the scope of this text. However, it is perhaps worth observing that the following identities can be derived.

$$\text{arcsinh } A \leftrightarrow \circledast A+(1+A*2)*0.5 \leftrightarrow \circledast A+4\circ A$$
$$\text{arccosh } A \leftrightarrow \circledast A+(\bar{\ }1+A*2)*0.5 \leftrightarrow \circledast A+\bar{\ }4\circ A$$
$$\text{arctanh } A \leftrightarrow 0.5\times\circledast(1+A)\div 1-A$$

Observe that the logarithm and square root of a negative number do not exist and therefore that the equivalent expressions confirm the previously stated domain restrictions.

4-21 Summary of Transcendental Functions

Table 4-4 gives a summary of the transcendental functions. Note the following: The dyadic ○ functions are unusual in the sense that the left-hand argument determines the function; the domain restrictions are quite varied and are important attributes of the functions. Also note that in the illustrations of the trigonometric functions the argument $A\leftarrow 0\ 0\ 0.1666\ 0.3333$ is intended to represent fractions of π; A is the vector $0,(\pi\div 6),(\pi\div 3)$. It is assumed you know the trigonometric functions for these values. Results for all the illustrations are given to only a few significant digits, to conserve space. Arguments of the trigonometric functions are in radians; results of the inverse trigonometric functions are in radians.

The dyadic ○ functions can be used in reduction. As an example

$$\circ / \ 2\ 2\ ,A$$

will give the cosine of the cosine of a scalar A. Each element of the argument, except the last one on the right, must be an integer from $\bar{\ }7$ to 7. Care must be exercised in observing domain restrictions.

4-22 Scalar Functions in the Inner and Outer Products

Sections 3-19 and 3-20 contain introductory descriptions of the outer and inner products. There, all the illustrations of these operators were in terms of the scalar functions + and ×. Having now introduced all the scalar functions, we can say that the *dyadic* form of any scalar function can be used with these operators.

CONCLUSION

The capability provided by the scalar functions is very fundamental to APL. Accordingly, the scalar functions must be learned very thoroughly by anyone wishing to attain proficiency in the language. Much proficiency will be attained through subsequent programming experiences, and to facilitate such learning concise tabulations of the various classes of scalar functions are included in this chapter. These tables constitute a summary of the chapter, and should be used freely for reference.

Although there are wide differences among the scalar functions with respect to the computations they carry out, they have three characteristics in common:

(a) When an argument is an array, a scalar function acts on each element of the array as if it were a scalar.

148 / Scalar Functions

    (b) The conditions for compatibility of shapes of arguments are the same for each dyadic scalar function.

    (c) The function symbol for each dyadic scalar function can be used with the reduction and outer and inner product operators.

Consideration of the floor, ceiling, and relational functions engenders an interest in the subtle effects produced by roundoff errors. The automatic inclusion of the comparison tolerance in the operation of these functions tends to suppress roundoff errors. While the comparison tolerance is very important, making these functions behave as expected most of the time, you must keep in mind that roundoff errors exist and that it is possible for an error to be so large as to override the comparison tolerance in certain cases.

Problems--Chapter 4

Comment: Each of the following problems can be programmed using nothing more than the material included through Chap. 4. This is mentioned because in some cases your first inclination may be to use techniques of branching or looping, as described in Chap. 5. These problems are designed to emphasize the imaginative use of arrays, so you should study a problem until you see how array concepts apply, and develop an algorithm accordingly. Also, be alert to possibilities for using defined functions developed in the text as subfunctions in your solutions.

4-1 Assume that the accompanying graph shows how a set of "raw scores" is to be converted to course grades.

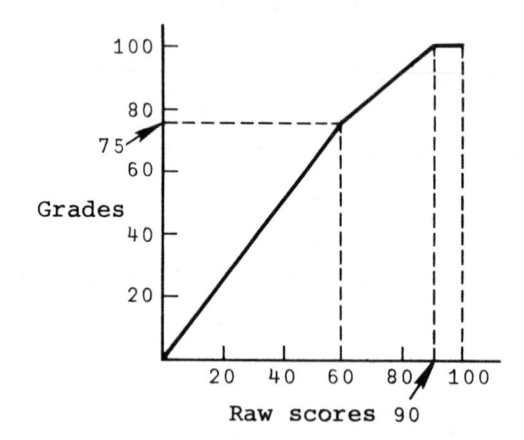

Construct a monadic function called *GRADE* which will take a vector of raw scores as its argument, and produce a corresponding vector of course grades as a returned value. Results are to be rounded to the nearest integer, in the usual manner.

4-2 Design two functions meeting the following specifications.
    (a) A monadic function named *MULT3*, to take an array argument of integers and return a value which has 1 for each integer in the input which is a multiple of 3, ¯1 for each integer of the input which is one less than a multiple of 3, 0 for each integer which is one greater than a multiple of 3.
    (b) A monadic function named *FRACTION*, to take a scalar or vector argument of numbers having fractional parts (such as 8.73 or ¯8.73) and return a value in which the integer part is removed (giving, respectively, 0.73 or ¯0.73 as the result in this example).

4-3   Construct a monadic function called *REPLY* which will take a character scalar or vector as its argument. The returned value is to be 1 if the argument is `'YES'`, ¯1 if the argument is `'NO'` and 0 for any other input. Note that it is not satisfactory merely to test the first two or three characters; `'YESTERDAY'` or `'NOT'` are to yield 0 as returned values.

4-4   Design a monadic function *TYPE* which will take an argument which is a scalar or array of either numerical or character type. The result is to be the printed word *NUMERICAL* if the argument is of numerical type, or the printed word *CHARACTER* if the argument is of character type.

4-5   Design a monadic function *CHARNUM* which will take as its argument an array of characters. These characters may be letters of the alphabet, numerals, or other characters such as spaces and punctuation marks. The function is to give a printed result, giving the number of letters and the number of single-digit numerals. For example,

```
      CHARNUM 'THERE ARE 35 MEN AND 41 WOMEN IN THE CLASS'
NUMBER OF LETTERS = 29
NUMBER OF NUMERALS=  4
```

4-6   Suppose you have an array of integers (positive, negative, or zero). You are to design a monadic function *ODDEVEN* which will take such an array as an argument and produce a printed result as illustrated in the example

```
      ODDEVEN ¯2 5 0 9 6 4 ¯3
NUMBER OF ODD NUMBERS =  3
NUMBER OF EVEN NUMBERS=  4
```

4-7   Suppose you have an array of numbers which you wish to analyze to determine how many are positive, how many are negative, and how many are zero. Write a monadic function *POSNEG* which will take such an array as an argument and print a result as illustrated in the example

```
      POSNEG 5.7 ¯3.4 0 4.3 ¯0.5 2.53 0
NUMBER OF POSITIVE NUMBERS =  3
NUMBER OF NEGATIVE NUMBERS =  2
NUMBER OF ZERO NUMBERS     =  2
```

4-8   You are to create a monadic function *NUMBDIGIT* which will take a numerical argument of nonnegative integers and return a value which is an array of the same shape as the argument such that each element is the number of digits required to write the corresponding element of the argument. For example

```
      NUMBDIGIT 34  1034637  4285  0
2  7  4  1
```

4-9   This problem is to compute the law of cosines for a triangle. It is to be done with a dyadic function giving a returned value. The left-hand argument is to be a two-element vector representing the lengths of two sides of a triangle, and the right-hand argument is to be the angle between them, in degrees. The result is to be the length of the third side. Call the function *LAWCOS*.

4-10 Design a monadic function *TRIANGLE* taking as its argument a vector of three numbers. The function is to determine whether those three numbers can be the sides of a triangle; if not, it is to return an empty vector; if so, it is to compute the three angles of the triangle. The result is to be returned as a 2 by 3 matrix: the lengths of the sides in the first row; opposite angles (in degrees) in the second row.

4-11 Suppose you are given a vector of mixed numbers such as 5.77 4.21 8.46. You are to define a dyadic function *HALFRND* which will take such a vector as an argument and yield an explicit result in which the elements of the vector are rounded to the nearest integer or integer plus one-half. For the example given above, the result would be 6 4 8.5. The criterion to be used for determining the result is the following (using *I* to represent an integer):

150 / Scalar Functions

> Make the result I if N is in the range $(I-0.25) \leq N < (I+0.25)$
> Make the result $I+0.5$ if N is in the range $(I+0.25) \leq N < (I+0.75)$

4-12 Suppose you are given an array of characters which can include numerals, such as: '*THE PRICE FOR 2 ITEMS IS 34.56, AND THE PRICE FOR 4 ITEMS IS 58.64*'. You are to design a monadic function *CONVNUM* which will take such an array as its argument and convert all the numerals to a numerical vector, as an explicit result. For example, if V is the vector given above, the function is to give

```
        CONVNUM V
2   34.56   4   58.64
```

The result is a numerical vector of four elements.

4-13 Define a monadic function which will take a character matrix as its argument, analyzing it to determine how many of each letter of the alphabet occur. The result is to be a printed matrix which will list the letters (vertically on left, with the numbers of their occurrences to the right. Call the function *LETTERCOUNT*.

4-14 You are given a character vector of words separated by one or more spaces. You are to design a monadic function *WORDMAT* to take such a vector as its argument and produce, as an explicit result, a matrix having one word in each line. The dimension of the horizontal axis is to equal the length of the longest word. Use the function *REMS* defined in example 4-5 as a subfunction.

4-15 Design a dyadic function *INTERSECT* which will find the point of intersection of two lines in the $x - y$ plane. The function is to be dyadic: the left-hand argument will be two sets of coordinate points which define the first line, and the right-hand argument will be a similar set of coordinates of two points defining the second line. Each of these input values will be a vector of four elements, for example 4 3 6 2 (meaning one point has coordinates $x = 4$, $y = 3$ and the second point has coordinates $x = 6$, $y = 2$). The result is to be a returned value, which will be an empty vector if the lines are parallel.

4-16 Design a dyadic function *ANGLE* which will find the angle of intersection between two straight lines in the $x - y$ plane. It is to be a dyadic function with arguments as defined in Prob. 4-15. The function will give a returned value, which will be an empty vector if the lines are parallel.

4-17 Design a dyadic function *DIST* giving a returned value, which will compute the distance in the $x - y$ plane of a specified point from any specified line (including one which is horizontal or vertical). The distance is to be measured perpendicularly from the point to the line. A vector of the x and y coordinates of the point will be the left-hand argument and the right-hand argument is to be a four element vector (the x and y coordinates of one point on the line and then the x and y coordinates of another point on the line).

4-18 Design a dyadic function *CENTER* which will locate the center and find the radius of a circle passing through three specified points in the $x - y$ plane. The argument on the left will be the three x coordinates of the points, and the argument on the right will be the corresponding y coordinates. The function is to give an empty vector as the returned value if the points are in a straight line. Otherwise, the returned value will be a three-element vector consisting of the radius, the x coordinate of the center, and the y coordinate of the center.

4-19 Suppose a character variable *NAMES* is a matrix of names, one name to each line. Also, let N be a character vector of one name which may or may not be in *NAMES*. You are to design a dyadic function *SEARCH* which will take N as a left-hand argument and *NAMES* as a right-hand argument. The explicit result is to be the row index number of the location of N in *NAMES*, if it can be found, or an empty vector if it cannot be found. Include the possibility that the number of characters in N might be less than the horizontal dimension of *NAMES*.

4-20 Imagine a set of points situated in a plane, specified in a polar coordinate system. The coordinates of these points can be stored in a matrix, with distances from the origin in the first row and angles in the second row. The

special case of a single point will have the distance from the origin as the
first element of a vector, and the angle as the second element. You are to design a monadic function *POLTOREC* which will take such an array as an argument and give an explicit result (of the same rank) which specifies the rectangular coordinates of the same points. If the result is a matrix, the x coordinates should be in the first row and the y coordinates in the second row. If the result is a vector, the x coordinate should be the first element, and the y coordinate the second. There are functions given in the examples in the text which are appropriate subfunctions for this problem.

4-21 Imagine a set of points in a plane, specified in a rectangular coordinate system. The coordinates of these points can be stored in a matrix, with the x coordinates in the first row and y coordinates in the second row. The special case of a single point will have the x coordinate as the first element of a vector and the y coordinate as the second element. You are to design a monadic function *RECTOPOL* which will take such an array as an argument and give an explicit result (of the same rank) which specifies the polar coordinates of the same points. If the result is a matrix, the first row should be the distances of the points from the origin and the second row should be the principal values of the angles (angles greater than $-\pi$ and less than or equal to π). If the result is a vector the first element should be distance from the origin. There are functions given in the examples in the text which are appropriate subfunctions for this problem.

4-22 Let *V* be a vector of numerical elements which are all different and arranged in increasing order. An example of *V* might be 3 4.5 7 10. Let *X* be a scalar, vector, or matrix in which each element is not smaller than the first element of *V* and not larger than the largest element in *V*. An example of *X* might be
6 3 10 4.2 9. For each element of *X*, let the words "lower index" refer to the index number in *V* (in origin 1) of the largest element in *V* which is not larger than that element of *X*. For the sample given above, the lower index numbers are 2 1 4 1 3. Design a dyadic function *LOWINDEX* which will take a vector such as *V* as its left-hand argument and a scalar or vector such as *X* as its right-hand argument. Its returned value should be the lower indices for values of *X* in *V*, as defined above. The shape of the returned value is to be the same as the shape of *X*.

4-23 Imagine a graph of values of some dependent mathematical variable y plotted against an independent variable x. Let *MF* be a two-rowed matrix which represents the relationship between y and x. The first row of *MF* will be sample values of x, in increasing order, and the second row will be corresponding values of y.
(a) Design a dyadic function *INTERP* which will take *MF* as its left-hand argument and a variable *X* (consisting of one or more values of x) as its right-hand argument. The explicit result is to be values of y corresponding to the elements of *X*, obtained by linear interpolation. Note that *X* can be a scalar or a vector. Assume all elements of *X* are within the range of values in *MF*[1;], but allow elements of *X* to be repeated, and in any order. An example is

```
      MF
1   3   8
2   6   4
      MF INTERP 2  4  2
4   5.6  4
```

If you have the function *LOWINDEX* described in Prob. 4-22, use it as a subfunction. Be sure *INTERP X* will work if element of *X* is the same as the last element of *MF*[1;].
(b) The specifications for *INTERP* given in (a) do not include the possibility that *X* can have elements outside the range of values in *MF*[1;]. Such inadmissible values cannot produce results. Create a modified version *MODINTERP* which takes the same arguments as *INTERP*, but will accept a right-hand argument *X* having inadmissible elements. The function is to remove these inadmissible elements and return a matrix in which the first row is the set of admissible elements of *X*, and the second row contains the corresponding interpolated results. Use *INTERP* as a subfunction.

4-24 The relationship between a dependent mathematical variable y and an independent variable x can be thought of as a graph. Suppose there is a collection of sample points on the x axis of such a graph arranged in increasing order, in the first row of a matrix MF. The values of x are not necessarily uniformly spaced. Also, let the corresponding values of y be in the second row of MF. Any two points on the x axis, within the range of values of x in the first row of MF, will form a vector X. You are to define a dyadic function $GRAPHAREA$ which will take MF as a left-hand argument and X as a right-hand argument. The explicit result is to be the area under the graph (in the usual sense) between the points given in X, if the elements in X are in increasing order. If the elements in X are in decreasing order, the result is to be the negative of the result that would be obtained if they were in increasing order. In computing the area, assume data points are joined by straight lines, and if elements of X lie between the data points in the first row of MF, use linear interpolations. Functions $INTERP$ described in Prob. 4-23 and $LOWINDEX$ described in Prob. 4-22 can be useful in this problem.

4-25 The government of a fictional country wants to use APL to compute income taxes. The tax will be graduated, and specified by a matrix such as

```
       RATE
1000   5000   10000
  10     18      30
```

The first row gives "break points" in incomes (in the monetary units of the country) and the second row gives percentage tax. The interpretation is as follows: There is no tax below 1000, from 1000 to 5000 the incremental tax is 10%, from 5000 to 10000 the incremental tax is 18%, and above 10000 it is 30%. The meaning of "incremental" is illustrated by the following examples.

Income	Computation of tax (in APL notation)
3000	0.10×3000-1000
8000	(0.10×5000-1000)+0.18×8000-5000
13000	(0.10×5000-1000)+(0.18×10000-5000)+0.30×13000-10000

You are to design a dyadic function TAX which will take a matrix such as $RATES$ on the left and a vector of incomes for individuals on the right. The explicit result is to be a vector of the corresponding taxes for those individuals. The matrix $RATES$ given above is merely illustrative; it can have any number of columns and entries that are different from the example. However, the amounts in the first row must be increasing from left to right.

4-26 For this problem it is necessary for you to know a few basic facts about probability. For a random experiment, such as tossing a coin or rolling a die, there are various possible outcomes. A probability, represented by a number between 0 and 1, is associated with each outcome (the outcome "3" when rolling a die has a probability 1÷6). For two random experiments (not necessarily the same) for which the outcome of one experiment *does not* affect the outcome of the other, the probability of a given outcome from one experiment and a given outcome from the other *both* occurring is the product of the probabilities of the two outcomes. Also, if each outcome *prevents* the occurrence of the other, the probability that *either* outcome will be obtained is the sum of the probabilities of the individual outcomes. Finally, if an outcome has the probability p, the probability of not obtaining that outcome is $1 - p$.
(a) You are to design a monadic function $TOSS$ which will take a positive integer (say N) as its argument. The function is to return a vector, for N tosses of a coin, in which successive elements are the probabilities that the number of heads obtained will be 0, 1, 2, etc. up to N. Note that the number of ways H heads can be obtained in N tosses is the number of combinations of N things taken H at a time.
(b) Create a dyadic function $PTOSS$ which will take a positive integer (say N) as its right-hand argument and a positive integer D less than or equal to $\lfloor N \div 2$ as its left-hand argument. The function is to return the probability that the number of heads received in N tosses will be between $(\lfloor N \div 2) - D$ and $(\lceil N \div 2) + D$, inclusive. Thus,

2 $PTOSS$ 40

will give the probability of obtaining 18, 19, 20, 21, or 22 heads. The result is one number. Use *TOSS* as a subfunction.

4-27 This problem depends on the facts about probabilities given in the introductory paragraph of Prob. 4-26. You should read that paragraph before proceeding. Consider a multiple-choice examination consisting of Q questions, each question having C choices. You are to design a dyadic function *TESTPROB* which will take C as the left-hand argument and Q as the right-hand argument. Assume Q is an even number. The function is to return the probability of answering half the questions correctly by making random guesses. Note that the number of ways R questions can be right in a test of Q questions equals the number of combinations of Q things taken R at a time. Experiment with the function, to obtain an impression of how this probability varies with the length of the test and the number of choices.

4-28 Write a dyadic function *MEMB* which will simulate the primitive function membership, for vector arguments. Note: if you write this in a certain way it will also work for arguments of ranks higher than 1, but understanding how this is possible involves concepts from Chap. 6.

4-29 For this problem it is assumed you know how to compute a bowling score. Write a monadic function *BOWL* that will take as its argument a vector of the numbers of pins knocked down on successive rolls for a complete game. The length of the vector will be influenced by the number of strikes, since there is only one roll in any frame having a strike. Part of the algorithm involves determining how to pair the elements of the vector so that pairs will correspond to the individual frames. This is necessary in order to be able to locate spares. The returned value is to be the score for the game.

Chapter 5

BRANCHING AND ITERATION

INTRODUCTION

All programs considered up to this point have the property that the computer executes the statements in the order of their line numbers. However, as was shown in Chap. 1, there are algorithms which require different orders of execution under different circumstances. An iterative process is an important example: a certain sequence of statements is executed repeatedly until a prescribed stopping criterion has been met (such as attainment of a desired accuracy), and then the operation proceeds to a different set of statements, or stops. In order to execute program steps out of sequence it is necessary to have a computer instruction which will cause a jump from one line to some line other than the next one. An instruction which accomplishes the jump is called a *branching* statement.

There are two kinds of branching operations: *unconditional* branching, which always causes a jump to the same line, and *conditional* branching for which a control variable determines which line is executed next. The diamond-shaped boxes in the flow charts in Chap. 1 symbolize conditional branches.

The present chapter begins with a treatment of techniques for writing statements which produce branching. Later, the discussion moves on to a consideration of iterative processes, for which branching is an essential ingredient. Also, the basic concepts of "structured programming" are introduced, through the development of two control structures which provide the equivalent of branching without explicit branching statements. These are realizations of the *IF-THEN-ELSE* and *FOR-UNTIL-DO* statements employed in some of the algorithms in Chap. 1.

Branching is essential to many programming tasks, but should be used only when necessary. In APL, many problems that seem at first appraisal to require branching can be done without it by virtue of the wide variety of computations and manipulations that can be done with arrays. You should keep this thought in mind when planning an algorithm.

Beginning with this chapter, the exercise problems in the margin are discontinued, on the assumption that your knowledge is sufficiently good at this point as to not require this facility for page by page checking of your progress. You are encouraged to generate your own questions, and also refer to the problems at the end of the chapter. Some of those problems are arranged according to related section numbers in the text, to facilitate reference to them.

5-1 Unconditional Branching

The basic statement for branching is the right-pointing arrow →, with a value on the right which is the number of the next line to be executed. We shall call this the *target* line. The following program is contrived to illustrate branching (it has no other use).

```
      ∇ SHOWBRANCH
[1]   'ONE'
[2]   →5
[3]   'THREE'
[4]   →7
[5]   'TWO'
[6]   →3
[7]   'FOUR' ∇

      SHOWBRANCH
ONE
TWO
THREE
FOUR
```

This "useless" function serves to show that →5 on line [2] causes operation to jump to line [5], etc. In reality, this demonstration program is written in poor style. A much better version is

```
      ∇ SHOWBRANCH
[1]   'ONE'
[2]   →A
[3]   X:'THREE'
[4]   →RT
[5]   A:'TWO'
[6]   →X
[7]   RT:'FOUR' ∇
```

In a display, statements having line labels are displayed one position to the left of the normal position. However, when the function is created, they can be in the normal position.

Each of the variables A, RT, and X is a local variable called a *line label*. When a name is used in this way (placed immediately to the right of a line number and followed by a colon) the computer automatically makes it a local variable and assigns to it the corresponding line number. Line labels should *not* be listed in the header line. Any name can be used as a line label so long as it is not the same as another local variable used by the function or a global variable.

Consider label A. Since it is on line [5], A will have the value 5. Therefore, →A on line [2] is equivalent to →5. The reason for saying the second program is better than the first is evident when we consider the possibility of editing at some future time. Suppose line [1] is removed by editing, causing each line number to decrease by one. In the first version each of the branch statements must also be changed, because the number of each target line will decrease by one. In the second version, the values of the line labels will always be the same as their corresponding line numbers, even when the line numbers change.

A line label is always a scalar. However, → can have a vector on its right; in that case all elements except the first are ignored. That is, →5 9 4 is exactly the same as →5.

The value to the right of the branch arrow can be an empty vector. In that case the branch is to "nothing" (not zero). Accordingly, there is no branching and progress is to the line immediately following.

156 / Branching and Iteration

The branch statement

$\rightarrow 0$

will cause "exiting" from the program, because no statement line is ever numbered 0. (Any integer not a line number can also be used for the same purpose.)

5-2 Conditional Branching

Consider the function

```
      ∇ Z←A COMPARE B
[1]   Z←∧/,A=B ∇
```

which will return the value 1 if the arguments are identical arrays, and zero if they are of the same shape but not otherwise identical. If the arguments are of different shapes (unless one of them is a single element) the $A=B$ operation is impossible; there will be an error report and a suspension.

Suppose we want to make this function "suspension proof." If the arguments are not compatible, the line involving $A=B$ is to be skipped, and the returned value is to be an empty vector (implying no result). Also, in this case the function is to print a suitable explanatory message. A conditional branch is needed, to skip ∧/,A=B if the arguments are not compatible. A suitable function is

```
       ∇ Z←A COMPARE1 B;C
[1]    C←(ρρA)≠ρρB
[2]    →C/L1
[3]    C←∨/(ρA)≠ρB
[4]    →C/L2
[5]    Z←∧/,A=B
[6]    →0
[7]    L1:'RANKS DIFFER'
[8]    →L3
[9]    L2:'SHAPES DIFFER'
[10]   L3:Z←ι0 ∇
```

The control variable C is specified on line [1]: the value is 1 if the ranks are different, 0 if they are the same. Referring to line [2], $L1$ is a line label having the value 7, and 1/7 is the one-element vector 7, and 0/7 is an empty vector. Thus, if C is 1, there is branching from line [1] to line [7]; if C is 0, computation proceeds to line [3]. Note that there is an unconditional branch on line [8], so the assignment $Z←ι0$ will be made.

On line [3] the control variable takes on a new meaning: it is 1 if the shapes are different and 0 if the shapes are the same. Line [4] is a conditional branch, similar to line [2] except that the target line is the one with the label $L2$.

This program illustrates the use of a Boolean control variable, and a branch which occurs only if the control value is 1. The possibility exists that both arguments can be scalars, and so we should check whether the function will work properly for that case. If A and B are scalars, line [1] will be 0≠0, which is correct. On line [3], (ρA)≠ρB yields an empty vector, and ∨/ι0 yields 0. Thus, this line also works correctly, and we conclude that the function accepts scalar arguments.

Some of the steps of this function can be combined, to give the shorter form

```
        ∇ Z←A COMPARE2 B
[1]     →((⍴⍴A)≠⍴⍴B)/L1
[2]     →(∨/(⍴A)≠⍴B)/L2
[3]     Z←∧/,A=B
[4]     →0
[5]     L1:'RANKS DIFFER'
[6]     →L3
[7]     L2:'SHAPES DIFFER'
[8]     L3:Z←⍳0 ∇
```

There are many other ways to produce the equivalent of $C/L1$. A few of them are: $L1×⍳C$ (in origin 1), $C⍴L1$, and $C↑L1$.

There is some advantage to making a general purpose defined function for branching, such as

```
        ∇ Z←A IF B
[1]     Z←B/A ∇
```

With this, the first two lines of COMPARE2 would be

```
[1]     →L1 IF (⍴⍴A)≠⍴⍴B
[2]     →L2 IF ∨/(⍴A)≠⍴B
```

This allows a branching statement to be written with a natural syntax, namely: go (somewhere) if (something is true). It also allows the target line labels to be located on the left, where they are easily scanned by the eye, when checking a program.

The conditional branching just described is in accordance with a two-valued logic: namely, branch to a specified target, or not branch. Branching can also be in accordance with an n-valued control variable, say one that can have values 0, 1, 2. In this case, 0 will mean no branch, 1 will mean go to one particular target line, 2 will mean go to a different target line. A version of COMPARE which uses a 3-valued control variable is (in origin 1)

```
        ∇ Z←A COMPARE3 B;C;RB;RNE;SNE
[1]     RNE←(⍴⍴A)≠RB←⍴⍴B
[2]     SNE←(~RNE)∧∨/(RB↑⍴A)≠RB↑⍴B
[3]     C←RNE+2×SNE
[4]     →(C=⍳2)/L1,L2
[5]     Z←∧/,A=B
[6]     →0
[7]     L1:'RANKS DIFFER'
[8]     →L3
[9]     L2:'SHAPES DIFFER'
[10]    L3:Z←⍳0 ∇
```

In line [1], RNE is 1 if the ranks are not equal; and in line [2], SNE is 1 if the ranks are equal and the shapes are not equal. Note that $(RB↑⍴A)≠RB↑⍴B$ is used instead of $(⍴A)≠⍴B$ because $⍴A$ and $⍴B$ may be of different lengths (when the ranks of A and B are the same, $RB↑$ has no effect). It is evident that C has the possible values:

  0   when the ranks and shapes are the same,
  1   when the ranks are different,
  2   when the ranks are the same and the shapes are different.

The left-hand argument of compression in line [4] is 0 0 if C is 0, 1 0 if C is 1, and 0 1 if C is 2. Thus, there is no branching if C is 0; and the target lines are, respectively, $L1$ or $L2$, for C equal to 1 or 2.

158 / Branching and Iteration

A defined function (for origin 1)*

```
     ∇ Z←A WHEN B
[1]  Z←(B=⍳⍴A)/A ∇
```

can be used to provide branching under multivalued control. With this, line [4] of the previous function would be

[4]   →(L1,L2) WHEN C

Example 5-1

Let us consider the quadratic equation (in conventional notation)

$$Ax^2 + Bx + C = 0$$

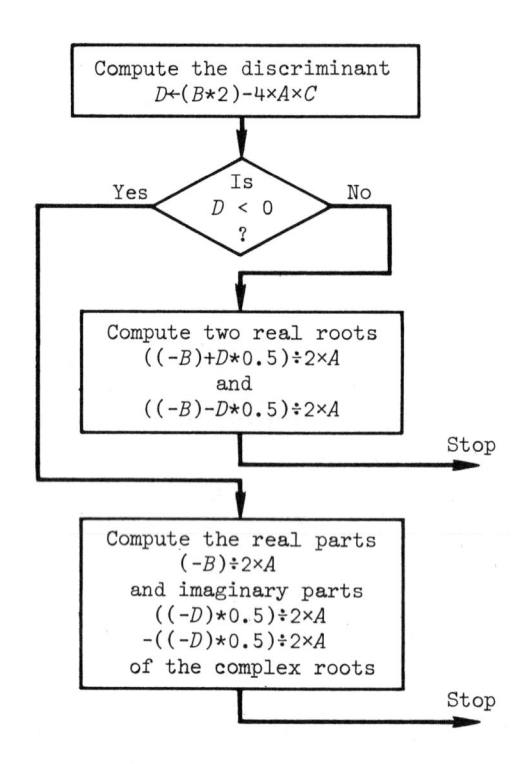

Figure 5-1 Flow chart for finding roots of a quadratic equation.

The quadratic formula leads to the algorithm described by the flow chart in Fig. 5-1. We shall translate this into a monadic function $QUAD$ which will take a vector of the coefficients (in the order A,B,C) as its argument. If the roots are real, they are to be returned as a two-element vector; if they are imaginary, they are to be returned

---

*The function $WHEN$ given in the text is sensitive to origin. A function that is independent of origin, and equivalent in a branching statement, is

```
     ∇ Z←A WHEN B
[1]  Z←⌽B↑A ∇
```

This function differs from the one in the text in that it returns a vector of more than one element if the right-hand argument is 2 or greater. The first of these elements is the one sensed by the branching arrow.

as a two-by-two matrix, with real parts in the first column and imaginary parts in the second column. It is convenient to use subfunctions QR and QC to find the real and complex roots, respectively. Each will be dyadic, taking the vector (A,B) as the left-hand argument and the square root of the *absolute value* of the discriminant as its right-hand argument. These functions can be written, in accordance with the directions in the flow chart, as

```
      ∇ R←G QR H
[1]   R←((-¯1↑G)+ 1 ¯1 ×H)÷2×1↑G ∇

      ∇ R←G QC H
[1]   R←((2ρ-¯1↑G),[1.5] 1 ¯1 ×H)÷2×1↑G ∇
```

(Note: In QC, $G[2]$ could have been used instead of $2\rho-\bar{1}\uparrow G$ because a scalar is permitted as an argument of laminate.)

The required function can now be written (in origin 1)

```
      ∇ R←QUAD P;D;DS
[1]   DS←(|D←(P[2]*2)-4××/P[1 3])*0.5
[2]   →IM IF D<0
[3]   R←(2↑P)QR DS
[4]   →0
[5]   IM:R←(2↑P)QC DS ∇
```

5-3 A Control Structure Equivalent of Conditional Branching

The function $QUAD$ described in example 5-1 can be realized without explicit branch statements by using the function execute, and indexing a character matrix of two rows, having the names QR and QC in the rows. This version is (in origin 1)

```
      ∇ R←QUAD1 P;M;D;DS
[1]   DS←(|D←(P[2]*2)-4××/P[1 3])*0.5
[2]   M←'QR',[0.5]'QC'
[3]   R←⍎'(2↑P)',M[1+D<0;],' DS' ∇
```

In this, QR and QC are the names of the subfunctions defined in example 5-1.

This is a quite satisfactory way to program this algorithm, but our objective is to convert this to the *IF-THEN-ELSE* from given in Chap. 1. The set of general purpose functions

```
      ∇ Z←IF A
[1]   Z←A ∇

      ∇ Z←A THEN B
[1]   Z←,B[1+⍎A;] ∇

      ∇ Z←A ELSE B;F
[1]   F←(ρ,A)⌈ρ,B
[2]   Z←(F↑B),[0.5]F↑A ∇
```

can be used in this way. (Note: underlines are used on $\underline{IF}$ to avoid conflict with the earlier function IF.) To see how they work, let us analyze

```
      ∇ R←QUAD2 P;D;DS
[1]   DS←(|D←(P[2]*2)-4××/P[1 3])*0.5
[2]   R←⍎IF 'D<0' THEN '(2↑P)QC DS' ELSE '(2↑P)QR DS' ∇
```

In line [2], '(2↑P)QC DS' ELSE '(2↑P)QR DS' will be executed first. From the

160 / Branching and Iteration

definition of *ELSE*, it is seen that this execution of *ELSE* returns the character matrix

```
(2↑P)QR DS
(2↑P)QC DS
```

which is therefore the right-hand argument of *THEN*. The role played by *THEN* is to index the matrix described above, with the row index computed from 1+⍕'D<0'. Finally, *IF* plays no role other than to transmit the result of *THEN*. *IF* is used merely to make the entire statement similar to a statement in English. *IF* returns a character vector, so ⍎ is required on line [2] of *QUAD2*.

The use of an underline on the input and output variables of *THEN* avoids possible conflicts with variables which are global to *THEN*. To explain, suppose the character value of *A* or *B* includes another *A* or *B* representing a global variable. The global value, which is required for *THEN* to operate correctly, will not be available within *THEN*. Such conflicts can be avoided by not using underlines on global variables.

The *IF-THEN-ELSE* structure can be used to provide multivalued control, by using the syntax *IF-THEN-ELSE-IF-THEN-ELSE* to whatever extent required. For example, suppose in the function for roots of a quadratic equation, we want to return an empty vector if the argument does not have three elements. This is handled by

Example 5-2

```
       ∇ R←QUAD3 P;D;DS
[1]    DS←(|D←((1↑¯2↑P)*2)-4××/2↑¯1⌽P←,P)*0.5
[2]    R←⍎IF '3≠⍴P' THEN '⍳0' ELSE IF 'D<0' THEN '(2↑P)QC DS' ELSE '(2↑P)QR DS' ∇
```

5-4 Program Loop

It frequently happens that a programming task requires the repeated execution of a certain number of steps. Two illustrations were given in Chap. 1. Such situations are handled by branching from the last of these steps back to the first, forming what is called a *loop*. The inclusion of a conditional branch which will stop the looping process at an appropriate time is essential. The conditional branch can be at the end of the loop, or at the beginning. Both possibilities are portrayed in Fig. 5-2. In each of these figures, the box labeled "Loop statements" represents one or a sequence of statements. The boxes labeled "Main program" refer to the program in which the loop is imbedded. The first "Main program" box normally includes the initialization of variables used in the loop. In cases where the loop is at the end of the program, the last box labeled "Main program" will not exist.

For most algorithms requiring a loop, either style can be used. However, sometimes we want a program that will work on degenerate cases for which no execution of the loop is wanted. The style shown in Fig. 5-2b handles such cases, because the test occurs first.

For some loops, the test for completion depends on a count of whether the loop has been executed a prescribed number of times, for others a test of accuracy of an approximate result is the criterion for completion. We shall illustrate both.

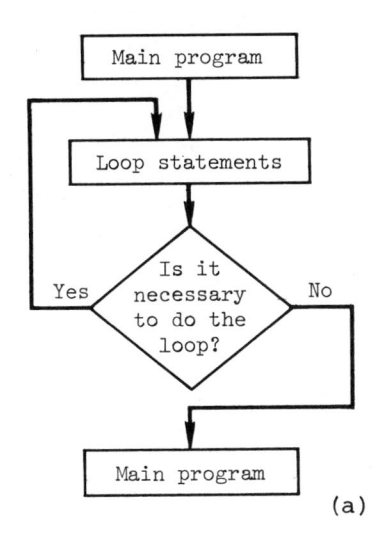

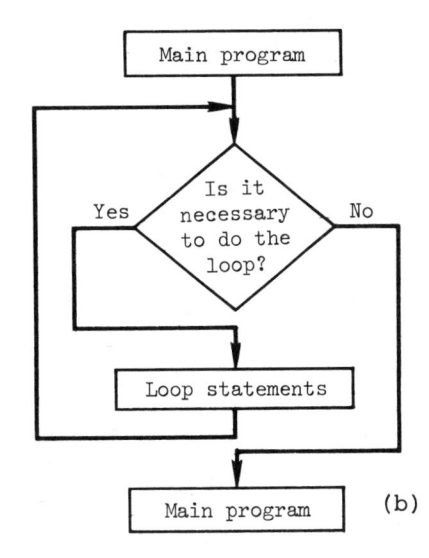

Figure 5-2 Two basic styles for a program loop.

5-5 Using a Loop to Evaluate a Polynomial

A method of evaluating a polynomial, based on array concepts, was given in Sec. 3-22. That method indicates that in APL the evaluation of a polynomial does not inherently require a loop. However, a loop-based solution is of pedagogical interest and also produces a program that is less subject to roundoff error in certain exceptional cases.*

As in Sec. 3-22, let C be the vector of coefficients of a polynomial in X, in the order of increasing powers of X. To consider a specific example, suppose we have

$C \leftarrow 5 \quad 3 \quad ^-4 \quad 2$

representing (in conventional notation)

$5 + 3X - 4X^2 + 2X^3$

Observe that this can also be written (again in conventional notation)

$5 + X(3+X(^-4+2X))$

The computations implied by this form can be represented in APL notation by the series of steps

$P \leftarrow 2$
$P \leftarrow ^-4 + X \times P$
$P \leftarrow 3 + X \times P$
$P \leftarrow 5 + X \times P$

---

*The method of evaluating a polynomial presented here can be done without a program loop, by using the primitive function *decode* described in Chap. 6. The loop is a "built in" part of that primitive.

162 / Branching and Iteration

The first of the above steps is $P \leftarrow C[\rho C]$, and the others are of the form

$P \leftarrow C[I] + X \times P$

where in this case I is successively 3, 2, 1 (in origin 1). This series of steps implies a program with a loop, as illustrated by the function $LOOPPOLY$ shown below. This function takes the vector of coefficients as its left-hand agrument, and the value of X as the right-hand argument.

```
      ∇ P←C LOOPPOLY X;I
[1]     P←C[I←ρC]
[2]   L:P←C[I←I-1]+X×P
[3]    →L IF 1<I ∇
```

This function will work if the right-hand argument is an array of any rank. The looping process stops when all elements of C have been indexed. This program is an example of the algorithm in Fig. 5-2a. Suppose we want the program to accept the degenerate polynomial consisting of a single number (the constant term). Such a "polynomial" is independent of X; the result is the constant term, for all values of X. Line [1] can be made to work if C is a scalar by first replacing C by $C \leftarrow ,C$. However, $C[I \leftarrow I-1]$ in the next line will yield $INDEX\ ERROR$. A program patterned after Fig. 5-2b, which will work for this special case, is

```
      ∇ P←C LOOPPOLY1 X;I
[1]    C←,C
[2]    P←C[I←ρC]
[3]  M:→0 IF 2>I
[4]    P←C[I←I-1]+X×P
[5]   →M ∇
```

Both of the functions given above work only in origin 1. A version which is independent of origin is

```
      ∇ P←C LOOPPOLY2 X
[1]    P←¯1↑C
[2]  M:→0 IF 1>ρC←¯1↓C
[3]    P←(¯1↑C)+X×P
[4]   →M ∇
```

Here, the stop occurs on line [2] when C is reduced to an empty vector.

These are examples where the number of times a loop is executed depends on a parameter of the data (the number of elements in C), not the accuracy of an answer.

5-6 Nested Loops

A program loop can be incorporated within another loop. To illustrate, suppose we want to evaluate a sequence of polynomials, of successively higher degree, derived from one set of coefficients. That is, if we have a vector C, we want to evaluate the polynomials for which the coefficients are

```
    C[1 2]            1st degree
    C[1 2 3]          2nd degree
    C[1 2 3 4]        3rd degree
    up to
    C                 degree ¯1+ρC
```

This can be done in a variety of ways. One program is (in origin 1)

```
      ∇ P←C MANYPOLY X;R;I;K
[1]   P←ρK←1
[2]   M:R←C[I←K←K+1]
[3]   L:R←C[I←I-1]+X×R
[4]   →L IF 1<I
[5]   P←P,R
[6]   →M IF K<ρC ∇
```
} loop 1 } loop 2

Loop 1 is said to be *nested* within loop 2. There are two "counting" variables: K for loop 1 and I for loop 2. Note that K is initialized only once, on line [1], but that I is initialized once for each value of K, on line [2]. Also, observe the initialization of P as an empty vector, and the building up of a vector of results on line [5]. This program illustrates that counting in a loop can be either up or down. I counts down but K counts up. A program equivalent to the above but more consistent with the nature of APL (assuming the previous LOOPPOLY exists) is

```
      ∇ P←C MANYPOLY1 X;K
[1]   P←ρK←1
[2]   L:P←P,((K←K+1)↑C) LOOPPOLY X
[3]   →L IF K<ρC ∇
```

In this case the nested loops are not visible, because one of the loops is in LOOPPOLY. This program is independent of the origin.

5-7 Successive Approximations

We shall now consider the use of a loop to carry out an iterative process for computing an answer by successive approximations. The problem relating to a spherical tank, described in Sec. 1-10, is used as an example (reference to that section is advised). Given a spherical tank of radius R, we are to find the height of water H to have a prescribed volume V.

To review the problem, the volume for a given height is (in conventional notation)

$$V = \pi H^2 (R - \frac{H}{3}) \qquad \text{valid for } H \text{ in the range from 0 to } 2 \times R$$

With V and R specified, this is a cubic equation in H. For positive V and R the equation has three solutions, but we are only interested in the physically meaningful one between 0 and $2 \times R$.

The method given in Sec. 1-10 is to introduce an auxiliary variable W, giving a pair of equations (in conventional notation)

$$W = H^2 \qquad (1)$$

$$W = \frac{V}{\pi(R - \frac{H}{3})} \qquad (2)$$

We are to obtain values for W and H which simultaneously satisfy both of these equations. The method of successive approximations illustrated in Fig. 5-3 (a repetition of Fig. 1-5) is to be used.

164 / Branching and Iteration

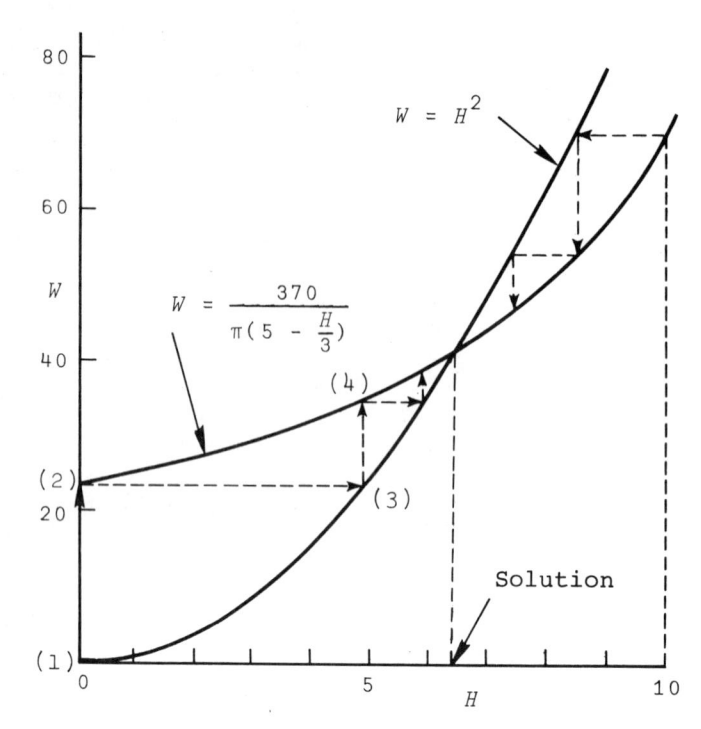

Figure 5-3 Iterative solution for two nonlinear relationships.

From here on we shall use APL notation. Assume a guess is made for H, say at point 1 on the H axis of Fig. 5-3. The APL statement

```
W←V÷○R-H÷3     H at point 1
```

is derived from Eq. (2) above and will produce W at point 2. Then, using this W in Eq. (1),

```
H←W*0.5
```

yields H at point 3. Then, H at point 3 can be a new starting point for the same process. It is intuitively evident from the figure that a sequence of values of H computed in this way approaches the value where the curves cross. The process is said to *converge* to a solution.

In the pair of steps

```
W←V÷○R-H÷3
H←W*0.5
```

the W is really superfluous. The two statements can be combined, giving

```
H←(V÷○R-H÷3)*0.5
```

As long as H on the right of ← is in the interval between 0 and $2\times R$ this statement will assign a new value to H which is closer to the solution than the previous one. This statement can be used repeatedly until adequate accuracy has been attained.

Let us write a program based on Fig. 5-2a. Clearly the line given above is the body of the loop. The preliminary "Main program" is the initialization $H←0$, and the specification of an error tolerance to be used in the test for completion. An arbitrary choice is made that the error in volume shall be less than 0.00001 times the volume of the sphere.

The function is to be dyadic, taking the radius of the sphere as the left-hand argument and the required volume as the right-hand argument. A possible definition is

```
      ∇ H←R TANK V;T
[1]   T←0.00001×○4×(R*3)÷3
[2]   H←0
[3]   L1:H←(V÷○R-H÷3)*0.5
[4]   →L1 IF T<V-H×H×○R-H÷3 ∇
```

Note the use of local variable T in the test for completion. By giving this value the name T, that name can be used in line [4] in lieu of repeated computation of its value.

There is a slight waste of computing time in the program above, to the extent that ○R-H÷3 is computed twice for each execution of the loop. This disadvantage can be overcome by assigning ○R-H÷3 to a name, as in the revised version

```
      ∇ H←R TANK1 V;T;M
[1]   T←0.00001×○4×(R*3)÷3
[2]   M←○R
[3]   L1:H←(V÷M)*0.5
[4]   →L1 IF T<V-H×H×M←○R-H÷3 ∇
```

Because the first use of M in the loop, on line [3], occurs prior to the specification of M on line [4], the initialization of M on line [2] is necessary. It is wise when writing a loop to remove redundant computing because there is the possibility that the loop may be executed many times for one execution of the function.

There are many other algorithms for solving problems by computing successive approximations. Such algorithms form a large part of the methodology of computing. The purpose here is to show one example where a looping process terminates after an answer meets a specified condition of accuracy.

The computation carried out by a program such as *TANK* is called an *iterative* process, and each execution of the loop is called an *iteration*. The number of iterations required to reach a solution to a specified degree of accuracy may depend on the solution being sought. For example,

```
      5 TANK 10
0.82063
```

converges in 3 iterations, but

```
      5 TANK 520
9.5130
```

requires 55 iterations. The first example may be said to converge rapidly, the second one slowly.

This observed difference in the rate of convergence for small and large V is worthy of attention. It illustrates the importance, when programming a loop, of being alert to possible modifications of the algorithm that will improve the rate of convergence. The examples given above suggest that the number of iterations required increases with the required volume. Accordingly, it is an improvement if we arrange the initialization so that the loop computes the height of the water *or* the airspace, whichever is smaller. If the height of the airspace is computed, it can be subtracted from the diameter, to give the answer. A modified function which does this is

166 / Branching and Iteration

Example 5-3

```
        ∇ H←R TANKM V;T;B;M
[1]     T←0.00001×○4×(R*3)÷3
[2]     V←V⌊B←(○4×(R*3)÷3)-V
[3]     M←○R
[4]     L1:H←(V÷M)*0.5
[5]     →L1 IF T<V-H×H×M←○R-H÷3
[6]     H←|H-(B=V)×R+R  ∇
```

5-8 Comment about Convergence

In writing an algorithm for computation by successive approximations, sometimes it is necessary to make a judicious choice to ensure convergence. When, as in the case of *TANK*, the problem can be formulated as a search for the point where two curves cross, the attainment of convergence depends on which curve is chosen as the starting point. For a general case the two possibilities are shown in Fig. 5-4. For the indicated starting value of X, if the first point is chosen on curve 1, the process will converge; if it is chosen on curve 2, the process will diverge (not converge). The proper choice was made in the algorithm for *TANK*. It is not necessarily true that any iterative process you might program will converge to a solution.

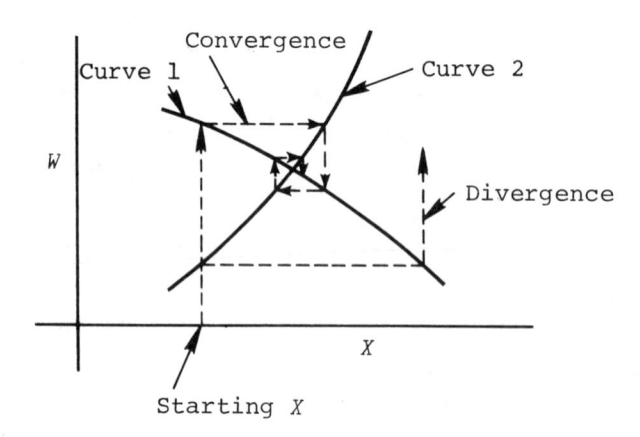

Figure 5-4 Convergence and nonconvergence of an iterative process.

A thorough consideration of the question of convergence of iterative processes is beyond the scope of this text. At this point it is sufficient for you to know that it is possible to program divergent processes, so you will be alert to the problem if you should accidentally do so. If you program a loop which is supposed to find a solution by successive approximations, and are not sure it will converge, it is wise to include a stop after some reasonable number of iterations (say 20). Otherwise, you may execute an "infinite loop"; a process that never stops. If you do not use such a precaution and do not obtain a completion of execution in a reasonable interval of time, interrupt the execution manually (see Appendix 6).

5-9 A Control Structure Equivalent to a Loop

In this section we shall discuss some possible ways to program a loop using the *FOR-UNTIL-DO* syntax described in Chap. 1. To consider the case of a polynomial, we begin with an example of the desired syntax, namely

```
      ∇ Z←P LOOPPOLY3 X;I
[1]   FOR 'Z←¯1↑P:I←⍴P' UNTIL 'I=1' DO 'Z←P[I←I-1]+X×Z' ∇
```

and then define *FOR*, *UNTIL*, and *DO* so as to make this possible. The expression in quotes between *FOR* and *UNTIL* contains two initialization statements, separated by a colon. The functions are to be designed so that in general there can be any number of initialization statements in this expression. The expression in quotes between *UNTIL* and *DO* is the test statement. The loop statement, to the right of *DO*, is to be executed until the test statement is true. Since these are to be general purpose functions, we shall make them independent of the index origin.

We shall construct *UNTIL* and *DO* so as to produce a character matrix in which the initialization statements form the first row, the test statement the second row, and the loop statement the third row. These operations are accomplished by simple vector and matrix manipulations. Two versions are given for each function, as follows:

```
      ∇ Z←A DO B                                    ∇ Z←A DO B
[1]   M←(⍴,A)⌈⍴,B                         or   [1]  M←(⍴,A)⌈⍴,B
[2]   Z←(2,M)⍴(M↑A),M↑B ∇                      [2]  Z←(M↑A),[¯0.5+⎕IO] M↑B ∇

      ∇ Z←A UNTIL B                                 ∇ Z←A UNTIL B
[1]   M←(⍴,A)⌈¯1↑⍴B                       or   [1]  M←(⍴,A)⌈¯1↑⍴B
[2]   Z←(3,M)⍴(M↑A),,(2,M)↑B ∇                 [2]  Z←(M↑A),[⎕IO] (2,M)↑B ∇
```

The versions on the left use primitive functions which are inherently independent of the origin. The versions on the right employ ⎕IO to provide that independence (?1 can be used in place of ⎕IO).

For the example *LOOPPOLY3* given above, the explicit result from *UNTIL* (and therefore the argument of *FOR*) will be the character matrix

```
Z←¯1↑P:I←⍴P
I=1
Z←P[I←I-1]+X×Z
```

A possible realization of *FOR*, which will carry out the initializations and form the loop, is

```
      ∇ FOR A;B;C
[1]   B←, 1 0 0 ≠A
[2]   L1:C←(B⍳':')-⎕IO
[3]   ⍎C↑B
[4]   →(0≠⍴B←(C+1)↓B)/L1
[5]   C←, 0 1 0 ≠A
[6]   B←, 0 0 1 ≠A
[7]   L2:⍎B
[8]   →(~⍎C)/L2
```

In this function, lines [2], [3], and [4] form a loop which executes the initialization statements sequentially, beginning with the one on the left. On lines [5] and [6], *C* and *B* are, respectively, assigned the character vector representations of the test statement and the loop statement. These statements are then executed in the loop formed by lines [7] and [8].

The function *FOR* will not work properly if any of the names for variables used in the initialization, test, and loop statements are the same as names of local variables in *FOR*. On the assumption that underlined names will not be used in these statements, the local variables in *FOR* have underlined names.

168 / Branching and Iteration

You will note that the structure described above cannot produce a loop having more than one statement line. If more than one statement line is required, the statements can be put in a niladic function whose name is used on the right of *DO*.

Example 5-4

A function for the tank problem can now be written as follows:

```
     ∇ H←R TANK1A V;M;T
[1]  FOR 'M←OR:T←1E¯5×○4×(R*3)÷3' UNTIL 'T>V-H×H×M←OR-H÷3' DO 'H←(V÷M)*0.5' ∇
```

The *FOR-UNTIL-DO* structure is a realization of a loop in the form of Fig. 5-2a. The word "until" implies execution *until* the stated condition is satisfied. For Fig. 5-2b, the pertinent word is "while." The loop will be executed *while* the stated condition is satisfied. A change to this structure is possible if the name of *UNTIL* is changed to *WHILE*, and *FOR* is changed to

```
     ∇ FOR A;B;C
[1]  B←, 1 0 0 ≠A
[2]  L1:C←(Bι':')-⎕IO
[3]  ⍎C↑B
[4]  →(0≠⍴B←(C+1)↓B)/L1
[5]  C←, 0 1 0 ≠A
[6]  B←, 0 0 1 ≠A
[7]  L2:→(~⍎C)/0
[8]  ⍎B
[9]  →L2 ∇
```

Now, the test is executed on line [7] prior to the execution of the loop statement. In terms of this second structure, the tank problem can be solved by the function

```
     ∇ H←R TANK2 V;M;T
[1]  FOR 'H←0:T←1E¯5×○4×(R*3)÷3' WHILE 'T<V-H×H×M←OR-H÷3' DO 'H←(V÷M)*0.5' ∇
```

It is inconvenient to require two different *FOR* functions. This problem is avoided in the improved set of functions for either structure, given in Appendix 9.

5-10 Bisection Method of Finding a Zero

We shall now discuss a general method of finding a point where a mathematical function of one variable becomes zero. It is a practical method, of use in its own right, but it also serves as a further example of a program loop.

Assume a dependent variable Y has a mathematical relationship to an independent variable X, such as represented by the curve in Fig. 5-5. A formula is assumed to be available (or perhaps an algorithm) such that Y can be determined for a given value of X. To be specific, assume there is an APL defined function *FN* such that

```
     Y←FN X
```

We are to find a value of X such that *FN X* is zero. In terms of the figure, we want the location of the point where the curve crosses the X axis.

The method depends on making a few trial computations of Y at arbitrarily chosen values of X. This is done enough times to locate two points $X1$ and $X2$ such that F has *different* algebraic signs at the two points. If the curve is smooth between $X1$ and $X2$ (has no jumps) it follows that Y must be zero at some point between $X1$ and $X2$. The curve could just as well be positive at $X1$ and negative at $X2$.

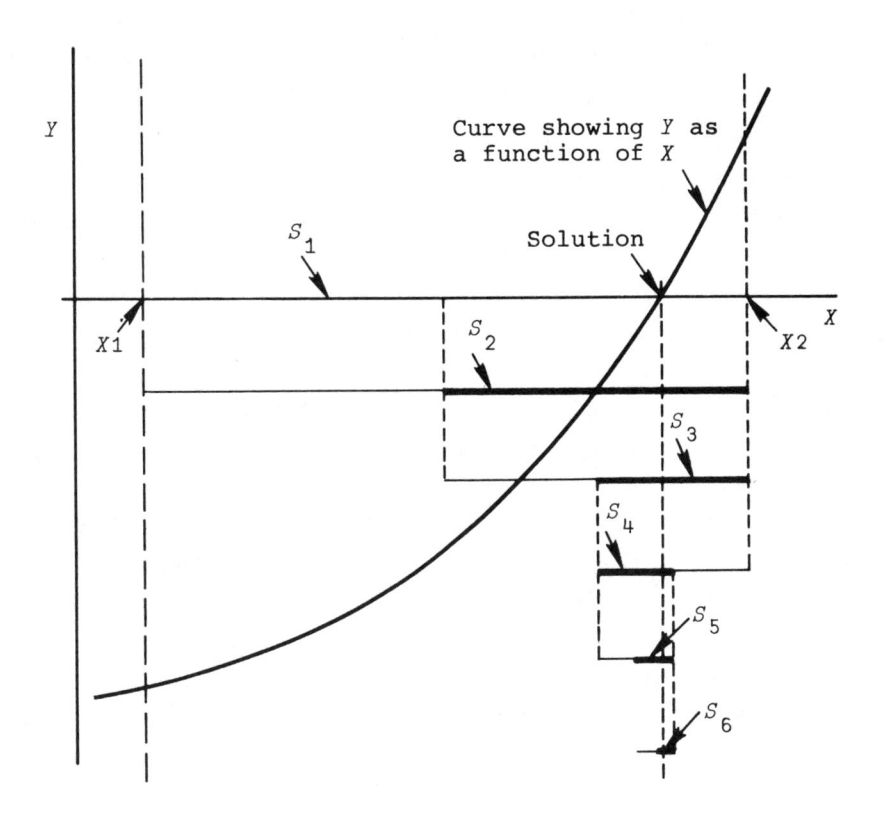

Figure 5-5 Illustration of the bisection method.

The general idea, given a starting interval (say S_1 from $X1$ to $X2$ in Fig. 5-5), is to determine in which *half* of that interval the axis crossing occurs. For the case shown, this is the right-hand half of S_1. Then, this half is called S_2, and the same process is repeated, as if S_2 were the starting interval. Thus, a sequence of intervals, decreasing in length by one half, is obtained such that the axis crossing is contained within each one. The exact position of the axis crossing is never found, but since the length of each interval decreases, the amount of uncertainty can be made as small as we want. The reason for calling this the "bisection" method is evident from this description.

Careful thought will reveal a possible exception to this process: if a crossing should happen to fall at the center of an interval, it will not be possible to pick either half. But it is not necessary, because if this happens, the answer has been found.

The description given above is made more precise in the following statement of the algorithm:

(a) Let S designate any interval which spans an axis crossing. Compute Y at the midpoint of S. If zero is obtained, call that midpoint the solution, and stop the process. If Y is not zero at the midpoint of S, determine the signs of Y at the left-hand end *and* at the midpoint. If these signs are different, designate the left-hand half of S as a new S, if these signs are the same, designate the right-hand half of S as a new S.

170 / Branching and Iteration

> (b) Repeat (a) until the length of S is less than the acceptable error in the answer. Finally, designate the midpoint of the last S as the result.

You will note that the algorithm calls for checking the signs of Y only at the left-hand end and at the midpoint. There is no check at the right-hand end. In doing this we are relying on the fact that there is known to be an axis crossing in the interval, and if it is not in the left half it must be in the right half.

This algorithm has a fixed rate of convergence, which is rather slow. Because of this slowness it is not an elegant method, and is not recommended for programs which must be run many times. Nevertheless, as long as two starting points are available for which Y has opposite signs, and if the curve is smooth, it will *always* find a solution. It is a "brute force" method which does not require extensive analysis of a problem to determine whether it will work.

The relationship between accuracy and the number of iterations can be estimated because with each iteration the interval is halved. Suppose N iterations are completed. If XL is the distance from X1 to X2, the length of the last interval is XL×2*-N. The exact solution is at some unknown point within this last interval, and the midpoint is chosen as an approximation for that unknown point. The midpoint cannot differ from the exact solution by more than half the interval, therefore, the error is no greater than one-half of XL×2*-N, and so it is true that

Magnitude of error < XL×2*-N+1

Using 16 steps, the factor 2*-N+1 is approximately 0.0000076.

It is possible that there will be an *odd* number of axis crossings in the interval, as shown by either of the two curves in Fig. 5-6. It is seen from the figure

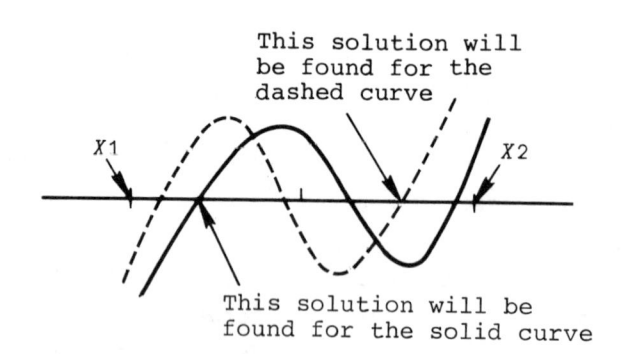

Figure 5-6 Examples of three zero crossings in the starting interval.

that in such a case only one solution will be found, starting with the interval from X1 to X2. To locate the others, different starting intervals are necessary.

The algorithm calls for a check of signs at the left-hand end and at the midpoint of each interval, to determine in which half of the interval the zero point is located. Let us define a subfunction called CKSIGN to perform the check. It will be monadic, taking as its argument the two-element vector of values of Y at the left-hand end and the midpoint of the interval. The returned value is to be 0 if the change in sign occurs in the left half of the interval, or 1 if the change in sign occurs in the right half of the interval. Since the computation is dependent on sign, the signum function ×Y is indicated, where Y will be a two element vector. The required subfunction is

```
      ∇ Z←CKSIGN Y
[1]   Z←=/×Y ∇
```

Let the main function be BISECT. It will be dyadic, taking the number of desired iterations as its left-hand argument, and the end points of the starting interval (a two-element vector) as its right-hand argument. The returned value is to be the approximate location of the axis crossing. The algorithm is realized by the function

```
      ∇ HS←N BISECT X;T;I;Y
[1]   I←0
[2]   HS←(1↑X)+ 0  0.5 ×--/X
[3]   Y←FN 1↑HS
[4]   L1:→L IF 1E¯15>|¯1↑Y←Y,FN¯1↑HS
[5]   HS←((T←1-2×CKSIGN Y)↑HS)+ 0  0.5 ×--/HS
[6]   Y←T↑Y
[7]   →L1 IF N>I←I+1
[8]   L:HS←¯1↑HS ∇
```

It would be preferable to use underlined local variables, to avoid possible conflicts with global variables in FN. In the following description, S is a vector of the end points of an interval, assuming the smaller value is the first element. S is used in the description but does not appear explicitly in the program.

Line 1: Initializes the counter I

Line 2: Specifies HS as the vector of the end points of the left half of S.

Line 3: Specifies Y as the value of the curve at the first element of HS.

Line 4: Creates Y as a vector of values of the curve at end points of HS, and terminates the loop if the second value (Y at the midpoint of the interval) is within $1E^{-}15$ of zero.

Line 5: Specifies T as 1 if the crossing occurs in HS; ¯1 if it does not. Also, respecifies HS as the new half interval.

Line 6: Respecifies Y as the value of the curve at the left-hand end point of the new HS.

Line 7: Terminates the looping when N iterations have been completed.

Line 8: Returns the second element of HS, which is the midpoint of the last S.

Example 5-5

As an application of BISECT, let us use it to solve the tank problem. We define the auxiliary function

```
      ∇ Z←FN H
[1]   Z←V-○H×H×R-H÷3 ∇
```

in which V and R are global. The function for solving the tank problem, using 16 iterations, can then be written

```
      ∇ H←R TANK3 V
[1]   H←16 BISECT 0,2×R ∇
```

172 / Branching and Iteration

Of course, there are many other ways to construct the *BISECT* function. In particular, it is suggested that you write a version using *FOR-UNTIL-DO* or *FOR-WHILE-DO*.

5-11 Secant Method of Finding a Zero

It was pointed out in the last section that the bisection method of finding a zero crossing is slow, but reliable in the sense that it will always converge. We now consider a method which has quite different characteristics; it converges rapidly when it converges, but in many cases it will fail to converge. It is called the *secant* method.*

Refer to Fig. 5-7a which shows a curve representing some mathematical relationship that can be computed by $Y \leftarrow FN\ X$, if *FN* is suitably defined. For *FN*, assume X can be a scalar or vector. Suppose we know that $X1$ and $X2$ are two values near the zero crossing. Let X be the vector $X1,X2$. Then,

$Y \leftarrow FN\ X$

will be a vector of the two elements $Y1$ and $Y2$. The two data points ($X1$ and $Y1$) and ($X2$ and $Y2$) can be used to construct the *secant* shown extended in the figure until it intersects the axis at $X3$.

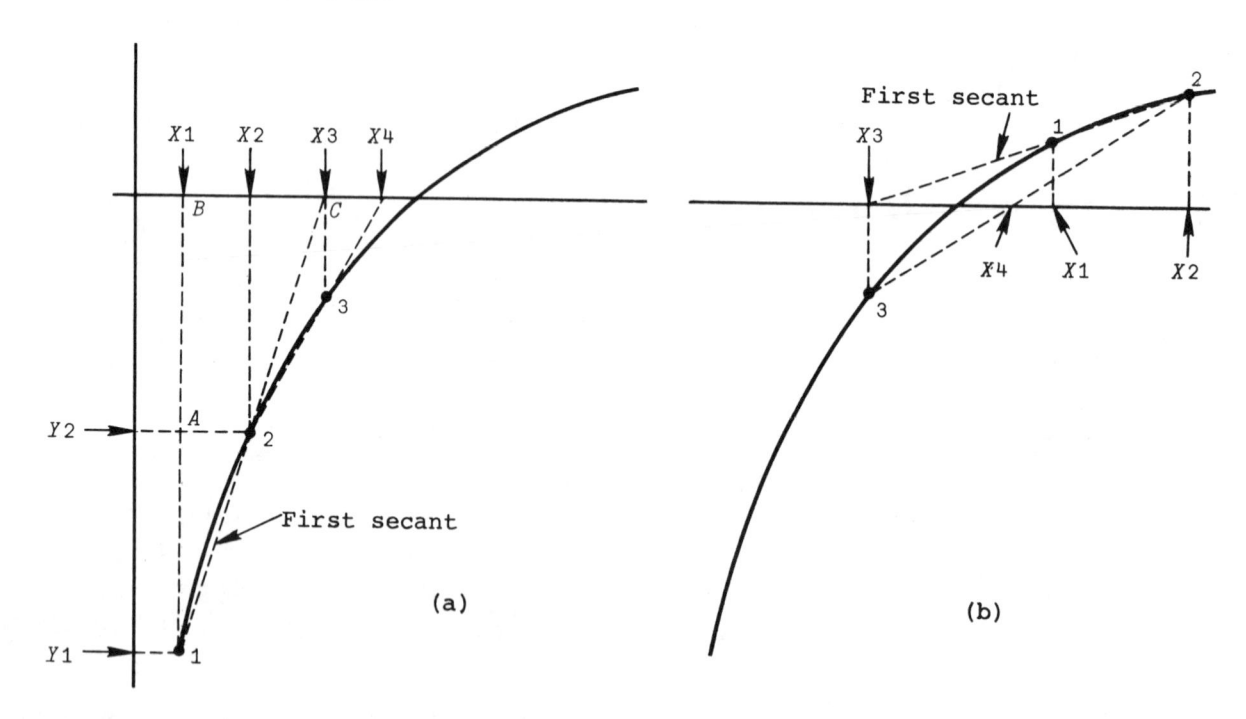

Figure 5-7 Examples of convergence for the secant method.

---

*The secant method is closely related to the well known Newton-Raphson method, which uses the derivative rather than finite differences. The secant method is chosen for illustration because calculus is not considered a prerequisite.

Next, we let X be the vector $X2,X3$ and compute a new vector Y (now consisting of $Y2,Y3$) by again using $Y \leftarrow FN\ X$. This process can be continued, obtaining additional points $X4$, $X5$ etc. which eventually converge to the zero crossing, in this example.

The constructions in Fig. 5-7b show the beginning of a sequence starting with two points to the right of the zero crossing. In this case there is an occasional jump from one side of the zero crossing to the other, but there is still convergence. The initial points can also be on opposite sides of the zero crossing. Since we do not know the location of the zero crossing, we do not know which case will prevail at the beginning.

A cautionary comment concerning convergence is necessary. Whether or not the process converges depends on how close $X1$ and $X2$ are to the zero crossing, and sometimes on how close together they are. An extreme case where $X1$ and $X2$ are inappropriately chosen is shown in Fig. 5-8. In this case the secant does not intersect the X axis. The secant method is satisfactory if the approximate location of a zero crossing is known at the start. For example, we might envision using a few iterations of the bisection process, with the result of that used to specify starting conditions for the secant method.

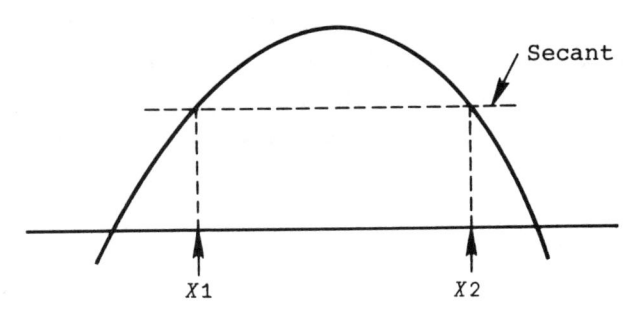

Figure 5-8 A condition for which the secant method does not converge.

It can be shown that, if the secant method converges, *eventually* the error in the last computed value of X is less than the absolute value of the difference of the last two computed values. This property can be used in a test for completion.

The description above is the algorithm for the secant method, except for the lack of a description of how to obtain the point where the secant intersects the X axis. Using $X1$ and $X2$ as an example, from the similar triangles $1A2$ and $1BC$ in Fig. 5-7a, it follows that (in conventional notation)

$$\frac{X3 - X1}{Y1} = \frac{X2 - X1}{Y1 - Y2}$$

which, when solved for $X3$, gives

$$X3 = \frac{(Y1 \times X2) - (Y2 \times X1)}{Y1 - Y2}$$

Thus, in APL notation, if X is a vector of two elements (such as $X1,X2$) and $Y \leftarrow FN\ X$, then the intersection of the secant with the X axis is

$X3 \leftarrow (-/Y \times \phi X) \div -/Y$

The algorithm described above can be translated into the following dyadic function. The left-hand argument is the desired error tolerance, and the right-hand argument is a two element vector of the initial values of X.

174 / Branching and Iteration

Example 5-6

```
        ∇ Y←T SECANT X
[1]     Y←FN X
[2]     L:Y←(1↓Y),FN 1↓X←(1↓X),(-/Y×⌽X)÷-/Y
[3]     →(T<|-/X)/L
[4]     Y←⁻1↑X  ∇
```

This program shows only the essentials. To be practical, it should include a check for divergence, and for the possibility of -/Y being zero. Another version is

```
        ∇ Y←T SECANT X
[1]     FOR 'Y←FN X' WHILE 'T<|-/X' DO 'Y←(1↓Y),FN 1↓X←(1↓X),(-/Y×⌽X)÷-/Y'
[2]     Y←⁻1↑X  ∇
```

5-12 Use of Execute in Representing a Mathematical Relationship

The functions BISECT and SECANT described in the previous two sections are general-purpose functions. By this we mean that the mathematical relationship for which a zero crossing is to be found is represented by a general defined function FN. To change the problem being solved, it is necessary to redefine FN.

An alternative is to use a character representation of the name of the function to be investigated as an argument of BISECT or SECANT. This will require a rearrangement of the header line, making the left-hand argument a vector of three elements, consisting of what is now one element on the left and two on the right. To illustrate, we shall convert SECANT to the form given in the following example.

Example 5-7

```
        ∇ Y←X SECANTM F;T
[1]     T←1↑X
[2]     X←1↓X
[3]     Y←⍎F,' X'
[4]     L:Y←(1↓Y),⍎F,' 1↓X←(1↓X),(-/Y×⌽X)÷-/Y'
[5]     →(T<|-/X)/L
[6]     Y←⁻1↑X  ∇
```

This program is very similar to SECANT. The left-hand argument is a three-element vector: the tolerance for checking for completion, and the two initial values of X. These are extracted in lines [1] and [2] so that T and X are the same as previously. The other change consists of replacing FN by ⍎F followed by a character representation of what was the argument of FN in SECANT. The right-hand argument of SECANTM can be the name of any appropriate existing function, in quotes so it will be a character value.

Another way to use SECANTM is to let the right-hand argument be a character representation of the relationship for which a zero crossing is to be found. That is to say, this argument does not have to be a defined function. All that is required is that F be a character representation of a suitable executable statement. For example, if V and R are specified as global variables, and

```
        TK←'V-○H×H×R-(÷3)×H←'
```

is used as the argument of SECANT, the result will be a solution to the tank problem. Thus,

```
      V←200
      R←5
      (1E¯12, 5 6) SECANTM TK
4.2065
```

Note the introduction of variables which are global to *SECANTM*. These can be local to a main function, in which *SECANTM* is used as a subfunction. Thus, we can define

```
      ∇ H←R TANK4 V
[1]   H←((1E¯5×o4×(R*3)÷3),0,2×R) SECANTM 'V-oH×H×R-(÷3)×H←' ∇
```

In this program the test value $1E¯5×o4×(R*3)÷3$ was chosen to make *TANK4* equivalent to the previous examples.

This is not an exhaustive treatment of the various possibilities of using execute to provide general purpose functions, but it is complete enough to illustrate its efficacy. It is advised that you keep execute in mind in applications such as this.

5-13 Recursive Functions

We shall now consider a way to program an iterative process by having a function "call itself" as a subfunction. Such a function is said to be *recursive*. As a first illustration, consider the iterative evaluation of a polynomial previously described in Sec. 5-5. It was shown there that if C is a vector of coefficients, in increasing powers of X, the value of the polynomial at X is (in origin 1, for the case where ρC is 4)

```
      C[1]+X×C[2]+X×C[3]+X×C[4]
```

An equivalent way to write this is

```
      (1↑C)+X×(1↑1↓C)+X×(1↑2↓C)+X×1↑3↓C
```

This second statement is in a convenient form upon which to base a recursive definition.

Example 5-8

Consider the function

```
      ∇ Z←C POLYR X
[1]      →0 IF 1=ρZ←C
[2]      Z←(1↑C)+X×(1↓C) POLYR X ∇
```

and suppose

```
      2 6 ¯3 4 POLYR 5
```

is executed. The branching on line [1] is ignored because the vector C has four elements, and therefore an attempt is made to execute line [2]. However, line [2] includes

```
      6 ¯3 4 POLYR 5
```

which calls for *POLYR* to be executed again. Meanwhile, the first execution of *POLYR* becomes suspended. This process repeats. The second execution of *POLYR* will become suspended because it calls for the execution of

```
      ¯3 4 POLYR 5
```

176 / Branching and Iteration

and finally this calls for the execution of

    4 *POLYR* 5

where 4 is a one-element vector. *POLYR* now exits from line [1], returning the value 4. Observe that because 1↓*C* is the left-hand argument of *POLYR* in line [2], each execution calls for one less element in the argument on the left.

At the instant when 4 *POLY* 5 is about to be executed, the situation is as described in the following table.

	C	1↑*C*	ρ*C*
1st suspension	2 6 ¯3 4	2	4
2nd suspension	6 ¯3 4	6	3
3rd suspension	¯3 4	¯3	2
4th execution	4	4	1

Local variable *C* has a different value for each suspension. The suspended functions go to completion in the reverse order in which they are called. Thus, as the third suspension goes to completion, it returns 17, as a result of

    ¯3+5×4

and as the second suspension goes to completion it returns 91 as a result of

    6+5×17

Finally, completion of the first suspension gives

    2+5×91

Thus, it is seen that the combined operation of four executions of *POLYR*, initiated by

    2 6 ¯3 4 *POLYR* 5

produces the equivalent of

    2+5×6+5×¯3+5×4

From this example it is seen that the effect of using recursion is to produce the equivalent of one statement line. The length of that line depends on some parameter of the problem, in this case the number of elements in *C*. It is also possible to use recursion where the length of the equivalent statement line depends on how many computations are required to attain a desired accuracy. Thus, it is possible to define a recursive equivalent of *SECANT*, as in the following example.

Example 5-9

We are to define a recursive function *SECANTR* which will take the same arguments as *SECANT* and produce the same result. One possible realization is

```
        ∇ Y←T SECANTR X
[1]     →L IF T<|-/X
[2]     Y←¯1↑X
[3]     →0
[4]     L:Y←FN X
[5]     X←(1↓X),(-/Y×⌽X)÷-/Y
[6]     Y←T SECANTR X ∇
```

Again we use FN to represent the relationship between Y and X for which we are to find a zero crossing. In this case, executions of $SECANTR$ remain suspended until the branch out of the function occurs on line [3]. This last execution produces the answer, as a returned value. As each of the other suspensions goes to completion no further computations are done; each completion of a suspension merely does an assignment, creating a new returned value. Inspection of lines [4] and [5] shows that these carry out calculations called for by the algorithm for the secant method given in Sec. 5-11. There is one slight difference compared to $SECANT$. In $SECANTR$, both elements of Y are computed on each iteration whereas in $SECANT$ one old element is held over from the previous iteration.

The version of $SECANTR$ above was written on several lines, for clarity. A more concise form is

```
      ∇ Y←T SECANTR X
[1]     →L IF T<|-/X
[2]     Y←¯1↑X
[3]     →0
[4]   L:Y←T SECANTR (1↓X),(-/Y×⌽X)÷-/Y←FN X ∇
```

Having developed the concept of a recursive function definition as a means of programming an iterative process, it is natural to consider its advantages and disadvantages compared with a looping process. From a practical standpoint the methods are essentially equivalent, but conceptually they are different. In some ways the idea of recursion is conceptually more satisfying, but for the inexperienced it may seem to be more subtle. From the standpoint of the computer there is not much difference in execution times, but recursive functions require more workspace because of the suspensions.

5-14 Input-Controlled Loop

Suppose there are two global vectors for storing two sets of data. To be specific, suppose the data are obtained from a series of measurements of time and temperature, over the duration of one day. Each value of time can be one number, the number of minutes since midnight. We want to store these data in the variables

   $TIME$

and

   $TEMP$

One way to do this is to initialize each one as an empty vector, and then use a defined function having evaluated input and a loop, to take an input of one value of time and one value of temperature in each execution of the loop.

A simple version of such a function is

```
      ∇ STORE;A
[1]   L:A←⎕
[2]     TIME←TIME,A[1]
[3]     TEMP←TEMP,A[2]
[4]     →L ∇
```

After each completion of a loop, the computer will type

☐:

and await the input of a new *pair* of numbers, time and temperature. The question now arises as to how to stop the process, when further input of data is not wanted. One way is to type the right arrow

☐:
    →

which will always cause an exit on a call for evaluated input. However, let us design the program so this will not be needed. At the same time, a check will be included to prevent errors due to typing the wrong number of items of data.

We note that two items of data is the correct number. Therefore, we choose the following design criteria:

(a) The input of any *single* number shall terminate the looping.

(b) If more than two items are entered at any one time, the computer shall return the message *INCORRECT DATA*, do nothing with the incorrect data, and prepare to accept input again.

The program is now modified as follows:

```
      ∇ STORE;A
[1]   L:→M IF 2=ρ,A←☐
[2]     →0 IF 0=ρρA
[3]     'INCORRECT DATA'
[4]     →L
[5]   M:TIME←TIME,A[1]
[6]     TEMP←TEMP,A[2]
[7]     →L ∇
```

Two points are illustrated by this example:

(a) A loop is sometimes useful in a process (usually not one of successive approximation) where looping is under the control of the user at all times, by virtue of a test of input data which determines whether to continue.

(b) In such an application, the function should be designed with enough checks to avoid mistakes due to improper input. A mistake should cause execution of the function to terminate rather than an APL error report.

This is an appropriate example for illustrating the *IF-THEN-ELSE* format. Suppose we define the auxiliary function

```
      ∇ ADD
[1]   TIME←TIME,A[1]
[2]   TEMP←TEMP,A[2] ∇
```

Then, a possible program equivalent to *STORE* given above is

```
      ∇ STOREM;A
[1]   L:↟IF '2=ρ,A' THEN 'ADD' ELSE IF '0=ρρA←☐' THEN '→0' ELSE '''INCORRECT DATA'''
[2]     →L ∇
```

Observe that the message *INCORRECT DATA* has three quote symbols on each side. This is because the character value *'INCORRECT DATA'* is itself within quotes, and therefore requires an extra quote symbol on each side.

CONCLUSION

Branching is fundamental to computer programming, since it provides a means for choosing between two or more sequences of program steps, depending on the value of a control variable. In particular, a test and a branch are essential parts of a loop or a recursively defined function, to ensure that operation will stop.

Concerning the branch operation itself, it is true that APL does not have an inherent operator to accomplish conditional branching; a conditional branch is programmed by placing a suitable statement to the right of the branch arrow →. However, defined functions such as *IF* and *WHEN* (as given in the text) provide a convenient syntax. Also, although branching can be done using line numbers rather than line labels, it is emphatically recommended that line labels always be used, to avoid problems arising from changes in line numbers which can occur when a function is edited.

In contrast to the *IF* and *WHEN* functions given in the text, which merely simplify the syntax of a statement line, the *IF-THEN-ELSE* and *FOR-UNTIL-DO* structures permit the equivalents of conditional branching and looping to be accomplished without writing actual branch statements. The decision steps are imbedded in the functions *THEN* and *FOR*, and are generated when these functions are executed.

There are two kinds of process for which a loop or recursive definition is used:

(a) Repetitive process which are inherently finite, such as the term-by-term evaluation of a polynomial.
(b) Repetitive processes which involve approaching an answer in successive approximations; processes which are inherently infinite but are stopped after a finite number of iterations.

In APL, array structures can usually, but not always, be used to avoid loops of type (a). The test for completion of such a looping process is based on the known number of times it is to be done. Algorithms requiring computation by successive approximations always require a loop or recursive definition, and are usually characterized by a test for completion based on the attainment of a certain prescribed degree of accuracy.

One of the main objectives of this chapter is to present some typical program solutions for problems involving successive approximations. Through examples, you were introduced to the essential features: the necessity of adopting an appropriate algorithm, concern for rate of convergence (the number of iterations required to reach a satisfactory result) and choice of a criterion for testing for the stop. But in details the chapter must be regarded as rather superficial. Methods of computing by successive approximations are many and varied, and are the subjects of entire books.

180 / Branching and Iteration

Problems--Chapter 5

Problems Related to Secs. 5-1 through 5-3

5-1 Concerning a line label:

(a) It is a (local/global) _____ variable.
(b) Its name (can/cannot) be the same as another variable in the program.
(c) It (should/should not) be listed in the header line.

5-2 (a) Write a branch statement that will exit from a program. _____
(b) What will the statement →'' do? _____
(c) If a line having a label P has the statement →P+1, explain what this statement will do. _____

5-3 In *COMPARE*1 in Sec. 5-2, what is the value of $C/L1$ if $(\rho\rho A)$ equals $\rho\rho B$? _____ What is this value if $\rho\rho A$ does not equal $\rho\rho B$? _____

5-4 Rearrange *COMPARE*1 of Sec. 5-2 using $C \leftarrow (\rho\rho A)=\rho\rho B$ and $C \leftarrow \wedge/(\rho A)=\rho B$ as the control variables on lines [1] and [3] of the version in the text. Do not use ~C.

5-5 Write a version of *IF* which uses only the primitive dyadic ρ.

5-6 In *COMPARE*3 of Sec. 5-2, show how indexing could be used on line [4]. Be sure you get an empty vector when C is 0.

5-7 For each of the following executions of *COMPARE*3, as given in Sec. 5-2, on the blanks to the right give the values of the variables indicated.

	RNE	SNE	C
(2 3 ρι6) *COMPARE*3 2 3 ρ8	_____	_____	_____
(2 3 ρι6) *COMPARE*3 2 3	_____	_____	_____
(2 3 ρι6) *COMPARE*3 2 4 ρ8	_____	_____	_____

5-8 For the function *WHEN* given in the text, what result is produced if B is an integer greater than ρA?

5-9 Referring to *QUAD* in example 5-1, change line [2] to

[2]   →*IM IF* $D \geq 0$

and make any compensating changes in lines [3], [4], and [5].

5-10 (a) In *THEN* of Sec. 5-3, what are the possible values of ⌶4?
(b) Write a version of *THEN* that is independent of origin.

5-11 In *QUAD*3 of example 5-2 change line [2] using *IF* '$D \geq 0$' etc.

5-12 Write programs *IFF* and *THEN* which will be used in the syntax

  IFF 'Condition' *THEN* 'Statement'

This is to execute the statement and proceed to the next line, if the condition is true; otherwise, proceed to the next line. For properties of ⌶ see Sec. 7-10.

Problems Related to Secs. 5-4 through 5-6

5-13 Assume

    2 4 ¯3 1 *LOOPPOLY* 2

is executed. Trace its operation, writing the value of P after each passage through the loop.

Branching and Iteration / 181

5-14 Do Prob. 5-13, but with 2 3 as the right-hand argument of *LOOPPOLY*.

5-15 Rewrite *LOOPPOLY* of Sec. 5-5 so it will operate in origin 0.

5-16 Write line [3] of *LOOPPOLY*1 in Sec. 5-5, using an equality in the argument of *IF*.

5-17 Assume

       2 4 ¯3 1 *LOOPPOLY*2 2

is executed. Trace its operation, writing the value of *P* and *C* after each passage through the loop.

5-18 Modify either *MANYPOLY* or *MANYPOLY*1 given in Sec. 5-6 so that the highest degree polynomial will be evaluated first.

5-19 (a) Modify *MANYPOLY* of Sec. 5-6 so that it will operate in origin 0.
(b) Modify *MANYPOLY* of Sec. 5-6 so that it will operate in either origin.

Problems Related to Secs. 5-7 through 5-9

5-20 Referring to *TANK* in Sec. 5-7, assume line [2] is changed to H←2×R. Make any other necessary changes.

5-21 Change *TANK*1 of Sec. 5-7 so that it will begin the iterations with the equivalent of *H* having the value 2×R.

5-22 Modify *TANK*1 of Sec. 5-7 so that upon completion there will be a print of the number of iterations.

5-23 Write a function *TANKMS* which will be equivalent to *TANKM* of Sec. 5-7, but using *TANK*1 as a subfunction.

5-24 Write a function, using the method of finding the intersection of two curves, to obtain the value of *X* for which *X* equals *-X.

5-25 Values of *X* for which (5×X*0.5)-(1+X*2) equals 0 can be found by searching for the points of intersection of two curves. Write a separate defined function for finding each value of *X* for which the expression above is 0.

5-26 Write a program using *TANKM* of Sec. 5-7 as a subfunction which will use a loop to find a vector of heights corresponding to a vector of specified volumes. The function is to be dyadic, taking the radius as the left-hand argument and the vector of volumes as the right-hand argument.

5-27 The function *TANKM* of Sec. 5-7 will work if the right-hand argument is a vector of volumes. The result will be a corresponding vector of heights. However, the iterative process treats all elements of *V* simultaneously, so there is a question as to whether the test on line [5] is adequate for all cases. If *T* is the error tolerance, determine whether the errors are: (a) all greater than or equal to *T*; (b) all less than or equal to *T*; or (c) some greater and some less than *T*.

5-28 Write a function *LOOPPOLY*4 using the syntax *FOR-UNTIL-DO*, but using take and drop rather than indexing as in *LOOPPOLY*3 in Sec. 5-9. That is, use *FOR-UNTIL-DO* to carry out the same processes as *LOOPPOLY*2.

5-29 Write a function *LOOPPOLY*5 using the syntax *FOR-WHILE-DO*, using take and drop rather than indexing. That is, use *FOR-WHILE-DO* to carry out the same process as *LOOPPOLY*2.

5-30 This question refers to the first version of *FOR* given in Sec. 5-9.
(a) Use indexing on lines [1], [5], and [6] but retain independence of origin.
(b) Change line [5] so that line [8] can be →(⍳C)/L2.

182 / Branching and Iteration

5-31 This question refers to the first version of *FOR* given in Sec. 5-9.
   (a) Explain why ravel is used on lines [1], [5], and [6].
   (b) Explain why it is not possible to change line [5] to $C \leftarrow \text{⍬}, 0\ 1\ 0\ /\underline{A}$ and then omit the execute function on line [8].

Problems Related to Secs. 5-10 through 5-12

5-32 For the function *BISECT* given in Sec. 5-10, rewrite line [5] using indexing in origin 1 instead of take.

5-33 The function *BISECT* given in Sec. 5-10 takes as its right-hand argument a two-element vector representing two points on the axis of the independent variable. In the analysis given in the text it is assumed that the first element of this argument is smaller than the second. Consider the other possibility, that the first element is larger than the second, analyzing the operation to determine whether the correct result will be obtained.

5-34 For *BISECT*, as given in Sec. 5-10, to work properly the signs of the mathematical function represented by *FN* must be different for the two starting values of the independent variable.

   (a) Predict what result will be obtained from

       4 *BISECT* 2 4

       if the curve does not cross the axis between 2 and 4.
   (b) Modify *BISECT* so as to reject a case where the signs of *FN* at the beginning points are the same. During rejection there should be a print of the message *INADMISSIBLE CASE*, and the returned value should be an empty vector.

5-35 Modify the function *BISECT*, given in Sec. 5-10, so it will operate by testing the right-hand half of each of the successively halved segments of the independent variable. Assume the end with the smaller value is on the left.

5-36 For *BISECT* as given in Sec. 5-10, the left-hand argument is the number of iterations desired. Modify this function to take a tolerance of the independent variable as the left-hand argument, such that upon completion it will be known that the error is less than that tolerance.

5-37 It is mentioned in the text that whether or not the operation of *SECANT*, as given in Sec. 5-11, converges depends on having the starting values close to a zero crossing. Design a modified version that will terminate operation if there is no evidence of convergence after 10 iterations, or if at any time $-/Y$ is zero. If there is no convergence for either reason, the function should print the message *DOES NOT CONVERGE* and return an empty vector.

5-38 Use *SECANTM* as given in Sec. 5-12 to obtain zero crossings for:

   (a) $X - * - X$
   (b) $+/\ \bar{}12.5\ 27\ \bar{}4.5\ 1\ \times X * 0\ 1\ 2\ 3$

5-39 Write a modified version of *BISECT*, called *BISECTM*, which will use execute in a manner similar to *SECANTM*, using a character representation of *FN* on the right.

5-40 Explain why a space is required as the first character in the vector catenated to $\underline{F}$ in lines [3] and [4] of *SECANTM*.

5-41 Write a version of *SECANTM* equivalent in its operation to the one in Sec. 5-12, but using indexing instead of take and drop.

Problems Related to Secs. 5-13 and 5-14

5-42 The function *POLYR* given in Sec. 5-13 will not work for the degenerate case of a polynomial consisting of only a constant term. Modify it so it will work for this case.

5-43 Write a version of *POLYR* equivalent in its operation to the one in Sec. 5-13, but using indexing instead of take and drop.

5-44 Write a monadic recursive function *TANKR* to solve the tank problem by the method given in Sec. 5-7. Let the radius of the tank and the required volume be global variables, and let the height of water be the argument.

5-45 Write a recursive function *BISECTR* which will perform the same task as *BISECT* given in Sec. 5-10. The arguments will be the same as for *BISECT*.

5-46 Modify the function *STORE* given in Sec. 5-14 in such a way that termination of operation will occur if the input is a return (which produces an empty vector on character input).

5-47 Modify *STORE* as given in Sec. 5-14 so that data entered can be more than one pair of numbers. For each pair, the first number will be a value of time and the second a value of temperature. Thus, in this case, a vector having an odd number of elements greater than 2 will be rejected as *INCORRECT DATA*.

5-48 Modify *STORE* as given in Sec. 5-14 so that if the input is a vector not having two elements it will be rejected (as in the text) and also arrange that the data will be rejected if the time element of the input is negative.

5-49 Write a version of *STORE* having the properties specified in Prob. 5-48, but using the *IF-THEN-ELSE* format.

General Problems

5-50 Suppose the input to a certain program is to be a vector of nonnegative even integers (zero is accepted). Construct a monadic function called *TEST* which will check whether its input conforms to these conditions: If it does, that vector is to be the returned value; if it does not, the message *INADMISSIBLE DATA* is to be printed, and the returned value is to be an empty vector.

5-51 A monadic function called *CHANCE* is to be constructed which will simulate the throw of a pair of dice. The right-hand argument is to be the number you want the "throw" to produce (2 to 12). The result is to be a printed line (no returned value). This line should be: if the "throw" does not match the argument, the number produced by the "throw" followed by *LOSE*; if the "throw" agrees with the argument, *WIN*; if the argument is outside the range 2 to 12, *IMPOSSIBLE*.

5-52 Write a function *CHANCE*1 which is equivalent to the function *CHANCE* described in Prob. 5-51. However, write it in the *IF-THEN-ELSE* format.

5-53 Write a monadic function *DICE* that will take as its argument an integer from 2 to 12 inclusive. The function is to simulate repeated throws of a pair of dice until the sum on the pair of throws equals the argument of the function. The returned value will be the number of throws required.

5-54 It can be shown that given two positive numbers N and r_n,

$$r_{n+1} = \tfrac{1}{2}(r_n + \frac{N}{r_n})$$

is closer to the square root of N than r_n. Write a monadic function *ROOTL* which will take N as an argument, and use a loop to carry out the algorithm. Use 1 as the first value of r. Make your own decision concerning the criterion for termination. The square root of N is to be the explicit result.

184 / Branching and Iteration

5-55 Write a function *ROOTR* which will be recursive, to carry out the algorithm described in Prob. 5-54. Make the function dyadic, taking an approximate value of the square root of *N* as the left-hand argument, and *N* as the right-hand argument. The square root of *N* is to be the explicit result.

5-56 Given a vector such as 4 8 3 6 5, the expression (in conventional notation)

$$\cfrac{1}{4 + \cfrac{1}{8 + \cfrac{1}{3 + \cfrac{1}{6 + \cfrac{1}{5}}}}}$$

is called a continued fraction. An APL statement for this is

÷4+÷8+÷3+÷6+÷5

Write a monadic function *CFL* using a loop which will perform this computation, and give a returned value. The argument is to be a vector of any dimension.

5-57 Referring to Prob. 5-56, write a monadic recursive function *CFR* which will take the given vector as its argument and return the value of the continued fraction.

5-58 Euclid's algorithm is the classic procedure for finding the greatest common divisor of two positive integers *X* and *Y*. A description of the algorithm is as follows:

(1) Divide *X* by *Y* and obtain the remainder *R*.
(2) Test whether the remainder is zero. If it is, *Y* is the greatest common divisor, and the process should stop.
(3) If the remainder is not zero, designate the previous *Y* as *X*, and designate the remainder *R* as *Y*.
(4) Repeat step 1.

Write a monadic function *EUCLIDL* taking *X* and *Y* as a vector argument, and returning the greatest common divisor. The program should employ a loop.

5-59 Refer to Euclid's algorithm as described in Prob. 5-58. Write a recursive function *EUCLIDR* which will find the greatest common divisor of two positive integers. Make the function dyadic, with *X* and *Y* as the arguments.

5-60 The accompanying diagram portrays the intersection of two halls in a building. The problem is to find the longest beam that can be carried around the corner, if it remains horizontal. Wall dimensions *A* and *B* are given.

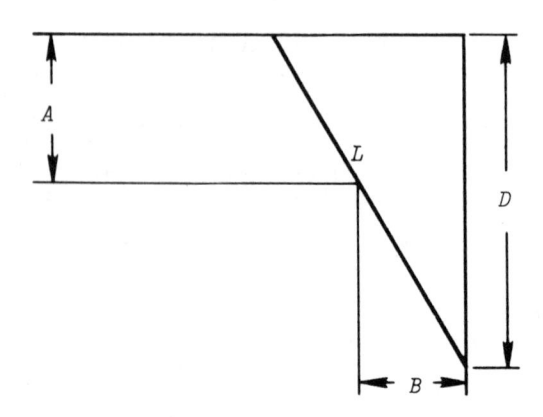

At any distance D it can be shown that the length of line L is given by

```
      ∇ L←FL D
[1]   L←(((B×D÷D-A)*2)+D*2)*0.5 ∇
```

You should confirm this. An algorithm which will find the value of D which makes L a minimum is as follows:

(1) Choose a starting value of D, and a small increment of D, say I.
(2) Compute the two-element vector L←FL $D,D+I$.
(3) Test >/L.
    (a) If it is 1, replace D by $D+I$ and return to step 2.
    (b) If it is 0, test whether I is less than the acceptable error. If it is, stop, otherwise replace I by ¯0.5×I and return to step 2.

Write a dyadic function $BEAM$ which will take A and B as its arguments and return the length of the longest possible beam that can be carried around the corner.

5-61 In example 3-2 a function $ADDLINE$ was developed for adding a line to a matrix. Improve that function so it will have the following additional features: The left-hand argument is to be allowed to be a scalar or vector of line numbers (numbered in the finished matrix), for the lines to be added. These are not necessarily in increasing order. The function will then accept a corresponding number of quote-quad inputs, one at a time. Also, a check is to be included to make sure all specified row numbers are within acceptable range, and that there are no repeated numbers. If the line numbers do not pass this test, the function is to print the message $IMPROPER$ $LINE$ $NUMBERS$, and the returned value is to be the original matrix, unchanged.

Chapter 6

EXTENDED SCALAR AND MIXED FUNCTIONS

INTRODUCTION

Introductory treatments of the extended-scalar functions formed by combining a scalar primitive with one of the three operators (reduction, outer product, inner product) are given in Secs. 3-12, 20, 21. What remains to be done concerning these functions is to establish how they work for the general case where arguments are not restricted in ranks, and to introduce a fourth extended scalar function obtained from the *scan* operator.

Those primitive functions of the language which are not scalar or extended scalar are called *mixed* functions. The mixed functions exhibit a wide variety of relationships among shapes and ranks of arguments and of results; for many of them the shape of the result depends on the numerical value of an argument.

Quite a few mixed functions have been introduced in previous chapters, without their having been labeled "mixed". For some of them the previous descriptions are adequate, and therefore are not given further treatment. These are:

Name of function	Symbol	Reference
Reshape	Dyadic ρ	Sec. 3-3
Shape	Monadic ρ	Sec. 3-6
Index generator	Monadic ι	Sec. 2-8
Ravel	Monadic ,	Sec. 3-5
Grade up	Monadic ▲	Sec. 3-16
Grade down	Monadic ▼	Sec. 3-16
Membership	Dyadic ϵ	Sec. 4-14
Execute	Monadic ⍎	Sec. 2-23

The other mixed functions previously introduced but only partially described are: catenate, laminate, indexing, take, drop, reverse, rotate, transpose, format. The present chapter completes the descriptions of these functions and introduces the remainder of the mixed functions.

Some of the functions are difficult to describe in complete generality. For that reason you should study this chapter in two steps. First, study the numerical examples and work out examples for yourself. Second, after you have gained experience with specific examples, study the abstract presentations of the general properties; methods of computation, compatibility conditions, and shapes and ranks of the results. These abstract generalities will be easier to learn after you gain some practical experience.

While working with the mixed functions, be alert to the ranks and shapes of the arguments and the results. Your understanding of these functions can be considerably enhanced by an awareness of conditions which arguments must satisfy to be compatible, and how the rank and shape of a result relates to the ranks and shapes of the arguments.

Part A - EXTENDED SCALAR FUNCTIONS

Each extended scalar function employs a scalar primitive in conjunction with an operator. In the rather general treatment here we do not wish to be committed to any one scalar function. Accordingly, the letter s will be used to represent *any* scalar primitive (in the case of the inner product, which employs two scalar primitives, r and s will be used). The scalar functions used with these operators are dyadic.

6-1 Reduction   / REDUCTION

Reduction for vectors and matrices is covered thoroughly in Secs. 2-17 and 3-12, and so here we give an example for rank 3, and then proceed to the generalization for an array of any rank. We shall use the array

```
     A
 1  2  3  4
 5  6  7  8

 9 10 11 12
13 14 15 16

17 18 19 20
21 22 23 24
```

as an example. There is a reduction corresponding to each axis. Using + for the illustration,

```
+/[1]A ↔   1+9+17    2+10+18   3+11+19   4+12+20  ↔  27 30 33 36
           5+13+21   6+14+22   7+15+23   8+16+24     39 42 45 48

+/[2]A ↔   1+5       2+6       3+7       4+8       ↔   6  8 10 12
           9+13     10+14     11+15     12+16          22 24 26 28
          17+21     18+22     19+23     20+24          38 40 42 44

+/[3]A ↔   1+2+3+4        5+6+7+8       ↔  10 26
           9+10+11+12    13+14+15+16       42 58
          17+18+19+20    21+22+23+24       74 90
```

General Case

Let the general case be represented by

   s/[J]B

where J in the axis operator [J] must be in the range $1 \leq J \leq \rho\rho B$ (in origin 1). The result is produced by placing s between successive elements along axis J, removing that axis from the result. Thus, the rank of the result is 1 less than the rank of B. An exception occurs in the limiting case when B is a scalar; then, the result of s/B is the scalar B. Also, if B is a vector of one element, the result is the value of B, as a scalar.

188 / Extended Scalar and Mixed Functions

Returning to the general case, removing the J th axis means that the shape of the result is obtained from the shape of the argument by removing the Jth element.

In APL notation, except when B is a scalar,

Rank of result: ¯1+⍴⍴B

Shape of result: (J≠⍳⍴⍴B)/⍴B

The notation s/B (without an explicit axis operator) always means reduction over the last (highest numbered) axis. Similarly, s⌿B means reduction over the first (lowest numbered axis). These abbreviated notations are independent of origin.

The result obtained for reduction on an empty vector depends on s. For some s such a reduction is not possible, but when it is possible the result is the *identity value* for s. An identity value is defined as follows: I is an identity value for s if, for any A in an admissible domain, AsI ↔ A or IsA ↔ A (in some case, both). To illustrate, A+0 ↔ A (and 0+A ↔ A) and so the identity value for + is 0. For some primitives I can be defined on only one side. For example, A-0 ↔ A, but 0-A does not equal A. The functions ○, ⍟, ⍣, and ⍱ have no identity values and if used in reduction over an empty vector will produce a *DOMAIN ERROR* report.

Thus, for admissible functions

s/⍳0 ↔ I

In some systems a reduction over an empty array produces a logical extension of this, if the axis of reduction is the only one with zero dimension. Some examples are:

```
+/[1] 0 3 ⍴6 ↔ 0 0 0

+/[2] 4 0 ⍴6 ↔ 0 0 0 0

+/[1] 0 3 4 ⍴6 ↔ 0 0 0 0
                  0 0 0 0
                  0 0 0 0

+/[2] 2 0 4 ⍴6 ↔ 0 0 0 0
                  0 0 0 0

+/[3] 2 3 0 ⍴6 ↔ 0 0 0
                  0 0 0
```

The following table gives the identity values for all admissible cases.

Table 6-1

s	Identity value	Identity relationship	s	Identity value	Identity relationship
+	0	A+I or I+A	∨	0	A∨I or I∨A
-	0	A-I	∧	1	A∧I or I∧A
×	1	A×I or I×A	>	0	A>I
÷	1	A÷I	≥	1	A≥I
*	1	A*I	<	0	I<A
|	0	I|A	≤	1	I≤A
⌊	Largest number	A⌊I or I⌊A	=	1	A=I or I=A
⌈	-Largest number	A⌈I or I⌈A	≠	0	A≠I or I≠A
!	1	I!A		Boolean values only, for A	

Extended Scalar and Mixed Functions / 189

The words "largest number" mean the largest number the computer can produce: + and - that number are machine-dependent "representations" of +∞ and -∞.

Reduction with - is of interest because, in conventional phraseology, it produces the effect of alternating signs. Thus, for a vector V

$\quad$ -/V ↔ (Sum odd-numbered elements) - (Sum even-numbered elements)

Similarly, for divide

$\quad$ ÷/V ↔ (Product odd-numbered elements) ÷ (Product even-numbered elements)

6-2 Scan   ✗ SCAN

Scan employs the operator symbol \ with a symbol for a scalar function to its left and the argument to its right. When the argument has rank greater than 1, an axis operator is included between \ and the argument. In the following numerical examples + is used as representative of the general scalar function s. Axis designations are in origin 1.

Vector

If V is

```
       V
2   8  6  3
```

$\quad$ +\\V ↔ 2,(2+8),(2+8+6),2+8+6+3 ↔ 2   10   16   19

and similarly for the other arithmetic primitives.

Matrix

For a matrix, there is a scan along each axis. Thus, for

```
    M
2  8  3  2
4  1  7  5
6  5  4  3
```

```
+\[1]M ↔    2        8        3        2      ↔  2   8   3   2
           2+4      8+1      3+7      2+5        6   9  10   7
          2+4+6    8+1+5    3+7+4    2+5+3      12  14  14  10

+\[2]M ↔  2   2+8   2+8+3   2+8+3+2   ↔   2  10  13  15
          4   4+1   4+1+7   4+1+7+5       4   5  12  17
          6   6+5   6+5+4   6+5+4+3       6  11  15  18
```

Array of Rank 3

Consider the array

```
     A
 1   2   3   4
 5   6   7   8

 9  10  11  12
13  14  15  16

17  18  19  20
21  22  23  24
```

190 / Extended Scalar and Mixed Functions

There are three possible scan operations, as follows:

```
+\[1]A ↔      1           2           3           4        ↔      1      2      3      4
              5           6           7           8               5      6      7      8

              1+9         2+10        3+11        4+12           10     12     14     16
              5+13        6+14        7+15        8+16           18     20     22     24

              1+9+17      2+10+18     3+11+19     4+12+20        27     30     33     36
              5+13+21     6+14+22     7+15+23     8+16+24        39     42     45     48

+\[2]A ↔      1           2           3           4        ↔     1      2      3      4
              1+5         2+6         3+7         4+8            6      8     10     12

              9          10          11          12              9     10     11     12
              9+13       10+14       11+15       12+16          22     24     26     28

             17          18          19          20             17     18     19     20
             17+21       18+22       19+23       20+24          38     40     42     44

+\[3]A ↔      1          1+2         1+2+3       1+2+3+4    ↔    1      3      6     10
              5          5+6         5+6+7       5+6+7+8         5     11     18     26

              9          9+10        9+10+11     9+10+11+12      9     19     30     42
             13         13+14       13+14+15    13+14+15+16     13     27     42     58

             17         17+18       17+18×19    17+18+19+20     17     35     54     74
             21         21+22       21+22+23    21+22+23+24     21     43     66     90
```

Example 6-1

We shall illustrate a simple application of add scan on a vector. Suppose M is a character matrix of single words of different lengths, such as

```
      M
TIME
IS
OF
THE
ESSENCE
```

Assume the number of columns in M equals the number of letters in the longest word. We are to create a monadic function FV that will take such a matrix as an argument, and return a vector of these words, with single spaces between them, as in the example

```
      FV M
TIME IS OF THE ESSENCE
```

We shall write an algorithm in APL notation, beginning with

```
NC←+/LC←' '≠M
```

This produces matrix LC and vector NC which, for this case, are

```
      LC
1 1 1 1 0 0 0
1 1 0 0 0 0 0
1 1 0 0 0 0 0
1 1 1 0 0 0 0
1 1 1 1 1 1 1
      NC
4 2 2 3 7
```

Elements of NC are the numbers of letters in the words. Note that

  $(,LC)/,M$

will place the words in a vector form, but without spaces. If we had the vector

1 1 1 1 0 1 1 0 1 1 0 1 1 1 0 1 1 1 1 1 1 1

it could be used as the left-hand argument of expansion on $(,LC)/,M$. This was the approach used in example 4-5, to insert spaces to the right of punctuation marks. However, rather than to create this Boolean vector, we shall use indexing and grade up to accomplish the same result. As a simple example of the method, suppose we have a vector $V \leftarrow 'ABCDEF'$ and want spaces to the right of C and E. This can be done by executing the statement

  $(V,2\uparrow' \ ')[\blacktriangle(\iota\rho V),\ 3\ 5]$

where (in origin 1) 3 5 is a vector of the indices of C and E. The result of grade up will be 1 2 3 7 4 5 8 6, in which 7 and 8 are indices for spaces.

 To apply this technique to the present problem, observe that

  $+\backslash\bar{\ }1\downarrow NC$

produces the index numbers of the ends of words in $(,LC)/,M$. The last element of NC is dropped because we do not want a space after the last word. Using these ideas, the function MV can now be written

```
     ∇ Z←MV D;LC;IZ
[1]    Z←ρIZ←+\¯1↓+/LC←' '≠D
[2]    Z←((LC/,D),Z↑' ')[▲(ι+/LC←,LC),IZ] ∇
```

In writing the function it is unnecessary to introduce the name NC.

General case

 Let the general case be represented by

  $s\backslash[J]B$

where J in the axis operator must be in the range $1 \leq J \leq \rho\rho B$ (in origin 1). Let R represent the result. The shape of R is the same as the shape of B. To give a general statement as to how the computations are done, let

  $R[;\ldots;I;\ldots;]$

represent an indexing operation, where the dots stand for undesignated numbers of semicolons, and the scalar index I is a particular index number for the Jth axis. This subarray is specified as follows:

  $R[;\ldots;I;\ldots;] \leftrightarrow s/[J]B[;\ldots;\iota I;\ldots;]$

 In similarity with reduction, the axis operator can be omitted for the first and last axes. In the notation of origin 1, it is possible to use

  $s\backslash B$ for $s\backslash[1]B$ and $s\backslash B$ for $s\backslash[\rho\rho B]B$

For any scalar function, scan on an empty vector returns an empty vector, and scan on a scalar value returns that scalar.

6-3 Outer Product

Here we shall generalize the description of the outer product, repeating the vector case, and extending the treatment to arguments of higher ranks. The general case is written using s to represent any primitive scalar function, as

$A \circ .s B$

In writing out these examples we shall use a symbolic notation in which functions have arguments shown as *displays*. While this is not a proper notation for computing, it simplifies the exposition. Examples of numerical results are obtained using × for s.

Two vectors

```
                              Equivalent to           Result (for s ↔ ×)

2  8  6  3 ∘.s 5  9  4  ↔   ┌─ ─ ─ ─┐
                            │2  2  2│ s │5  9  4│  ↔   10  18   8
                            │8  8  8│   │5  9  4│      40  72  32
                            │6  6  6│   │5  9  4│      30  54  24
                            │3  3  3│   │5  9  4│      15  27  12
                            └─ ─ ─ ─┘
                                  └─ 4  3 ρ 5  9  4
```

Vector on the left, matrix on the right

```
2  8  6  3 ∘.s 5  9  4  ↔   ┌─ ─ ─ ─┐
         1  7  3            │2  2  2│ s │5  9  4│  ↔   10  18   8
                            │2  2  2│   │1  7  3│       2  14   6
                            ├─ ─ ─ ─┤
                            │8  8  8│   │5  9  4│      40  72  32
                            │8  8  8│   │1  7  3│       8  56  24
                            ├─ ─ ─ ─┤
                            │6  6  6│   │5  9  4│      30  54  24
                            │6  6  6│   │1  7  3│       6  42  18
                            ├─ ─ ─ ─┤
                            │3  3  3│   │5  9  4│      15  27  12
                            │3  3  3│   │1  7  3│       3  21   9
                            └─ ─ ─ ─┘
                                  └─ 4  2  3 ρ 5  9  4
                                              1  7  3
```

Matrix on the left, vector on the right

```
2  8  6  3 ∘.s 5  9  4  ↔   ┌─ ─ ─ ─┐
4  1  9  7                  │2  2  2│ s │5  9  4│  ↔   10  18   8
                            │8  8  8│   │5  9  4│      40  72  32
                            │6  6  6│   │5  9  4│      30  54  24
                            │3  3  3│   │5  9  4│      27  27  12
                            ├─ ─ ─ ─┤
                            │4  4  4│   │5  9  4│      20  36  16
                            │1  1  1│   │5  9  4│       5   9   4
                            │9  9  9│   │5  9  4│      45  81  36
                            │7  7  7│   │5  9  4│      35  63  28
                            └─ ─ ─ ─┘
                                  └─ 2  4  3 ρ 5  9  4
```

Two matrices

```
2  8   ∘.s  9  7  4   ↔  |2  2  2| s |9  7  4|  ↔  18  14   8
3  5        3  5  9      |2  2  2|   |3  5  9|      6  10  18
6  4                     
                         |8  8  8|   |9  7  4|     72  56  32
                         |8  8  8|   |3  5  9|     24  40  72

                         |3  3  3|   |9  7  4|     27  21  12
                         |3  3  3|   |3  5  9|      9  15  27

                         |5  5  5|   |9  7  4|     45  35  20
                         |5  5  5|   |3  5  9|     15  25  45

                         |6  6  6|   |9  7  4|     54  42  24
                         |6  6  6|   |3  5  9|     18  30  54

                         |4  4  4|   |9  7  4|     36  28  16
                         |4  4  4|   |3  5  9|     12  20  36
```

3 2 2 3 ρ 9 7 4
            3 5 9

The general case*

The key to understanding the above examples is the reshape function shown below the boxed array on the right of s. This reshape function produces the array indicated. In terms of the general notation

$A∘.sB$

it will be found that each of these reshape functions is

$((ρA),ρB)ρB$

The general case of the outer product can be constructed by carrying out the following steps:

(1) Create the array $((ρA),ρB)ρB$.
(2) To the left of the array created in 1, draw boxes to represent another array having the same shape as the array from 1.
(3) Compute the number N of elements in B (this is $×/ρB$).
(4) In the normal reading order, fill in the empty boxes obtained in 2; the first N elements are repetitions of the first element of A, the next N elements are repetitions of the second element of A, etc. until the boxes are filled. This will exhaust the elements of A.
(5) Do the scalar operation s between these arrays. The result is the outer product.

---

*The outer product is equivalent to the following:
   $(((ρρA)⌽ιρ(ρB),ρA)⍉((ρB),ρA)ρA)s((ρA),ρB)ρB$
This statement uses the dyadic transpose, discussed in Sec. 6-13.

194 / Extended Scalar and Mixed Functions

The outer product has no compatibility conditions, except for whatever limit the computer places on rank. The rank of the result is the sum of the ranks of the arguments, and the shape of the result is the catenation of the shapes of the arguments. In APL notation these are:

Rank of result: $(\rho\rho A)+\rho\rho B$

Shape of result: $(\rho A),\rho B$

These generalizations apply if either argument is a scalar, in which case the outer product reduces to the ordinary scalar function.

6-4 Inner Product

This section develops the general case for the inner product. It includes a repetition of the previous treatment of Sec. 3-21, but in a notation which lends itself to generalization. We shall use the general notation

$A r.s B$

where r and s represent scalar functions (r and s are not necessarily different). We shall develop specific examples from which a procedure for the general case can be inferred. As in the case of the outer product, we shall use a symbolic notation in which arguments of functions are shown as displays. Numerical results on the far right of the examples are obtained using + for r and × for s. In the examples, axis operators are in origin 1.

Two vectors   Equivalent to   Result (for r ↔ +, s ↔ ×)

```
    3 8 6 r.s 2 9 7 ↔ r/[1] ⌈3 8 6⌉ s ⌈2 9 7⌉ ↔ 120
                                         │
                                         └─ 3ρ 2 9 7
```

Vector on the left, matrix on the right

```
    3 8 6 r.s 2 1 ↔ r/[1] ⌈3 3⌉ s ⌈2 1⌉ ↔ 120 67
              9 5         │8 8│   │9 5│
              7 4         │6 6│   │7 4│
                                    │
                                    └─ 3 2 ρ 2 1
                                             9 5
                                             7 4
```

Matrix on the left, vector on the right

```
    2 9 7 r.s 3 8 6 ↔ r/[2] ⌈2 9 7⌉ s ⌈3 8 6⌉ ↔ 120 67
    1 5 4           │1 5 4│   │3 8 6│
                                │
                                └─ 2 3 ρ 3 8 6
```

Extended Scalar and Mixed Functions / 195

Two matrices

```
2 9 7  r.s  4 2   ↔  r/[2] ┌─────┐ ┌───┐  ↔  78  111
1 5 4       7 8         │2  2│ │4  2│     43   62
            1 5         │9  9│ │7  8│
                        │7  7│ │1  5│
                        │    │ │    │
                        │1  1│ │4  2│
                        │5  5│ │7  8│
                        │4  4│ │1  5│
                        └─────┘ └───┘
                              ↑
                          └── 2 3 2 ρ 4 2
                                      7 8
                                      1 5
```

Matrix on the left, rank 3 array on the right

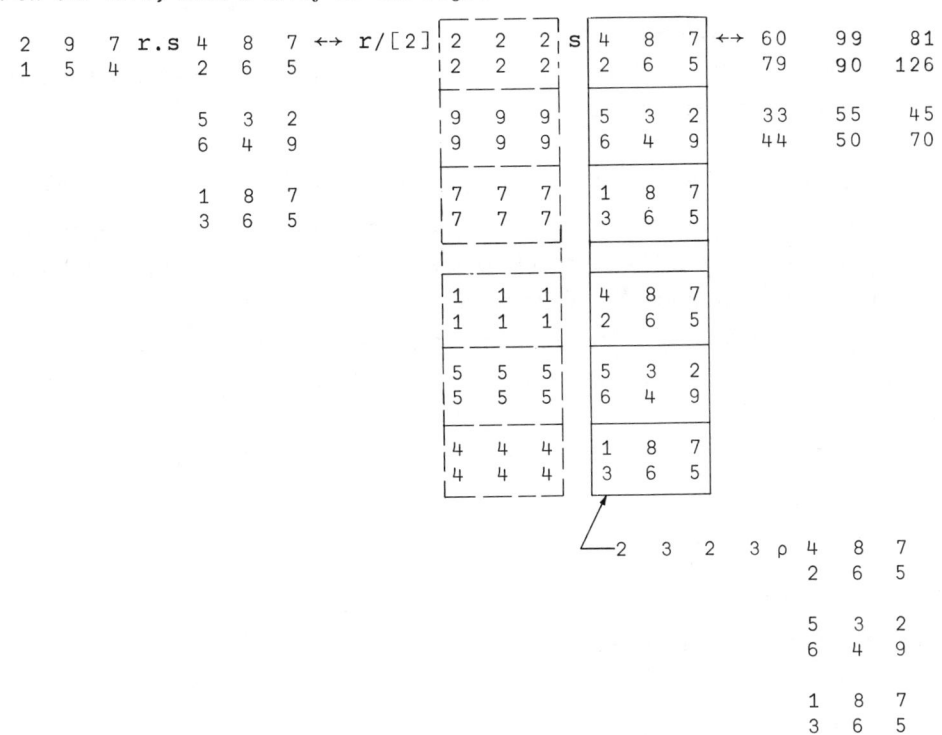

```
2 9 7  r.s  4 8 7  ↔  r/[2] ┌───────┐ ┌───────┐  ↔  60  99  81
1 5 4       2 6 5         │2 2 2│ │4 8 7│     79  90 126
                          │2 2 2│ │2 6 5│
            5 3 2         │     │ │     │     33  55  45
            6 4 9         │9 9 9│ │5 3 2│     44  50  70
                          │9 9 9│ │6 4 9│
            1 8 7         │     │ │     │
            3 6 5         │7 7 7│ │1 8 7│
                          │7 7 7│ │3 6 5│
                          │     │ │     │
                          │1 1 1│ │4 8 7│
                          │1 1 1│ │2 6 5│
                          │     │ │     │
                          │5 5 5│ │5 3 2│
                          │5 5 5│ │6 4 9│
                          │     │ │     │
                          │4 4 4│ │1 8 7│
                          │4 4 4│ │3 6 5│
                          └───────┘ └───────┘
                                ↑
                            └── 2 3 2 3 ρ 4 8 7
                                          2 6 5

                                          5 3 2
                                          6 4 9

                                          1 8 7
                                          3 6 5
```

The general case*

In terms of the notation

$Ar.sB$

the general condition for compatibility is

---

*The inner product is equivalent to the following, when A and B are not scalars:
   r/[ρρA](((1-ρρB)φι¯1+ρ(ρB),ρA)⍉((1↓ρB),ρA)ρA)s((¯1↓ρA),ρB)ρB
This statement uses the dyadic transpose, discussed in Sec. 6-13.

¯1↑⍴A ↔ 1↓⍴B

That is, the dimension of the last axis of A must equal the dimension of the first axis of B. However, there is an exceptional case: If A or B is a scalar or vector of one element, it is automatically extended by repetition to a vector of dimension compatible with the other argument.

In each of the examples above, the array structure shown on the right of s is obtained from the reshape function ((¯1↓⍴A),⍴B)⍴B. This expression gives the shape of the result, except when A or B is a scalar, or one-element vector. Also, it is found that for each example (in origin 1) the axis operator is [⍴⍴A]. With this information we can write the steps for producing the inner product (excluding the exceptional case) as follows:

(1) Create the array ((¯1↓⍴A),⍴B)⍴B.
(2) To the left of the array created in 1, draw boxes to represent another array having the same shape as the array from 1.
(3) Compute the number N as ×/1↓⍴B.
(4) In the normal reading order, fill in the empty boxes obtained in 2; the first N elements are repetitions of the first element of A, the next N elements are repetitions of the second element of A, etc. until the boxes are filled. This will exhaust the elements of A.
(5) Do the scalar operation s between the arrays obtained in 1 and 4.
(6) Do the reduction r/[⍴⍴A] on the array obtained in 5. The result is the inner product.

Excluding the exceptional case noted above, in APL notation the properties of the result are:

Rank of result: 0⌈¯2+(⍴⍴A)+⍴⍴B

Shape of result: (¯1↓⍴A),1↓⍴B

If one of the arguments is a scalar or one-element vector P, then,

Pr.sB ↔ r/PsB

Ar.sP ↔ r/AsP

Part B - MIXED FUNCTIONS

Most of the mixed functions provide means for manipulating the internal structures of arrays. These manipulations deal predominantly with: combining arrays, selecting parts of arrays, rearranging elements in a variety of ways, and inserting new elements. A few of the mixed functions do not fit into these categories. Some of the mixed functions are treated completely in earlier chapters and are not included here. A list of these, with references, is given in the introduction to this chapter.

6-5 Catenate

Catenation for vectors and matrices is treated in Sec. 3-4, including the special cases where one argument is of lower rank than the other. This function also accepts arrays of ranks higher than 2, with catenations being possible along each axis. The general case can be described under two compatibility conditions.

General case 1: Both arguments of the same rank (1 or higher)

The catenation

   A,[I]B

is possible if (in origin 1) I is an integer from 1 to ⍴⍴A, inclusive, and the dimensions of corresponding axes of A and B are the same except possibly the Ith. In APL notation this condition is

   (I≠⍳⍴⍴A)/⍴A ↔ (I≠⍳⍴⍴B)/⍴B

The result is obtained by appending B to A along axis I, producing a result having the same rank as the arguments, and having all dimensions of axes the same as the arguments except the Ith whose dimension is the sum of the dimensions of the Ith axes of the arguments. In APL notation,

   Rank of result: ⍴⍴A

   Shape of result: S after S←⍴A
                            S[I]←S[I]+(⍴B)[I]

If the axis operator is omitted, the highest axis number is implied.

General case 2: Ranks differ by 1, or one argument is a scalar

   Now consider

   A,[I]B

where A and B are not of the same rank. The operation is possible if the ranks differ by exactly 1 *or* if one argument is a scalar. If the ranks differ by 1 the shape of the argument of smaller rank must equal the shape of the argument of larger rank *with the Ith element removed*. I is an axis number for the argument of larger rank.

The result can be written in terms of General case 1. To describe how this is done, let R be the shape vector obtained by taking the shape of the argument of larger rank and replacing its Ith element by 1. Then, the results are as follows:

   A,[I]R⍴B   if   ⍴⍴A > ⍴⍴B

or

   (R⍴A),[I]B   if   ⍴⍴A < ⍴⍴B

These expressions merely state that the scalar, or array of lower rank, is extended to form an array which is compatible under the previous case. This extended array has dimension 1 for the Ith axis. In this case the dimension of the Ith axis of the result is 1 greater than the dimension of that axis in the array of larger rank. In APL notation, if C stands for whichever of A and B is of the higher rank.

   Rank of result: ⍴⍴C

   Shape of result: S after S←⍴C
                            S[I]←S[I]+1

6-6 Laminate

The lamination of vectors was treated in Sec. 3-4. In the present section we shall consider the extension to ranks higher than 1.

Matrices

Using the examples

```
    M1
2   8   3   1
4   1   7   5
6   5   4   3
```

and

```
    M2
6   3   5   6
8   2   9   2
2   7   6   4
```

there are three applications of laminate, as follows:

```
    M1,[0.5]M2
2   8   3   1
4   1   7   5
6   5   4   3

6   3   5   6      Shape of result: 2  3  4
8   2   9   2                        ↑
2   7   6   4                        └Axis added
```

```
    M1,[1.5]M2
2   8   3   1
6   3   5   6

4   1   7   5      Shape of result: 3  2  4
8   2   9   2                           ↑
                                        └Axis added
6   5   4   3
2   7   6   4
```

```
    M1,[2.5]M2
2   6
8   3
3   5
1   6

4   8
1   2
7   9              Shape of result: 3  4  2
5   2                                     ↑
                                          └Axis added
6   2
5   7
4   6
3   4
```

In these examples, which are for origin 1, 0.5 can be any number between 0 and 1 (exclusive), 1.5 can be any number between 1 and 2 (exclusive), 2.5 can be any number between 2 and 3 (exclusive). In origin 0, the ends of these ranges are 1 less than given above.

General case

For the general case (in origin 1)

$A,[N]B$

can be done if ρA equals ρB and N is a noninteger between 0 and $1+\rho A$. The rank of the result is 1 greater than the rank of A, and the new axis is inserted between axis $\lfloor N$ and axis $\lceil N$ of A. This inserted axis always has dimension 2. A and B are combined along the new axis as in a catenation. To interpret the word "between" in the statement above when $\lfloor N$ equals 0 (or $\rho\rho N$), imagine A temporarily has an axis 0 (or $1+\rho\rho A$).

Rank of result: $1+\rho\rho A$

Shape of result: $((\lfloor N)\uparrow\rho A),2,(\lfloor N)\downarrow\rho A$

There is also a special case. Laminate can be done when one argument is a scalar, no matter what the rank of the other argument. In such a case, the scalar is extended by repetition to the shape of the other argument. Then, the description given above applies, and the statements for the shape and rank of the result are valid if A is interpreted as that argument which is not a scalar.

6-7 Take and Drop

The functions take and drop are described for vectors and matrices in Sec. 3-15. We shall now extend these functions to the general case, beginning with examples for rank 3, in terms of the array

```
       A
  1   2   3   4
  5   6   7   8

  9  10  11  12
 13  14  15  16
```

Two examples of take are

```
       ¯1  ¯3   2 ↑A
  0   0
  9  10                 Take 1 page from high index end
 13  14                 Take 3 rows from high index end
                        Take 2 columns from low index end
```

and

```
       3   2  ¯5 ↑A
  0   1   2   3   4
  0   5   6   7   8

  0   9  10  11  12     Take 3 pages from low index end
  0  13  14  15  16     Take 2 rows from low index end
                        Take 5 columns from high index end
  0   0   0   0   0
  0   0   0   0   0
```

Two examples of drop are

```
       1   1  ¯2 ↓A
 13  14                 Drop 1 page from low index end
                        Drop 1 row from low index end
                        Drop 2 columns from high index end
```

200 / Extended Scalar and Mixed Functions

and

```
      ¯1   0   1  ↓A            Drop 1 page from high index end
       2   3   4                Drop no rows
       6   7   8                Drop 1 column from low index end
```

In the descriptions above, the words "low index end" and "high index end" refer to the range of indices for a given axis. Thus, for a vector the low index end is on the left; for a matrix the low index end for axis 1 is on the top.

On numeric arrays, a take of more elements than the dimension of an axis produces zeros for the extra elements. A similar situation for a character array produces spaces.

General case

The general cases

$A↑B$

and

$A↓B$

both require the condition that A shall be a vector having the property $\rho A \leftrightarrow \rho\rho B$, except for two degenerate cases: If B is a vector, A can be a scalar or one-element vector; if B is a scalar, A can be a scalar or vector of any number of elements. The elements of A must be integers. For take, the elements of A determine how many index positions are taken from the corresponding axes of B. For drop, the elements of A determine how many index positions are dropped from corresponding axes of B.

Signs of the elements of A operate in the same manner as when B is a vector: Positive numbers take or drop beginning at the low index end of an axis, negative numbers take or drop beginning at the high index end of an axis.

In APL notation, the ranks and shapes of the results are

Rank of result: ρ,A

Shape of result of take: $|,A$

Shape of result of drop: $0\lceil(\rho B)-|,A$ or $0\lceil 1-|,A$ if B is a scalar

6-8 Compression

Compression for vectors is described in Sec. 4-19, and so here we extend the function to higher ranks, and consider the general case. The examples are in origin 1.

Matrix

Using

```
       M
   1   2   3   4   5
   6   7   8   9  10
  11  12  13  14  15
  16  17  18  19  20
```

an example of compression along axis 1 is

```
      1 0 1 0 /[1]M
   1  2  3  4  5           Keep rows 1 and 3 of all columns
  11 12 13 14 15
```

and an example of compression along axis 2 is

```
      0 1 0 0 1 /[2]M
   2   5
   7  10
  12  15                   Keep columns 2 and 5 of all rows
  17  20
```

Array of rank 3

For an array such as

```
       A
   1   2   3   4
   5   6   7   8
   9  10  11  12

  13  14  15  16
  17  18  19  20
  21  22  23  24
```

there are three possible axes along which there can be compression. An example for axis 1 is

```
      0 1 /[1]A
  13 14 15 16
  17 18 19 20              Keep page 2 of all rows and columns
  21 22 23 24
```

and an example for axis 2 is

```
      1 1 0 /[2]A
   1  2  3  4
   5  6  7  8
                           Keep rows 1 and 2 of all pages and columns
  13 14 15 16
  17 18 19 20
```

Finally, an example of compression along axis 3 is

```
      0 1 1 0 /[3]A
   2   3
   6   7
  10  11
                           Keep columns 2 and 3 of all pages and rows
  14  15
  18  19
  22  23
```

General case

In the general notation (in origin 1)

   I/[J]A

I is a Boolean vector, A is a numeric or character array of any rank, and the axis

202 / Extended Scalar and Mixed Functions

index J is in the range from 1 to $\rho\rho A$, inclusive. The dimension of I must equal the dimension of the Jth axis of A. The function performs the operation of removing those index positions along axis J which correspond with the index positions of zeros in I. The dimension of axis J of the result equals $+/I$.

In APL notation, the compatibility condition is

$\rho I \leftrightarrow (\rho A)[,J]$

and the specifications of the results are (in origin 1)

Rank of result: $\rho\rho A$

Shape of result: $((J-1)\uparrow\rho A),(+/I),J\downarrow\rho A$

There are two special cases which violate the relationships given above: I can be a scalar 0 or 1, or A can be a scalar. If I is a scalar, it is automatically extended by repetition to a vector of length $(\rho A)[J]$. Thus, $1/[J]A$ is equivalent to A, and $0/[J]A$ is empty with zero dimension for axis J. If A is a scalar, it is automatically extended by repetition to length ρI, so I/A is equivalent to $I/(\rho I)\rho A$. If I and A are scalars, the result is the same as if they were one-element vectors.

The alternate notation

$I \neq A$

can be used for compression along the first axis of an array of any rank, and

I/A

can be used for compression along the last axis of an array of any rank.

6-9 Expansion

Expansion on vectors is treated in Sec. 4-19. In this section we deal with the general case, including examples for ranks 2 and 3. Examples are in origin 1.

Matrix

Consider the matrix

```
    M
1   2   3   4
5   6   7   8
9  10  11  12
```

An example of expansion along axis 1 is

```
     0 1 1 0 1 \[1]M
0    0    0    0
1    2    3    4        Zeros in new rows 1 and 4
5    6    7    8
0    0    0    0
9   10   11   12
```

and an example of expansion along axis 2 is

```
     1 1 0 0 1 1 0 \[2]M
1    2    0    0    3    4    0
5    6    0    0    7    8    0     Zeros in new columns 3, 4, and 7
9   10    0    0   11   12    0
```

Array of rank 3

        Using

           A
        1 2 3 4
        5 6 7 8
        9 10 11 12

       13 14 15 16
       17 18 19 20
       21 22 23 24

for illustration, there can be expansion along any one of the three axes. An example along the first is

          1 0 1 \[1]A
        1 2 3 4
        5 6 7 8
        9 10 11 12

        0 0 0 0
        0 0 0 0   Zeros in new page 2
        0 0 0 0

       13 14 15 16
       17 18 19 20
       21 22 23 24

Along the second and third axes, examples are:

          1 0 1 1 0 \[2]A
        1 2 3 4
        0 0 0 0
        5 6 7 8
        9 10 11 12
        0 0 0 0   Zeros in new rows 2 and 5

       13 14 15 16
        0 0 0 0
       17 18 19 20
       21 22 23 24
        0 0 0 0

and

          0 1 0 0 1 1 1 \[3]A
        0 1 0 0 2 3 4
        0 5 0 0 6 7 8
        0 9 0 0 10 11 12   Zeros in new columns 1, 3, and 4

        0 13 0 0 14 15 16
        0 17 0 0 18 19 20
        0 21 0 0 22 23 24

General case

    In the general notation

        I\[J]A

I is a Boolean vector, A is a numeric or character array of any rank, and the axis J is in the range from 1 to ⍴⍴A, inclusive (in origin 1). I must satisfy the condition

204 / Extended Scalar and Mixed Functions

that the number of 1's must equal the dimension of axis J of A. The function inserts zeros at index positions along axis J of the result to correspond with locations of zeros in I. The dimension of axis J of the result equals the dimension of I. In APL notation, the compatibility condition is

$$+/I \leftrightarrow (\rho A)[J]$$

and the specifications of the results are (in origin 1)

Rank of result: $\rho\rho A$

Shape of result: $((J-1)\uparrow\rho A),(\rho I),J\downarrow\rho A$

Not included in the above is the special case where A is a scalar. Then, A is automatically extended by repetition to a vector of compatible length $+/I$, and therefore in that case $I\backslash A$ is equivalent to $I\times A$ (or $I\times A$ if I and A are both scalars).

When expansion is on a character matrix, spaces are inserted in index positions corresponding to zeros in the left-hand argument.

6-10 Index Function

The index function is rather thoroughly treated in Sec. 3-13, and used there in simple forms in many examples. Therefore, the remaining task is to deal with its general properties; treating the indexing of an array of any rank with index values which may themselves be arrays of any ranks.

As a beginning, let V be a vector, say

$V\leftarrow$'ABCDEFGHIJ'

and consider two other arrays

```
    I1
2   5   3
6   8  10

    I2
7   5
1   3
2   9

4   6
5   7
4   3
```

Using these as index values in V, we get

```
    V[I1]                    V[I2]
BEC                          GE
FHJ                          AC
                             BI

                             DF
                             EG
                             DC
```

These examples show that the shape and rank of the result depend on the shape and rank of the *index value*, not on the array being indexed. To continue this line of thought, observe the following equivalencies:

Extended Scalar and Mixed Functions / 205

$V[I1] \leftrightarrow (\rho I1)\rho V[,I1]$

$V[I2] \leftrightarrow (\rho I2)\rho V[,I2]$

Writing the results for the statements on the right above will confirm the equivalence in each case. The reason for including this step is to demonstrate that in the equivalent form on the right, the shape information concerning the index value is put "outside", as an argument of reshape, while the *ravels* of the index values are used in the index function.

As the next step in complexity, now suppose we have the matrix

```
      M
ABCDEFGHIJ
KLMNOPQRST
```

First we note that $M[1;I1]$ and $M[1;I2]$ (or $M[2;I1]$ and $M[2;I2]$) are basically similar to $V[I1]$ and $V[I2]$ because $M[1;]$ and $M[2;]$ are vectors. Therefore, these do not require consideration. For $M[;I1]$ and $M[;I2]$, which are equivalent to $M[1\ 2;I1]$ and $M[1\ 2;I2]$, we have

```
     M[;I1]                    M[;I2]
BEC                         GE
FHJ                         AC
                            BI
LOM
PRT                         DF
                            EG
                            DC

                            QO
                            KM
                            LS

                            NP
                            OQ
                            NM
```

A still more complicated example of indexing a matrix with matrix index values is

```
      M[2 2 ρ 1 2 2;I1]
BEC
FHJ

LOM
PRT


LOM
PRT

BEC
FHJ
```

An investigation of these three examples will show the validity of the following equivalencies:

206 / Extended Scalar and Mixed Functions

```
M[;I1] ↔ M[1 2;I1] ↔ (2,ρI1)ρM[1 2;,I1]
M[;I2] ↔ M[1 2;I2] ↔ (2,ρI2)ρM[1 2;,I2]
M[2 2 ρ 1 2 2;I1] ↔ (2 2,ρI1)ρM[1 2 2 1;,I1]
```

Thus, in all cases so far considered, indexing with index values of ranks higher than 1 can be reduced to the simpler indexing with vector index values. A reshape operation whose left-hand argument is the catenation of the *shapes of the index values* restores the structure.

Without further examples, we extend this principle to the general case. If A is an array of rank N, and $I1, I2,...IN$ are index values of any ranks, then

```
A[I1;I2;...;IN] ↔ ((ρI1),(ρI2),...,ρIN)ρA[,I1;,I2;...;,IN]
```

Of course, if the full range of indices of any axis is wanted, the index value for that axis will be left blank, and the dimension of that axis of A will be used in the corresponding place in the argument of reshape in the equivalent form on the right.

We conclude that for the general case, in the notation used previously,

Rank of result: `+/(ρρI1),(ρρI2),...,ρρIN`

Shape of result: `(ρI1),(ρI2),...,ρIN`

It is evident that indexing can provide a rich assortment of results from a given array. You should be aware that for certain cases indexing can produce the same results as compression or take or drop; but indexing is more general. For operations that can be performed by compression, take, or drop, those functions are to be preferred over indexing; they are faster, and less sensitive to rank because of the necessity of including the proper number of semicolons when using the index function.

6-11 Reverse

The function reverse was described for vectors and matrices in Sec. 3-17. In the present section we shall extend it to the general case.

Array of rank 3

Considering the example of an array of rank 3

```
       A
 1    2    3
 4    5    6
 7    8    9

10   11   12
13   14   15
16   17   18
```

reverse can be executed with respect to any one of three axes, as in the following (in origin 1):

```
        φ[1]A                    φ[2]A                    φ[3]A
    10  11  12                7   8   9                3   2   1
    13  14  15                4   5   6                6   5   4
    16  17  18                1   2   3                9   8   7

     1   2   3               16  17  18               12  11  10
     4   5   6               13  14  15               15  14  13
     7   8   9               10  11  12               18  17  16
```

General case

In terms of the general notation

    φ[J]A

the value of J in the axis operator is an integer in the range from 1 to ρρA, inclusive (in origin 1). There is no change in shape or rank. The result is obtained by reversing the positions of the elements along axis J.

The axis operator can be omitted in two cases: reverse with respect to the first axis can be designated by

    ⊖A

and

    φA

means reverse with respect to the last axis.

6-12 Rotate

The operation of the function rotate for vector and matrix right-hand arguments was treated in Sec. 3-17. In the present section we shall consider an example of rank 3, and then give a description of the general case (in origin 1).

Array of rank 3

The array

```
         A
     1   2   3   4
     5   6   7   8

     9  10  11  12
    13  14  15  16

    17  18  19  20
    21  22  23  24
```

will be used for illustration. If we think about rotation along axis 1, there are eight vectors within the array which are candidates for rotation. Specified by their elements, they are 1 9 17, 2 10 18, 3 11 19, 4 12 20; and 5 13 21, 6 14 22, 7 15 23, 8 16 24. The left-hand argument must specify a rotation for each of these, and will be a matrix. An example, written symbolically, is

208 / Extended Scalar and Mixed Functions

```
1  0  2 ¯1  ⌽[1]A ↔   9   2  19  20
2 ¯1  0  1            21  22   7  16

                      17  10   3   4
                       5   6  15  24

                       1  18  11  12
                      13  14  23   8
```

The row `1 0 2 ¯1` specifies rotations for matrix `A[;1;]`, and `2 ¯1 0 1` specifies rotations for matrix `A[;2;]`.

Similar examples for axes 2 and 3 are

```
1  0 ¯1  1  ⌽[2]A ↔   5   2   7   8      2  1  ⌽[3]A ↔   3   4   1   2
0 ¯1  0  1            1   6   3   4      0 ¯3             6   7   8   5
1  0  0 ¯1                               3 ¯1

                      9  14  11  16                       9  10  11  12
                     13  10  15  12                      14  15  16  13

                     21  18  19  24                      20  17  18  19
                     17  22  23  20                      24  21  22  23
```

In these examples it is observed that the shape of the left-hand argument is `(J≠⍳3)/⍴A`, where `J` is the number of the axis and 3 is the rank of `A`.

General case

The left-hand argument of

`R⌽[J]A`

where `A` is of any rank must be an array of integers satisfying the compatibility condition

`⍴R ↔ (J≠⍳⍴⍴A)/⍴A`

An attempt to write the properties of the general case leads to messy notation. Instead, we shall assume rank 4 is high enough to represent the general case. If `A` is rank 4, `R` will be rank 3, and picking axis 2 as a typical case, if

`D←R⌽[2]A`

then

      Scalar Vector

`D[K;;L;M] ↔ R[K;L;M]⌽A[K;;L;M]`

The direction of rotation of this vector is subject to the usual dependence on sign of the left-hand argument. If the sign is positive, rotation is toward the end of the axis having low index numbers; if it is negative, rotation is in the other direction.

A similar expression applies for other axes. In the notation above, `K`, `L`, and `M` are scalars within the ranges permitted by the shape of `A`. The point made by the formulation is that rotation of an array is a collection of rotations of vectors.

There is a special case which violates the compatibility condition: For any rank on the right, the left-hand argument can be a scalar or one-element vector. Then, the computer executes the function as if the one element on the left were replicated as an array of shape compatible with the argument on the right. Thus, using the previous `A`,

```
         1⌽[3]A ↔  1    1 ⌽[3]A ↔   2   3   4   1
                   1 1              6   7   8   5
                   1 1
                                   10  11  12   9
                                   14  15  16  13

                                   18  19  20  17
                                   22  23  24  21
```

Rotation along the first and last axes can be designated respectively by ⊖ and ⌽ without explicitly showing the axis operator.

6-13 Monadic and Dyadic Transpose

The function transpose has two forms: monadic and dyadic. The monadic form with matrix argument is treated in Sec. 3-18. The purpose here is to introduce the dyadic form, and to consider the monadic and dyadic forms for arguments of ranks higher than 2. The analysis is in origin 1.

Matrix

Consideration of the dyadic transpose of a matrix will be in terms of the example

```
       M
 1   2   3   4
 5   6   7   8
 9  10  11  12
```

From Sec. 3-18 we have the monadic transpose

```
       ⍉M
 1   5   9
 2   6  10
 3   7  11
 4   8  12
```

The first example of the dyadic transpose is

```
    2  1 ⍉M
 1   5   9
 2   6  10
 3   7  11
 4   8  12
```

It is evident that this is the same as ⍉M. However, for the dyadic transpose the left-hand argument explicitly states what axes are interchanged. To explain how, let the left-hand argument of the above (namely 2 1) be given the name T. Then the fact that $T[1]$ is 2 means that axis 1 (the *index* value of $T[1]$) of the argument transposes to axis 2 (the *indexed* value of $T[1]$) in the result. Similarly $T[2]$ having the value 1 means that axis 2 of the argument transposes to axis 1 of the result.

Since 2 1 ⍉M and ⍉M give identical results, it would seem that the dyadic transpose is superfluous in the case of a matrix. However, this is not completely true. $T⍉M$ is useful in cases where under different conditions a transpose is sometimes wanted and sometimes not, under computer control. For example,

```
       (K⌽ 1  2)⍉M
```

will execute a transpose when K is 1, and not when K is 0.

210 / Extended Scalar and Mixed Functions

Array of rank 3

We shall use the array

```
        A
  1   2   3   4
  5   6   7   8

  9  10  11  12
 13  14  15  16

 17  18  19  20
 21  22  23  24
```

for illustration. One example of a dyadic transpose on this array is

```
    T←3 1 2
    T⍉A
 1   9  17
 2  10  18
 3  11  19
 4  12  20

 5  13  21
 6  14  22
 7  15  23
 8  16  24
```

How this result is obtained will now be explained. First, observe the following interpretation of T.

$T[1] \leftrightarrow 3$ means that axis 1 of A becomes axis 3 of the result.
$T[2] \leftrightarrow 1$ means that axis 2 of A becomes axis 1 of the result.
$T[3] \leftrightarrow 2$ means that axis 3 of A becomes axis 2 of the result.

Then, we note that the dimensions of each axis will remain fixed when the axis number changes. Thus, the shape of the result is

$(\rho A)[2],(\rho A)[3],(\rho A)[1] \leftrightarrow 2\ 4\ 3$

A more graphical description of how to obtain the shape of the result is to write the three vectors

```
    3  1  2  ←──────── The vector T
    3  2  4  ←──────── The shape of A
    2  4  3  ←──────── The shape of the result
```

The third of these vectors is obtained from the other two: an element of the first vector determines the index position in the third vector of the corresponding element of the second vector.

The method of obtaining the shape of the result is essential to an understanding of the dyadic transpose, and so we pursue it a bit further. If R is the result of $T⍉A$, each of the above approaches is summarized by

$(\rho R)[T[I]] \leftrightarrow (\rho A)[I]$ where $1 \leq I \leq \rho \rho A$

which can be written in the more concise form

$\rho R \leftrightarrow (\rho A)[⍋T]$

Extended Scalar and Mixed Functions / 211

On the basis of this procedure for finding the shape of the result, we can develop an algorithm for predicting the result of a dyadic transpose operation. The algorithm is this: First, determine the shape of the result, and draw a set of boxes of proper dimensions as determined by that shape. Second, choose $A[1;1;1]$ as a starting point and read along any axis of A while writing the elements along the transposed axis in the result. Next, do the other axes, starting from the same point. Then, use any one of the elements covered in this way as another starting point, and continue the process.

This algorithm is illustrated by the following partially completed result, for the example we have been using:

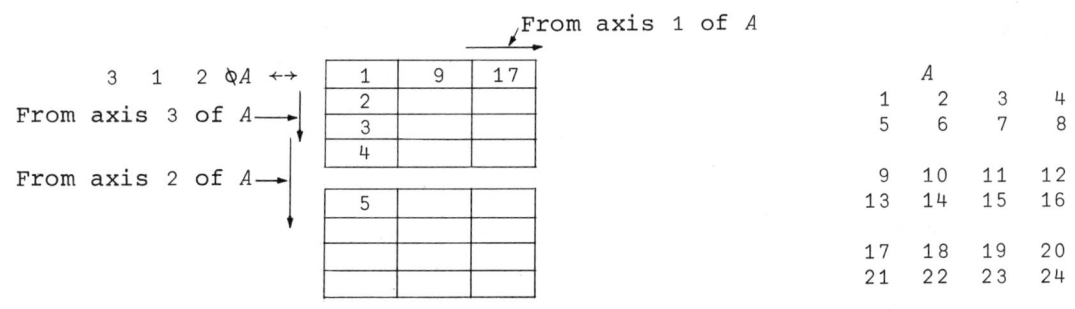

```
                      From axis 1 of A
                     ┌──────────────────┐
   3  1  2 ⍉A  ↔     │  1  │  9  │ 17  │
                     ├─────┼─────┼─────┤
From axis 3 of A ──→ │  2  │     │     │
                     ├─────┼─────┼─────┤
                     │  3  │     │     │
                     ├─────┼─────┼─────┤
                     │  4  │     │     │
                     └─────┴─────┴─────┘
From axis 2 of A ──→ ┌─────┬─────┬─────┐
                     │  5  │     │     │
                     ├─────┼─────┼─────┤
                     │     │     │     │
                     ├─────┼─────┼─────┤
                     │     │     │     │
                     ├─────┼─────┼─────┤
                     │     │     │     │
                     └─────┴─────┴─────┘
```

```
         A
  1   2   3   4
  5   6   7   8

  9  10  11  12
 13  14  15  16

 17  18  19  20
 21  22  23  24
```

With this beginning, the other elements readily fall into place; for example, element 5 can be the next starting point.

It is left as an exercise for you to confirm that, using the same argument A on the right,

```
     2   3   1 ⍉A
 1   5
 9  13
17  21

 2   6
10  14
18  22

 3   7
11  15
19  23

 4   8
12  16
20  24
```

The general case can now be described. For

$T⍉A$

it is necessary that T have the following properties:

$\rho T \leftrightarrow \rho\rho A$

$1 \leftrightarrow \wedge/(\iota\rho T)\epsilon T$

The second of these means that in origin 1 each integer from 1 to ρT inclusive (0 to $^-1+\rho T$ in origin 0) must be present in T.

The transpose $T⍉A$ produces an array having the properties:

212 / Extended Scalar and Mixed Functions

    Rank of result: ⍴⍴A

    Shape of result: (⍴A)[⍋T]

In either origin, the elements along axis I of A transpose to axis T[I] of the result. An alternate phrase is to say that axis I "maps" onto axis T[I].

General monadic transpose

    The monadic transpose of an array is described in terms of the dyadic transpose. For the case of rank 3,

    ⍉A ↔ 3 2 1 ⍉A

and for the general case

    ⍉A ↔ (⌽⍳⍴⍴A)⍉A

In words, the monadic transpose reverses the order of the axes.*

Example 6-2

    Suppose N is a character array of rank 3, carrying perhaps the following information:

    Page 1: Names of people
    Page 2: Telephone numbers
    Page 3: Street addresses
    Page 4: Cities, states, and zip codes

Corresponding rows of the various pages refer to the same person. For the description above, the first axis would be of dimension 4. But we assume this dimension can have any value, depending on the number of items of information stored for each person.

    We are to write a monadic program PRLIST which will take such an array as an argument and print a matrix in which each row is of the form:

    Name, Telephone number, Street address, State and zip code

In origin 1, such a function is

```
     ∇ PRLIST M;S
[1]    S←1⌽⍴M
[2]    ((1↑S),×/¯2↑S)⍴ 2 1 3 ⍉M ∇
```

In this function, 2 1 3 ⍉M rearranges the array so that in the result each page refers to one person. Each page will be

    Name
    Telephone number
    Street address
    City, state, and zip code

---

*In some of the early APL systems, the monadic transpose interchanges the last two axes.

This array is in a form which can be reshaped into the desired matrix. The left-hand argument of the reshape function is equivalent to (ρM)[2],(ρM)[1]×(ρM)[3].

6-14 Reduced Dyadic Transpose

A variation of the dyadic transpose allows a left-hand argument having repeated axis numbers and yields a result of reduced rank. This is a rather complicated function to describe in the general case, and so we give several examples.

Matrix

```
         M
    1    2    3    4
    5    6    7    8
    9   10   11   12
   13   14   15   16

        1   1 ⍉M
   1    6   11   16
```

In similarity with the regular dyadic transpose, the left-hand argument 1 1 indicates that axis 1 of the argument becomes axis 1 of the result, and also that axis 2 of the argument becomes axis 1 of the result. Both axes of the argument map onto one axis, giving a result which is the *vector* of diagonal elements because each element of the diagonal has the same index position on each axis.

It is not necessary for the matrix to be square. Thus,

```
         N
    1    2    3    4
    5    6    7    8
    9   10   11   12

        1   1 ⍉N
   1    6   11
```

Array of rank 3

In terms of the array

```
         A
    1    2    3    4
    5    6    7    8

    9   10   11   12
   13   14   15   16

   17   18   19   20
   21   22   23   24
```

three examples of the reduced dyadic transpose are:

```
    1  1  2 ⍉A              2  1  1 ⍉A              2  1  2 ⍉A
 1    2    3    4         1    9   17              1   10   19
13   14   15   16         6   14   22              5   14   23
```

Observe that the dimension in the result, of an axis obtained from several axes of the argument, is the minimum of the dimensions of those several axes. Thus, for the third of the examples above, axes 1 and 3 of the argument (of dimensions 3 and 4, respectively) map onto axis 2 of the result, having the dimension 3⌊4.

214 / Extended Scalar and Mixed Functions

General case

The conditions for compatibility in the reduced dyadic transpose

$R \mathbin{\lozenge\mkern-5mu\backslash} A$

are

$\rho R \leftrightarrow \rho \rho A$

$1 \leftrightarrow \wedge/(\iota \lceil/R)\epsilon R$

The second of these conditions ensures that there will be no gaps in the axis numbers in R.

The rank of the result is $\lceil/R$. A rather complicated expression is required to give the shape of the result, but in any specific case the dimension of an axis of the result is the minimum of the dimensions of the axes which map onto it.

6-15 Decode

The dyadic function *decode* (represented by the symbol $\bot$) takes arguments which are subject to a condition for compatibility similar to the condition for the inner product. We begin with an example, using the vector arguments

```
A←2 8 6 7
B←4 2 3 5
A⊥B
```
1454

This can be produced by the mathematically equivalent statement*

```
((8×6×7),(6×7),7,1)+.× 4 2 3 5
```
1454

To generalize, we specify the auxiliary variable

```
AA←⌽×\⌽(1↓A),1
AA
```
336 42 7 1

which is the left-hand argument of the equivalent given above. Thus, in terms of AA $A \bot B$ is equivalent to

$AA+.\times B$

It is to be noted that the first element of A does not enter into the computation of AA, so the result of $A \bot B$ is independent of the first element of A. However, this first element must exist, to satisfy compatibility.

The special case where all elements on the left are the same is of particular interest. For example

---

*The computer does not necessarily make the calculation in this way, but this statement is conceptually useful in showing the nature of the function encode. In some cases, due to roundoff errors, this statement may not be computationally equivalent.

```
        6  6  6  6 ⊥ 4  2  3  5
959
```

is equivalent to

```
    (4×6×6×6)+(2×6×6)+(3×6)+5
```

which is seen to be an evaluation of the polynomial (in conventional notation)

$$5 + 3x + 2x^2 + 4x^3$$

at $x = 6$. When this computation is wanted, it is possible to use

```
    6⊥ 4  2  3  5
```

The computer extends the scalar 6 by repetition to a length compatible with the vector on the right. A scalar on the right will similarly be extended automatically to match a vector on the left.

Vector on the left, matrix on the right

    Consider the matrix M

```
       M
    4  2
    2  6
    3  4
    5  3
```

and the execution

```
         2  8  6  7 ⊥M
    1454   955
```

This result is the catenation of the results of 2 8 6 7 ⊥ 4 2 3 5 and 2 8 6 7 ⊥ 2 6 4 3.

Matrix on the left, vector on the right

    If we have the matrix

```
         N
    2  8  6  7
    4  6 ¯3  3

         N⊥ 4  2  3  5
    1454  ¯220
```

is equivalent to the catenation of the results of 2 8 6 7 ⊥ 4 2 3 5 and 4 6 ¯3 3 ⊥ 4 2 3 5.

    An important special case occurs when the left-hand argument is a matrix of one column, say

```
        (3  1 ρ 2  3  4)⊥ 4  2  3  5
    51  140  305
```

The computer extends this left-hand argument to the matrix

```
    2  2  2  2
    3  3  3  3
    4  4  4  4
```

216 / Extended Scalar and Mixed Functions

Therefore, the result is the polynomial $5 + 3x + 2x^2 + 4x^3$ evaluated at $x = 2$, 3, and 4. This is a very convenient way to evaluate a polynomial.

Two matrices

Using the previously specified M and N,

```
    N⊥M
1454   955
 ¯220  ¯147
```

From the previous cases, (using notation in origin 1) it is evident that the first row is the result of $N[1;]⊥M$, and the second row is the result of $N[2;]⊥M$.

General case

The function decode is structurally similar to the inner product. The general compatibility condition for

   $A⊥B$

is

   $¯1↑ρA ↔ 1↑ρB$

Also, as for the inner product, A or B may be a scalar no matter what the rank of the other argument. The computer automatically extends such a scalar, by repetition, to a vector of compatible length. Furthermore, the arguments are compatible if $¯1↑ρA$ is 1 or $1↑ρB$ is 1, for any rank of the other argument. Whichever of these axes has dimension 1 is automatically extended by repetition to the compatible dimension. Assuming the general compatibility condition is satisfied, $A⊥B$ is equivalent to

   $(⌽×\⌽(((-ρρA)↑1)↓A),1)+.×B$

The result has the following properties

Rank of result: $0⌈¯2+(ρρA)+ρρB$

Shape of result: $(¯1↓ρA),1↓ρB$

Although all illustrations are with positive integers, decode accepts nonintegers and negative values.

Example 6-3

For an application of decode, suppose we have a matrix $TIME$ of any number of rows and 4 columns. Each row represents time measured from some reference point, in weeks (1st column), days (2nd column), hours (3rd column), and minutes (last column). We are to define a monadic function $ELAPSE$ which will take such a matrix as an argument and return a vector of the equivalent times, in weeks.

The decode function is used, with the left-hand argument

   1 7 24 60

where 1 is arbitrary, and 7 24 60 are, respectively, the numbers of days per week, hours per day, and minutes per hour. However, we must remember the similarity with the inner product, and arrange to have weeks, days, hours, minutes read vertically.

The function can be written

```
     ∇ T←ELAPSE P
[1]    T←(1  7  24  60 ⊥⌽P)÷10080 ∇
```

Division by 10080 (the number of minutes in a week) is necessary because the operation of decode yields time in minutes.

6-16 Encode

As an introduction to the function encode we consider a numerical example. Suppose we are given a scalar number such as 2733, and a vector such as 8 7 6 12. This vector is arbitrary except that, for the present, we want the product of the elements to be greater than 2733. In the following sequence of steps, each line is numerically equivalent to the one above it (you should confirm this). The value of each line is calculated by the APL rule for computation.

```
2733
(9+12×227)
9+12×(5+6×37)
9+12×5+6×(2+7×5)
9+12×5+6×2+7×(5+8×0)
```

Unneeded parentheses are included to help in the interpretation: In each line the expression within parentheses is equivalent to the last number on the right in the line above. It is interesting to note that, aside from the + and × signs, the last line contains the numbers of the original vector, in the reverse order 12 6 7 8, and a new set of numbers (those underlined). In effect, the number 2733 has been "encoded" in terms of the two vectors

```
   A←8  7  6  12
   B←5  2  5  9     The reverse of the numbers underlined above.
```

An analysis of the last line of the tabulation above will show that this encoding is such that the decode function

```
      A⊥B
2733
```

produces the original number.

The process we have just described is carried out by the dyadic function *encode* (represented by the symbol ⊤). For the example,

```
      8  7  6  12 ⊤2733
5  2  5  9
```

It is useful to consider further the nature of the calculations done by the encode function, by constructing a defined function which is equivalent. We continue to use the numerical example, and observe that 9+12×227 is calculated from 2733 in the two steps

```
      12|2733
9
      (2733-9)÷12
227
```

218 / Extended Scalar and Mixed Functions

Then the next line is computed from

```
      6|227
5
      (227-5)÷6
37
```

and so on. It is evident that this is a recursive process: The number 2733 is treated in a certain way to produce 227; this in turn is treated in the same way (but using 6 instead of 12) to produce 37, etc.

The following recursive function carries out this process.*

```
       ∇ Z←C ENCODE N;R;K
[1]    →(0<ρ,C)/L
[2]    Z←ι0
[3]    →0
[4]    L:Z←((¯1↓C)ENCODE (N-R)÷K),R←(K←¯1↑C)|N ∇
```

A ENCODE B simulates *A⊤B*. To demonstrate this, we shall trace the execution of *ENCODE* as follows:

```
      8 7 6 12 ENCODE 2733
      (8 7 6 ENCODE 227),12|2733
      (8 7 ENCODE 37),(6|227),9 ←──────── 9 is 12|2733
      (8 ENCODE 5),(7|37),5 9 ←────────── 5 is 6|227
      ((¯1↓8) ENCODE 0),(8|5),2 5 9 ←──── 2 is 7|37
5 2 5 9
```

The last execution of *ENCODE* is with ¯1↓8 (an empty vector) as the left-hand argument, and reference to the definition shows that the returned value is also empty. Therefore, the last execution contributes nothing to the accumulated vector 5 2 5 9.

When we first introduced our numerical example we mentioned that ×/8 7 6 12 is greater than 2733. We shall now consider what happens if that condition is not met, by using 6 12 as the left-hand argument. We get

```
      6 12 ENCODE 2733
      (6 ENCODE 227),12|2733
      ((¯1↓6) ENCODE 37),(6|227),9
5 9
```

Now consider

```
      6 12 ⊥ 5 9
69
```

showing that in this case decode is not an inverse of encode.

Observe that in the previous case the right-hand argument of the last execution of *ENCODE* is 0, but that in the case above this argument is 37. When this last argument is not 0, the process is *truncated*. For the nontruncated case**

---

*The encode function depends on the residue function. Therefore, if a computer uses a nonstandard definition of residue, encode will behave differently than described here. However, differences will occur only if there are negative elements in *A*. See the footnote on page 126.
**For all cases, it is generally true that

```
      A⊥A⊤B  ↔  (×/A)|B
```

However, there are some exceptional cases involving negative elements in *A* for which the equivalence is to (-×/A)|B. For the nontruncated case, (×/A)|B ↔ B.

$B \leftrightarrow A \perp A \top B$

The question naturally arises as to whether $A \top A \perp B$ is equal to B. This is true if A and B are nonnegative integers such that each element of A is greater than the corresponding element of B, with an exception for the first element of A if it is 0.

When B and all elements of A are positive, making $\times/A$ greater than B will ensure there is no truncation. Another way to ensure there will be no truncation is to use 0 as the first element on the left. Thus, now we have

```
      0   6   12 ENCODE 2733
     (0    6 ENCODE 227),12|2733
     (0 ENCODE 37),(6|227),9
     ((¯1↓0) ENCODE 0),(0|37),5   9
37   5   9
```

To explain the last step, it must be remembered that $0|37 \leftrightarrow 37$ and so the last argument of ENCODE is 37-0|37, which is zero. The process is not truncated, and

```
      0   6   12 ⊥ 37   5   9
2733
```

When a leading zero is used on the left, the first element of the result is that part which remains after the steps preceding the nonzero element of A are completed.

An elementary application is to convert a time (in hours) to weeks, days, and hours. For example,

```
      0   7   24 ⊤637
3   5   13
```

means 637 hours is equivalent to 3 weeks, 5 days, and 13 hours. Another useful application is to convert a decimal number to a vector of its separate integers, as in

```
      10   10   10   10 ⊤287
0   2   8   7
```

or to convert a decimal number to a vector representation of its binary equivalent, as in

```
      2   2   2   2   2   2 ⊤43
1   0   1   0   1   1
```

Encode accepts positive and negative noninteger arguments. However, there may be some problems due to roundoff errors, with noninteger arguments. It is interesting to make a comparison of

```
      10   10   10 ⊤873
8   7   3
```

and

```
      10   10   10 ⊤¯873
1   2   7
```

It is apparent that 127 (obtainable from 10⊥ 1 2 7) is the decimal complement of 873. A similar result is possible using a base number other than 10.

Array arguments

Some insight into the possibilities of array arguments is obtained by considering a vector on the right. For example,

220 / Extended Scalar and Mixed Functions

```
      10   10   10 T 287   563
  2   5
  8   6
  7   3
```

This is to be compared with 10 10 10 T287 ↔ 2 8 7 and 10 10 10 T563 ↔ 5 6 3. For a matrix on the right, an example is

```
       10   10   10 T 2   2 ρ 287   563   27   814
  2   5
  0   8

  8   6
  2   1

  7   3
  7   4
```

To consider further examples, we shall use

```
       A
  10   15
  10   15
  10   15
```

as a left-hand argument. Then,

```
     AT287
  2   1
  8   4
  7   2

       AT 287   563
  2   5
  1   2

  8   6
  4   7

  7   3
  2   8

         AT 2   2 ρ 287   563   27   814
  2   5
  0   8

  1   2
  0   3

  8   6
  2   1

  4   7
  1   9

  7   3
  7   4

  2   8
 12   4
```

General case

For the general consideration of

$A \top B$

we first observe that there are no compatibility conditions. Furthermore, reference to the previous examples shows that

Rank of result: $(\rho\rho A)+\rho\rho B$

Shape of result: $(\rho A),\rho B$

With respect to these properties, encode is similar to the outer product. For each element on the right, encoding is done for each vector along the *first* axis on the left. The result of that encoding is then displayed along the *first* axis of the result.

Example 6-4

Suppose the manager of a business wishes to store in a computer the following information concerning each item purchased:

(1) Month, day, and year the order was placed.
(2) Month, day, and year of delivery.
(3) Price of the item.

Assume dates are coded: 0 to 11 for months, 0 to 30 for days, and 0 to 99 for years (assuming the 20th century). Also, to avoid decimal fractions, assume prices are in cents. Seven numbers are to be stored for each item. We shall now describe how memory space can be saved, by using decode to represent these seven numbers as one stored number.

A monadic function *PACK* is to be defined to take a vector of seven elements, in the order:

Price, Three elements for delivery date, Three elements for order date

as its argument, and return a scalar representing this vector. The function is

```
     ∇ R←PACK N
[1]    R←0 12 31 100 12 31 100 ⊥N ∇
```

This function can be used each time a new item is added to the list. In this way the record for I items can be in a vector of length I rather than a matrix of shape I,7.

Of course, on occasion the data stored in this way will be wanted in its original form. A function which will return the original 7 elements is

```
     ∇ R←UNPACK N
[1]    R←0 12 31 100 12 31 100 ⊤N ∇
```

Observe that each element (except the first) on the left of ⊥ is greater than the maximum possible corresponding element on the right, and that the elements of both are nonnegative. This ensures that *UNPACK* will recover the data used as the argument of *PACK*. Of course, this pair of functions will work correctly only if the result of *PACK* does not have more significant digits than the machine can store.

6-17 Index Of

The function *index of* (represented by the dyadic ⍳) gives the index positions in a vector left-hand argument of elements which correspond in the right-hand argument. For example (in origin 1),

```
        2 8 5 ⍳ 5 8
3 2
```

The result carries the information that 5 (the first element in the right-hand argument) is in index position 3 in the left-hand argument, and that the 8 of the right-hand argument is in index position 2 on the left.

Two possibilities are not covered by the above example: the repetition of a number on the left, and the appearance of a number on the right which is not found among the elements of the vector on the left. The first of these cases is represented by

```
        2 8 5 8 ⍳ 5 8
3 2
```

indicating that when there is a repetition on the left, the result is the lowest index number of the repeated element. An example of the second case is

```
        2 8 5 ⍳ 6 5 8
4 3 2
```

The 6 in the right-hand argument is not found on the left, and for that element the corresponding element in the result is 1 greater than the number of elements in the argument on the left. Thus, for all cases the dimension of the result is the same as the dimension of the right-hand argument.

These examples of the index of function are for origin 1. In origin 0, the results would be 1 less than those shown here.

Either argument can be numeric or of character type. If the types are different, each result will be one greater than the largest index number in the argument on the left. The left-hand argument must be a vector but the right-hand argument can be of any rank. As another example, if

```
      P
INDEX OF
WORKS ON
MATRICES
```

then

```
      'ABCDEFGHIJKLMNOPQRSTUVWXYZ' ⍳ P
 9  14   4   5  24  27  15   6
23  15  18  11  19  27  15  14
13   1  20  18   9   3   5  19
```

Note the appearance of 27 (1 greater than the dimension of the alphabet) in positions corresponding to spaces in the right-hand argument.

In the general case

```
    A ⍳ B
```

A must be a vector but B can be of any rank. The rank and shape of the result is the same as for B. The comparison tolerance operates on this function.

Example 6-5

Alphabetizing a list of words is a standard problem in computing. Suppose we have a matrix *NAMES* having a name on each line. Possibly each line consists of a last name, a comma followed by a space, and a first name followed by spaces to fill up the line.

Consider the defined function, to be executed in origin 0,

```
    ∇ Z←REPWORD N
[1]   Z←28⊥⍉' ,ABCDEFGHIJKLMNOPQRSTUVWXYZ'⍳N ∇
```

If we execute

```
    REPWORD 'SMITH'
12608885
```

This is the result of

```
    28⊥ 20  14  10  21  9
```

where the vector 20 14 10 21 9 contains the indices in the vector ' ,ABC etc.' obtained from the "index of" function (the transpose will not affect this vector). The argument 28 is the number of letters in the alphabet plus 2 (for the space and comma). Now suppose

```
      NAMES
SMYTH
SMITH
      P←REPWORD NAMES
      P
12621429  12608885
```

The change of the 3rd letter from *I* to *Y* increases the corresponding index number, and hence decode yields a larger number. The transpose is necessary so that the right-hand argument of decode will have index numbers along the first axis. In the last example, that argument will be

```
    20  20
    14  14
    10  26
    21  21
     9   9
```

The size of each number obtained from *REPWORD* will be an indication of the position of the corresponding word in an alphabetized list. Thus, grade up can be used on the result of *REPWORD* to give the indices in *NAMES* for an alphabetized list. For the example,

```
      NAMES[⍋12621429  12608885;]
SMITH
SMYTH
```

It appears that

```
      NAMES[⍋REPWORD NAMES;]
```

is sufficient to put the names in *NAMES* in alphabetical order. However, from the nature of decode, it is evident that for a name of *N* letters the largest integer obtainable from *REPWORD* is

```
    28⊥N⍴27
```

which can be shown to equal (28*N)-1. If this number requires more significant binary
digits than the machine is capable of handling, some letters on the right-hand end of
the names will be lost, and not heeded in the alphabetizing process. If a machine employs B binary digits, the largest integer is (2*B)-1. Thus, we have the condition

  28*N < 2*B

  N < 28⍟2*B

for B = 56 this gives N < 11.65. In the case of a machine using 56 bits, alphabetizing can only be with respect to the first 11 letters in a name.

  Let us assume N is 11 and consider alphabetizing with respect to 22 letters.
This can be done by first alphabetizing with respect to the first 11 letters and then,
using a loop, alphabetizing with respect to letters 12 through 22 each group of names
for which the first 11 letters are the same. The function

```
        ∇ Z←REPEAT Y
[1]     Z←((¯1⌽~Z)∧Z←(¯1↓Y=1⌽Y),0)/Y
[2]     Z←Z∘.=Y
```

will be used as a subfunction. It takes a vector argument and produces a Boolean
matrix in the manner of the example

```
        REPEAT 201   563   563   800   927   927   927   981
0 1 1 0 0 0 0 0
0 0 0 0 1 1 1 0
```

There is a row for each set of repeated numbers, and in each row a 1 corresponds in
position to one of the repeated numbers. If there are no repetitions in the argument,
the result is an empty matrix with zero rows.

  A possible function for alphabetizing with respect to 22 letters is (in origin 0)

```
        ∇ W←ALPH N;NR;GUNR;F;RM;RNI
[1]     NR←REPWORD((1↑⍴N),11)↑N
[2]     W←N[GUNR←⍋NR;]
[3]     F←⍳¯1↑⍴RM←REPEAT NR[GUNR]
[4]     L:→(0=1↑⍴RM)/0
[5]     RNI←RM[0;]/F
[6]     NR←REPWORD 0 11 ↓W[RNI;]
[7]     W[RNI;]←W[RNI[⍋NR];]
[8]     RM←1 0 ↓RM
[9]     →L ∇
```

  Line [1] produces the vector NR of numerical representations of the first 11
letters of the names. In line [2] grade up of NR is the index value for the first
axis of N and so W becomes a list alphabetized with respect to the first 11 letters.
Line [3] produces a Boolean matrix RM having a row for each group of names having the
same first 11 letters. Line [4] branches out of the function if RM has no rows, as
will be the case if there are no repetitions. Within the loop, line [5] converts the
first row of RM to index numbers RNI, line [6] obtains the numerical representations
(for the repeated cases) of the last 11 letters, and line [7] rearranges these names
by alphabetizing the last 11 letters. Line [8] removes the first row of RM, and looping continues until there are no longer any rows in RM.

  This program would use less memory if it were made niladic and with no returned
value. The matrix to be alphabetized would be global. Then, it would be unnecessary

Extended Scalar and Mixed Functions / 225

for a local copy to be made of a large variable. As another observation, note that repetitions of short names (less than 12 letters) will cause an unneeded execution of the loop. It is left for you, as an exercise, to exclude such a case from the loop.

6-18 Deal

The function *deal* (represented by the symbol ? in dyadic form), when written

```
    A?B
```

is subject to the condition that A and B must be nonnegative scalar integers, with A less than or equal B. The result is a random selection of A numbers from the set ⍳B, without replacement. Thus, some possible results are (in origin 1)

```
        4?6
5   1   3   4

        4?6
2   4   6   5
```

The function is sensitive to origin because ⍳B is origin dependent. If A is zero, the result is an empty vector. Deal is not classified as a scalar function because it does not accept array arguments.

6-19 Matrix Divide

The function *matrix divide* (using the symbol ⌹ formed by overstriking ⎕ and ÷, in dyadic form) basically provides the solution to a set of linear algebraic equations. To illustrate, suppose we have a set of equations (in conventional notation)

$$3x_1 + 2x_2 + x_3 = 1$$
$$x_1 + 4x_2 + 2x_3 = 3$$
$$x_1 + 2x_2 + 4x_3 = 2$$

in the unknown variables x_1, x_2, and x_3. The mathematical information in these equations can be expressed in APL notation in terms of the variables

```
        A
1   3   2

        M
    3   2   1
    1   4   2
    1   2   4
```

and the "unknown" vector X having as elements the unknown x_1, x_2, and x_3. The equivalent of the above set of equations is that

```
    A-M+.×X
```

shall yield a vector of 0's. The function matrix divide yields X to meet this condition. For this example,

```
    X←A⌹M
    X
¯0.2   0.7   0.2
```

226 / Extended Scalar and Mixed Functions

If the determinant of M is zero, the equations have no unique solution (because they are then linearly dependent) and the message DOMAIN ERROR will be obtained. The condition for compatibility is $\rho A \leftrightarrow 1\uparrow\rho M$.

Special cases

While the description given above covers the basic nature of matrix divide, there are several special cases. Assume M is square and nonsingular and that A is a matrix (not necessarily square) having the same number of rows as M. For example, if

```
    A
1       2.2
3       2.4
2       3.2
```

and M is the same as above,

```
       A⌹M
¯0.2       0.4
 0.7       0.2
 0.2       0.6
```

Individual columns of the result are equivalent, respectively, to $A[;1]⌹M$ and $A[;2]⌹M$. The shape of the result is $(1\downarrow\rho M),1\downarrow\rho A$.

The definition of $A⌹M$ extends to the case where M is not square but for which the following conditions are met:

(1) The number of rows of M is greater than the number of columns.
(2) The columns of M are linearly independent (no column is a scalar multiple of another column).
(3) The dimension of the first axis of A equals the dimension of the first axis of M.

For A and M meeting these conditions,

$A⌹M$

is equivalent to

$((\lozenge M)+.\times A)⌹(\lozenge M)+.\times M$

This equivalence is useful because it shows that $A⌹M$ for the case where M is nonsquare can be reduced to the case where the right-hand argument is square, by virtue of the fact that $(\lozenge M)+.\times M$ is square. However, the interpretation of the result is more important. If A is a vector of length equal to $1\uparrow\rho M$,

$R \leftarrow A⌹M$

R will be computed to meet the condition that (when A is a vector)

$+/(A-M+.\times R)\star 2$

will be a minimum. In this case there are too many equations represented by M to be solved in the sense of $A-M+.\times R$ being a vector of 0's, as when M is square (we used X instead of R for the case where M is square). Instead $M+.\times R$ is a *least square* approximation of A.

A numerical example is

```
      M
 3   7  ¯2
10   2  15
 8  13  ¯2
13  ¯2   7
      A
1  2  3  4
   R←A⌹M
   R
0.363455  ¯0.0168334  ¯0.106385
   A-M+.×R
¯0.185300  ¯.00510494  0.0984268  ¯0.0138818
   -/(A-M+.×R)*2
0.0442428
```

If A is a matrix meeting the conditions for compatibility, the above analysis applies as if each column of A were a vector left-hand argument. The result is a matrix of shape (1↓⍴M),1↑⍴A for which the first column is A[;1]⌹M, the second column is A[;2]⌹M, etc. For example,

```
   A
1  2
2  3
3  4
4  1
   A⌹M
 0.363455    0.0552330
¯0.0168334   0.293815
¯0.106385    0.123956
```

When A is a matrix and R←A⌹M, then

    +/,(A-M+.×R)*2

is a minimum. Whether A is a vector or matrix, the shape of the result is (1↓⍴M),1↑⍴A.

Although the function matrix divide is basically useful for a matrix on the right, the following equivalencies apply for degenerate cases. If A and B are vectors,

    A⌹B ↔ (+/A×B)÷+/B*2

and if A and B are scalars

    A⌹B ↔ A÷B

except that 0⌹0 is not permitted. In both cases, the result is a scalar.

General case

All of the cases of A⌹B are covered by the condition (1↑⍴A) ↔ 1↑⍴B for compatibility, and ≥/⍴B is 1.

Rank of result: 0⌈¯2+(⍴⍴A)+⍴⍴B

Shape of result: (1↓⍴B),1↑⍴A

228 / Extended Scalar and Mixed Functions

Example 6-6

Suppose we have a plot in the x-y plane of a set of points. Let X be the vector of x coordinates of the points, and Y the vector of the y coordinates. We are to obtain the coefficients of the polynomial (in conventional notation)

$$a_0 + a_1 x + a_2 x^2 + \ldots + a_N x^N$$

which will minimize the sum of the squares of the differences between the polynomial at each x and the corresponding value of y. The degree N is any value less than ¯1+⍴X.

We begin by specifying the nonsquare matrix (in origin 0)

```
P←X∘.*⍳N+1
```

Each row of P is a vector of one element of x, to successive powers up to N. If a vector C of the coefficients of the polynomial were known,

```
P+.×C
```

would be a vector of values of the polynomial at all elements of X. However, C is not known but is to be determined so that

```
+/(Y-P+.×C)*2
```

will be a minimum. This is the sum of the squares of the "errors" by which the polynomial differs from elements of Y at the corresponding elements of X. From the description of matrix divide it is evident that the solution is

```
C←Y⌹P
```

The polynomial so determined is said to be a *least square* approximation of the set of data.

6-20 Matrix Inverse

The function *matrix inverse* (using the symbol ⌹ in monadic form) is defined in terms of the function matrix divide. Specifically, if a matrix M meets conditions which permit it to be used in matrix divide (that is, ¯1↑⍴M less than or equal 1↑⍴M, and columns are linearly independent), the matrix inverse of M is defined by

```
⌹M ↔ I⌹M
```

where I is a *unit matrix* of shape 1 1 × 1↑⍴M (a unit matrix is zero everywhere except for 1's on the main diagonal). It can be shown that the matrix inverse has the following properties:

```
⍉⌹⍉⌹M ↔ M
(⌹M)+.×M ↔ Unit matrix of shape 1 1 × ¯1↑⍴M
(⌹M)+.×A ↔ A⌹M
```

where A is any matrix which is compatible with M in $A⌹M$. This last identity shows that the matrix inverse can be used to give the same result as matrix divide, but (⌹M)+.×A is slower and uses more workspace. If M is square, the first two of these become

Extended Scalar and Mixed Functions / 229

⌸⌸M ↔ M

(⌸M)+.×M ↔ M+.×⌸M ↔ Unit matrix, same shape as M

An example for a nonsquare matrix is

```
      M1
 3    7   ¯2
10    2   15
 8   13   ¯2
13   ¯2    7
      ⌸M1
 0.0040737   ¯0.0419371    0.0191025    0.0964869
¯0.0279923    0.0404038    0.0455469   ¯0.0655685
¯0.0078735    0.0891983   ¯0.0180508   ¯0.0556889
```

and for the square matrix

```
      M
 3    2    1
 1    4    2
 1    2    4
      ⌸M
 0.4         ¯0.200000    0
¯0.066667     0.366667   ¯0.166667
¯0.066667    ¯0.133333    0.333333
```

This function also gives results for scalar and vector arguments. If B is a scalar,

⌸B ↔ ÷B

and for a vector B (not all zeros),

⌸B ↔ B÷+/B*2

For all cases of ⌸B,

Rank of result: ⍴⍴B

Shape of result: ⌽⍴B

6-21 Dyadic Format

The monadic function format (using the symbol ⍕ formed by overstriking ⊤ and ∘) was introduced in Sec. 2-24. That form converts a numeric array to a character array, but provides no control of format for the individual columns. The dyadic form employs the left-hand argument to provide such control. In general, the left-hand argument is a vector having *two* elements for each column of the array to be printed. The array is the right-hand argument. The first of each pair of elements on the left is the width of the "field" for the corresponding column, and the second element is the number of digits to the right of the decimal point. The width of field is the total number of spaces occupied by the column (including the decimal point, negative sign, and any blanks on the left). For the variable (displayed numerically)

```
   M
2.5      3.67
6.9     ¯4.32
```

two examples are

230 / Extended Scalar and Mixed Functions

```
        5   1   8   3  ▼M
  2.5     3.670
  6.9    ¯4.320

        9   2   6   1  ▼M
  2.50    3.7
  6.90   ¯4.3
```

In the second case, note the rounding to the nearest last digit.

If the same format is desired for each column, only one pair of numbers is required on the left, as in

```
      5   1  ▼M
  2.5   3.7
  6.9  ¯4.3
```

The use of 0 for the width of field indicator will cause the spacing to be adjusted so there is at least one space between numbers. Also, a scalar left-hand argument is interpreted as being preceded by a zero. Examples are

```
        3   1   0   3  ▼M
  2.5     3.670
  6.9    ¯4.320

        3 ▼M
  2.500   3.670
  6.900  ¯4.320
```

The last example is equivalent to 0 3 ▼M. When a field width is specified, and is not zero, it must be large enough to accommodate the numbers to be printed. For example, 4 3 ▼M would be impossible because (with a leading space) a field of 7 is required for ¯4.320. If a field specification is too small, *DOMAIN ERROR* results.

A floating point format is possible: The number of digits is specified as a negative number, of absolute value equal to the number of significant digits desired. The field includes the exponential part. Thus,

```
        5   1   9  ¯2  ▼M
  2.5    3.7E00
  6.9   ¯4.3E00
```

For ranks higher than 2, the format specifications apply to each page. For example,

```
        8   3   9   4  ▼M,[0.5]⌽M
  2.500     3.6700
  6.900    ¯4.3200

 ¯3.670     2.5000
 ¯4.320     6.9000
```

The dyadic format function is very useful because it permits the spacing of columns of tabulated data in a manner appropriate to the numbers in the columns, or perhaps in accordance with the lengths of column headings.

CONCLUSION

To a great extent, the "power" of APL to reduce complex problems to manageable size resides in the functions described in this chapter. Many of the functions are

Extended Scalar and Mixed Functions / 231

subtle, become very complex with arrays of high rank, and some of the generalities about them are included only by inference. You must discover much about these functions through your own experience and therefore practice with them should be regarded as an important adjunct to the text. These functions have a potential for solving problems that you can come to understand only through extensive experience.

Particular note is made of the importance of compatibility conditions, and the relationship between rank and shape of a result and properties of the arguments. These relationships are summarized for the various functions, but learning them should be through experience more than by memorization. This chapter, in particular, should be used as a reference document.

A summary word about axis operators is in order. Those functions which require an explicit designation of an axis operator are, of course, sensitive to origin. However, for some there is a special notation for either the first or last axis, which is not sensitive to origin. The use of these designations sometimes has an advantage in providing functions which are insensitive to rank as well as origin. One of the features of the notation for arrays is the possibility of writing programs which will work for arrays of any ranks. In general, it is good policy to create such programs even though at the time of writing this property may not seem important.

Problems--Chapter 6

Comment: This chapter deals with sophisticated procedures for using arrays. The following problems are designed to provide you with experience in using these procedures. Wherever there is a statement that you should not use branching or looping, you should comply. To do so may make the problems more challenging, but that is the intent. Wherever possible, make your functions independent of origin.

6-1 The display

    ORANGE
    BOX
    PAPER

is typical of a matrix (or one page of an array of rank higher than 2) having only one word to a line. The rearrangement

    ORANGE
       BOX
     PAPER

is said to be "justified on the right." You are to design a monadic function *JUSTIFY* which will accept such an array (of any rank, 2 or higher) as an argument and produce, as an explicit result, the form justified on the right. The dimension of the last axis can be greater than the length of the longest word. The function is not to employ looping or branching.

6-2 This problem is similar to Prob. 6-1, but involves more than one word to a line. The display

    ORANGE SODA
    PAPER BOX
    ANY OTHER WORD

232 / Extended Scalar and Mixed Functions

is typical of a matrix or one page of an array of any rank higher than 2. The rearrangement

```
   ORANGE SODA
    PAPER BOX
ANY OTHER WORD
```

is said to be "justified on the right." The dimension of the last axis may be greater than the length of the longest line of words. There is not more than one blank space between words, but there may be punctuation. Design a monadic function *JUSTIFIER* that will take an array such as described above as an argument. It is to give the arrangement justified on the right as an explicit result. There is to be no branching or looping.

6-3 You are to design a monadic function *DASH* which will take an array of any rank in which each row is a group of words separated by single spaces. The number of words per line is not necessarily the same for each line. The returned value is to be the same array, but with spaces between words replaced by dashes (negation symbols). Any spaces following the last word in a line are not to be replaced. Use no looping or branching.

6-4 For this problem it is assumed that you have the functions *WORDMAT* described in Prob. 4-14, *REMS* given in example 4-5, and *ALPH* described in example 6-5. You are to define a function *ALPHVEC* which will alphabetize the words in a vector. The returned value is to be a vector in which the words are in alphabetical order, with single spaces between them. Use *ALPH* and *WORDMAT* as subfunctions. Do not use branching or looping.

6-5 Refer to the function *ALPH* described in example 6-5. Revise it so that if there is a group of names which are the same, and having less than 12 letters, they will not be processed in the loop.

6-6 The display

```
ORANGE RED BLUE
PAPER PEN INK
CLASS STUDENTS

RAIN CLOUDY SUNSHINE
TRAVEL TRAIN BUS CAR
TREE FLOWERS PLANTS
```

is typical of an array of rank 2 or higher, having one or more words in each row. The dimension of the last axis can be greater than the length of the longest line of words. There are single spaces between words.

(a) Write a monadic function *WORDCOUNT* which will take such an array as an argument and return a numeric array of one rank less than the argument, giving the numbers of words in the rows. For the example above, the result would be

```
3  3  2
3  4  3
```

(b) Write a dyadic function *SELECT* which will take an array as in the above as a right-hand argument. The left-hand argument will be a positive integer N equal to or less than the largest number of words in any line. The explicit result is to be an array of the same rank as the argument, but with a single word in each row, that word being selected as the Nth word of the row. For any row of the argument having fewer than N words, the corresponding row of the result should be blank. As an example, for the array above, and 2 as the left-hand argument, the result would be

RED
PEN
STUDENTS

CLOUDY
TRAIN
FLOWERS

The dimension of the last axis of the result should equal the length of the longest word. You will probably find it convenient to use *WORDCOUNT* as a subfunction. These functions are to be written without loops or branching.

6-7 You are to design a monadic function *REMSA* which will remove extra spaces between words in the rows of a character array. For example, the argument might be the array given in Prob. 6-6, but with extra spaces between some of the words. Use *REMS* given in example 4-5, and looping in terms of the *FOR-UNTIL-DO* structure. The returned value is to be the array (of the same rank as the argument) without extra spaces, and no extra spaces on the right of the last word of the longest row. Note: you are encouraged to try writing a function to accomplish this result without looping.

6-8 For this problem it is assumed you have *REMSA* described in Prob. 6-7. Write a monadic function *SHIFTL*1 which will take an array such as the one given in Prob. 6-6 as an argument. In the explicit result, each row is to begin with the second word in the argument, and the first word of the argument is to be shifted to the end of the row, but with only one space preceding it. Any row having only one word should be unchanged. Use *REMSA* as a subfunction. There should be no looping or branching in *SHIFTL*1 (this does not count looping in *REMSA*).

6-9 You are to define a monadic function *EDIT* which can be used for text editing, by which is meant inserting or deleting words in a line of words. Its argument is to be the character vector you want to edit, for example

B←'THE BIG BROWN FOX JUMPED OVER THE FENCE'

An example of execution of *EDIT* is

EDIT B
THE BIG BROWN FOX JUMPED OVER THE FENCE
  D AD   *A*

The computer types the line to be edited, and then below this you type letters *D* and *A* in accordance with the editing you want to accomplish. The letters *D* and *A* are entered on a quote-quad input. *D* under the first letter of a word means delete the word; *A* under a space means add a word (or words) at that point. The program is to allow a quote-quad input once for each *A*, for entering the word (or words) to be added. These might be

LARGE
HIGH STONE

The returned value is to be the corrected line. In this case it would be

THE LARGE FOX JUMPED OVER THE HIGH STONE FENCE

Checks should be included to make sure each *D* is under the first letter of a word, and each *A* is under a space. If either of these conditions is not met, the message *A OR D IN WRONG POSITION* is to be printed, and then the line to be edited is to be displayed again, for a second try.

6-10 Consider the problem of using the terminal to plot a graph. Suppose X is a vector of any length less than or equal 101, whose elements are values of an independent variable x. A vector Y has corresponding values of the dependent variable y. Let *XN* and *YN* be corresponding normalized variables, obtained from X and Y, respectively, such that *XN* and *YN* each has a range 0 to 100 (inclusive) rounded to the nearest integer, in the usual manner.

234 / Extended Scalar and Mixed Functions

(a) Create a dyadic function *GPH* which will take *XN* as a left-hand argument and *YN* as a right-hand argument. The returned value is to be a character matrix of shape 51 101. Each index number of the horizontal axis represents *one* unit of the variable *XN*; each index number of the vertical axis represents *two* units of the variable *YN*. In this matrix, the mark _ (the underbar) will be used as a marker for an even element of *YN*, and the mark - (negation symbol) will be used as a marker for an odd element of *YN*. A partial display for *XN*←0 2 4 6 8 and *YN*←→4 3 2 1 0 is

```
-
  _ _
      -
        _
```

(b) Design a monadic function *GRAPH* which will take a matrix of two rows and any number of columns not greater than 101 as an argument. The first row of this matrix represents values of *X*: the second row values of *Y*. The elements of *Y* and *X* represent a relationship to be plotted by the function. Elements of *X* and *Y* are unrestricted, except that when *X* is normalized in the manner described in (a), there shall be no repeated elements. Use *GPH* as a subfunction and produce a result which is a print of the data points produced by *GPH*, but augmented with a border around the outside (making a matrix of shape 53 103), using the symbols | and _, respectively, for the vertical and horizontal sides. Below this rectangle there should be printed two lines such as

RANGE OF X: ¯3.45 *TO* 26.56
RANGE OF Y: 29.63 *TO* 89.45

where the numbers representing the ranges are derived from *X* and *Y*. There is to be no branching or looping in either function.

6-11 Define a niladic function *CARDS* which will produce a deal of 13 playing cards to each of 4 persons, from an ordinary 52 card deck. Use the letters *S, H, C, D* to designate suits, numbers 2 to 10, and *A, J, Q, K* respectively for ace, jack, queen and king. The hands are to be printed in four columns in the manner indicated below. For each hand list all clubs first, all diamonds second, all hearts third and all spades last. List the cards in the order *A*, 2, 3, 4, 5, 6, 7, 8, 9, 10, *J, Q, K* in each suit. There is to be no returned value. An example of the print format is:

```
 2C    7D    KD    3D
10H   10S    4S    6D
etc.
```

This function is to use no looping or branching.

6-12 A number expressed as a ratio of two integers is said to be in rational form. You are to define a dyadic function *RADD* which will add two rational numbers, add two compatible sets of rational numbers, or add one rational number to each of a set. For a single rational number, say 2÷3, the representation will be the vector 2 3; for a set of rational numbers, say 2÷3, 5÷4, 4÷9, the representation will be the matrix

```
2  5  4
3  4  9
```

Numerators are in the first row, denominators are in the second row. Examples are

```
        3  2 RADD 1  4
7  4

        2  3 RADD 2  3 ρ 4  3  1  1  2  4
14  13  11
 3   6  12

       (2  3 ρ 2  8  6  3  9  5) RADD 2  3 ρ 4  3  1  1  2  4
14  43  29
 3  18  20
```

The function is to give a returned value. For some examples, the algorithm for adding rational numbers will give a result not in reduced form; numerator and denominator will have a common factor. In such a case, numerator and denominator should be divided by that common factor (see Prob. 5-58). Looping may be used to divide each number pair of the results by their greatest common divisor.

6-13 You are to design a monadic function which will take an array of numbers as its argument. Some of the elements of this argument will be repeated. The returned value is to be a vector of all numbers in the argument, but without repetition, in ascending order. Thus, if the argument is 8 5.2 3 9 5.2 3, the result is to be 3 5.2 8 9. Call the function $NOREP$. No looping or branching is to be used.

6-14 For this problem it is assumed you have function $NOREP$, from Prob. 6-13. Suppose you have an array of numbers, many of which are repeated. Typically, it might be statistical data, such as the heights of 1000 randomly selected people, to the nearest centimeter. You are to design a monadic function $DISTRIB$ which will take such an array as an argument. The returned value is to be a two-column matrix: all the separate heights found in the array in the first column (in increasing order); in the second column, the number of occurrences of the heights in corresponding rows of the first column. Use $NOREP$ as a subfunction. There is to be no looping or branching.

6-15 A palindrome is an item of writing that reads the same from either end. You are to create a monadic function $PALDRM$ which will take a two-element vector of positive integers as its argument. If these integers are denoted $N1$ and $N2$, the returned value is to be a list of all integers between $N1$ and $N2$ (inclusive) whose squares are palindromes. The function shall use no loops. On your computer, determine the largest number whose square can be accurately represented in numeric form.

6-16 Define a dyadic function $MULT$ which will multiply two integers of up to 14 decimal digits each and express all digits of the product, as a character representation. It is assumed that your machine is accurate to 15 decimal digits. The product of two numbers of 14 digits will require 27 or 28 digits. This is why the output must be a character representation. The function can be written in two forms; with inputs as character representations of the original numbers, or with numerical inputs. Take your choice; each one has interesting features. Negative numbers are to be admitted. Hint: break the numbers into two parts, and use encode. The function is to employ no branching or looping.

6-17 This problem has to do with the representation of a positive number X in hexadecimal floating point form (binary mantissa, and exponential multipliers which are powers of 16). The representation is

$$X = M \times 16^N$$

In conventional notation, where N is an integer, and M is in the range

$$16^{-1} \leq M < 1$$

Taking the logarithm to base 16 of both sides of the equation above, and solving for N, gives

$$N = \log_{16} X - \log_{16} M$$

and in view of the range of M,

$$\log_{16} X < N \leq 1 + \log_{16} X$$

Thus, in APL notation,

$N \leftarrow 1 + \lfloor 16 \circledast X$

You are to define a monadic function $BINARY$ which will take a scalar X as an argument and print (no returned value) a character vector which is the binary representation of X. The mantissa should come first, with a leading binary point, then a space followed by a four bit binary representation of N. In the event of a positive exponent, the first bit on the left of the representation for N is to be zero; in the case of a negative exponent the first bit on the left is to be 1, and the representation of N should be the two's complement of $|N$. (The two's complement is obtained by interchanging 0's and 1's for all positions to the left of the last 1 on the right.) Thus, $|N$ will be represented by 3 bits. Design the function for a mantissa of 27 bits. Here are some examples:

```
      BINARY 20.54
0.000101001000101000111101011 0010
      BINARY 2936
0.101101111000000000000000000 0011
      BINARY 0.0002834
0.000100101001001010101001101 1110
```

In the last case, the 1110 representation for N means ¯2. For those interested, a further refinement is suggested, to accommodate negative values of X. If X is negative, the mantissa should have a leading 1, to the left of the binary point, and the body of the mantissa should be the 2's complement of $|X$. There is to be no looping.

6-18 Define a function *STLINE* which will give the best straight-line approximation to a set of points in the $x - y$ plane, in the sense that the sum of the squares of the deviations of the points from the line, in directions parallel to the y axis, shall be a minimum. The function is to be dyadic; the argument on the left will be a set of x coordinates of the points, and the argument on the right will be the corresponding set of y coordinates. The output will be a returned value giving the intercept and slope of the line. Use no looping or branching.

6-19 Write a dyadic function *MEMB* which will completely simulate the primitive function membership. It is to accept arguments of any rank on either side. No looping or branching is to be used, and of course, the primitive membership may not be used.

6-20 Suppose the elements of a vector Y are the y coordinates of a set of data points corresponding to equal increments of x. The number of elements in Y is to be odd. In the manner of the accompanying figure, one way to interpolate between points is to pass a succession of parabolas through sets of three adjacent points. Each parabola is to be specified as if it had an origin at the data point in the middle, as is shown for one case in the figure. This establishes a temporary set of coordinates for each parabola, which we shall call x' and y'.

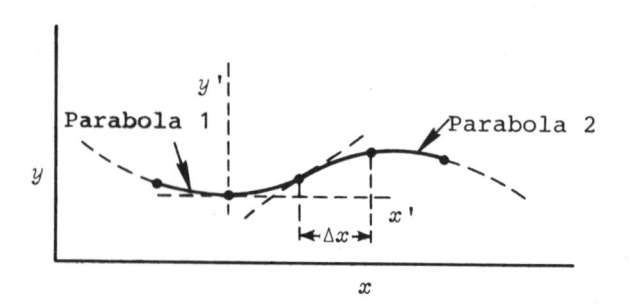

Since the parabola goes through the origin of the primed coordinate system, the expression for it has no constant term and is (in conventional notation)

$$y' = Ax' + B(x')^2$$

For each parabola A and B can be found because it is known that it must pass through the two points at its ends. Define a dyadic function *PARAB* which will take the scalar increment in x as a left-hand argument, and the vector Y as a right-hand argument. The returned value is to be a matrix having one row for each parabola, and three columns. The first column is to be values of y at the centers of the parabolas, the second column is to be values of A, and the third column is to be values of B. There is to be no looping or branching.

6-21 For this problem it is assumed you have the function PARAB described in Prob. 6-20. It deals with a set of values of y spaced at uniform points on an x axis. The number of values of y is odd. Let XY be a vector of the increment of x, the initial value of x, the values of y. Design a dyadic function PARABINTERP which will use the parabolic approximation described in Prob. 6-20 for the purpose of interpolating between data points. The left-hand argument will be an array X of values of x at which interpolated values are wanted. The right-hand argument will be XY as described above. The elements of X are to be within the range determined by the distance between data points on the x axis, and the number of points. If any element of X is outside that range, the function is to do no computing, other than to return an empty vector and print OUT OF RANGE. If all elements are acceptable, the returned value is to be the interpolated values of y, in an array having the same shape as X. Use no looping, and use PARAB of Prob. 6-20 as a subfunction. The function is to work properly if an element of X is one of the data points.

6-22 For this problem it is assumed you have the function PARAB described in Prob. 6-20. You are to construct a dyadic function CURVLGTH which will take the same arguments as PARAB: an increment of an independent variable x on the left, and a vector representing a set of values of y, for equally incremented values of x, on the right. The number of elements of the right-hand argument must be odd. The returned value is to be the length of the curve passing through the points, as approximated by the sum of the lengths of the parabolas. In the notation of Prob. 6-20, the length of any one parabola is given in terms of the parameters A and B for that parabola, which are obtainable from PARAB, by the following formulas derived from calculus (in conventional notation)

$$H = 2 \times B \times \Delta X$$

$$F = \sqrt{1 + (A+H)^2} \qquad\qquad G = \sqrt{1 + (A-H)^2}$$

$$L = \frac{\Delta X}{2H}\left[A(F-G) + H(F+G) + \ln \frac{F+A+H}{G+A-H}\right] \qquad \text{if} \quad B \neq 0$$

$$L = 2 \times \Delta X \times \sqrt{1+A^2} \qquad\qquad \text{if} \quad B = 0$$

These computations should be done simultaneously for all segments on the matrix of A and B parameters, so that the total length can be found without looping. However, the possibility that some B elements might be zero must be taken into consideration. This necessitates writing one APL statement that will give the correct length of a segment for all values of B. No looping or branching should be used.

6-23 For this problem it is assumed you have the function CURVLGTH described in Prob. 6-22.

(a) You are to use CURVLGTH in a modified version CURVLGTHM. The new function is to take a character name of some function which computes a vector of values of y for a curve for which the length is wanted. The left-hand argument will be a two-element vector giving the beginning and ending values of x. The number of data points will be fixed at 15.

(b) Use CURVLGTHM with characters 'OO' representing a Pythagorean function as the right-hand argument, and the left-hand argument chosen to cover the arc of one-eighth of a circle, as shown in the accompanying figure. Compare 4× the result with π.

238 / Extended Scalar and Mixed Functions

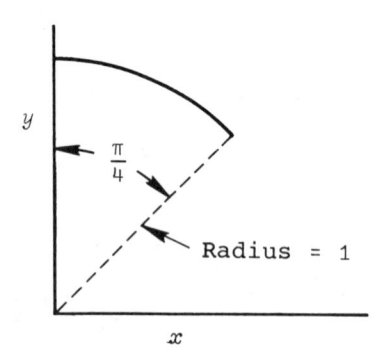

Note that *CURVLNGTH* or *CURVLENGTHM* cannot be used for a curve that has a vertical part (as where the circle intersects a horizontal diameter) because a parabola cannot fit such a case. Therefore, the length of a semicircle cannot be computed directly.

6-24 For this problem it is assumed you have the function *CURVLGTH* described in Prob. 6-22. The accompanying figure portrays a chain or very flexible rope hanging between two supports which are at the same height. For the coordinate axes shown, the equation for the curve is (in conventional notation)

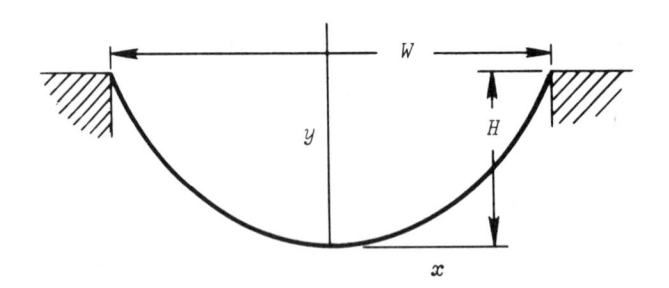

$$y = \frac{e^{\alpha x} + e^{-\alpha x}}{2} - 1$$

where α is a parameter which must be chosen to fit the given values of W and H. Write a dyadic function *CHAIN* which will take the two-element vector W,H as its right-hand argument, and an odd scalar integer on the left which determines the number of data points to be used in using *CURVLGTH* as a subfunction to compute the length of the chain. For a fixed set of W and H parameters (preferably with H greater than W) run the function with different numbers of data points, and compare the results.

6-25 The modern (Gregorian) calendar began on Oct. 15, 1582 (a Friday). Since that beginning, a year has been designated a leap year if it is an integral multiple of 400, or if it is an integral multiple of 4 and not an integral multiple of 100. Design a monadic function which will serve as a perpetual calendar in the sense that it will give the day of the week corresponding to any data. The date will be a three-element numeric vector consisting of the number of the month, the number of the day of the month, and the year. The function is to accept such a vector (for the case of one date) or a matrix of shape $N,3$ for N dates, where each row of this matrix is a date. The result is to be a print of the date followed by the day of the week. Make this a matrix, even if the argument is one date. Call the function *PERPCAL*. An example is

```
      PERPCAL 2 3 ρ 7 4 1776 12 7 1941
   7     4  1776  THURSDAY
  12     7  1941  SUNDAY
```

Write this function without looping or branching.

Chapter 7

REFINEMENTS

INTRODUCTION

The basic ideas relevant to the creation and use of defined functions are given in Chap. 2. Furthermore, the primitive functions are treated in Chaps. 3, 4, and 6; and the uses of branching, looping, and control structures are described in Chap. 5. Thus, at this point you should be able to write useable, but perhaps not elegant, programs for a wide variety of algorithms.

The APL language is very rich in alternatives; it is usually true that many programs can be constructed for a given algorithm, and that within a given program there usually are many ways to construct a statement to perform a required operation. In this chapter we shall consider certain questions of "style" as they affect choices among alternatives. We shall also deal with some new concepts; particularly the representation of a function as a character matrix, and the use of shared variables.

There are no absolute criteria for judging a program to be "good" or "bad", but we can list characteristics which, if improved, can be said to improve a program. These characteristics are:

(1) The ease with which a person skilled in APL, but who did not write the program, can decipher it.
(2) Convenience to the user: for two otherwise equivalent programs, the one requiring the fewer instructions to the user would be the better, and the one presenting the fewer opportunities for misuse would be the better.
(3) The use of memory space; for two otherwise equivalent programs, the one requiring less memory space would be the better.
(4) Running time; for two otherwise equivalent programs, the one requiring less central processor time would be the better.
(5) Considerations of accuracy; for two otherwise equivalent programs, the one that is more free of spurious results due to roundoff errors would be the better.

In dealing with refinements in program writing pertaining to the above criteria, many of the points dealt with are subtle. This means that the reader is expected at this point to have a good knowledge of the fundamentals.

7-1 Types of Defined Functions

The objective of this section is to summarize the concepts relevant to the design of defined functions, developing a perspective appraisal of information given earlier.

In general, a defined function processes data (does arithmetic computations or other manipulations). Accordingly, there must be means whereby data can "enter" and "leave" a function. That is to say, there must be an "interface" permitting the transfer of values between statements internal to the function and the workspace environment or the person using the function.

The most common method of arranging an interface between a function and its workspace is the use of input and output variables. A function having input variables takes values in a workspace as arguments, transferring values of the arguments to the input variables. Such a function is subject to the same syntax as a primitive function. A function which has an output variable returns the value of the output variable to the workspace. That value is the value of the output variable at the instant execution goes to completion; the output variable may have other values during execution.

In some applications it is desirable to have data enter a function through the direct intervention of the person using the function, very often in response to a command to the user incorporated in the program and displayed as the program runs. Such a request for input is usually employed when the data to be entered are obtained from some observation made by the user, such as data obtained from an experiment or information obtained from another person (as in a program used in a bank to keep records). Interfacing of this type, which is between the function and the user, can be through an evaluated input (using the quad input ⎕) or a character input (using the quote-quad input ⍞). The quad input causes ⎕: to print at the margin, and takes a value either explicitly typed or the result of an executable statement which can include global variables. The quote-quad input gives no printed signal (⎕: does not appear) and accepts entries starting at the margin. The input is automatically a character value, although it is entered without using the quote symbols. For those applications where evaluated or character input is convenient it is often sufficient to have a printed result (no returned value). This is a kind of output, but it does not go to the workspace; it is an output directly to the eye of the user.

Another way the internal statements of a function can communicate with a workspace is through the use of global variables, by virtue of the fact that a global variable is valid in a workspace and within any function in which it is used. Thus, a global variable can serve to transfer data into a function. Also, a global variable can be assigned a computed result within a function and, when execution stops, that value will be available in the workspace, as the value of the global variable. Global variables should be used for inputs and outputs only in special situations, where there is a particular reason for doing so. This is often the case when using the control structures described in Chap. 5. Then, the "global" variables are usually local to a main function and global to subfunctions which appear as arguments of the control functions.

The header line of a function identifies the input and output variables. All cases are summarized in the following table, using the name *FN* to represent any function. The output variable is *R*, and the input variables are *A* and *B*.

	Explicit result (Returned value)	No explicit result (No returned value)
Niladic	∇ R←FN	∇ FN
Monadic	∇ R←FN B	∇ FN B
Dyadic	∇ R←A FN B	∇ A FN B

7-2 Ease of Reading

The factors which affect the readability of a program are inherently nonquantitative and are highly dependent on the preferences of the reader. Therefore, it is not possible to make much of a generalization about readability. However, most persons skilled in APL would agree that programs that use arrays and functions in ways that minimize the number of programmed operations tend to be easier to read. This is to say, for example, that a skilled person can interpret an outer product more readily than its equivalent loop. Also, it is usually true that a program that uses subfunctions is easier to read than one that does not, at least if the subfunctions are well defined so as to represent clearly definable portions of the algorithm.

It is the nature of APL that many operations can be coded into a one-line statement. To do this is good practice if the sequence of operations of the statement bears a logical relationship to the requirements of the algorithm. However, it is not good style to contrive artificially to make long statement lines; they tend to be hard to read.

Sometimes, to improve a program in one way is to degrade it in another. The choice of names for variables is an example of this phenomenon. A program is more readable if each name represents only one variable, but sometimes a certain variable is not needed beyond a certain point in the program. In such a case, when the variable has large dimensions there may be significant saving of memory space by reusing the name of that variable, thereby releasing the memory space required for its previous value. As a general rule, readability is degraded by the reuse of a name, but sometimes it may be necessary. If a name is reused, that fact should be acknowledged with a comment line. In fact, comment lines should be regarded as important aids to readability.

7-3 Convenience to the User

In general, if a defined function is misused the result will be a wrong answer or an aborted operation with an associated error report. Judgement as to how convenient it is to use a defined function depends to some extent on who is the user. A person knowledgeable in APL can readily interpret an error report and diagnose the difficulty, but this may not be true if the user is a layman. When a function is designed to be used by a layman, possible errors should be anticipated by the programmer in such a way as to avoid aborted operations.

A typical misuse of a monadic or dyadic function is to use it with an improper argument; a character value when it should be numeric (or vice versa) or a value having the wrong rank or shape. Two design procedures are available to minimize problems of this kind:

(1) Include in the program a test for appropriateness of input value(s). If this test detects an improper input there should be a branch to provide a message describing the error, followed by →0 to exit from the function.
(2) Use programming techniques that make the function insensitive to rank and shape of its argument(s).

One general principle to observe, when making a function insensitive to rank, is to avoid indexing. This is because indexing inherently implies a rank, by virtue of the number of semicolons within the brackets. Take, drop or compression can often provide rank-independent selections in lieu of indexing, but not always. For example, if A is an array of any rank

$$((^{-}1\downarrow\rho A),2)\uparrow A$$

will be equivalent to $A[1\ 2]$ if A is a vector, $A[;1\ 2]$ if A is a matrix, $A[;;1\ 2]$ if A is of rank 3, etc.

A check as to whether an input to a function results from a character or numeric argument can be accomplished by the statement

$$0=1\uparrow 0\uparrow,A$$

When A has a numeric value, $0\uparrow,A$ produces an empty vector of numeric type, and 1 take on that empty vector produces zero; the result for the entire statement is then 1. When A has a character value, $0\uparrow,A$ produces an empty vector of character type, and 1 take on that empty vector produces a space; the result of the entire statement is then zero.

When the input to a function is by way of a quote or quote-quad input it is particularly important to include adequate checks for validity of the input value. Such functions are frequency designed to be used in business applications, perhaps by non-skilled persons who would be confused by an APL error report. Each such program application will have its own unique requirements.

7-4 Memory Space Utilization

A defined function occupies part of a workspace by virtue of its being represented by an assemblage of characters. We shall call this the static space required by a function, as distinct from the dynamic requirement which is the maximum space required while the function is running. The dynamic requirement is greater than the static (except in the most trivial cases) because while the function is running there are calculated values which must be stored temporarily, and usually there are local variables having values which must be stored. In this section we shall deal with techniques for minimizing both of these space requirements. The principles discussed here can often be ignored, but they can be very important for problems dealing with variables having large dimensions.

For a reasonable program, the static space requirement is pretty much dictated by the algorithm it represents. In general, anything you can do to reduce the number of characters required to represent a program will reduce the static requirement, such as using short variable names. There is a slight amount of "overhead" with each line, and so two statement lines require slightly more space than one statement line which is twice as long. However, the saving accomplished by using one line is not great, and it is not good policy to make lines so long that they are almost impossible to read.

The greatest potential for space saving in the design of a program is in the dynamic requirement. Tracking down the last bit of wasted space can be an exercise in sophistication not appropriate for a beginner, but we shall illustrate the principles by writing several versions of one example. Suppose we consider the following pair of statement lines, which could be part of a longer program. Variables A, B, and C are assumed to be local, and so storage of their values is part of the dynamic requirement.

```
[1]    A←2×C←⌽⍳500        Version 1
[2]    B←A+C×C
```

We shall discuss this and subsequent examples in terms of a machine requiring 4 bytes of storage per integer and 8 bytes per mixed number (number with a fractional part). Each variable requires a small amount of "overhead" to store the name and shape information, but we shall neglect this. Therefore, C is a vector of 500 integer elements, requiring 2000 bytes. Thus, line [1] creates a block of 4000 bytes of memory (2000 each for A and C). On line [2], $C \times C$ temporarily creates another 2000 bytes, which are released as soon as $C \times C$ is added to A and stored as B. Thus, the maximum space required to compute these two lines is 6000 bytes, and when the execution is completed, 6000 bytes are utilized for the three variables A, B, and C.

We are interested in the possibility of saving space in this operation. Suppose the value given C on line [1] is not needed after line [2] is completed. Then, a more reasonable sequence would be

```
[1]    A←2×C←⌽⍳500        Version 2
[2]    C←A+C×C
```

This is an example of the *reuse* of a variable name; C is reused instead of introducing another name B. This pair of lines still requires 6000 bytes during execution, but the *final* space requirement, for variables A and C, is 4000 bytes.

In both of the previous examples, A is computed on line [1] on the assumption that it will be needed in subsequent lines, as on line [2]. If line [2] is the only place A is needed, it might be better to use

```
[1]    C←⌽⍳500            Version 3
[2]    C←(2×C)+C×C
```

Again, 6000 bytes are required during computation, but only 2000 are required when computation is complete. This is an example of using an *unnamed computed value* ($2 \times C$) as an argument.

Sometimes it is possible to change the mathematical form of a statement to accomplish the same result but with different space requirements. For example, the last version is mathematically equivalent to

```
[1]    C←⌽⍳500            Version 4
[2]    C←C×2+C
```

244 / Refinements

This requires only 4000 bytes during execution and 2000 for the storage of C after execution is complete.

Now go back to version 3 and suppose

[1] $C \leftarrow \phi \iota 500$ Version 5
[2] $C \leftarrow (2 \times C) + C \star 2$

is used. This is a poor form in this case (where all elements of C are integers) because $C \star 2$ will produce a temporary value of *mixed* numbers (with zero fractional parts). Each mixed number requires 8 bytes. As a result execution of this pair of steps requires 8000 bytes, and 4000 are needed for storage. This is an example of a waste of memory space by using an *inappropriate* primitive function.

To carry this last example further, you might think of using $\lfloor C \star 2$ in order to convert $C \star 2$ to integers, as in

[1] $C \leftarrow \phi \iota 500$ Version 6
[2] $C \leftarrow (2 \times C) + \lfloor C \star 2$

Version 6 still requires 8000 bytes during execution, but after execution the requirement is 2000 bytes, compared with 4000 for version 5.

When space is at a premium, statements should be analyzed according to the principles illustrated here. Very often, space can be saved at the expense of computing time; for example, by computing $\phi \iota 500$ each time it is needed, instead of giving it a name.

If the name of a variable previously having a value of large dimension(s) is to be reused, it may be necessary first to give it a new value of zero dimension. For example, suppose a variable

   $T \leftarrow \phi \iota 500$

is to be reused, with the assignment

   $T \leftarrow 10 \; 50 \; \rho \iota 50$

The total space required will be 4000 bytes (2000 bytes to compute $10 \; 50 \; \rho \iota 50$ and 2000 bytes required by the former value of T), and after completion the requirement will be 2000 bytes. However,

   $T \leftarrow \iota 0$
   $T \leftarrow 10 \; 50 \; \rho \iota 50$

will require only 2000 bytes during execution.

Sometimes it is feasible to convert mixed numbers to integers, when the fractional part has a fixed number of digits. For example, numbers representing dollars and cents (as in 69.37 452.87) can be stored in less space, by multiplying by 100 and using $\lfloor$ to give integers (6937 45287). Of course, multiplication by 0.01 is necessary to regain the actual numbers; an example of the trade-off between memory requirements and computing time. Also, values which are only 0 or 1 should be stored in Boolean form. For example, if A is a vector of integers, each element of $2 | A$ will be 0 or 1, but not Boolean. The same numbers can be stored in much less space by computing $1 = 2 | A$, but the space used during computation will be slightly larger than that required for $2 | A$.

Keep in mind the fact that certain computations with integer arguments will produce mixed numbers. For example, 2×2 produces an integer 4, while 2*2 produces the mixed 4.0.

To summarize space considerations when storing numerical arrays, the following points are noted: The requirement for storing a given number of elements is smallest for Boolean numbers, next for integers (up to a certain maximum size) and then mixed (floating-point) numbers. Furthermore, you cannot always determine the nature of a number from the way a computer prints it. For example, numbers which print 0 or 1 may or may not be Boolean, and a number which prints as 6 may or may not be an integer. In cases such as the above, the type of number in the computer memory depends either on how the number was entered (say, 6 vs. 6.0) or how it was computed.

The use of input variables will cause some waste of space when the argument of a function is a named variable. For example, suppose we have a monadic function

```
     ∇EXAMPLE H
[1]  statement line changing H
```

and suppose there is a global variable

```
    X←⌽⍳500
```

When the operation

```
    EXAMPLE X
```

is executed, local variable H is created as a duplicate of X, doubling the storage requirement compared with a function which would use the global variable X in the statement line. On the other hand, there is no waste of space by doing

```
    EXAMPLE ⌽⍳500
```

because now there is no permanent global variable. Although input variables are a convenience, it may be necessary to avoid them in certain cases, to avoid the duplication of memory space entailed in their use.

7-5 Running Time

The amount of computer time required to obtain a solution is an important consideration in the design of a program, particularly when the program requires extensive calculations. Different programs for solving the same problem can exhibit wide variations in running time. The amount of programming effort that is reasonably expended in achieving fast execution depends to some extent on the number of times a program will run. For example, if a program is to be used only a few times it does not make much difference whether it takes 1 second or 0.1 second. However, if it is to be run a large number of times (say 10000) there could be a significant difference.

The running time required to achieve a solution can depend on the algorithm, particularly when there is computation by successive approximations and rate of convergence is a factor. However, a given algorithm can have different program realizations having different running times. In this section we shall consider some of the factors affecting running time.

246 / Refinements

(a) Arithmetic operations are faster than transcendental

There are only a few instances where this principle is important, but they occur frequently. One of the most important is to use $A×A$ instead of $A*2$. In addition to being faster, if A is an integer, the result of $A×A$ will be an integer (if it is not too large) whereas $A*2$ will always be a mixed number. As another example, if you have $A←*B$ and also want $*-B$, it is faster to compute $÷A$.

(b) Logic functions are faster than arithmetic functions

If A and B are Boolean values, $A×B$ gives the same result as $A∧B$, and $1⌊A+B$ gives the same result as $A∨B$. However, the logic functions should always be used for operations in logic.

(c) Indexing is relatively slow

When possible, compression or take or drop should be used to extract elements, rather than indexing. For example $1↑A$ is faster than $A[1]$, and for a matrix A of shape 3 4, it is faster to do $1\ 1\ 0/A$ than $A[1\ \ 2;]$.

(d) Avoid loops

Avoiding loops is one of the most fruitful ways of minimizing computer time. However, a program without a loop usually requires more space than one with a loop, so the trade-off between computing time and space requirement may be very important.

(e) Mathematically equivalent combinations of primitives may run at different speeds

Some primitives are mathematically equivalent to combinations of others, and some combinations are mathematically equivalent to other combinations. However, it is possible that mathematically equivalent statements will run at different speeds. The evaluation of a polynomial provides an example. A polynomial with coefficients C (in decreasing powers) can be evaluated at a vector of values of X (in origin 0) by

$(X∘.*⍳⍴C)+.×⌽C$

or by using decode

$(((⍴X),1)⍴X)⊥C$

The statement using decode runs considerably faster, and also requires less memory space; this is one case where an increase in speed does not result in an increased memory requirement.

(f) Assign frequently calculated values to names

If a program requires the same calculation many times, and if there are no restrictions on memory space, it is a good idea to assign this calculated value to a name the first time the calculation is made, and then to use that name subsequently where that value is wanted. This technique is particularly important if an extensive calculation is required to produce the value. In many cases, the first computation of such a value occurs within a statement line, and assignment to a name can be made at that point, as an imbedded assignment.

7-6 Roundoff Errors

Roundoff errors do not occur with integers, unless they are so extremely large as to require floating point representation. On the other hand, it is generally true that roundoff errors occur when computations are done with mixed numbers, which are always in floating point form, because a given machine allows only a finite number of binary digits. The main difficulty is that errors tend to grow larger in certain types of computations, sometimes in ways that are very difficult to trace. The analysis of errors forms a large part of the extensive subject of numerical analysis; an exhaustive treatment is beyond the scope of this text.

In spite of the complexity of the problem, it is possible to provide the following relatively simple guidelines for minimizing errors. Keep in mind that these guidelines have to do with choices among various statements which are equivalent mathematically but differing in computed results. The case of 10÷5 vs. 10×0.2 is an example; mathematically they are the same but 10×0.2 has a roundoff error, 10÷5 does not.

(a) Errors tend to increase with multiplication

Some numbers can be represented by a finite number of significant digits (less than the number of digits allowed) and some require an infinite number of digits. In the decimal system (allowing six decimal digits, for example) 6÷5 can be represented accurately by 1.2, but 4÷3 can be represented only approximately by 1.33333. Assuming you are more familiar with the decimal system than the binary, we shall use the decimal system for illustration. It should be noted, however, that some numbers that do not have roundoff errors in the decimal system do have roundoff errors in the binary system; 6÷5 is an example. As a binary number it has an infinitely repeating fractional part: namely, 1.00110011... etc.

Continue to think in terms of six decimal digits, and assume any positive number represented in the machine has been "rounded" to the nearest last digit. That is, 1÷3 would be 0.333333 and 2÷3 would be 0.666667. Also, assume a power of 10 is represented separately, so that 10÷3 would be $0.333333E1$ and 1÷30 would be $0.333333E^{-}1$. Thus, any computer number N_c will be equal to $N_{cm} \times 10^n$ where N_{cm} (the mantissa) is $0.1 \leq N_{cm} < 1$, and n is an integer. In conventional notation (for the 6 digit case),

$$N_{cm} - 0.0000005 \leq N_m < N_{cm} + 0.0000005$$

$$N_{cm}(1 - \frac{0.0000005}{N_{cm}}) \leq N_m < N_{cm}(1 + \frac{0.0000005}{N_{cm}})$$

where N_m is the mantissa of the (generally unknown) actual number. Furthermore, for all possible cases, the smallest value of N_{cm} is 0.1. Thus, we can give the "worst case" estimate that N_m is always in the range

$$N_{cm}(1 - 0.000005) \leq N_m < N_{cm}(1 + 0.000005)$$

We have gone through these steps to establish the general notation

248 / Refinements

$$N_{cm}(1 - \varepsilon_m) \le N_m < N_{cm}(1 + \varepsilon_m)$$

where the maximum *relative error* ε_m depends only on the number of significant digits and the number system. In practice, the number of significant digits is chosen large enough to make ε_m very small.

Now suppose there are computer approximations N_{cm} and M_{cm} for two positive unknown numbers N_m and M_m (again dealing with mantissas because exponents are not involved in errors). We have

$$N_{cm}(1 - \varepsilon_m) \le N_m < N_{cm}(1 + \varepsilon_m)$$

$$M_{cm}(1 - \varepsilon_m) \le M_m < M_{cm}(1 + \varepsilon_m)$$

and multiplying these gives (approximately)

$$N_{cm}M_{cm}(1 - 2\varepsilon_m) \le N_m M_m < N_{cm}M_{cm}(1 + 2\varepsilon_m)$$

This is approximate because the very small ε_m^2 obtained from expanding $(1 \pm \varepsilon_m)^2$ has been dropped. This seems to indicate that when two floating point numbers are multiplied, the maximum relative error doubles. This would be true if $N_{cm}M_{cm}$ were the actual computer result of this multiplication. However, this is also subject to possible roundoff error, and if P_{cm} is the actual computer result (the only number that is known),

$$P_{cm}(1 - \varepsilon_m) \le N_{cm}M_{cm} < P_{cm}(1 + \varepsilon_m)$$

and therefore

$$P_{cm}(1 - 3\varepsilon_m) \le N_m M_m < P_{cm}(1 + 3\varepsilon_m)$$

where the small number $2\varepsilon_m^2$ has been neglected. A similar result is obtained for negative numbers, but with the inequalities reversed.

We have shown that the *maximum possible* error in the result of multiplying two numbers is three times the maximum possible error in each of the numbers. However, this is not to say that the error is actually that large; for any given case the actual error can be considerably less, or even zero. If a machine automatically rounds a result to the nearest last digit, as compared with dropping digits, errors tend to be very much less than the maximum. However, the possibility that multiplication will cause an increase in the relative error always exists. In some cases a number raised to an integer power is more accurate than the equivalent repeated multiplication.

(b) A situation where errors can be dominant

Even with the possible degradation of accuracy in a multiplication, with the large number of significant digits used by most computers, such errors are not serious except when there is subtraction of two numbers which are nearly equal. This can be illustrated by a calculation done on an actual computer, using the variables

```
A←2*16
B←(6×÷3)*16
```

Mathematically, A and B are equivalent, but there is a difference in their computed values due to the roundoff error in `6×÷3`. The relative error in B (obtained on a particular computer) is

```
      (A-B)÷A
1.77636E¯15
```

Now suppose another value

```
      C←A-(1-1E¯10)×B
```

is computed. If there were no error in B, this computation would yield $A \times 1E^{-10}$. Thus, the relative error in C is

```
      (C-A×1E¯10)÷A×1E¯10
1.77075E¯5
```

Emphasis is on the fact that the relative error in C is $1E10$ times the relative error in B. (If your computer performs differently on this example, try `B←(6×1-2÷3)*16`.)

This is a contrived example, in the sense that one would not normally use `6×÷3` to represent 2. However, sometimes approximations arise as a result of complicated computations for which it is difficult to trace the errors. Therefore, it is best to avoid differences of mixed numbers which are nearly equal, or at least to be alert to possibilities of large relative errors when such computations are made.

(c) Do not expect too much from the comparison tolerance

When the comparison tolerance is involved, whether or not it will operate so as to give an expected result depends on the size of the error compared with (approximately) the comparison tolerance multiplied by the absolute value of an argument. Errors are somewhat system dependent but the following examples are typical:

```
      100=¯99900+300000×÷3
0
      1000=¯99000+300000×÷3
1
```

Both statements are mathematically true, but in the first one the error is larger than 100 multiplied by the comparison tolerance.

The residue function can yield errors with mixed numbers as in the example (obtained on a system which does not use comparison tolerance in the residue function)

```
      1|0.2×⍳10
0.2 0.4 0.6 0.8 1 0.2 0.4 0.6 0.8 1
```

Each 1 should be zero. The correct result can be obtained by revising the computation so the residue will have integer arguments, as in

```
      0.1×10|2×⍳10
0.2 0.4 0.6 0.8 0 0.2 0.4 0.6 0.8 0
```

7-7 Branching on Inequalities

If I is an integer, there will be no difficulty in using an equality in branching, as in

```
      →(4=I)/L
```

250 / Refinements

However, if a variable K is a mixed number, due to the possibility of a roundoff error, a branching statement such as

$\rightarrow(0.4=K)/L$

may operate differently than expected, depending on the roundoff errors in 0.4 and K in relation to the comparison tolerance. If, for some reason, you want to use mixed numbers as arguments with a branch on an equality, you can contrive to use an inequality instead. For example, with a loop in which K is initialized at 0,

$\rightarrow(0.4=K\leftarrow K+0.1)/L$

can be replaced by

$\rightarrow(0.35<K\leftarrow K+0.1)/L$

The case where a loop is to be executed until a certain value (a mixed number) becomes zero is particularly important. The value may never actually attain zero. Accordingly, a small number (say $1E^{-}15$) should be chosen for use in

$\rightarrow(1E^{-}15>|F)/L$ instead of $(0=F)/L$

or

$\rightarrow(1E^{-}15<|F)/L$ instead of $(0\neq F)/L$

7-8 Roundoff Errors in Computed Index Numbers

A comparison tolerance which is not controlled by $\Box CT$ operates in cases where an index number, used for indexing an array or in an axis operator, is a mixed number. Thus, if $K\leftarrow 6\times\div 3$, $A[K]$ is equivalent to $A[2]$ without regard to the setting of $\Box CT$.

7-9 Ambiguous Arguments of Dyadic Functions

Consider the two statements

$A\leftarrow 4$
$(A\leftarrow A\times A)+A$

Although A is specified on the first line, its value in the second line as the right-hand argument of $+$ is ambiguous. Its value cannot be determined from the execution rule. The execution of $+$ is delayed until the statement in parentheses is executed, assigning 16 to A, making 16 clearly the left-hand argument of $+$. However, the rule of execution does not stipulate whether the interrupted execution of $+$ includes a storage of 4 as the value of A, or if the right-hand argument is not sensed until the $+$ is executed, in which case A will have the value 16. Thus, there are two possible results from this statement: 20 and 32.

Because of the ambiguity noted above, a dyadic function should never have as its left-hand argument the same name as on the right, if it is *reassigned* within parentheses on the left. While a statement which violates this principle may work on a given computer, a program including it may not be transferable to another computer.

7-10 Uses of Execute

The primitive function execute was introduced in Sec. 2-23, with emphasis on its use in producing a computed result from a character representation of a computable statement such as '3+4'. The general applicability of execute is now emphasized, as we point out that the character vector can be *any* executable statement. For example, if

```
      X←'''ABC'''
      X
'ABC'
      ⍎X
ABC
```

and

```
      Y←5
      ⍎'Y'
5
```

Also,

```
      ⍎'Y←',⍕5
      Y
5
```

Execute makes it possible to do an "indexing-like" operation with vectors, selecting among a set of vectors according to the value of some variable. For example, suppose there exists a set of vectors $V1$, $V2$, and $V3$, and a variable I having the value 1, 2, or 3. The Ith vector can be obtained by executing

```
      ⍎'V',⍕I
```

and the Kth element of the Ith vector is

```
      (⍎'V',⍕I)[K]          or          ⍎'V',(⍕I),'[K]'
```

An assignment to the Ith vector can be done with

```
      ⍎'V',(⍕I),'←',⍕ 4 6 8
```

In the examples above, note that ⍕ must be used on a numeric value if it is part of the argument of ⍎. It is recalled that ⍕ of a character value produces that character value unchanged. Therefore,

```
      ⍎'V',(⍕I),'←',⍕P
```

can be used whether P is a character or numeric value, and I could be a character value (say for "indexing" VA, VB, etc.).

If an argument of execute is not an executable character vector, an error report is received. However, there are three types of arguments for which execute produces no result and no error report. These are: a character vector beginning with '→', a vector of spaces, or an empty character vector. If, in a function, execute is on the left-hand end of a line, with such an argument, that line has no effect. However, an attempt to execute

```
      A←⍎''
```

will produce *VALUE ERROR* because no value is produced by ⍎'' (or ⍎' ' or ⍎'→5').

252 / Refinements

The fact that execute of a vector of spaces produces no result is pertinent to any one of the functions FOR given in Sec. 5-9 or Appendix 9. Normally, FOR sequentially applies the execute function to one or more character vectors representing the initialization statements. However, for the special case where there is no initialization statement, the value '' will be used as the left-hand argument of UNTIL or WHILE, and will be converted by that function to a vector of spaces which then becomes an argument of execute in FOR. Thus, it is seen that the FOR-UNTIL-DO or FOR-WHILE-DO structures can be used even when there is no initialization statement.

7-11 APL Functions as Experimental Tools

It has been well established that the result produced by a function can be the argument of another function. This fact enables APL to be used in an experimental mode in those situations where defined functions are available for solving parts of problems. Very often, such functions can be combined, in "chain" fashion, to produce results without writing a function for the purpose.

To illustrate this principle, suppose we have the function

```
       ∇ Z←A NEWZERO B
[1]    Z←(B,0)-(0,B)÷A ∇
```

This function is pertinent to the problem of having a certain polynomial, say (in conventional notation)

$$p_1(x) = a_0 + a_1 x + a_2 x^2 + a_3 x^3$$

and creating a new polynomial $p_2(x)$ having the same zeros as $p_1(x)$ and same value at $x = 0$, and also having an additional zero at $x = XZ$. If C is the vector of coefficients of $p_1(x)$, then (as can be seen by carrying out the algebraic manipulations) the coefficients of $p_2(x)$ are given by

```
       XZ NEWZERO C
```

There is a restriction that XZ cannot be zero.

It is evident that the degree of the starting polynomial is immaterial. In particular, for a zeroth degree C will be a constant. Suppose we want the coefficients of a polynomial having the value 2 at $x = 0$, and zeros at 1, ¯4, and 6. The desired result is obtainable from

```
       C←1 NEWZERO ¯4 NEWZERO 6 NEWZERO 2
       C
2 ¯1.83333 ¯0.25 0.0833333
```

The use of APL in this mode has an "experimental" aspect to the extent that a user can readily make trials which can enhance learning (particularly in mathematics, and the mathematical sciences). For example, one can try

```
       C←6 NEWZERO 1 NEWZERO ¯4 NEWZERO 2
```

to observe that the results are the same. Also, suppose a function POLY is available, which evaluates a polynomial of coefficients as the right-hand argument at values specified as the left-hand argument. We will obtain

```
      6  1  ¯4 POLY C
0 0 0
```

Also, the fact that the coefficient of the highest powered term is the constant term divided by (¯1*number of zeros)×(product of zeros) can be confirmed by

```
      2÷×/ 6  1  ¯4
¯0.083333
```

Of course, the same experiment could be done in steps, as

```
      C←6 NEWZERO 2
      C
2  ¯0.333333
      C←¯4 NEWZERO C
      C
2  0.166667  ¯0.0833333
      C←1 NEWZERO C
      C
2  ¯1.83333  ¯0.25  0.0833333
```

However, the chaining of functions is sometimes so convenient that when this is a significant possibility arguments should be chosen accordingly. Thus, it would be less convenient to use *NEWZERO* if the arguments were interchanged.

To give further illustrations of this mode of using APL would involve excursions into the details of specific subject areas. However, this simple example provides a hint as to possibilities, particularly for applications in education and research.

7-12 System Variables

System variables are shared between a user's workspace and the APL system environment. They provide a means for controlling the workspace parameters. Three of them (⎕PP, ⎕IO and ⎕PW) have been considered previously, but they are described again here. System variables can be incorporated within defined functions, and can be localized in a header line. You may find differences in what system variables are available in your computer, but in general the system variables are:

⎕CT Comparison Tolerance

The value of the system variable ⎕CT is the comparison tolerance employed by the system in those functions which rely on the comparison tolerance. In a clear workspace ⎕CT normally has the value 1E¯13, but its value can range from 0 to 1.

⎕IO Index Origin

The system variable ⎕IO can have 0 or 1 as its value. Its value is the origin in which the system operates. In a clear workspace ⎕IO automatically has the value 1.

⎕LX Latent Expression

The system variable ⎕LX takes a character vector as its argument, containing information which can be used to control an action when the workspace is loaded. This can be a print of a message, or a function execution to be initiated or resumed. Possible specifications of ⎕LX are:

```
      ⎕LX←'''message'''
      ⎕LX←'name of a function'
      ⎕LX←'→⎕LC'
```

254 / Refinements

For the meaning of □LC, see below. The first of these will cause the message within the inner quotes to be printed, the second will initiate execution of the function named in the statement, and the third will resume computation of the suspended function whose line number appears in □LC. The action specified in this way occurs when the workspace is next loaded. In a clear workspace the value of □LX is an empty character vector.

□PP Printing Precision

The system variable □PP can have an integer from 1 to the maximum number of significant digits of the computer. This value determines the number of significant digits printed in numerical outputs. In a clear workspace the value of □PP is normally 10.

□PW Printing Width

The value assigned to the system variable □PW determines the maximum number of characters in a printed line of output. In a clear workspace it has a value appropriate to a particular computer.

□RL Random Link

The operation of the random number generator depends on a certain number called the "link." This number is the value of the system variable □RL. It can be assigned any positive integer less than or equal to the largest integer that can be represented.

□AI Account Information

While an account is active, the system variable □AI has a numeric vector value which carries information about the current work session: identification number, computer time, connect time, and keying time.

□AV Atomic Vector

The value of the system variable □AV is a character vector of all possible keyboard characters (control "characters" such as "return" may be included).

□LC Line Counter

The value of the system variable □LC at any time during a work session is automatically a vector containing line numbers of statements in execution or of suspended functions. The one currently being executed appears first. In a clear workspace the value is an empty vector.

□TS Time Stamp

The value of the system variable □TS is the date (year, month, day) and time of day (hour, minute, second, millisecond).

□TT Terminal Type

The value of the system variable □TT is a numerical coding of the type of terminal you are using.

□UL User Load

The value of the system variable □UL at any time is the number of users connected to the system.

⎕WA Workspace Available

The value of the system variable ⎕WA at any time is the number of unused bytes in the active workspace.

⎕TC Terminal Control

On some systems, ⎕TC is a vector of the following nonprinting "characters" which produce a control: backspace, new line, line feed.

⎕HT Horizontal tab settings

This variable takes a vector of integers up to the value of the printing width. These integers represent tabulation positions. In a clear workspace its value is an empty vector.

7-13 System Functions

The *system functions* provide means for changing the workspace environment. Unlike the system *commands* described in Appendix 1, the system functions can be used in APL statements, and therefore within defined functions, in the same manner as the primitives. They may be slightly different in different computer systems, or may not all be available, but in general they are described as follows:

⎕CR Canonical Representation of a function

The monadic function ⎕CR takes the name of an existing defined function as a character argument. The explicit result is a character matrix containing the header line (without ∇) and statement lines of the function (without line numbers). For example, if the function

```
       ∇ Z←MEAN N
[1]    Z←(+/N)÷ρN ∇
```

exists,

```
       MM←⎕CR 'MEAN'
       MM
Z←MEAN N
Z←(+/N)÷ρN
```

The value of MM is called a *canonical* representation of the function. If the argument of ⎕CR is a name not representing an existing unlocked function, the returned value is an empty array of shape 0 0.

The function ⎕CR can be used in conjunction with another system function ⎕FX described below, which produces a defined function from a canonical representation. Possible uses for a canonical representation are to allow active editing (changing it through any pertinent operation on a matrix) or storage in memory as a matrix.

⎕FX Fixing a function from its canonical representation

Assume the matrix MM described above exists. It could have been obtained by using ⎕CR, or in any way that a matrix can be formed (say by reshape or laminate). Then, execution of

```
       ⎕FX MM
```

will create (fix) a defined function under the name given in the first row of MM (in this case MEAN). The value returned by ⎕FX is the name of the function created, as a character vector. The name of the function cannot conflict with any existing use of the name other than an existing nonexecuting and nonsuspended function. An existing function by that name, unless it is in a state of execution or suspension, will be replaced by the form produced by □FX. If no function by that name exists, one will be created. The argument must be a character matrix in proper form for conversion, but it can differ from the canonical form by the inclusion of nonsignificant spaces. Rows consisting of nothing but spaces are not accepted. If the argument has a row which is not a valid statement, no function will be created, and □FX will return the number of the row in which the error was detected.

If □FX is used within a defined function, the function created by □FX can be made local to the host function, by including its name in the header line, in similarity with a local variable.

□EX Expunge

The system function □EX is monadic and takes a character scalar, vector or matrix as its argument. Each row of this value is the name of a function or variable in the active workspace. The execution of □EX causes those objects named in its argument to be expunged (erased), with the exception that suspended functions will not be erased. The function returns a Boolean vector having a 1 for each object expunged. Thus, if A is a matrix of three names of which the third is a suspended function, □EX A will return the value 1 1 0 and erase the first two objects. A group (see Appendix 1) cannot be erased by □EX.

□NL Name List

The system function □NL is either monadic or dyadic. The monadic form accepts a numeric scalar or vector restricted to the numbers 1, 2, or 3 as its argument. The returned value is a character matrix of object names in the active workspace (including local variables of any function being executed) selected by categories in accordance with the argument of □NL. In that argument, the integers 1, 2, and 3 mean, respectively, labels, variables and functions. Thus, □NL 2 3 will return a value which is a matrix list of the variables and functions.

In the dyadic form, the left-hand argument is a scalar or vector of letters of the alphabet, as a character value. The listing of objects is then confined to names beginning with the letters in the left-hand argument. The nature of the right-hand argument is the same as for the monadic case.

□NC Name Classification

The system function □NC is monadic and returns as a value a classification of active objects listed in a character matrix argument. The classification is the same as for □NL, with the addition that 0 means the corresponding name is available for use, and 4 means it is not available. In general, the argument of □NC is a matrix of names of objects but it can be a vector or scalar in the case of a single name.

□DL Delay

The system function □DL is monadic, taking as its argument a scalar value of time in seconds. The function produces a delay in execution approximately equal to the value of the argument, subject to slight variations due to varying demands on the system. The returned value is the actual delay.

7-14 A Function for Creating a One-Line Function

The system function $\square FX$ can be used to provide an alternative method of defining functions which can be written in one line. Such a method is useful to a person who wishes to create and use APL functions without learning the mechanics of the function definition mode.

We begin with an illustration of what we want, using the example of *HYPOTENUSE* as given in Sec. 2-13. We assume there is a function *DEFN* (to be defined below) which will take the information about the function to be created, on a quote-quad input. For example,

```
      DEFN
HYPOTENUSE:((α×α)+ω×ω)*0.5
```

will create *HYPOTENUSE*. The non-APL characters α and ω are always used, respectively, for the left-hand and right-hand arguments. This avoids possible conflicts with names of other variables or functions used in the statement line. The name of the function being created and its statement are separated by a colon. The function created will produce an explicit result. Having done this operation, the version of *STRING* given at the end of Sec. 2-18 can be created, by executing

```
      DEFN
STRING2:+/((α÷2)+ ¯1  ¯1 ×1↑ω) HYPOTENUSE ¯1↑ω
```

We shall now describe a simple version of *DEFN*, but one which does not permit recursive definitions*. The function is

```
      ∇ DEFN;H;F;S;I;A;W;□IO
[1]   □IO←1
[2]   H←⍞
[3]   F←'Z←',(S←H⍳':')↓H
[4]   H←(¯1+S)↑H
[5]   H←'Z←',((2×∨/A←'α'=F)↑'X'),H,(¯2×∨/W←'ω'=F)↑'Y'
[6]   F[A/S←⍳⍴F]←'X'
[7]   F[W/S]←'Y'
[8]   S←(⍴H)⌈⍴F
[9]   S←□FX(S↑H),[0.5]S↑F
```

In line [3] of this function the character representation of the assignment to the output variable *Z* is catenated to the function statement line, which is still in terms of α and ω. Line [4] extracts the function name, and in line [5] the header line is completed by adding the assignment to the output variable, and the input variables *X* and *Y* which correspond, respectively, to α and ω. Note that *X* or *Y* is included only if α or ω exists in *F*. Thus, if the function being defined is monadic, there will be no α in *F*, and *X* will not appear in the header line. (A more complete version

---

*A more elegant function for this purpose, which includes the possibility of a recursive definition, is given in "Elementary Analysis" by K.E. Iverson; APL Press, 1976.

258 / Refinements

of *DEFN* would include a check to make sure α is not used if a monadic function is wanted.) Lines [6] and [7] cause 'α' and 'ω' to be replaced, respectively, by '$\underline{X}$' and '$\underline{Y}$', and finally line [9] forms a character matrix of the function and fixes it as a defined function.

A function defined by using *DEFN* is limited to one line, and there is no way to establish local variables other than the input and output variables. Underscores are used on the input and output variables to minimize possible conflicts with other named variables used in the statement. The name used for the function is subject to the same restrictions as for □*FX*.

7-15 Shared Variables

An APL *shared variable* system permits the interaction of two processors by virtue of variables that are made common to the two processors. A processor may be an active workspace, or some other entity of the computer environment not necessarily part of the APL system. In this section we shall deal with the sharing of a variable between two active workspaces identified by two user numbers. Sharing is a bilateral arrangement between only two users, but one user may simultaneously share a different variable with each of several other users. However, there is a system-dependent limit on the number of variables that may be shared.

The basic purpose of sharing variables is to permit two users to process one set of data. This may involve computations of different kinds leading to results pertinent to each of the sharing partners, or it may involve interactions where each user may change the shared data. There are three operations which are unique to the sharing of variables and for which there are appropriate system functions to be described. These operations are:

   (1) Establishment of a shared variable.
   (2) Control of its use: when each user may read a shared variable, or assign a value.
   (3) Termination of sharing.

We proceed to discuss the details of these operations.

7-16 Establishing a Shared Variable

Suppose two users, one with number 989898 and the other with number 121212 wish to establish sharing of a variable named *XP*. One user must make an offer, then the other must accept the offer. For example, suppose user 989898 makes an offer first, by executing

      121212 □*SVO* '*XP*'
1

This demonstrates the use of the function *shared variable offer* □*SVO*. It is evident that the left-hand argument is the identification number of the user with whom sharing is desired. The right-hand argument is the name of the variable to be shared, as a character value. The function returns a value, called the *degree of coupling*, which

indicates the state of sharing. The result 1 indicates an offer is pending but not
accepted. If at a later time user 121212 executes

```
      989898 ⎕SVO 'XP'
2
```

the returned value 2 (the degree of coupling) indicates that sharing is complete: user
121212 has accepted the offer made by user 989898. Note that an offer and an acceptance use the same function and syntax. Which execution of ⎕SVO is an offer and which
is an acceptance depends on which occurs first.

After sharing has been established, one of the users (say 121212) can *set* the
variable (assign a value), as

```
      XP←5
```

Then, the other user (989898) can *use* the variable (test its value, or use its value
in a computation), as

```
      3×XP
15
```

At any time, the common value of a shared variable is the value assigned to it in the
last set, by either user. A set *or* use is called an *access*.

Although the examples show ⎕SVO used with a scalar on the left, and a character
vector on the right, multiple offers can be made in one execution of ⎕SVO if a vector
of user numbers appears on the left, and a corresponding matrix of names of variables
is on the right.

This description indicates the essential steps, but there is the practical matter
of timing. Unless they are operating with synchronized clocks, each potential sharer
must make the offer repeatedly until the result 2 is obtained. Therefore, it is convenient to have a program that will do this automatically. Such a program is

```
      ∇ R←A SHARE B;N;T;D
[1]     N←⁻1↓A
[2]     T←(⁻1↑A)÷2
[3]     I←0
[4]   L:→(∧/2=R←N ⎕SVO B)/0
[5]     D←⎕DL 2
[6]     →(T≥I←I+1)/L ∇
```

This function can be used to make repeated offers to N users, for a prescribed interval of time. The left-hand argument is a vector of N+1 elements: the vector of user
numbers catenated with the desired duration of the search (in seconds). The right-
hand argument is a character vector or matrix of N names of variables to be shared,
respectively, with the owners of the user numbers in the left-hand argument. The
function runs until the alloted time has elapsed, or until all offers have been accepted. Line [5] provides a delay of 2 seconds, and so the function makes the offers,
waits 2 seconds and makes them again etc., if necessary. The returned value is a
scalar or vector of the degrees of coupling for the variable or variables. Thus, if
there is an overlap of the time intervals during which two such functions operate,
sharing will be established. If two users execute the following, at approximately
the same time,

```
      121212 600 SHARE 'XP'
2
      989898 600 SHARE 'XP'
2
```

each will eventually receive 2 as a response. This example shows that the function
□SVO can be used to make the *same offer* repeatedly. If sharing is not established,
the offers initiated by SHARE remain in effect, to the degrees of coupling indicated
by the explicit result.

The monadic use of □SVO, with the name of a variable as its argument, will return
the degree of coupling, but its use does not constitute an offer.

In the operations described above, it is necessary that the shared variable have
the same name in the workspace of each user. The shared variable may be global or
local. However, in some cases it may be impractical for both users to use the same
name. In that case it is possible to use a *surrogate* name for the purpose of sharing.
The surrogate name is included as a second word in the vector (or row of a matrix)
following the name of the workspace variable in the character argument of □SVO. Thus,
the sequence

```
      121212 □SVO 'A SN'       By user 989898
1
      989898 □SVO 'Z SN'       By user 121212
2
```

will establish sharing between the users, via the surrogate name SN. The shared variable will be A to user 989898 and Z to user 121212; there is no variable named SN.
For example, if user 989898 executes

```
      A←12
```

then, for user 121212

```
      Z
12
```

The name of a variable of one user can be a surrogate name for the other user,
as in

```
      121212 □SVO 'A'
1
      989898 □SVO 'Z A'
2
```

A user can use the dyadic □SVO to search for offers, but only if the user number
of the potential offerer and the variable name (or surrogate) are known. There can
be situations where a user does not know what other users might be making offers, or
names of variables being offered. Then, □SVO cannot be used to detect an offer. The
monadic function *shared variable query* □SVQ provides needed information in such cases.
When used with an empty vector as an argument, it returns a vector of user numbers of
those who have outstanding offers to the user executing □SVQ ⍳0. □SVQ can also take
a user number as its argument. For example,

```
      □SVQ 555444
AB
CDE
```

returns a matrix of names of variables (`AB` and `CDE`) offered by user `555444` but not yet accepted.

The monadic ⎕SVQ provides information about *incoming* offers. Some systems include a dyadic form of ⎕SVQ which provides information about *outgoing* offers. The left-hand argument is the degree of coupling for which the query is being made. The right-hand argument is either empty or a vector of user numbers. The result is either a vector of user numbers (in the case of an empty vector on the right) or an array of names. This response only pertains to offers for sharing having the degree of coupling designated on the left.

Immediately after sharing is established, if neither user has made a previous assignment to the shared variable, it will have no value. If one of the sharing users has previously assigned a value, that value will appear to both users. If both users have made prior assignments, that value assigned by the user making the first offer will prevail.

A general offer, to all users on the system, can be made by using 0 as the left-hand argument of ⎕SVO. However, such an offer must be answered by an offer that is specific.

One user may employ the same surrogate in a succession of offers to another user, or in several offers to other users, provided that the variables associated with the multiple use of the surrogate have different names.

7-17 Access Control

The fact that two users have access to a variable introduces unique problems concerning which users can set or use a variable, and when. For example, suppose user 121212 wishes to transmit two different values (say, 5 and 7) sequentially to user 989898 via the shared variable `XP`. If user 121212 executes two assignments

```
    XP←5
    XP←7
```

it is necessary to have a wait after the first set, to give user 989898 time to use the value 5. This wait can be accomplished automatically if user 121212 first executes

```
    1 0 0 0 ⎕SVC 'XP'
1 0 0 0
```

This action establishes a constraint whereby the second set (`XP←7`) by user 121212 cannot be executed without an intervening access (use or set) by user 989898. Thus, `XP←5` will be executed, and the computer will delay the execution of `XP←7` until the value 5 of `XP` is used by user 989898. Note in the example above that ⎕SVC returns its left-hand argument as an explicit result.

Also, there must be a way to ensure that the two uses of `XP` by user 989898 are separated by a sufficient interval of time to allow user 121212 to make the second set (`XP←7`). User 121212 can add this constraint by executing

```
    1 0 0 1 ⎕SVC 'XP'
1 0 0 1
```

In the illustrations above, the values 1 0 0 0 and 1 0 0 1 are examples of the *access control* vector. A 1 provides a constraint of a nature determined by its position in the vector. To explain the constraint associated with each position, suppose we consider the access control vector of a user called "me" in relation to another user called "you." The four possible constraints are as follows:

- $AC[1]=1$ means XP cannot be set twice in succession by "me" without an intervening access (use or set) by "you."
- $AC[2]=1$ means XP cannot be set twice in succession by "you" without an intervening access by "me."
- $AC[3]=1$ means XP cannot be used by "me" without a prior set by "you."
- $AC[4]=1$ means XP cannot be used by "you" without a prior set by "me."

The value of the access control vector can be determined by using $\Box SVC$ in monadic form. Thus, for the previous example, user 121212 would obtain

```
      □SVC 'XP'
1 0 0 1
```

The access control vector is shared by the two users. However, it may have a different appearance to each one because what is "me" to user 121212 is "you" to user 989898. Thus, for the same access control vector as above, user 989898 will obtain

```
      □SVC 'XP'
0 1 1 0
```

The interpretation of the vector 0 1 1 0 seen by user 989898, in terms of the above table, is obtained by regarding user 121212 as "you" and 989898 as "me."

The control vector can be set by either user, or jointly by the two. However, each user can only increase the amount of constraint imposed by the other, and can do so only after using $\Box SVO$ for the variable being controlled. A scalar 1 as a left-hand argument is equivalent to 1 1 1 1, and a scalar 0 is equivalent to 0 0 0 0. The latter will remove any constraints previously imposed by the user who executes it.

Controls can be set on a group of N variables by using an N rowed matrix of their names on the right and a corresponding N by 4 Boolean matrix on the left.

Further explanation of access control is given in Appendix 10. The possibility of constraints provided by access control has implications for the use of variables in program statements. Two statements which are equivalent may not be equivalent in a sharing mode. For example, if A has a constraint preventing two successive uses, $A \times A$ is not equivalent to $A*2$, because $A \times A$ requires two uses of variable A.

7-18 Retraction of Sharing

The monadic function *shared variable retraction* $\Box SVR$, used with a variable name (or matrix of variable names) as an argument, reduces the coupling to zero for each variable in the argument. This 0 is the degree of coupling for the user who executes $\Box SVR$. For each of the previous sharers the degree of coupling will then be 1. The function $\Box SVR$ returns a scalar or vector giving the degrees of coupling prior to the action of $\Box SVR$.

Retraction is automatic if the variable is erased (or expunged), a new workspace is loaded, a user signs off, or a shared variable which is local to a function goes out of existence when execution of that function terminates.

7-19 Illustration of Shared Variable Operations

Suppose a central office is to receive hourly reports of temperatures from a number of weather stations, and is then to report back to each station the mean value of those temperatures. This describes a simple procedure that can be accomplished by using shared variables. To be specific, suppose the central office is user number 99999 and there are five stations with numbers 10101 through 10105. The central office will operate a function *MONITOR*, and each station will operate a function *REPORT*. Each will execute the appropriate function approximately on the hour, using *SHARE* to provide operation for up to 10 minutes.

Each reporting station will execute

```
      ∇ W←REPORT T;A
[1]   W←⍳0
[2]   →L IF 2=99999 600 SHARE 'T DATA'
[3]   'SHARING NOT ESTABLISHED'
[4]   →0
[5]   L:A←0 0 1 0 □SVC 'T'
[6]   W←T ∇
```

and the central station will execute

```
      W←MONITOR SN;T;N;N1;N2;SH
[1]   T←⍴SN
[2]   W←⍳0
[3]   N←'V',(T,1)⍴'12345'
[4]   →L1 IF ∨/2=SH←(SN,600) SHARE N,(T,5)⍴' DATA'
[5]   'NO SHARINGS ESTABLISHED'
[6]   →0
[7]   L1:N←(SH=2)/N
[8]   N2←N1←,N
[9]   L2:W←W,⍎2↑N1
[10]  →L2 IF 0<⍴N1←2↓N1
[11]  W←⌽(+/W)÷⍴W
[12]  L3:⍎(2↑N2),'←',W
[13]  →L3 IF 0<⍴N2←2↓N2
[14]  T←□SVR N ∇
```

Each function attempts to establish sharing (by the execution of *SHARE*), using *DATA* as the surrogate. In *REPORT* the variable name is *T*. In *MONITOR* V1, V2 through V5 are, respectively, the variable names for the data received from stations 10101 through 10105. In each operation of *REPORT* the argument is the temperature being reported, and for *MONITOR* the argument is a vector of the numbers of the stations from which reports are expected. If a station does not establish sharing with the central office during the 10 minutes of operation of *SHARE*, *REPORT* prints the message *SHARING NOT ESTABLISHED* and returns an empty vector. If *MONITOR* establishes sharing with no stations, it prints the message *NO SHARINGS ESTABLISHED* and returns an empty vector. *MONITOR* is designed to proceed if it establishes sharing with at least one station.

If *MONITOR* establishes some sharing, it collects the temperature data from the sharing stations, and computes the mean value. The mean is then transmitted to each sharing station and also is the explicit result of *MONITOR*.

The following comments pertain to specific details of the functions. In *REPORT*, if sharing is established, *SHARE* returns 2 and line [5] is executed, assigning the value 0 0 1 0 to the access control vector. The input variable for each *REPORT* is the shared variable, and so it has its proper value as soon as sharing is established. By virtue of the position of 1 in the access control vector, the completion of line [6] of *REPORT* will be delayed until *T* has been set (with the mean value) by *MONITOR*.

In *MONITOR*, on line [3] *N* is created as a character matrix of the variable names (*V1* through *V5*). This matrix, augmented on the right by catenation of a compatible matrix of repetitions of the surrogate name *DATA*, serves as the argument of *SHARE* on line [4]. Variable *SH* is the degree of coupling, and branching to line [7] occurs if there is at least one 2 in *SH*. In case sharing was not established with all of the stations, *N* is reduced to a matrix of variables for which there is sharing. Line [8] creates two vectors *N1* and *N2*, as the ravels of *N*. Thus, successive pairs of elements of *N1* (or *N2*) are the names of variables in workspace 99999 for the data being transmitted from the stations.

Lines [9] and [10] of *MONITOR* constitute a loop for creating *W* as a numeric vector of the temperatures transmitted from the stations. Note that execute is necessary because each operation of 2↑*N1* produces a character representation of the name of one of the variables. Then, the mean is computed on line [11], converted to a character representation by the use of monadic format, and assigned to the shared variables in the loop formed by lines [12] and [13]. The retraction operation on line [14] would not be needed if the variables *V1* through *V5* were local to *MONITOR*.

In the operations of functions *REPORT* and *MONITOR* it is a matter of chance which one makes the first offer. However, it makes no difference because if *REPORT* makes the first offer it is not released from the operation of *SHARE* until the offer has been accepted. The operation of *MONITOR* with respect to any offer it makes first is similar, except that provision is made for eliminating variables corresponding to any stations that do not reply. Another style for *MONITOR* would use ⎕*SVQ* to determine what offers are coming in from the stations. After an interval of searching, *MONITOR* would then accept offers from the responding stations.

While this example is relatively simple, it shows that the use of shared variables introduces the factor of timing for those operations that involve interactions among users. The degree of coupling and the access control, combined with the delay function, are the devices by which controls of timing are established.

CONCLUSION

This chapter introduces a few fundamental properties of APL, particularly in the sections on system variables and functions, and shared variables. However, the main thrust is toward matters of style: a consideration of those factors which affect value judgements when making decisions concerning alternatives in programming. The ways in which programming choices affect execution time and memory space requirements is an example; another is the fact that mathematically equivalent statements are not always equivalent in the presence of roundoff errors. The previous chapters were quite specific in describing the features of the language. Many of those descriptions included implications concerning alternatives, but not much help in the actual making of choices. The present chapter provides some of the information omitted from the previous chapters.

In providing a glimpse of the vista of creative things that can be done with APL, this chapter is intended to serve as a "launching platform" from which it is expected that you will progress in the development of your own style. No exercise problems are included because it is deemed preferable to encourage you to explore in a free manner the implications of the ideas presented. There are ample opportunities for such exploration in the problems given at the ends of the previous chapters. In particular, it is suggested that you review your solutions to the more sophisticated problems you have done, to see in what ways they may change as a result of your experience in studying this chapter.

Chapter 8

CONCERNING STRUCTURE

INTRODUCTION

Some of the most significant applications of computing involve the management of data. By this we mean the storage of large amounts of data, retrieving parts of the data, and modifying it from time to time to keep it up to date. Data management tends to involve relatively simple arithmetic calculations, but the logical operations tend to be complicated. Programs for data management are usually operated by people who are not skilled in the art of computing. Therefore, the programs they use should be constructed with checking devices which anticipate mistakes, preventing the occurrence of error reports in the computer language and an associated suspension. Also, checks should be provided which will minimize the chance of storing incorrect data.

In this chapter we shall consider a relatively simple problem, the addition of an item to an inventory. The essential operation is quite simple; merely the addition of a row to a matrix. Our entire attention in this chapter will be directed at the design of an algorithm and programs which will provide nearly trouble-free operation. Furthermore, the approach will be structured in the sense that the *IF-THEN-ELSE* structure will be used instead of branching.

8-1 Description of a Data Base

The information contained in the following table is typical of data which would be used by the manager of a retail store (say a hardware store).

Descriptive name of item	Code Number	Unit Price	Reorder Number	Number on Hand
Wood saw	2501	6.90	6	8
Sheet metal hammer	3601	4.65	15	22
Metal saw	2502	7.25	6	7
Power saw	2503	35.00	4	5
Sledge hammer	3602	9.25	5	7
Claw hammer	3603	5.85	12	15
Step ladder	4101	15.90	3	4
Extension ladder	4102	53.40	2	4

The first two digits of the code number are common for a given type of item (36 for all hammers, etc.) so that these two digits can be used in sorting the items by general categories. The reorder numbers represent judgements made by the manager as to how many of each item should always be on hand. When the number on hand gets down to the reorder number, a new supply should be ordered.

There are many operations which might be done on such a list of items in the course of doing business. Some examples are:

(1) Add new items at the bottom of the list.
(2) Correct the list to take care of sales, replenishment, or change of price.
(3) Remove items from the list, as in the case of an item no longer stocked.
(4) Determine what items should be reordered.
(5) Determine the total value of the stock on hand, or the subtotal for a given category.
(6) Print lists of item names and data, arranged according to designated categories.

We shall deal with only the first item.

The first question to be decided is how to store the data. Perhaps the first thought would be to use two matrices, one of characters for the item names and a numeric matrix for the item data. However, we shall store the numeric data in character form, so that names and data can be stored in one matrix. To avoid storing a decimal point, prices will be stored in cents. The following arbitrary limitations will be placed on the various entries:

(1) An item name will not be more than 20 characters, and will always have enough spaces on the right to make a vector of 20 elements.
(2) The code number will always be 4 decimal digits.
(3) The price will not be greater than 999999 cents. When less than 6 digits are needed, the corresponding number of spaces will be on the left of the number.
(4) The reorder number will not be greater than 99. If the number is only 1 digit, the space will be on its left.
(5) The number on hand will not be greater than 999. If less than 3 digits are required, the corresponding number of spaces will be on the left of the number.

In view of these specifications, the first two lines of the storage matrix corresponding to the first and second items of the table will be

```
WOOD SAW             2501    690 6  8
SHEET METAL HAMMER   3601  46515 22
```

Notice that there is no separation between adjacent numbers if the one on the right has a full complement of digits, as in 46515 where 465 is the price and 15 the reorder number. The numbers align vertically, with the following index positions (in origin 1) along axis 2,

268 / Concerning Structure

Index Positions
- 1 through 20   Item name
- 21 through 24   Code number
- 25 through 30   Price (in cents)
- 31 through 32   Reorder number
- 33 through 35   Number on hand

We shall call this matrix *INV* (for inventory). It will be a global variable so far as this analysis is concerned. The dimension of the first axis of *INV* will be the number of items stored, and therefore will vary with the size of the inventory. The second dimension will always be 35. Accordingly, *INV* will be initialized as

   INV←0 35 ρ' '

8-2 Specifications for an Algorithm

The basic requirement is to design a function which will take an item name and the four items of associated numerical data, on a quote-quad input, and add it as a new row at the bottom of *INV*. The following features are to be included:

(1) If an error is detected in the input, a message indicating the nature of the error should appear, and only that part of the input containing the error should be required on a further input operation.

(2) Exiting from the program should be possible at *any* request for input, merely by doing a return, or entering only spaces.

(3) No modification of *INV* should occur until all information has been entered correctly.

(4) An appropriate message should be transmitted if an attempt is made to enter an item name or code number which already exists in *INV*, and an opportunity should be provided whereby the incorrect item can be entered again.

(5) The first of the four data numbers must have exactly 4 digits, and the others must be respectively not more than 6, 2 and 3, with a decimal point permitted only in the second number (price). Also, the price can have no more than two digits to the right of the decimal point. An appropriate message should be transmitted if there is an error in the data, and an opportunity should be provided to enter it again.

(6) The user should be free of concern about format. For example, it should make no difference how many spaces are inserted between words or numbers, it should make no difference whether or not punctuation is used in the item name (it will be stored without punctuation), and the use of the decimal and trailing zeros in the cents column of the cost should be optional in appropriate cases (there should be no difference between 34.6 and 34.60; and 34, 34., 34.0, and 34.00 should all be equivalent).

(7) On the input of the name, it should be necessary to type only the name itself, without adding spaces at the end to make up the 20 characters required by the format.

The item name is stored without punctuation because of the necessity of searching to determine whether a new item name already exists in the list. It would increase the complexity to require standardization of punctuation.

The algorithm will be developed in APL notation. First we define pertinent programs for making the tests and modifications in accordance with the specifications given above. Then these programs will be put together by using *IF-THEN-ELSE* a sufficient number of times to fulfill all requirements.

8-3 Subprograms for Testing and Modifying Inputs

It is assumed that the name of an item might include a numeral. Therefore, we cannot use a differentiation between letters and numerals to identify the name in the input string. Accordingly, a person using the program will be instructed to use a colon as a separator, at the end of the name. An example of the expected input is

```
    WOOD SAW:2501 6.90 6 8
```

With one exception, each testing program will be designed to return 1 if the criterion is met, and 0 if not. Functions will generally be displayed in canonical form, and are designed for operation in origin 1.

(a) Check for separation of item name and data

This test will determine whether the input includes one, and only one, colon. It is assumed that the colon will be used for no other purpose, and therefore should occur only once. An appropriate function, taking the character vector being checked as its argument, is

```
Z←COLON N
Z←1=+/':'=N
```

(b) Check of length of item name

The item name is to be not more than 20 characters (including spaces between words). Therefore, we will need the program

```
Z←LENGTH N
Z←21>ρN
```

to provide the test. The argument is the character vector of the name.

(c) Check for name only

The specifications state that if the name has too many characters or is a repeat, only the name should be reentered. Therefore, a check is needed to avoid the inadvertent entry, as a correction, of the numerical data with the name. For this check we shall assume that if data are inadvertently entered they will be preceded by a colon. This check can be accomplished by

```
Z←ONLYNAME N
Z←∧/':'≠N
```

which takes the character vector being checked as its argument. This check will incorrectly pass a character vector of a name followed by data, if there is no colon. (A way to avoid this possible error is suggested in Prob. 8-1.)

270 / Concerning Structure

(d) Check for repetitions

Checks are to be made to ensure that an item name or code number is not repeated. The same function can be made to serve both purposes, by making it dyadic, with a vector of the column index numbers in INV of the entity being checked as the left-hand argument ($\iota 20$ for names; $20+\iota 4$ for code numbers). The character vector being checked will be the right-hand argument. An appropriate function is

```
Z←A CKLIST N
Z←∧/(((ι35)∊A)/IVN)∨.≠N
```

In this, INV is a global variable.

(e) Check of data

A check of the numerical data part of the input is complicated by the fact that the decimal point is optional in the price (for those cases where it is not required). Because of this, it is convenient to have one program which removes the decimal point (if one exists) converting the price to cents, and also checks the data. A suitable program is

```
      ∇ Z←CKDATA N;IS;R;SP;IP
[1]   Z←''
[2]   →0 IF~∧/N∊'0123456789. '
[3]   →0 IF 2≤ρIP←(~R←'.'≠N)/ιρN
[4]   N←R/N
[5]   →0 IF 4≠ρIS←(' '=N,' ')/ι1+ρN
[6]   →0 IF(∨/(IP≤IS[1]),IP>IS[2])∧1=ρIP
[7]   SP←5 7 3 4 -IS-0,¯1↓IS
[8]   IP←1↑(IP-1),IS←¯1+IS[2]
[9]   →0 IF(2<IS-IP)∨(0≠1↑SP)∨0>⌊/1↓SP
[10]  Z←(IS↑N),((2-IS-IP)ρ'0'),IS↓N ∇
```

This program differs from the other testing programs to the extent that an empty vector is returned if the input fails to meet any one of the tests incorporated in the program. The argument is the character representation of the data, with all extra spaces removed. If all the tests are passed, the returned value is the data, with any decimal point removed and any required zeros added to the cost item. The program operates as follows:

Line [2]: Exits from the function if the input includes a character other than a numeral, space or decimal point.

Line [3]: Specifies IP as a vector of the index position of any decimal point(s) in the input vector, and exits from the function if there is more than one decimal point. IP is an empty vector if there is no decimal point.

Line [4]: Removes the decimal point if one exits, otherwise makes no change.

Line [5]: Specifies IS as a vector of index numbers of spaces in the vector of character data augmented by a space on the right. Exits from the function if the dimension of IS (the number of numbers in the vector N) does not equal 4.

Line [6]: Exits from the function if the original input includes a decimal point and the decimal point does not lie within the second number or immediately on its right. To interpret ∨/(IP≤IS[1]),IP>IS[2], note that after removal of the decimal point on line [4], IP is the index of the character immediately to the right of the original location of the decimal point.

Line [7]: Specifies a variable SP which is a vector of the maximum numbers of characters allowed for each number (4 6 2 3 minus the actual numbers of characters in each number computed from ¯1+IS-0,¯1↓IS).

Line [8]: Specifies variable IP as the index of the character immediately to the left of the "latent" decimal point. If there was a decimal point, this index is 1 less than the previous IP; if there was no decimal point this index is IS←¯1+IS[2], the index of the last character of the second number.

Line [9]: Exits from the function if any one of the first, third or fourth numbers exceeds its allowed number of characters (0>⌊/1↓SP) or if the 1st number is not exactly 4 characters (0≠1↑SP) or if there are more than two characters in the 2nd number to the right of the "latent" decimal point (2<IS=IP).

Line [10]: Adds the required number of zeros to the right of the "latent" decimal point. This number is 2-IS-IP. Since there is an exit from line [9] if IS-IP is greater than 2, 2-IS-IP cannot be negative.

(f) Removal of punctuation marks and extra spaces

The function

```
Z←REMP N;T
T←N∈'0123456789ABCDEFGHIJKLMNOPQRSTUVWXYZ '''
Z←T\T/N
```

takes a character vector as its argument and removes every character except numerals, letters, spaces, and the apostrophe. Its operation is straightforward. Any character removed is replaced by a space. It is assumed that an apostrophe might be wanted in an item name.

Extra spaces, either included in the original input or inserted by REMP, are removed by the program

```
Z REMS N;T
T←' '≠N←N,' '
Z←¯1↓(T∨¯1⌽T)/N
```

which takes a character vector of words as its argument. The criterion for removing a space is that it is removed if there is a space to its left.

(g) Justifying the data items

The data which has been deemed acceptable by CKDATA will be a character representation of four numbers, with certainly four digits for the first one. There may be any number of digits (up to certain maxima) in the other items, and they will be separated by single spaces. Therefore, the numbers will not necessarily be positioned correctly for incorporation in INV. The problem of adjusting positions of the last three numbers is complicated because it may be necessary to insert or remove spaces, depending on circumstances.

272 / Concerning Structure

As an example, suppose the data vector DA returned by $CKDATA$ is

```
      DA
3426 475 11 9
```

In order to conform to the format of INV it is necessary to convert this to

```
3426   47511   9
                └─two spaces
          └─no spaces
      └─three spaces
```

In terms of this example, the general plan is to use compression to convert the input to

3426475119

and then to use expansion with the left-hand argument

$$EX \leftarrow 1\ 1\ 1\ 1\ 0\ 0\ 0\ 1\ 1\ 1\ 1\ 1\ 0\ 0\ 1$$

We make the tentative observation that one way to create EX (again for this specific example) is

$$EX \leftarrow \sim(\iota 15) \in 5\ 6\ 7\ 13\ 14$$

To consider how the vector 5 6 7 13 14 (the index numbers of the desired zeros) can be obtained, let ADS be a three-element vector whose elements are the numbers of leading spaces required for the last three numbers (3 0 2 in the example). Also, let the following variables be specified:

$$MS \leftarrow \lceil/ADS$$
$$W \leftarrow {}^{-}1 + \iota MS$$

Then, again using the example for illustration,

```
       5  11  13 ∘.+W
  5   6   7
 11  12  13
 13  14  15
```

produces a matrix each row of which contains possible index numbers of spaces in the final form (or zeros in EX), except that there will be one or more unwanted index numbers in rows of this matrix corresponding to elements of ADS which are smaller than MS. Elements of the vector 5 11 13 are the first index numbers of the last three items of data, assuming each one has a full complement of digits. A means for removing the unwanted index numbers is evident from considering

```
    ADS∘.>W
1 1 1
0 0 0
1 1 0
```

which has zeros in positions corresponding to the unwanted index numbers. Thus, the desired vector of index numbers is produced by

$$(,ADS\circ.>W)/, 5\ 11\ 13\circ.+W$$

If no spaces are required, W will be empty, but the properties of the outer product and compression are such that the last statement will then yield an empty vector, which will be the correct right-hand argument of $(\iota 15)\epsilon$.

A possible program for this algorithm is

```
Z←JUSTIFY N;U;S;ADS;W
S←(~U←' '≠N←N,' ')/ι1+ρN
ADS←7 3 4 -(1↓S)-⁻1↓S
S←, 5 11 13 ∘.+W←⁻1+ι⌈/ADS
Z←(~(ι15)∈(,ADS∘.>W)/S)\U/N
```

The elements of 7 3 4 used in this program are 1 greater than the numbers of digits required for the last three numbers.

8-4 A General Input Function

The nature of the algorithm is that, in addition to the original input of data, there may be requests to the user for corrections. Accordingly, it is convenient to have a general purpose input function that will serve for all cases. Each input will be associated with a test, a message requesting corrected input if the test is not passed, and a program to be executed next, if the test is passed.

The functions to be executed if the tests are passed will be named $SP1$, $SP2$, through $SP10$. A suitable input function is

```
A INPUT B
MESSAGE[A[1];]
⍎B,'←⎕'
⍎IF 'v/'' ''≠⍎B' THEN ('SP',▼A[2]) ELSE ''
```

Functions $\underline{IF}$, $THEN$, $ELSE$ are defined in Sec. 5-3. The right-hand argument of $INPUT$ is the character representation of the variable to which the input is to be assigned. Thus, if we want the input to be assigned to N, the right-hand argument of $INPUT$ will be $'N'$. The left-hand argument is a two element vector of positive integers: The first element is the index number of the row in matrix $MESSAGE$ which carries the message to be printed. The second element is the numerical suffix for the SP function to be executed next. The statement $'v/'' ''≠⍎B'$ yields $'0'$ if the quote-quad input is nothing but spaces or is empty (as in the case of a return only); otherwise $'1'$. The right-hand argument of $ELSE$ is an empty vector, and so if nothing is entered on the quote-quad (except possibly spaces) the last line of $INPUT$ reduces to $⍎''$ which is "nothing."

The matrix of messages will be

```
    MESSAGE
ITEM NAME:DATA
COLON MISSING
NAME TOO LONG
NAME ONLY
NAME IN USE
DATA NOT IN PROPER FORM
CODE NUMBER IN USE
```

8-5 The Program Realization

Let us agree on the following variables:

>   *IN* complete input (name and numerals)
>   *NA* item name
>   *DA* and *DM* numeric data (in character form)
>   *CN* code number (in character form)

The main function is

```
ADDITEM;IN;NA;DA;CN;DM
1  1 INPUT 'IN'
```

In spite of its brevity, this is the main function in the sense that it is the function executed by the user. The program operates by virtue of a sequence of calls of a set of subfunctions (*SP*1 through *SP*10). Each subfunction determines which subfunction is to be executed next. Some of the subfunctions involve decisions based on the operation of *INPUT*, in which an appraisal of the user's input determines which subfunction is executed next through the appending of an appropriate number as a suffix to *SP*. In this way, a rather complicated set of decisions is handled without branch statements. This is an example of structured programming.

When *ADDITEM* is executed, the message *ITEM NAME:DATA* will be printed and the user will enter the pertinent information. Assuming something is entered, progress will be to *SP*1, which is to make a check as to whether a colon is included as a separator. Thus, this function can be

```
SP1
⍎IF 'COLON IN' THEN 'SP2' ELSE '2  1 INPUT ''IN'''
```

If *COLON* yields 1, *SP*2 is executed next; if *COLON* yields 0, '2 1 INPUT ''IN''' is executed, with the message *COLON MISSING* being printed. In the latter case, if a new entry is made, *INPUT* will cause *SP*1 to be executed again; if nothing is entered ⍎'2 1 INPUT ''IN''' is equivalent to ⍎'', *SP*1 produces no result, and there is no further action.

Now assume that the data has been entered with the colon included, so that *SP*1 will cause *SP*2 to be executed. *SP*2 will separate the item name from the item data. A suitable form for *SP*2 is

```
SP2;T
T←IN⍳':'
NA←(T-1)↑IN
DA←T↓IN
SP3
```

so that *NA* will be the item name and *DA* the data. *SP*3 is to check whether the item name is not greater than 20 characters. Thus,

```
SP3
⍎IF 'LENGTH NA←REMS REMP NA' THEN 'SP4' ELSE '3  5 INPUT ''NA'''
```

Note that the argument of *LENGTH* is the value of *NA* after punctuation and extra spaces have been removed. If the length is satisfactory, *SP*4 will be executed next. If not, the message *NAME TOO LONG* will be printed due to the execution of '3 5 INPUT ''NA''' and if a new entry is made,

```
SP5
⍎IF 'ONLYNAME NA' THEN 'SP3' ELSE '4  5 INPUT ''NA'''
```

will be called for. If the new entry to *NA* does not include a colon, *SP*3 will be executed again, making another check of the length of name. If *NA* includes a colon, `'4 5 INPUT ''NA'''` will cause the message *NAME ONLY* to be printed, and after a further input, *SP*5 will be called for again.

Eventually, *NA* will pass the test for length in *SP*3, and then

*SP*4
◆IF `'(ι20) CKLIST NA←20↑NA' THEN 'SP6' ELSE '5  5 INPUT ''NA'''`

will be executed, making a check of whether the item name now exists in the list. If the name is in the list, `'5  5 INPUT ''NA'''` will cause the message *NAME IN USE* to be printed, and a corrected name can then be entered. The new entry will then be checked in *SP*5 and *SP*3.

When the name has been accepted by *SP*4, execution will proceed to

*SP*6
◆IF `'0≠ρDM←CKDATA REMS DA' THEN 'SP7' ELSE '6  6 INPUT ''DA'''`

which uses *CKDATA* to determine whether the data are in proper form, in accordance with the description in Sec. 8-3e. If the form is not correct, the message *DATA NOT IN PROPER FORM* will be printed and a corrected input will be accepted for further checking in *SP*6. Note that the operator might make the mistake of entering the name with the data at this point, but a separate check of this possibility is not needed because *CKDATA* will reject such an erroneous input. When the data have been accepted,

*SP*7
`CN←4↑DM`
`DM←4↓DM`
*SP*8

and

*SP*8
◆IF `'(20+ι4) CKLIST CN' THEN 'SP9' ELSE '7  10 INPUT ''CN'''`

will assign the code number to *CN*, respecify *DM* as the remaining data, and check whether the code number is in use. If the code number is in use, `'7  10 INPUT ''CN'''` will cause the message *CODE NUMBER IN USE* to be printed, and will accept a new input of the code number. The new code number will then be catenated with the other data in *SP*10 and rechecked in *SP*6. The remaining functions are

*SP*9
`INV←INV,[1]NA,JUSTIFY CN,DM`

*SP*10
`DA←CN,(¯1+DAι' ')↓DA`
*SP*6

Note that if more than the code number is entered in response to `'7  10 INPUT ''CN'''`, *SP*10 will cause *DA* to have too many items and therefore to be rejected by *CKDATA* in *SP*6.

8-6 Files

The preceding solution to a data management problem has been given only in terms of the task of programming, as an exercise in the application of the APL language.

In a practical situation, files would probably be used to store the data. Whether this is true would depend on the size of the data base in relation to the size of the workspace. In general, a file is a storage facility outside of a workspace, and having a capacity much larger than a workspace, in which values can be stored and recalled. In a file a value does not carry its APL name; being identified through some sort of indexing scheme. File systems do not necessarily have standardized characteristics on all APL systems and if you have need for a file system you should obtain information about it from your local computer personnel. The point of these few comments about files is to alert you to the fact that it may be necessary or convenient to use files in certain applications.

The use of a file will influence programming to the extent that extra steps are required to store data in a file, and to retrieve it. Also, if a value in a file is larger than can be contained in a workspace, it may be necessary to break that value into components, each of which can be stored and retrieved independently. In such a case it would be necessary to program a search as a repetitive process, searching one component at a time.

CONCLUSION

Although this chapter is written in terms of a specific hypothetical example of data management, it serves to emphasize two important points. The first is the **emphasis on accuracy, designing an algorithm with anticipation of possible user errors.** This is an important feature because a data base can be very large, making it difficult to locate errors, and because important decisions may depend on accuracy. The second point is the simplifications provided by a structured approach made possible through the use of subfunctions for testing, and the *IF-THEN-ELSE* format for handling the logic. The alternative, using a main program with explicit branching is considerably more complicated (see Prob. 8-2).

In a large establishment employing a data management system such as this, it might be convenient to allow data to be entered, processed, or read by more than one operator. This can be accomplished by using shared variables.

Problems--Chapter 8

8-1 The function *ONLYNAME* is designed to reject an input consisting of an item name followed by data, when only the name is wanted. However, it succeeds only if the input includes a colon. As an improvement we suggest a different version of *ONLYNAME* which will reject the input if the name and data are typed without a colon separating them, and perhaps with no space between the name and the code number. In thinking about a criterion for a test, we recognize that a simple test for the existence of numerals is not adequate: the name might include numerals (as in 100 watt lamp). A reasonable criterion is that the last six characters of a name will certainly include at least one letter of the alphabet. Use this criterion in the design of a modified function *ONLYNAME*.

8-2 Construct one main program to replace *ADDITEM*, which will use the various programs described in Sec. 8-3 as subfunctions, but using explicit branch statements rather than *IF-THEN-ELSE*. The performance is to be the same as for *ADDITEM* as given in the text. As an aid in writing this program, you should make a flow chart.

8-3 Write a monadic function *UPDATE* which can be used to change the data for an item (except the code number). The code number will be the argument. Use subprograms to provide suitable checks, using quote-quad input. Also, in recognition of the danger of changing the wrong item, include a print of the code number and require that the operator give the positive response *YES* before proceeding. Thus, a typical operation would be

    UPDATE 4369
DO YOU WANT TO MAKE CHANGES FOR 4369
YES
ENTER DATA
26.45 16 24

8-4 Write a version of *INPUT* that will allow making entries on the same line as the computer instruction. That is, use bare output.

8-5 Revise the set of functions given in this chapter so as to store the names in a character matrix and the data in a numerical matrix of four columns.

8-6 The version of *ADDITEM* given in the text is used once for each addition of an item (name and data). Modify it so that one operation will permit continuing entry of items. The following conditions are to be met: As soon as one item is successfully entered, the program is to ask for a new item. To exit, as when all new items have been entered, arrange that the typing of an unlikely entry (such as *ZZZ*) will cause operation to terminate.

8-7 Consider a system for handling the data base described in this chapter, where the data is under the control of a central office, but using shared variables so that additions can be made by several people. The central office is to make a continual search for offers, so that a person making an offer to share will not have to wait more than five seconds for a reply.

Appendix 1

WORKSPACE MANAGEMENT

In the descriptions given in this appendix it is assumed that you know how to sign on to the computer. The procedure for signing on is system dependent, and so about the only general statement that can be given is that you must have obtained authorization to use the computer by having been given a valid user number and perhaps a password. The details of the procedure for signing on should be obtained from someone in your local environment.

A workspace is an object (a certain amount of computer memory) which is identified by the user number of the person who "owns" the workspace, and a name. A workspace must have a name because a user may have a *library* in which there is more than one workspace. The size of a workspace, in terms of the amount of information it can store, is system dependent, but is generally large enough to store many functions and variables. A time sharing system generally has *public libraries* which contain programs of general interest. A workspace in a library is *saved*, meaning that its functions and variables will be available at some future time.

A1-1 The Active Workspace

Whenever you are signed on to the computer you will be in communication, through your terminal, with an *active* workspace. This is the only workspace with which you can communicate directly. You are able to use objects from the workspaces in your library, the libraries of other users, or the public libraries, by making your active workspace a *copy* of all or part of one of the library workspaces. Also, you can permanently save work you have done by replacing one of your library workspaces by a copy of your active workspace. An active workspace *goes out of existence* upon signing off.

It is important that you form a mental image of the active workspace in relation to library workspaces, as suggested by the accompanying diagram. In this diagram, it is assumed that you have two workspaces (having names *ABC* and *XYZ*) in your private library. The double-headed arrows between these workspaces and the active workspace indicate that the contents of these workspaces can be moved in either direction. Except in unusual situations (where you might be authorized to place objects in a public library), contents can be moved from libraries outside your private library into your active workspace, but not in the other direction. It is never possible for you to move the contents of your active workspace to the library of another user.

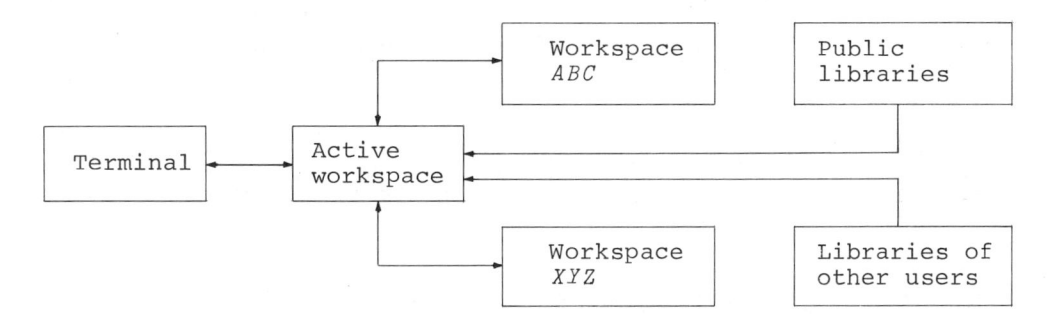

Emphasis is on the fact that you communicate only with the active workspace, and that the active workspace disappears when you sign off. Therefore, when you produce a new object (such as a function) which you want to save for future use, it must be transferred to a library workspace. Much of this appendix is devoted to describing how this is done.

A1-2 System Commands

The contents of workspaces are moved in and out of the active workspace by the use of system commands. A system command is an instruction which you give to the computer which is not part of the APL language and cannot be incorporated in a defined function. A system command always begins with the right-hand parenthesis: the symbol). For example,)SAVE is a system command. System commands are used for a variety of operations other than the shifting of contents of workspaces. The computer gives a printed response to a system command which is pertinent to the nature of the command.

System commands are not as well standardized among APL systems as is the APL language. Therefore, it is not possible to give descriptions of system commands that will be completely valid for all systems. However, the descriptions given are typical, and variations from them will generally be minor. If your system appears to have system commands which do not exactly conform to the descriptions given here, obtain further information from your local computer personnel.

A1-3 Workspace Identification

In general, a workspace is identified by the user number of a library, and a name. The name can be any combination of letters and numerals, except that the first character must be a letter; it can be the same as the name of an object in the workspace. The current name of the active workspace can be determined by executing

)WSID

The computer responds by printing the name of the active workspace. If the workspace was obtained from a library other than yours (see Sec. A1-8) the number will also be included in the response. The letters WSID stand for workspace identification. The names of workspaces in your private library can be obtained by executing

)LIB

You can have any name for the active workspace; its name does not have to be the same as one of the library workspaces. To change the name of the active workspace to

280 / Workspace Management

PQR you would do

)*WSID PQR*

after which the computer will respond with the previous name.

  The *CLEAR* workspace is a special case. It is created by executing

)*CLEAR*

The result is an active workspace with no contents, other than certain system variables such as □*PP*, □*IO*, □*PW*, □*RL*, □*CT*, and no name. The index origin is 1 in a clear workspace, and the comparison tolerance is normally $1E^-13$. Values of the other system variables may be system dependent. (Note: Some of the older APL systems do not have system variables by that name, but in such systems a clear workspace has the same properties in terms of initial values for the printing precision, etc.)

  When you first sign on, the workspace is clear.

A1-4 Creating a Library Workspace

  Assume you have just signed on, so that the active workspace is clear, and that you want to create a library workspace *ABC* in which there is a variable *X* having the value 5, and a library workspace *XYZ* in which there is a variable *Y* with the value 7.

  First, the specification

  X←5

can be done so that the workspace now has the object *X* in it. Then, the system command

)*SAVE ABC*

will create the library workspace *ABC* with the same contents as the active workspace, and will also change the name of the active workspace to *ABC*. Thus, after this has been done you will have two identical workspaces, one active and the other in the library. The printed response gives the time of day, the date, and name of the workspace.

  An equivalent procedure consists of the two steps

)*WSID ABC*
)*SAVE*

Actually, the)*WSID* command will be followed by a computer response not shown here.

  In the second procedure there would be no difference between)*SAVE* and)*SAVE ABC*, illustrating that)*SAVE* without a workspace name operates as if the name of the active workspace had been included. It would not be possible to omit the name *ABC* in the first procedure because no name had previously been established for the workspace.

  Under the condition that you have room for a new workspace in your library, when you execute)*SAVE ABC* the name of the active workspace is not important. For example, if you execute

)*WSID PQR*
)*SAVE ABC*

the first command has no permanent effect. As soon as)*SAVE ABC* is executed the library workspace is created and the name of the active workspace changes to *ABC*. If your library quota has been exhausted, the name of the active workspace does make a difference (see Sec. A1-5).

Having created one library workspace, let us consider how to create the second, having the object *Y*. By executing

)*CLEAR*

the active workspace is returned to the same status as when you signed on. Therefore, you can specify

$Y \leftarrow 7$

and execute

)*SAVE XYZ*

to create the second workspace, and change the name of the active workspace to *XYZ*.

In these examples, the specifications of *X* and *Y* are not part of the save operation. They were included so each workspace would contain an object. The specifications could have been omitted. You can save a workspace having no contents.

A1-5 Conditions for Saving a Workspace

Continuing to think in terms of the previous example, where two workspaces *ABC* and *XYZ* have been placed in your private library, suppose you have been authorized to have only two workspaces. If you try to create a third library workspace, you will obtain the following:

)*CLEAR*
)*SAVE PQR*
NOT SAVED, WS QUOTE USED UP

When doing a save command it is important that you read the message. Beginners frequently lose objects inadvertently because they use an incorrect name when trying to save, and ignore the *NOT SAVED* message. If a sign off occurs after such a message, the contents of the active workspace will be lost.

The command

)*SAVE*

which is equivalent to)*SAVE* [name of the active workspace], will be successful if the name of the active workspace is also the name of a workspace in your library, *or* if there is an unused workspace in your allocation. The command

)*SAVE* [name of a workspace]

can be done if the name used is the name of the active workspace *and* is also the name of a library workspace, *or* if there is an unused workspace in your allocation.

The save command can be executed while a function is awaiting evaluated input. The computer will then make a new request for input.

A1-6 Loading a Workspace

In the example given in Sec. A1-4, you have created two library workspaces and after the second save command the name of the active workspace is XYZ. Suppose you now want the active workspace to be a copy of the library workspace ABC. This is accomplished by executing

)LOAD ABC

This command wipes out the existing active workspace, replacing it by the contents of ABC (in this case, merely the variable X). The name of the active workspace is then the name of the workspace that was loaded. At the completion of the load command, your library workspace ABC and your active workspace ABC would be identical. However, if you specify another variable

    $A \leftarrow 10$

this will exist in your active workspace but *not* in the library workspace. Thus, although your active workspace may have the same name as a library workspace, their contents are not necessarily the same. However, if you execute)SAVE after specifying A, the library workspace will again be the same as the active workspace.

The description above enables us to make an important general statement. An active workspace and a library workspace having the same name will necessarily have the same contents only *immediately* after a)LOAD command or a)SAVE command.

Loading a workspace from a library other than your own is described in Sec. A1-8. If the system variable $□LX$ in the workspace being loaded has an executable statement as its character value, that statement will be executed automatically when the workspace is loaded. In general, always load a workspace as soon as you sign on.

A1-7 Copying Objects

Objects can be brought into your active workspace from a library workspace by using the command)COPY. The object copied can be a whole workspace or some of the objects in the workspace. For example, suppose you have previously done)LOAD ABC so that your active workspace is also ABC, and you have the variable X, as specified in Sec. A1-4. You also have in your library the workspace XYZ in which there is a variable Y. Now, if you execute

)COPY XYZ

you will copy all the objects in XYZ and add them to those already existing in ABC. Thus, in the example, you will now have two variables, X and Y. There is an exception: If there is an object in the copied workspace having the same name as an object in the active workspace before the copy is executed, this object will be replaced by the one that is copied. The copy command does not change the name of the active workspace. Copying an entire workspace differs from)LOAD in the following ways: Whereas)LOAD makes the active workspace an exact duplicate of the one loaded from the library (including a change in the name of the active workspace),)COPY augments the active workspace with objects in the library workspace (replacing objects if there is duplication of names) and does not change the name of the active workspace. Also,

)$COPY$ does not carry the state indicator and symbol table of the copied workspace, and a latent expression (value of $\Box LX$) cannot be activated with the copy command.

It is possible to copy selected objects from a library workspace by listing the names of the objects following the name of the workspace. For example, if there are objects (variables or defined functions) AX and HGS in workspace ABC, executing

)$COPY\ ABC\ AX\ HGS$

will add objects AX and HGS to your active workspace, or replace them if they existed previously.)$COPY$ can be executed when a function is awaiting evaluated input.

The copy command is sometimes a convenient device for rectifying a mistake. For example, suppose you sign on and forget to load a workspace, and create some objects that you want to save. If you have used your workspace quota, it is not possible to save the active workspace under a new library name, and if you save it under the name of an existing library workspace name, it will replace the contents of that workspace. However, if the names of your new objects are different from the names of objects in one of your library workspaces (say ABC) you can execute)$COPY\ ABC$,)$WSID\ ABC$ and)$SAVE$. As another example, suppose workspace ABC has been loaded, and you have made changes in an existing function (say FN) in that workspace. Suppose you make many changes, and then find you want the original form after all. Instead of changing the function back to its original form, it can be recovered by executing)$COPY\ ABC\ FN$.

There is another version of the copy command, called *protected copy*. It "protects" existing objects in your active workspace to the extent of not copying any objects having the same names. Thus, if you have an object AX in your active workspace and you execute

)$PCOPY\ ABC\ AX\ Y$

only Y will be copied.)$PCOPY$ can be used on a whole workspace.

When there is a frequent need to copy a certain collection of objects, it is convenient to use a system command which forms an object called a *group*; a collection under one name of a group of objects. Thus, if a workspace has objects (variables or functions) A, AX, and Y which form a related "package" they can be grouped under one name (say COL) by executing

)$GROUP\ COL\ A\ AX\ Y$

After having done this, a copy of the one object COL will result in each of its constituent objects being copied. A group is classified as an object in a workspace. If, at a later time, you want to add an object RS to this group, it can be done by

)$GROUP\ COL\ COL\ RS$

A1-8 User Numbers and Passwords

You can load or copy from workspaces not in your personal library. When doing so it is necessary to enter the user number as the first entity on the right of the $LOAD$ or $COPY$, as in

)$LOAD$ 123456 ABC

284 / Workspace Management

If there is a password associated with the user number, it should not be used.

If a workspace is locked, its password must be used in any)*LOAD* or)*COPY* command. If it is not used, the message *WS LOCKED* is printed.

A workspace can be locked by establishing a password (a "key" to the lock) at the time of executing a save command. For this it is necessary to include the name of the workspace as part of the save command, following it by a colon and the password. The password can be any name of your choice, and can be all numerals. Once a password has been applied to a workspace, it remains until it is changed by doing the same operation with a different password. Thus, a given password is established only once; it is not used on subsequent save commands.

A password can be removed (unlocking the workspace) by a similar process, but using only the colon following the name of the workspace.

A1-9 Dropping a Workspace

A workspace can be removed from your library by using the command)*DROP* followed by the name of the workspace. You can only drop workspaces from your personal library; if you attempt to drop a workspace from any other library you will receive the response *IMPROPER LIBRARY REFERENCE*. After you have removed a workspace from your library, the amount of unused workspaces in your authorization increases by one.

The drop command can be used in renaming a library workspace. If you want to change the name of library workspace *ABC* to *DEF*, execute

)*LOAD ABC*
)*DROP ABC*
)*WSID DEF*
)*SAVE*

The first step is important because it saves the workspace in active form while the library workspace is dropped.

A1-10 Monitoring the Contents of the Active Workspace

Especially when a workspace contains many objects, it is useful to be able to determine the names of those objects. There are system commands for this purpose.

The command

)*VARS*

provides an alphabetized list of names of existing global variables. Since this applies to the active workspace, any objects added after loading a workspace will be included in the list. If the command includes a letter of the alphabet, as in

)*VARS G*

it will list the global variables, beginning with that letter.

The command

)*FNS*

provides a similar listing of the defined functions, also alphabetized. If this is followed by a letter, the listing begins with that letter.

An alphabetized listing of groups is obtained by executing

)GRPS

A letter of the alphabet can be included, to cause the listing to begin with that letter.

If there is a group with the name COL, the command

)GRP COL

will provide a listing of the objects in that group.

The commands which pertain to the symbol table and state indicator are described in appendices 5 and 6.

The system variables are parameters of a workspace, and can be tested to determine their values. See Chaps. 2 and 7 for additional details. For systems which do not have system variables, there are system commands)DIGITS,)ORIGIN, and)WIDTH. For example,)ORIGIN gives the present origin, and)ORIGIN 0 changes the origin to 0.

A1-11 Removing Objects from a Workspace

The system command

)ERASE [names of objects]

will remove the named objects from the active workspace. If an object listed with)ERASE is a group, all objects in the group will be erased. Therefore, care should be used in erasing a group. To disperse a group (eliminate the group without erasing its objects), execute)GROUP followed by the name, and nothing else. It is possible to erase a suspended function, and doing so will result in the message SI DAMAGE.

For the removal of global variables and nonsuspended functions,)ERASE has the same effect as the system function □EX (expunge).

A1-12 Signing Off

A work session is terminated by executing the system command

)OFF

If this is followed by a colon and a password, that password is applied to the number and must be used when signing on in the future. The number is then locked. A password can be changed by using the new password when signing off, or can be removed by using only a colon when signing off. Once a password has been established,)OFF is used (without a password) until such time as the password is to be changed or removed.

Another way to sign off is

)CONTINUE

This action terminates the work session and also makes a copy of your active workspace which will automatically be your active workspace when you sign on the next time. This restored active workspace will be in exactly the same state as when you signed off. It is convenient to use)CONTINUE in the event you must terminate a work session before the execution of a function is complete. You can interrupt the function (see appendix 6), sign off with)*CONTINUE*, and resume where the function left off when you sign on again. If your connection to the computer is accidentally interrupted, and in some cases of computer failure, the computer will protect your active workspace by automatically doing the equivalent of)*CONTINUE*. The command)*CONTINUE* can be used on a request for evaluated input.

When signing off, it is possible to use

>)*OFF HOLD*

or

>)*CONTINUE HOLD*

In either case, the inclusion of the word *HOLD* maintains the telephone connection. This is useful if you or someone else wants to sign on again, within a few minutes.

Appendix 2

ERROR REPORTS

An error report occurs when the execution of an APL statement terminates because something is wrong. The following list of error reports is in four groups: group 1, there is an error in an APL statement, or something has been typed wrong; group 2, one of the system resourced has become exhausted; group 3, an error has been made in defining a function; group 4, the system has failed. In general, the required remedial action is evident from the nature of the report. Different computing systems may exhibit slight variations from the following list.

A few of the error report messages also appear as trouble report messages, and are therefore covered also in appendix 3. For example, *WS FULL* can occur as the result of the execution of an APL statement (an error report) or as the result of trying to copy too much into a workspace (a trouble report).

Group 1

DOMAIN ERROR
   An APL statement calls for the execution of a function with an improper argument, as in division by zero, or a logic function with an argument other than 0 or 1.

ENTRY ERROR
   In some systems this is *CHARACTER ERROR*. An illegal character has been entered or received. This is also a trouble report.

INDEX ERROR
   An index value is out of range.

LENGTH ERROR
   A dyadic function has arguments whose shapes are not compatible (for that function).

RANK ERROR
   A dyadic function has arguments whose ranks are not compatible (for that function).

SYNTAX ERROR
   The statement is not executable because of improper syntax: For example, there are unpaired parentheses, or the function symbol has been omitted between two variables.

VALUE ERROR
   A name has been used in a statement as if it were a variable, but without a prior specification.

288 / Error Reports

□xy *IMPLICIT ERROR*
> Here, xy refers to any of the pairs of letters pertinent to a system variable having a restricted range for its value. The error report indicates an attempt to use such a system variable if it has been assigned an improper value, or the use of the variable is localized without an assignment.

Group 2

INTERFACE QUOTA EXHAUSTED
> An attempt has been made to share more variables than authorized.

NO SHARES
> The shared variable facility is not available.

SYMBOL TABLE FULL
> Too many names have been used (see appendix 5). This is also a trouble report.

WS FULL
> The memory space allocated to the workspace has been exhausted: There are too many objects in the workspace, one or more variables is too large, or there is a large number of suspensions. This is also a trouble report.

Group 3

DEFN ERROR
> The symbols ∇ or □ have been used incorrectly. Common reasons for this report are an attempt to define a new function using the name of an existing variable or function, or an attempt to display a locked function.

SI DAMAGE
> A suspended function has been edited in such a way that its continued execution is not possible. Examples are: the name of the function is changed, or a line label is changed. This is also a trouble report.

Group 4

INTERRUPT
> Execution has been suspended within an APL statement line for some reason other than an error in the statement. It may be due to computer action, or a strong interrupt (see appendix 6). A function can be restarted after an interrupt.

RESEND
> An error has occurred in the transmission of an entry. Make the entry again.

SYSTEM ERROR
> There has been an error in operation of the system. The execution of a function cannot be restarted after a system error has occurred. A system error usually has associated with it a print of some data, with a request that it be returned to the operator of the computer.

Appendix 3

TROUBLE REPORTS

A trouble report occurs when the computer cannot carry out a system command. There is one general trouble report

INCORRECT COMMAND

which occurs if a system command was typed wrong (say, misspelled) or a nonexistent command is given. The other trouble reports can be arranged in two groups: group 1, having to do with signing on; group 2, having to do with workspace management.

Group 1

ALREADY SIGNED ON
    The terminal is now operating on an APL number.
INCORRECT SIGN ON
    You have not followed the prescribed procedure for signing on.
NUMBER IN USE
    There may be unauthorized use of your number by someone else. Consult the operator of your system.
NUMBER LOCKED OUT
    For some reason you are not permitted by the computer center authorities to use your number. Consult them to find out the reason and initiate remedial action.
NUMBER NOT IN SYSTEM
    You have used an incorrect number or incorrect password.

Group 2

IMPROPER LIBRARY REFERENCE
    Usually occurs with an attempt to save a workspace in a library other than the library for your number.
NOT COPIED [names of objects]
    On a)*PCOPY* command, the objects listed are "protected" because they already exist in the workspace.
NOT FOUND [names of objects]
    The objects listed do not exist in a workspace from which you have attempted a)*COPY* command.
NOT GROUPED, NAME IN USE
    You have attempted to form a group using a name which is already in use for a variable or function.

NOT SAVED, THIS WS IS CLEAR
: A clear workspace has no name, and therefore cannot be saved in your library.

NOT SAVED, THIS WS IS [name of active workspace]
: You attempted a)*SAVE* followed by a name in your library which does not agree with the name of the active workspace.

NOT SAVED, WS QUOTA USED UP
: You have attempted to create a new library workspace, beyond your authorized quota.

SI DAMAGE
: A system command has invalidated the status of a suspended function. Examples are: erasing a suspended function, or replacing it by doing a copy command.

SYMBOL TABLE FULL
: A)*COPY* command has resulted in too many symbols (see appendix 5).

WS FULL
: As a result of a copy command, the memory space of the active workspace has been exceeded.

WS LOCKED
: In a load or copy command you have attempted to obtain a locked workspace, either without using a password, or using an incorrect password.

WS NOT FOUND
: In a load or copy command you have asked for a workspace that does not exist.

Appendix 4

NUMBER STORAGE

In this appendix the intent is to describe enough about the mechanism of storage of binary numbers in a machine to clarify observable differences in memory space utilization for various kinds of data. Computers are not all the same with respect to how they represent numbers, and so your computer may not operate exactly as described here. There are four types of entities that are represented in the machine as binary numbers, as follows:

(a) Alphanumeric characters.
(b) Boolean numbers.
(c) Integers.
(d) Floating-point numbers

The same basic binary computer "word" is used for each of the above. The length of a computer word (in binary digits or *bits*) varies among systems, but 32 binary digits is common. All inputs to a machine are converted automatically to binary numbers (even in the case of alphanumeric characters) and utilize one or more of the computer words. It is noted that a computer word has a large number of binary digits because on the average a binary number is 3.32 times as long as the equivalent decimal number. For example, the decimal number 91701 is 10110011000110101 in binary.

A4-1 Alphanumeric Characters

In a typical system, the number of different characters that can be encoded as binary numbers is 256 (or 2*8). Thus, the code for a character requires only 8 binary digits, a fraction of a computer word, and when a vector of characters is represented, there can be up to four characters per computer word (for the 32 bit word being considered).

A4-2 Boolean Numbers

A Boolean number can be only 0 or 1, and therefore requires only one bit. Therefore, in a vector of Boolean numbers there can be up to 32 elements per computer word. In connection with Boolean numbers, it is important to recognize that the machine gives a different recognition to integers that may be 0 and 1 and integers that can *only* be 0 and 1. For example, $A \leftarrow 4\uparrow 1\ 0\ 1\ 1\ 2$ will produce A as a vector of integers, but $B \leftarrow 1 = 4\uparrow 1\ 0\ 1\ 1\ 2$ will produce a vector of Boolean numbers.

292 / Number Storage

A4-3 Integers

An integer, no matter how small it is, occupies one computer word. Thus, the integer 1 and the integer 1E8 use the same amount of space. If the word is 32 bits, the largest integer than can be represented in that word is ¯1+2*31. This reserves one of the 32 bits for representation of the sign. This number is 2147483648. Whether or not a word length is 32 bits, the point is made that there is a limit to the size of an integer that can be stored in one computer word.

A4-4 Floating-point Numbers

The floating-point representation is used for mixed numbers, or entered numbers which are integers larger than can be represented in one computer word. In most machines a floating-point number occupies *two* computer words. Mathematically, two common forms for a floating-point representation are:

$M \times 2*E$ (binary)   and $M \times 16*E$ (hexadecimal)

M, called the *mantissa*, is less than 1 but as large as possible, and E is an integer. M and E are also signed numbers, and so it is evident that four components must be stored when representing a number in floating-point form: the mantissa and its sign, and the exponent and its sign. In the combined space of two computer words, two bits are required for the two signs, a certain number for the exponent (say 6 for a hexadecimal representation) and the remainder for the mantissa. Knowledge of these allocations permits a determination of the number of significant digits in the computations and the maximum number that can be represented. For two 32 bit words and an exponent of 6 bits (with two sign bits) there are 56 bits in the mantissa. With an average of 3.32 bits per decimal digit, this gives approximately 16 decimal digits. To consider the largest possible number, if the exponent is 6 bits in the hexadecimal representation, the largest value of E is 63 (111111 in binary) and the largest value of $16*E$ is approximately 7.237E75.

A4-5 Overhead

The descriptions given above refer to the space requirement for representation of a character or number. However values are assigned to names, and there is a certain amount of "overhead" of memory space required to store the name, and also the shape of the value.

A4-6 The Byte Unit

Although a bit is the fundamental unit of number length in binary representation, another unit called a *byte* is frequently used. The number of bits in a byte is system dependent, but typically there are eight bits in a byte. The system variable ⎕WA reports unused workspace, in bytes.

Appendix 5

SYMBOL TABLE

During the execution of an APL statement, a computer must determine the values associated with names of variables, and the codings associated with names of defined functions. This is done through the use of a *symbol table*. This is an object in your workspace which you do not "see", but its existence will be evident if the report

SYMBOL TABLE FULL

is received. This report means that over the history of your workspace you have created enough objects to exhaust the symbol table.

The symbol table may be full even though you now have only a few objects. A record of objects erased remains in the symbol table. The contents of the symbol table can be reduced to that required for your present objects by taking advantage of the fact that the symbol table is not copied. Thus, if your workspace is *XYZ*, and the symbol table is full, erase all unwanted objects and do the steps

```
)CLEAR
)COPY XYZ
)WSID XYZ
)SAVE
```

In some systems it is possible to modify the size of the symbol table by executing (in a clear workspace) the system command

)*SYMBOLS* [a positive integer]

The system permits only certain sizes for the symbol table, and so the size produced (and displayed as a response) may not agree with the number given. The command

)*SYMBOLS*

gives the size of the symbol table, and in some systems also the number of symbols in use.

Appendix 6

STATE INDICATOR

It is assumed you are aware of the information about suspended function given in Chap. 2: that an error in a statement in a defined function will cause the function to become suspended when it is run, and that there is a record of the suspension in the state indicator. In this appendix we give further consideration to suspensions, with emphasis on the situation when a subfunction becomes suspended.

First, we point out that a suspension can be caused intentionally by the operator, by depressing the key labeled *ATTN*. (There may be some variation among systems in the procedure for causing a suspension.) Depressing the *ATTN* key once is called a "weak" interrupt, and allows the completion of the statement line being executed when the interrupt signal is sent. Depressing the *ATTN* key twice constitutes a "stong" interrupt, and can cause termination of computation within a statement line.

Suppose a function *F1* uses another function *F2* as a subfunction, and execution of *F2* is suspended. Furthermore, suppose *F2* occurs on line [2] of *F1*, and *F2* is suspended on line [3]. Under these conditions, the state indicator will show

```
      )SI
F2[3] *
F1[2]
```

The asterisk is opposite the function that is suspended, but the listing of *F1*[2] indicates that execution of *F1* is suspended also, by virtue of the suspension of *F2*. In such a case, *F1* is said to be *pendant*. It is possible to have a list of more than one pendant function.

If a suspended function is modified, by editing or copying, so that execution of it cannot be continued, that fact is indicated by the report *SI DAMAGE*, and a change in the state indicator. After an *SI DAMAGE* message the state indicator either does not show the function name (only the asterisk) or shows the function name with ¯1 as the statement number (depending on the computer system).

During a suspension, the system command

```
    )SINL
```

gives the same display as)*SI*, but augmented by the names of variables local to each function listed.

A suspension is cleared either by branching to the line number of the suspension, as in

```
    →3
```

or by executing

>   →

which clears the suspension but does not continue the execution. Clearing a suspension also removes all related pendant functions from the state indicator. If there is more than one suspension (indicated by more than one asterisk) the procedure described above clears only the last one. A large number of suspensions can be cleared by the procedure described in appendix 5 for resetting the symbol table; that is, clear, copy, save.

While a function is suspended, its local variables are available for testing for values. This means that a global variable having the same name will not be available. For example, suppose *X* is local to a suspended function, and that its local value is 10, and there is also a global *X* having 15 as its value. During suspension,

>   *X*
10

but after the suspension is cleared,

>   *X*
15

A global variable having the *same* name as a local variable of a suspended function is said to be *shadowed* by the local variable.

Appendix 7

DISPLAYING AND EDITING

It is possible to change parts of a defined function by making insertions or deletions of whole lines or parts of lines. This means that parts of a function which are correct do not have to be retyped when making modifications, thereby avoiding the possibility of introducing new errors. Editing procedures differ somewhat among different systems. If the description in this appendix does not apply to your system, obtain information locally about how editing is done on your system. Generally, when you are editing a function you will also want to display it, and so information about creating a display (also given in Sec. 2-15) is included in this appendix.

A7-1 Displaying a Function

While the function definition is open, typing the symbols [☐] will cause a display of the entire function, including the header line. The symbols [☐] can be typed in the statement which opens the definition, as in ∇TEST[☐] which will cause a display of the function, and then leave the definition open; or ∇TEST[☐]∇ will open the definition, produce a display and then close the definition because of the inclusion of the second ∇. The essential information about this is:

    The first ∇ opens the definition
    [☐] produces a display
    The second ∇ closes the definition

Furthermore, [☐] will produce a display when it is typed any time while the definition is open, except that it cannot be included as part of a statement.

Portions of a function can be displayed, as indicated by the following examples:

    ∇TEST[7☐]   (or [7☐] after the definition has been opened)

will display line [7] only.

    ∇TEST[☐7]   (or [☐7] after the definition has been opened)

will display line [7] and all lines that follow.

When opening a definition, only the name of the function is typed following ∇, not the whole header line. Otherwise, the computer makes the interpretation that the definition of a new function is being attempted, and will respond with *DEFN ERROR* if a function by that name exists. The process of displaying can be interrupted by using the *ATTN* key, after which the definition will close or remain open in accordance with whether ∇ was typed following [☐].

A7-2 Editing a Function

To edit a function, the definition must be open. You can make changes during the initial writing of a function, or after the definition has been closed, by opening the definition again in the manner indicated above. There are four types of editing. In the following descriptions, it is assumed that the function definition is open.

(a) Deleting an existing line

To delete an existing line, type (in brackets) ∆ followed by the line number, and do a return. The line having the number you typed will then be deleted. While the definition remains open, that number will be missing if you do a display. However, when the definition is closed the computer automatically renumbers the lines so that they will be in continuous sequence on subsequent displays.

(b) Adding a new line

Type the number of the line to be added in brackets, followed by the new statement. An optional procedure is to type the line number followed by a return. This will cause the computer to print the line number you gave it. Then you can type the new statement. Unless the new line is at the end, it will be interleaved between existing lines. To accomplish that interleaving fractional line numbers must be used. For example, to insert a new line between existing lines [4] and [5] you can use [4.1] as the new line number. After that line has been inserted, the computer will type [4.2] in case you want a second line between [4] and [5]. Suppose you put in such a second line, and then decide you want one between these two you just inserted (before the definition is closed). You can do this by numbering the line [4.11]. When all editing of this type has been completed, and the definition is closed, the computer automatically renumbers the lines to integer values.

(c) Replacing a line

To replace a whole line, follow the same procedure as for adding a line, except use the number of the line to be replaced.

(d) Changing an existing line

Here we consider keeping part of a line, but making additions or deletions, or both. Type the line number followed by the quad followed by a number giving the approximate number of spaces from the margin to the point where you want to make a correction (all enclosed in brackets) in the manner [7☐30] indicating you want to make a change in line [7] 30 spaces from the margin. The computer will display the line, do an up-space, and then the printing head will move in the designated number of spaces (30 in this example) and stop. The changes you can make are deletions of part of the line, insertions of new characters, or both. If you want to delete part of the line, space forward or back (if necessary) to the location of the leftmost character to be deleted and then type / under that symbol. Continue in this manner until there is a symbol / under each character you want to delete. Then, execute a return and the computer will display the line with the designated characters deleted.

If you want to insert additional characters in the statement, without making deletions, move the printing head to the next position to the right of the spot where you want to make the insertion, and then type a digit from 1 to 9 or a letter of the alphabet. If you type a digit, the computer will create that many spaces for the insertion of new characters. If you type A it will provide 5 spaces, B will give 10 spaces, C 15 spaces, and so on. Since the letters give only multiples of 5, you may get more spaces than you want, but (unless you are editing a character vector) this causes no problem because the computer will remove unused spaces when the editing process is completed. After you have indicated the number of spaces required for the insertion, execute a return and the computer will retype the line with the spaces you designated, and will position the printing head at the left of the series of spaces. You then proceed to type the characters you want to insert, and execute a return when you are finished. The line has then been corrected. A line can be edited in more than one place in one operation.

As an example of editing, suppose an existing line is

[4] $X \leftarrow A+B*C+C$

and you wish to put parentheses around $A+B$ and remove $C+$, replacing it by $E-$. First, type [4□8] and execute a return. The number 8 is not crucial, it determines where the printing head stops (8 will cause it to stop under A in the statement) but if that number is wrong you can use the backspace or space bar to bring the printing head to the proper position. After the return, the computer will type the line, and you type under it as follows:

[4] $X \leftarrow A+B*C+C$
          1   1//2

After the return the computer will type

[4] $X \leftarrow \ A+B\ *\ \ C$

showing the spaces needed for insertion of the parentheses and $E-$, which you then type. After a return is executed, editing of the line is complete.

The header line is edited by using [0] as its line number. Editing the header line can include changing the name of the function.

After all editing has been done, of course the definition should be closed by typing ∇.

A7-3 Locked Functions

A function can be locked, so that it cannot be displayed or edited, by using the symbol ⍫ (∇ overstruck with ~) in place of ∇ when either opening or closing a definition. There is no procedure for unlocking a function, but a locked function can be erased. The only way a locked function can be changed is by erasing and replacing it. For a locked function, an error report does not include a display of the incorrect statement, and the stop and trace controls do not operate.

Appendix 8

STOP AND TRACE CONTROL

It is possible to cause a function to stop at a predetermined point so that you can test for values of local variables as they exist at that line. This provides an important aid to debugging a program. Suppose you want a program to stop after line [5] has been completed. To accomplish this, if the name of the function is *TEST*, specify a *stop control* variable with the number of the next line to be executed. If there is no branch on line [5], this would be

    S∆TEST←6

The name of the stop control variable is the name of the function with the prefix *S∆*. The value assigned to it is normally *one greater* than the number of the last line to be executed. If the last line to be executed is a branch, the target value for that branch should be used. After the stop described above, computation is resumed by

    →6

The stop control variable can also have a vector as its value. In that case, a stop will occur for each element in the vector, and resumption of computation after each stop is in the same manner as indicated above. A stop caused by the stop control variable is recorded in the state indicator, and removed from the state indicator when computation is resumed.

Another technique for analyzing the operation of a function is to schedule printouts of the results of certain lines which you can designate by specifying a *trace control* variable. The name of the trace control variable is the name of the function with prefix *T∆*. Thus, if you want to see the results produced at the completion of lines [5] and [9] of function *TEST*, you would specify

    T∆TEST←5 9

The printout obtained from the trace control gives only the *last* value produced on the designated statement line. If you want to see values of variables specified internally in the statement, use the stop control, or include ⎕← at appropriate points. The trace control does not interrupt operation of the function.

The stop and trace control variables can be specified as global variables, or they can be specified within a function. When they are no longer needed, they are removed by specifying them with the value 0. The operation)*ERASE* cannot be used for these variables. As objects in the workspace, they can be saved.

The stop and trace control objects are not ordinary variables. They cannot be used on the right of a specification arrow, and cannot be used as arguments of a function.

Appendix 9

CONTROL STRUCTURE FOR A LOOP

In this appendix, which is a supplement to Sec. 5-9, we give a set of functions for which one function *FOR* will work in either of the forms *FOR-UNTIL-DO* or *FOR-WHILE-DO*. Also, a loop having more than one statement line is to be permitted. The functions are

```
        ∇ Z←A DO B;M                              ∇ Z←A UNWH B;M
[1]     M←(ρ,A)⌈ρ,B                        [1]    M←(ρ,A)⌈¯1↑ρB
[2]     Z←(2,M)ρ(M↑A),M↑B ∇                [2]    Z←(3,M)ρ(M↑A),,(2,M)↑B ∇

        ∇ Z←A UNTIL B                             ∇ Z←A WHILE B
[1]     Z←('0',A) UNWH B ∇                 [1]    Z←('1',A) UNWH B ∇

        ∇ FOR A;B;C;T;E                           ∇ Z←RSC N;B;T;C
[1]     B←⎕FX 2 7 ρ14↑'W←X E YW←X'         [1]    T←(B←N=':')/C←⍳ρN
[2]     T←1↑B←, 1 0 0 ≠A                   [2]    N[T]←'E'
[3]     ⍎RSC 1↓B                           [3]    Z←(B,N,B←(+/B)ρ' ')[⍋T,C,T] ∇
[4]     C←, 0 1 0 ≠A
[5]     B←, 0 0 1 ≠A
[6]     →(~⍎T)/L2
[7]     L1:→(~⍎C)/0
[8]     ⍎RSC B
[9]     →L1
[10]    L2:⍎RSC B
[11]    →(~⍎C)/L2 ∇
```

A loop of several statements will be specified by separating the statements by colons in the right-hand argument of *DO*, as in the example '*G←K+I*2:I←I+1:K←K-1*'. A function *E*, which is local to *FOR*, is created on line [1] by using ⎕FX. It is

```
        ∇ W←X E Y
[1]     W←X ∇
```

Now consider the execution of

    G←K+I*2 E I←I+1 E K←K-1

Each argument on the right of *E* has no effect on the value returned by *E*. Thus, interpreting this statement by the usual rule shows that *K* will receive its new assignment, and then the function *E* on the right will return its left-hand argument (the value 1) which replaces the 1 in *I*+1. The execution of the *E* on the left will be similar. Therefore, each of the three statements will be executed, in a right-to-left order. The function *RSC* replaces each colon in a character vector by *E* surrounded by spaces. Thus, ⍎*RSC* '*G←K+I*2:I←I+1:K←K-1*' is equivalent to the example above. It is now seen that line [8] of *FOR* is capable of executing a series of statements. In a similar way, the loop of lines [2], [3], and [4] of *FOR* in Sec. 5-9 is replaced by line [3] of the *FOR* given above.

Appendix 10

ACCESS CONTROL

The control provided by $\Box SVC$ is accomplished through the interaction, in the computer, of two Boolean matrices, each of shape 2 2. These matrices are the *access state* matrix ASM (a record of what access last took place) and the *access control* matrix ACM (which represents the combined constraints imposed by the users).

The actual control is produced by the matrix

   $CM \leftarrow ASM \wedge ACM$

Matrices CM and ASM, cannot be displayed by a user. The meanings of the rows and columns of CM are indicated by the diagram

	User A	User B
Set		
Use		

In this diagram A and B identify the two users, and the words "set" and "use", respectively, mean assign a value to the shared variable, or use the value (as in a computation or a display). A number 1 in this matrix, *prevents* the action implied by its position. Thus, if there is a 1 in the upper left, user A cannot set the variable; if there is a 1 in the lower right, user B cannot use the variable. A zero permits the operation implied by its position.

The matrix ACM is set jointly by users A and B (through the use of $\Box SVC$). If we let CA be the control set by user A and CB the control set by user B (both are vectors),

   $ACM \leftarrow (2\ 2\ \rho CA) \vee \phi\ 2\ 2\ \rho CB$

The function reverse is necessary because the index positions in CA and CB in relation to the identification of "me" and "you" are the same for each user but are opposite in $,ACM$. If user A obtains a display of the access control vector, through the use of $\Box SVC$, the display will be

   $,ACM$

302 / Access Control

but for user B the corresponding display will be

    $,\phi ACM$

The nature of ASM is described in the following table:

Last action	Configuration of ASM	Can be changed by
Set by A	1 0 1 0	Set or use by B
Set by B	0 1 0 1	Set or use by A
Use by B after set by A Use by A after set by B Initial state	0 0 1 1	Set by A or B

If all elements of ACM are zero, ASM has no effect because the control is established by $ASM \wedge ACM$. However, suppose (through the action of either user) ACM has been given the value

    1 0

    0 1

From the initial state, user A can set the variable. Then, $ASM \wedge ACM$ will have a 1 in the upper left-hand corner, and therefore user A cannot make another set. Now suppose the variable is used by user B, thereby changing ASM to the third configuration shown above. Because of the 1 in the lower right-hand corner, user B cannot use the variable again until a zero appears in this position in ASM. Reference to the table above shows that user B can use the variable again after another set by user A.

Appendix 11

APL CHARACTER SET

Names of the APL Characters

In the following tabulation, items marked * are keyboard characters which are not in general used in the APL language. There are a few exceptions, in some systems.

¨	dieresis*	~	tilde	)	close paren	⍱	del stile
¯	overbar	↑	up	[	open bracket	⍲	delta stile
<	less	↓	down	]	close bracket	⌽	circle stile
≤	not greater	⍳	iota	⊂	open shoe*	⦵	circle slope
=	equal	○	circle	⊃	close shoe*	⊖	circle bar
≥	not less	*	star	∩	cap*	⊛	log
>	greater	→	right	∪	cup*	⌶	I-beam*
≠	not equal	←	left	⊥	base	⍨	del tilde
∨	or	α	alpha*	⊤	top	⊻	base null
∧	and	⌈	upstile	|	stile	⊽	top null
-	bar	⌊	downstile	;	semicolon	⍁	slope bar
÷	divide	_	underbar	:	colon	⌿	slash bar
+	plus	∇	del	,	comma	⍓	cap null
×	times	Δ	delta	.	dot	⌷	quote quad
?	query	○	null	\	slope	!	quote dot
ω	omega*	'	quote	/	slash	⌹	domino
ϵ	epsilon	⎕	quad	⍱	nor		
ρ	rho	(	open paren	⍲	nand		

Arrangement of the Keyboard

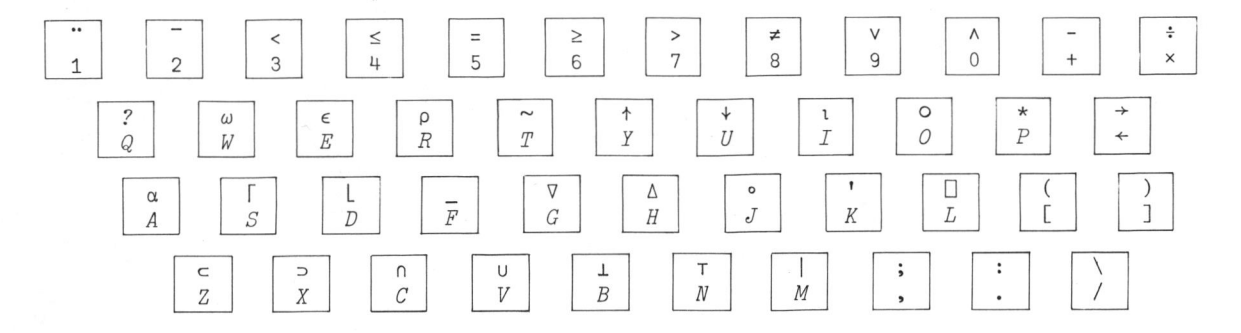

```
┌──┬──┬──┬──┬──┬──┬──┬──┬──┬──┬──┬──┐
│¨ │¯ │< │≤ │= │≥ │> │≠ │∨ │∧ │- │÷ │
│1 │2 │3 │4 │5 │6 │7 │8 │9 │0 │+ │× │
└──┴──┴──┴──┴──┴──┴──┴──┴──┴──┴──┴──┘
  ┌──┬──┬──┬──┬──┬──┬──┬──┬──┬──┬──┐
  │? │ω │ϵ │ρ │~ │↑ │↓ │⍳ │○ │* │→ │
  │Q │W │E │R │T │Y │U │I │O │P │← │
  └──┴──┴──┴──┴──┴──┴──┴──┴──┴──┴──┘
   ┌──┬──┬──┬──┬──┬──┬──┬──┬──┬──┬──┐
   │α │⌈ │⌊ │_ │∇ │Δ │○ │' │⎕ │( │) │
   │A │S │D │F │G │H │J │K │L │[ │] │
   └──┴──┴──┴──┴──┴──┴──┴──┴──┴──┴──┘
     ┌──┬──┬──┬──┬──┬──┬──┬──┬──┬──┐
     │⊂ │⊃ │∩ │∪ │⊥ │⊤ │\|│; │: │\ │
     │Z │X │C │V │B │N │M │, │. │/ │
     └──┴──┴──┴──┴──┴──┴──┴──┴──┴──┘
```

INDEX

Lower and upper case italics refer, respectively, to primitives and defined functions.

Aborted operation:
 avoidance of, 242
Absolute value, 33, 121
Access control:
 matrix, 301
 vector, 262
Access state matrix, 301
Account information, 254
Active workspace, 278
Algorithm, 6
Alphanumeric characters, 5, 291
And, 134
Arguments, 31
 ambiguous, 250
Arithmetic functions, 31
 domain restrictions, 129
 summary, 128
Assignment statement, 4, 5
Atomic vector, 254
Axis, 66
 operator:
  in catenation, 74
  in compression, 202
  in expansion, 203
  in reduction, 84
  in reverse, 96
  in rotate, 97

Bare output, 56
Binary numbers, 292
Bisection method, 168
Bit, 292
Boolean numbers, 23, 291
Branching, 154
 conditional, 156
 on inequalities, 249
 unconditional, 155
Byte, 292

Canonical representation, 255
Catenate, 47, 196
 compatibility, 47, 196
 rank and shape of result, 197
Ceiling, 119
 comparison tolerance in, 120
 comparison with floor and residue, 197
Central processor, 22

Character input, 55, 240
 exit from, 56
Character set:
 APL, 303
Character value, 30, 69
Clear workspace, 280
 properties of, 24, 280
Combination, generalized, 127
Comment lines, 57, 241
Comparison tolerance, 120, 253
 in floor and ceiling, 120
 in relational functions, 131
Compression, 137, 200
 compatibility, 202
 rank and shape of result, 202
Conditional branching, 156
Conjugate, 32
Continue command, 285
Control structure:
 equivalent of branching, 157
 equivalent of looping, 167, 168, 300
Copy command, 282
 compared to load command, 282
 protected, 283
Correcting typing errors, 25
Coupling of a shared variable:
 degree of, 258

Data base:
 example of, 266
Deal, 225
Decision making, 7
Decode, 214
 compatibility, 216
 rank and shape of result, 216
Defined functions, 38
 display of, 42, 296
 ease of reading, 241
 editing, 297
 monadic, 51
 types of, 239
Definition mode, 39
DEFN (defined function), 257
Degree of coupling, of shared variables, 258
Delay, 256
DeMorgan's theorem, 137
Display:
 of a function, 42, 296
 of a value, 66

305

DO (defined function), 167, 168, 300
Drop, 46, 93, 200
Dropping a workspace, 284
Dyadic functions, 32

ELSE (defined function), 159
Empty:
 array, 79
 vector, 30, 71
Encode, 217
 rank and shape of result, 221
 recursive definition, 218
Equal to, 129
Erasing objects, 285
Error reports, 287
Evaluated input, 54, 240
 exit from, 56
Execute, 55
 on empty vector, 251
 on vector of spaces, 251
 uses of, 251
Exit from input:
 character, 56
 evaluated, 56
Expansion, 138, 202
 compatibility, 203
 rank and shape of result, 204
Explicit result, 54
Exponent, 33
Exponentiation, 33
Expunge, 256

Factorial, 123
Files, 275
Fix (a function), 255
Floating-point:
 notation, 34
 numbers, 292
Floor, 117
 comparison tolerance in, 120
 comparison with ceiling and
  residue, 127
Flow chart, 8
FOR (defined function), 167, 300
Format:
 dyadic, 229
 monadic, 56
Functions:
 defined (see defined functions)
 primitive, 31

Global variable, 41
 used for input and output, 240
Grade down, 96
Grade up, 95
Greater than, 130
Greater than or equal, 130
Group, 283, 285

Header line, 39
Hexadecimal numbers, 292
Horizontal tab setting, 255
Hyperbolic functions, 145

Identity value:
 for scalar functions, 188
IF (defined function), 157
IF (defined function), 159
Imbedded assignment, 38, 246
Index function, 87, 204
 rank and shape of result, 206
Index generator, 30
Index of, 222
Index origin, 24, 253
Indexed value:
 specifying, 90
Inner product, 104, 194
 compatibility, 105, 196
 rank and shape of result, 196
 special cases, 196
Input:
 character, 54
 evaluated, 54
Input controlled loop, 177
Input variables, 39
Integer, 23, 292
Interrupt, 294
Inverse functions:
 hyperbolic, 145
 trigonometric, 143
Iterative process, 9, 163, 165

Keyboard:
 APL, 303

Label:
 line, 154
Laminate, 74, 198
 compatibility, 199
 rank and shape of result, 199
 scalar argument, 75
Latent expression, 253
Less than, 130
Less than or equal, 130
Library, 278
Line:
 inserting in defined function, 297
 label, 154
Line counter, 254
Listing objects, 284
Local variable, 41
Locked:
 function, 298
 workspace, 284
Logic functions, 133
 summary, 136
Loop, 160
 avoidance of, 246
 control structure equivalent, 166
 flow chart for, 161
 input controlled, 177
 nested, 162
 termination of, 13, 160

Mantissa, 35, 292
Matrix, 66
 formation by laminate, 74
 formation by reshape, 71

Matrix divide, 225
  compatibility, 227
  rank and shape of result, 227
  special cases, 225
Matrix inverse, 228
  special cases, 229
Maximum, 119
Membership, 131
Memory space utilization, 242
  overhead, 292
Minimum, 117
Mixed numbers, 23
Monadic functions, 32
  defined, 51

Name:
  reuse of, 241
  variable, 4
Name classification, 256
Name list, 256
Nand, 135
Negation, 33
Negative number, 33
Nested loop, 162
Niladic function, 54
Nor, 135
Not, 134
Number representation, 292

Offer:
  shared variable, 258
One-line function:
  function for creating, 257
Operator:
  axis, 74
  inner product, 104, 194
  outer product, 103, 192
  reduction, 46, 187
  scan, 189
Or, 134
Origin, 24, 253
Outer product, 103, 192
  compatibility, 194
  rank and shape of result, 194
Output variable, 40

Parentheses:
  effect on execution, 37
  superfluous, 37
Password, 282
Pendant function, 282
Polynomial, evaluation of, by:
  decode, 215
  inner and outer products, 106
  loop, 161, 167
  recursive function, 175
Printing precision, 24, 254
Printing values within
  a statement, 52
Printing width, 24, 254
Protected copy, 283
Pythagorean functions, 144

Quad input (see *evaluated input*)
Quadratic equation, roots of:
  defined function for, 159
  flow chart for, 158
Query:
  shared variable, 260
Quote-quad input (see *character input*)

Random:
  link, 124, 254
  numbers, 124
Rank, 66
Ravel, 75
Reciprocal, 32
Recursive functions, 175
Reduction, 46, 83, 187
  over an empty array, 85, 188
  over a scalar, 187
Relational functions, 129
  character values in, 130
Remainder, 125
Reshape, 69
Residue, 125
  comparison with floor and ceiling, 127
Respecification, 5
Retraction:
  of shared variable, 262
Returned value, 40
  (see also explicit result)
Reuse of names, 243
Reverse, 96, 206
Roll, 124
Rotate, 97, 207
Rounding:
  to nearest specified decimal digit, 119
Roundoff error, 120, 247
  examples, 248
  in multiplication, 247
Running time, 245

Scalar, 68
Scalar functions, 115
  compatibility, 116
Scaled notation, 34
Scan, 189
  on empty vector, 191
  on scalar, 191
Secant method, 172
  convergence, 173
Set:
  of shared variable, 259
Shadowed variable, 295
Shape, 47, 75
  of a scalar, 76
Shared variable:
  control, 259
  offer, 258
  query, 260
  retraction, 262
SI damage, 290
Signing off, 285
Signum, 32, 121
Specification, 5

308 / Index

State indicator, 45, 294
Stop control, 299
Structure in programming, 50, 154
Successive approximations, 163
  convergence, 166
Surrogate name:
  for shared variable, 260
Suspension:
  of functions, 43, 294
  removal of, 45
Symbol table, 290
Syntax, 4
System commands, 22, 279
System functions, 255
System variables, 24, 253

Take, 46, 92, 199
  compatibility, 199
  rank and shape of result, 200
Target line, 155
Terminal control, 255
Terminal type, 255
THEN (defined functions), 157
Time stamp, 254
Trace control, 299
Transcendental functions, 140
  summary, 146, 147
Transpose:
  dyadic, 209
    compatibility, 211
    rank and shape of result, 212
  monadic, 98, 212
  reduced dyadic, 213
    compatibility, 211
    rank and shape of result, 214
Trouble reports, 289
Truth table, 134

Unconditional branching, 155
UNTIL (defined function), 167, 300
Use:
  of shared variable, 259
User load, 254
User number, 22, 282

Variable, 4
  name, 26
  value, 26
Vector, 29, 66

WHEN (defined function), 158
WHILE (defined function), 168, 300
Working area available, 255
Workspace, 22, 278
  active, 278
  clear, 280
  creating a library, 280
  dropping, 284
  identification, 279
  loading from library, 282
  locked, 284

Index of Numbered Examples

2-1 Elevation of a point above a sphere, 47
2-2 Length of a string, 48
2-3 First modification of 2-2, 49
2-4 Second modification of 2-2, 50
2-5 Period of a satellite, 51
2-6 Monadic function for hypotenuse, 52
2-7 Mean value, 52
2-8 Function for hypotenuse, using evaluated input, 54
2-9 Function for hypotenuse, using character input, 55

3-1 Diagram for tic-tac-toe, 77
3-2 Adding a line to a numeric matrix, 78
3-3 Windchill effect on temperature, 82
3-4 Means of rows and columns of a matrix, 86
3-5 Modification of 3-4, to accept a scalar or vector argument, 86
3-6 Printing ordinal numbers, 89
3-7 Record of play, for tic-tac-toe, 91
3-8 Adding a line to a character matrix, 94
3-9 Area of a triangle, 98
3-10 Area under a linearly interpolated curve, 99
3-11 Successive differences for a set of data points, 101
3-12 Records for team sports, 101
3-13 Compound interest, 104

4-1 Rounding to the nearest specified decimal digit, 118
4-2 Moving haystacks, 122
4-3 Converting very small numbers to zero, 131
4-4 Identifying a leap year, 135
4-5 Converting a matrix of words to a standard form, 139
4-6 Radioactive decay, 141
4-7 General arctangent function, 144

5-1 Roots of a quadratic equation, 158
5-2 Modification of 5-1, using a control structure, 160
5-3 Height of water in a spherical tank, 166
5-4 Modification of 5-3, using a control structure, 167
5-5 Modification of 5-3, using the bisection method, 171
5-6 Secant method of finding a zero, 174
5-7 Modification of 5-6, using execute, 174
5-8 Recursive evaluation of a polynomial, 175
5-9 Modification of 5-6, using recursion, 177

6-1 Converting a matrix of words to a vector of the same words, 190
6-2 Printing a rearrangement of an array of rank 3, 212
6-3 Computing elapsed time, 216
6-4 Packing and unpacking numbers, 221
6-5 Alphabetizing a matrix of names, 223
6-6 Polynomial for a least squares fit, 228